AFRICAN C

SVZY
25.8.99
LONDON

AFRICAN CINEMA

Postcolonial and Feminist Readings

Edited by

Kenneth W. Harrow

Africa World Press, Inc.

P.O. Box 1892
Trenton, NJ 08607

P.O. Box 48
Asmara, ERITREA

Africa World Press, Inc.

P.O. Box 1892
Trenton, NJ 08607

P.O. Box 48
Asmara, ERITREA

Copyright © 1999 Kenneth W. Harrow

First Printing 1999

Book design: Krystal Jackson
Cover design: Jonathan Gullery

Library of Congress Cataloging-in-Publication Data

African cinema : postcolonial and feminist readings / edited by
    Kenneth W. Harrow.
         p.   cm.
    Includes bibliographical references, filmographies, and index.
    ISBN 0-86543-696-7 (hardbound).   -- ISBN 0-86543-697-5 (pbk.)
    1. Motion pictures--Africa.   2. Feminism and motion pictures-
-Africa.   I. Harrow, Kenneth W.
PN1993.5.A35A357   1998
791.43'096--dc21   98-37159
                                                                                        CIP

Chapters 1, 3, 6, 7, 8, 9, 10, were originally published in *Research in African Literature*, Volume 26, No. 3 and are reprinted with permission of Indiana University Press.

In memory of Djibril Diop Mambety.

CONTENTS

CONTENTS

PART THREE
THE QUESTION OF NATIONAL CINEMAS

PART FOUR
FEMINIST APPROACHES TO AFRICAN CINEMA

INTRODUCTION

THESE ESSAYS SPEAK DIRECTLY and compellingly to contemporary issues in African cinema. They address key aspects of
post-colonialism and feminism—the two major topics of interest
in current criticism. Issues of spectatorship, national identity,
ethnography, patriarchy, gender roles, and the creation of key film
industries, issues that animate the discussion of film today, are
central to this volume.

Postcolonialism has a special meaning when used in reference
to African cinema—a meaning that arises out of the particular his -
tory of colonialism and cinema in Africa. Although there were
filmmaking practices in Africa that date back to the colonial period,
the films generally viewed and discussed by students and critics of
African film are those directed by Africans, those made after inde -
pendence in the early 1960s. The essays on the formation of three
principal national film industries—those of Nigeria, Senegal, and
the lusophone countries—best exemplify the emergence of African
cinema when viewed from the optic of language or nation. In addi -
tion, studies of genre, patriarchal structures, spectatorship, and
representation, are central to the essays on women's films from
Algeria, West Africa, and the Sahel. Stephen Zack's study of Trinh
T. Minh-ha's *Reassemblage*, offers a brilliant meditation on difference, anthropology and Trinh's positioning in her seminal work.
Questions posed by post-colonial theory inform Jonathan Haynes's
study of one of Africa's most innovative new filmmakers, Jean-
Pierre Bekolo. A new approach to cinematic art grounded in a
specifically African aesthetic forms the subject of Keyan Tomaselli,
Arnold Shepperson and Maureen Eke's essay on orality in African
cinema. This is complemented by the studies of individual films,
such as *Wend Kuuni* (1982), *Yeelen* (1989), and *Sankofa* (1993),

films that have had a strong impact on how we think of African-centered aesthetics and visions of cinema, history, and tra-dition. Finally, Emilie Ngo-Nguidjol's bibliographic essay and Nancy Schmidt's filmographic essay provide invaluable informa-tion on sources dealing with African women directors.

It is important to recognize the inadequacy of regarding African cinema as having one clear moment of departure—say the cre-ation of the "first" African film—an honor often accorded to Paulin Vieyra and Mamadou Sarr's *Afrique sur Seine*, made in Paris in 1955. Cinema did not pass Africans by during the first half of the twentieth century, but the distribution of power within the indus-try replicated colonial structures, as in all other aspects of colonial society. Films were shown early in the century in South Africa, while other African states developed a limited infrastructure for the distribution of films by the 1930s and 1940s. Colonial authorities kept a tight control over what films were shown, but by the 1950s most African cities had movie theaters with considerable audi-ences. In their youth, pioneering African filmmakers like Sembène Ousmane or Oumarou Ganda were great enthusiasts of popular cinema, especially Westerns and crime films, that marked their imagination. At this stage Africans were the consumers, and Western studios were the distributors and sellers.

However, some of the colonial authorities, notably the British and Belgians, also saw virtue in creating film units in some of their colonies, with the goal of creating educational films—often doc-umentaries that would involve agricultural, medical, or social prac-tices, that would even instruct the audiences in correct comport-ment. Small groups that traveled from village to town would distribute the films. Significantly, Europeans directed the processes of filmmaking, but were assisted by Africans in a variety of ways. It was thus only natural that in the late colonial and early inde-pendence periods, as Africans began to assume positions formerly monopolized by the colonizers, they would eventually become filmmakers in their own right. Manthia Diawara (1992) has pro-vided some of the details of this early history of film production in Africa.

The installation of film production units was quite limited and uneven, but film showings grew rapidly, by mid-century extending throughout much of urban Africa. Further, although Africans were denied any directorial roles in this initial period, they were brought into the production units in minor capacities, as they were elsewhere in the colonial economy, with the logical consequence that as colonial ideologies advocated education and assimilation, Africans would eventually move into directorial roles. This is what happened in the 1950s and 1960s with a range of early directors, like Paulin Vieyra, Oumarou Ganda, Safi Faye, and later Sarah Maldoror, who had received training in Metropolitan cinematic institutes, and who had worked with such directors as Jean Rouch and Gillo Pontecorvo.

The important point is that cinema did not spring up all of a sudden in Africa after independence, but was widely known and appreciated during the colonial period. Its beginnings cannot be traced to an originary experience, but rather to a diffuse and differential set of practices, as occurred elsewhere.

In the 1950s, Africans began to aspire to create their own films. Others followed Vieyra's early efforts: Sembène Ousmane decided to extend into filmmaking his work as a committed writer. When the French refused to grant him a scholarship to study filmmaking, he turned to the Russians who accepted him, and later Souleymane Cissé and others, in their schools. The Russians' preference for socialist realism or socially conscious filmmaking was to have an influence on the practices of these influential African filmmakers.

The circumstances that surrounded African society and culture in the 1950s, the late colonial period, had a strong impact on the kinds of films that were to emerge. Early African films were predominantly committed to a social or political program—they constituted a *cinéma engagé* just as much African literature of the period saw itself as a *littérature engagée* or committed literature. The struggle for African independence was marked by radically different sorts of experiences. On the one hand, the major colonial powers all had recourse to the use of force to prevent Africans from participating in the political process. Brutal wars of repression were fought in Kenya, Algeria, Madagascar, and the Portuguese colonies, while the system of apartheid in South African grew increasingly harsh.

Despite these instances of bloody repression, there were great countervailing, pro-independence forces both within and outside of Africa. African political movements continued to be formed, with considerable success after World War II, so that even when

such leaders as Nkrumah, Kenyatta, or Bourghiba were imprisoned, their political movements managed to grow. Often the leaders would pass from prisoner to president, foreshadowing the
events that later would mark the career of Nelson Mandela.
European liberal parties tended to favor independence, in opposition to settler populations. In the case of Southern Rhodesia, this
opposition led to a unilateral declaration of independence by the
white population, thus delaying Zimbabwe's ascension to majority rule until 1980. However, most African colonies, with the
exception of the Portuguese colonies and South Africa, proceeded
peacefully toward a series of independences that would be achieved
in the late 1950s and early 1960s, beginning with the Sudan,
Morocco, and Tunisia in 1956 (the year following *Afrique sur
Seine*!) and Ghana in 1957. It was generally the case that first
African writers, and later African filmmakers, saw themselves
committed to the goals of decolonization, of independence from
European or Western hegemony.

Negritude, born in the 1930s, was the dominant literary movement of the 1940s, and remained so until the appearance of the
anticolonial literature of the 1950s. Initially, the concerns of
Negritude writers involved the affirmation of positive values for
Black people—the reaffirmation of the race, pride in the African
heritage. By the 1950s, concerns over racial pride were supplanted
by the demand for political rights and then for independence. The
radical strains of Negritude fed into the notion of a *littérature
engagée*—a literature whose major European voices included
Camus, Sartre, Ionesco and Genet, existentialist novelists and
dramatists of the absurd whose works attacked the banality and
compromises of bourgeois culture. Europeans did join sides in the
African struggle for independence, especially in the case of
Algeria. However, the major focus of the European intellectual
movements of the 1950s did not involve colonialism as much as
class struggle. Europe had served as the main battleground between
fascism and democracy, and once that conflict was resolved, whatever the flaws in the late colonial enterprise, African independence movements were regarded largely as peripheral to Europe's
major concerns over economic recovery, communism and the cold
war.

Africans, on the other hand, focused less on class divisions
than on political rights: after all, Africans themselves were less
divided by class than were the African and European populations.

The class problem was subsumed under the problem of colonial repression: resolution of the latter should bring a solution to the for-mer. A twin battle was fought, one against the ideologies of white supremacy that supplied the foundation for colonial practices, and the other for independence. Chinua Achebe and Camara Laye reconstituted African history and society along positive and human-istic lines, in opposition to prevailing white notions of Africans' inferiority. Mongo Beti and Ferdinand Oyono followed by Sembène Ousmane, Ngugi wa Thiong'o, and Cheikh Hamidou Kane, challenged the colonial enterprise by mocking its excesses or undercutting its epistemic presuppositions. In place of assimi-lation and acquiescence, they constructed a critique that aligned itself, for the most part, with revolutionary thought. Frantz Fanon was a high priest of the period; Algerian independence a triumph for the continent.

The rhetoric of racial pride and eventually of independence did not prepare Africans for the expropriation of fundamental rights by their own leadership, or for the legitimizations of such expro-priations, yet this is what occurred repeatedly in the decades fol-lowing independence. The positive emotions engendered by Negritude were channeled into statist ideologies, supported by the slogans of "authenticity," the African Personality, or its variants, and deployed by such rulers as Mobutu Sese Seko, Ahmadou Ahidjo, Kwame Nkrumah, and Leopold Senghor. Eventually even the most bloody of dictators, like Idi Amin or the Emperor Bokassa resorted to the rhetoric of racial pride and anticolonialism, while the FLN in Algeria turned into an entrenched autocracy.

The first group of African films to emerge in the late 1950s and 1960s were preoccupied with the need to escape from European hegemony—both political and psychological. Rouch's *Moi, un noir* (1958), an important predecessor, set the stage for Oumadou Ganda's entry into filmmaking, and Sembène's *Borom Sarret* (1963) were marked by a white-black binary. During the first stages of independence in the 1960s, even when colonialism had come to an end, there was a particular concern over acculturation and assim-ilation to white values and civilization—especially to French iden-tity. This issue carried through to the 1970s, as could be seen in Sembène's *La Noire de...*(1966); Djibril Diop Mambéty's *Touki*

Bouki (1973), and especially Sembène's *Xala* (1974). Even when the major characters in a film like Sembène's *Mandabi* (1968) lived at a distance from the Europeanized culture, there were always minor characters and bureaucrats who reiterated the effects of the colonial economy and who were pilloried as grotesque mimics of a foreign identity.

The uneven development of African independence assured that revolutionary values would inform African filmmaking as long as colonial domination continued. Thus, beginning with *The Battle of Algiers* (1966), the work of the Italian neorealist Pontecorvo, a body of politically committed, revolutionary films was created, utilizing the rhetoric of the 1950s. Such revolutionary filmmaking practices continued into the 1970s, with Sarah Maldoror's *Sambizanga* (1972), a film concerned with the MPLA's initial actions that launched the armed struggle against the Portuguese in Angola, and into the 1980s, with Flora Gomes's *Mortu Nega* (1988), dealing with the armed struggle in Guinea Bissau. And just as the discourses of racial pride or African integrity had been appropriated by the African leadership, so were the cultural representations of independence, of revolutionary struggle, turned into instruments of propaganda to prop up the state, especially in the case of Algerian cinema.

Starting in the late 1960s, and especially in the 1970s, the rhetoric of struggle began to turn from anticolonialism to protest against African elites, leaders, and state corruption, as well as against the acquiescence of the ruling classes in the face of European hegemony. Whereas the protests of the 1950s and 1960s were directed against European colonialists as outsiders, or against Europe itself as an outside force, now they were directed internally against African figures of authority—oppressive, domineering figures, including those who led the nation and the economy, as well as those who governed villages or families. The Great Father—be he political or familiar—defined the contours of a patriarchal system that increasingly preoccupied African filmmakers. Those who focused upon the figure of the oppressive father or husband included Jean-Pierre Dikongue-Pipa (*Muno Moto* [1975] and *Le Prix de la liberté* [1978]) and Mahama Johnson Traore (*Njangaan* [1975]). Traditional village authority was depicted as abusive, a familiar theme in much literature as well, as can be seen in Sembène's novella *Vehi Ciosane* (1965). Traore, as well as Sembène, depicted religious Muslim authorities, imams, or mal lams, as extensions of an abusive traditional patriarchy. Sembène developed this theme in various minor characters in *Tauw* (1970), and extended it in many of his films and novels, linking the abuses of the family patriarch with those of the social leaders. *Xala* (1974) might serve as a prime example, among many. Similarly, for Haile Gerima, the feudalized system functioned as the oppressive patri-arch (*Harvest 3000* [1974]), while for Kramo Lanciné Fadika, in his *Djeli* (1980), it was the Malinke caste system, and those figures who insisted upon upholding its restrictions, who maintained the functioning of the Law of the Father—even when it was grand-mothers or mothers who played this role.

Patriarchal assumptions undergirded by village traditionalism, perversely enough, served well the project of a modernism molded by colonial notions of European civilization. Throughout the con-tinent, and most especially in Muslim lands, the conflict over dom-inant values was played out in the arena of sexual politics. Muslim women were portrayed by Europeans as repressed, as the mis-treated property of benighted, backward men. Enlightenment was to be bought at the price of alienating the women from their tradi-tional roles, especially through education. The reactive, defiant, angry postures assumed by the African male avant-garde were translated into Negritudinist elaborations on the beauty of Mother Africa or the African dancer whose role was to inspire the Black (male) poet—there being no female poets or filmmakers to respond to the inspiration.

The relative distribution of gender roles in film production in Africa followed this same pattern through the 1960s and 1970s, despite the exceptional presence of Safi Faye or Sarah Maldoror. The strong male voices denouncing patriarchy—those of Sembène, Dikongue-Pipa, and later Souleymane Cissé, Idrissa Ouedraogo, and Cheikh Oumar Sissoko—were working through a naturalized discourse of modernism in which even the overt messages of neo-colonialism could be harmonized with European notions of pro-gressive thought. The absence of women writers and filmmakers was not coincidental. As long as men were there to defend the interest of women, to advance their cause, to speak for them, the naturalized patterns that could be traced back to Negritude remained intact. The voice of protest drowned out the whisper of gender difference.

This was a logical consequence of the choices originally made in the creation of the cinema of commitment. Its force lent authority to its choices, so that social realism, and its related modalities of socialist realism and neorealism, or even offshoots of *cinéma vérité*, tended to prevail. The assumption of realism had been almost universally accepted—only Djibril Diop Mambéty's work resisted it. And the corollary of a representational, mimetic cinema was equally dominant. The feminist challenge to such masculin-ist approaches could not be mounted in the 1960s and 1970s. The "truth" of *cinéma vérité* was marked, in fact, by the same set of contradictions that governed the cinema of commitment as well: the truthful image or voice that presented social problems, that gave voice to the wretched of the earth, to the oppressed masses, emerged as though by itself, as though without any mediating actions by the filmmaker, by his crew, his backers, his post-pro-duction units, or the distributors that then took charge of the film. Though lacking the hypocrisy of the African leaders, the film-makers fell into the same traps: they deployed a rhetoric that took its *prises de conscience* to be self-evident, transparent, while ignor-ing the implicit self-justification involved. Where the leaders man-aged to pillage the nation's wealth, or to maintain control over the reins of governance, the filmmakers, less greedy for personal profit, struggled to control the audience, the truth, and ultimately the direction of social change. Their motives did nothing to resolve their contradictory choice of a patriarchal praxis.

The financial constraints of production made it also seem nat-ural to follow the choices of neorealism—a mode of filmmaking that developed in Italy after World War II, when the Italian film industry was lacking in resources, and when the reconstruction of society was regarded as fundamental. Thus, the use of non-pro-fessional actors, location shooting, the absence of studios for film-ing, editing or post-production, and a dependency on foreign cap-ital for production, came to be the norm, even as it led certain filmmakers into inevitable contradictions. Sembène had to accept French money even as he cried out against neocolonialism; Kabore protested the urban development policies in *Zan Boko* (1988), while thanking the ministry for urban development in his credits; Cissé ended *Finye* (1982) with a successful student uprising, whereas in reality the student protests in Mali that had preceded the filming were met with brutal repression.

The 1980s and 1990s could not sustain the momentum that had brought the African ruling classes into power. The voices of a liberation struggle, or its successors, were now those of long-entrenched and often corrupt leaders: Senghor, Houphouet-Boigny, Bongo, Banda, Habyiramana, Bokassa, Kenyatta/Moi, Keita, Ahidjo/Biya, a series of Nigerian generals, etc. The 1980s saw the general deterioration of economic conditions, the relative impov - erishment of African societies, especially vis-a-vis the West, the commensurate increase of state corruption and oppression, the large scale violation of human rights, the general expansion of military rule, of police-state conditions, and the expropriation of national resources by multinational corporations with the con - nivance of ruling elites. The escalation of violence in such south - ern Africa states as Mozambique or Angola matched the exten - sive kleptocracies for which oil or diamonds provided the stakes. Eventually, even relatively poor countries—Liberia, Sierra Leone, Rwanda, Burundi—became the battlegrounds for control of resources, with seemingly unlimited descents into large scale vio - lence.

Within the cities, the conditions of life also deteriorated: a continual flood of rural emigration into the urban centers where jobs were not to be found, combined with the destructuring of social institutions, led to the steady increase of crime, the vast aug - mentation of slums, and the stagnation of city services: infra - structures deteriorated as corrupt governments refused to fund urban agencies. Life came to resemble the post-apocalyptic visions of Ben Okri or Calixthe Beyala. The local neighborhood alone provided a sense of belonging: the larger society remained threat - ening for most.

Under such conditions, African filmmakers and writers found themselves less and less concerned with foreign oppressors. Negritude, race consciousness, and African-centered identity were dead issues, doubly interred by their exploitation by remote and powerful rulers. A new vision for survival was needed, one that would go beyond such terms as *engagement* or commitment, one that would engage the conditions of life on a local scale, and not, as in post-colonialism, those involved with the great powers that were perceived as infinitely distant. The paths of mimesis, of real - ism—social, neo-, or *cinéma verité*—that rested upon the truth-fulness of representation, upon the conditions of representation itself, that formed the core of the earlier cinema, *The Battle of Algiers, Sambizanga, Emitai* (1971), *Xala*, or even *Finye* or *Wend Kuuni* (1982)—were no longer adequate to deal with the *quartiers*, the *bidonvilles* or shantytowns, the locations. The explosion of a vision that took the camera past engaged realism came in the the-atre and novels of Sony Labou Tansi, in V. Y. Mudimbe's novels marked by bitterness and disillusionment, and in the works of new Congolese, Zairois and Central African authors. It came in the return of the repressed, whose violence was expressed first in the 1970s in *Touki Bouki*, and reemerged with *Hyenas* (1992), and with the new generation of Bekolo and his peers.

Africa's leaders stood accused of torture in David Achbar's personal account of his father's imprisonment and torture in *Allah Tantou* (1991), with the one-time hero of independence, Sekou Touré, now generally discredited. Raoul Peck's celebration of Lumumba (*Lumumba* [1992]) struck a powerful note because of its indictment of the longstanding dictatorship of Mobutu. While Ken Saro-Wiwa stood up to the Nigerian military, Djibril Diop chal-lenged the entire African ruling class, and especially the Senegalese ruling classes and government, in *Hyenas* and *Le Franc* (1995).

The violence of the present age had called up a cinema of tremendous poignancy, crying out for a human face—not one that celebrated roots, but that mocked those who had abused the ideals of an earlier generation, installing a new age of selfishness and violence. The stress upon demystification was all the more poignant and terrible now because it was turned almost entirely inward. Gone was the concern over assimilation, except in a few vestigial moments of Sembène's cinema (*Le Camp de Thiaroye* [1987] and *Guelwaar* [1995]); gone the prevailing epistemes of revolt, commitment, good faith, or even self-sacrifice or commu-nity. Now came the time of bouki, the hyena, a trickster with a cynical mask, not to be worshipped, except from a romanticized distance, but to be feared. Post-engagement cinema is, like its lit-erary double, a cinema of negation and of love, as in the family sce-narios, the work of the children remembering their parents (*Allah Tantou* and *Lumumba*, or Salem Mekuria's *Deluge* [1996]). The appeal to an audience that felt itself increasingly helpless and with nothing left to lose might explain why the 1980s and 1990s also were marked by a tempo of increased demands for multipartyism, for an end to long-standing rulers, and to the right to voice or to print opposition views. This was the time that women began to make films, finally providing us with something more significant than Sembène's images of long-oppressed wives or daughters.

Perhaps the best way to understand post-engagement cinema is as that of a cinema that has begun to turn in the direction of women as the harbingers for Africa's future. African women film-makers are in the same position now that African women writers were in about ten to fifteen years ago. As with the early studies of African women's writing, like *Ngambika* (1986), scholarly work on African woman filmmakers has often included the ways out-siders portray women—outsiders here meaning non-Africans, like Trinh T. Minh-ha (*Reassemblage,* 1982) and Claire Denis (*Chocolat,* 1988), but also African men, like Cheikh Oumar Sissoko (*Finzan,* 1986) and Med Hondo (*Sarraounia,* 1987).

As with early women's literature in Africa, one finds much testimonial and pragmatic filmmaking practice, with examples ranging from the docu-dramas of the doyenne of women's films, Safi Faye, to the straightforward presentations of Anne-Laure Folly. However, the post-modern age of dialogical communica-tion has not by-passed the genius of other practitioners for whom silence, gaps, and bodily expression, so important in female dis-cursive theory, retain a central role in cinematic and feminist expression. Here the patient and loving attention provided Mozambican emigrant women laborers by Flora M'mbugu-Schelling (*These Hands* [1992]) sets a new standard in cinematic expressiveness, while Assia Djebar's films chronicling the women's background roles on the soundtrack of Algerian colo-nial history, and their vital places in 130 years of resistance in the Algerian revolution (*La Nouba des femmes du mont Chenoua* [1978] and *La Zerda ou Les Chants de l'oubli* [1980]), carry through the same daring, post-modernist feminist project as her recent writings on Algerian women.

We might wish to trace the origins of some of this work to the early "mothers" of African women's cinema, with filmmakers like Sarah Maldoror whose *Sambizanga* (1972) set an early standard. Maldoror is an "outsider," a Guadeloupian raised in France, mar-ried to an Angolan MPLA leader, in whose film adaptation of Luandino Vieira's revolutionary novel, *The Real Life of Domingos Xavier* (1978), the focus is changed entirely from the male pro-tagonist and martyr, Domingos, to his wife, Maria, and the women surrounding her. Maldoror's work has its roots in Pontecorvo, Italian neo-Realism, and such films as *The Battle of Algiers* (1966). Revolutionary and committed film, like the literatures of the 1950s and early 1960s, represent one dimension of women's cinema in Africa, paralleling the work of male filmakers like Gerima, Sembène, etc.

From another perspective, one could consider the matrilineage established by Safi Faye, whose own work we would trace back to the cinema verité of Jean Rouch with whom Safi Faye had originally worked. Faye's *Peasant Letter* (1975) has attained a quasi-canonical status, and has certainly influenced the direction taken by Folly, Anne Mungai, and others for whom the goal of chronicling "la condition féminine" still remains critical. Both men and women filmmakers have continued this program, so that issues like excision, polygamy, forced marriages, the oppression of unattached women, economic exploitation, religious and traditional sexism, and so on, are highlighted across a spectrum of works like Sissoko's Finzan (1986), Sembène Ousmane's *Xala* (1974), Folly's *Femmes aux yeux ouverts* (1993) and *Femmes du Niger* (1993), Kamal Dehane's *Femmes du Alger* (1993), Boureima Nikiema's *Ma fille ne sera pas excisée* (1990), Godwin Mawuru's *Neria* (1992) [with the collaboration of Tsitsi Dangarembga], and Alice Walker and Pratibha Parmar's *Women Warriors* (1994).

The issue of voice, the problematics of speaking for as opposed to speaking next to, as Trinh T. Minh-ha would have it in *Reassemblage*, remains central. In a larger sense, it is here that we can locate the unstated split between a post-modernist feminist theoretical position, and a modernist feminist reformist cinematic practice. The split can be seen in the different approaches taken by Walker and Parmar, in their *Women Warriors*, on the one hand, and Trinh T. Minh-ha, Djebar, or M'mbugu-Schelling on the other. In the former, there is little concern, except for occasional lip service, paid to the politics of representation or identity. Women are defined, their oppression detailed for them, their path to liberation laid out for them—sometimes by men, sometimes by non-Africans, sometimes by other African women. The problem of the subject and the subject position is displaced by the larger concern over social action: the goal of social reform is consistently presented throughout as though the issues of realism, representation, and voice had never been problematized in feminist theory.

More typical of the new direction of committed cinema is the intensely personal, the anguished personal testimony of filmmakers whose immediate families provide the occasion for demarcating the political. Raoul Peck's and David Achbar's family portraits as new forms of political cinema have their parallel with the cinema of Salem Mekuria whose powerful evocation of the turmoil in Ethiopia and its effects upon her family resulted in *Deluge*

(1996). Dangarembga's novel *Nervous Conditions* (1988) would seem to be the obvious fictional example of this approach; while her film *Everyone's Child* (1997) might be seen to mark the same key moment in her career, marking her turn towards filmmaking, as did Sembène's *Borom Sarret* and *La Noire de*....

Without leaving aside the social reformism of the above, Djebar has put forward a cinema of silence, a cinema of cries and songs, that echoes the combative stances taken by Algerian women in the streets, while M'mbugu-Schelling has done the same for exiled Mozambican women in *These Hands*. This is the cinema of the 1980s and 1990s, a cinema no less tenacious in its devotion to the cause of women's emancipation than are the films that still adhere to the older traditions of protest filmmaking.

Djebar, Faye, and dozens of other African women no longer stand alone as interlopers or newcomers in the male domain of African cinema. Although conventional male disparagement of women's professional accomplishments still represents a barrier to the financing of women's films, the persistence, and determination of dozens of women have resulted in what is now a substantial body of works. Nancy Schmidt has constructed a major filmography showing that "women are engaged in filmmaking throughout the subcontinent." She lists the names of almost one hundred women directors, and this does not even include North Africans. Most of the films were made in the 1980s or 1990s, although Safi Faye's earliest work dates to 1972, while Efua Sutherland collaborated in the creation of a film as early as 1967 and Thérèse Sita-Bella made a film in 1963. Schmidt has speculated that the higher visibility accorded African male filmmakers is due to the fact that women make far more documentary and television films than feature films. If that has been true up to now, it is certainly beginning to change with the efforts of Djebar, Mungai, Dangarembga, and other women of the 1990s for whom, like Sembène, filmmaking has come to accompany or even supplant their literary efforts.

Anne Mungai, Flora M'mbugu-Schelling, Tsitsi Dangarembga, Fanta Nacro, Anne-Laure Folly, Ngozi Onwurah, Salem Mekuria, Moufida Tlatli, and Yamina Benguigui, coming after the generation of Sarah Maldoror, Safi Faye or even Euzhan Palcy, constitute the core of an important new constituent body of filmmakers for whom the old masculinist vocabulary of engagement seems dated and inappropriate. Even though a portion of their work rests upon older scenarios of representation, they are in the process of creating a new cinematic vision, marking out the terrain within which the exciting work of Jean Pierre Bekolo (*Quartier Mozart* [1992] and *Aristotle's Plot* [1995], and the work of Jean-Marie Teno (*Afrique, Je te plumerai* [1992]) can find its place. We might associate that new space with Kristeva's chora, a "semiotic" or pre-symbolic site in which the rhythms, drives, and sympathies of a physical presence take precedence over the symbolic order of language and repression. Despite the advent of the symbolic order, with its transparent vision of a world subordinate to the logic of lan - guage and rationality, the semiotic, its forces and drives imbued with the sense of the maternal body, structures the patterns, traces and gaps that mark, more or less, the emergent women's cinema in Africa. Although this is more obvious in some cases than in others, in general we can assert that the new sensibility that informs the cinema of the 1990s owes as much to its attentiveness, its care - ful auscultation of women's voices and silences, as it does to a concern over "women's issues."

The new reference points that have emerged are being estab - lished by a core of women directors whose efforts to make films and to have them shown does more than duplicate that of the male directors of an earlier period. As was the case with the women writers of the 1980s, the women directors of the present period have redefined the boundaries of gender roles in cinema, and in the process are reconstituting cinematic praxis.

WORKS CITED

Achbar, David. *Allah Tantou* (1991).
Bekolo, Jean-Pierre. *Quartier Mozart* (1992).
—. *Aristotle's Plot* (1995).
Cissé, Souleymane. *Finye* (1982).
—. *Yeelen* (1989).
Dangarembga, Tsitsi. *Everyone's Child* (1997).
—. *Nervous Conditions*. London: The Women's Press, 1988.
Davies, Carole Boyce and Anne Adams Graves, *Ngambika*. Trenton, NJ: Africa World Press, 1986.
Dehane, Kamal. *Femmes du Alger* (1993).
Denis, Claire. *Chocolat* (1988).
Diawara, Manthia. *African Cinema*. Bloomington: Indiana University Press, 1992.
Dikongue-Pipa, Jean Pierre. *Muno Moto* (1975).

—. *Le Prix de la liberté* (1978).
Djebar, Assia. *La Nouba des femmes du mont Chenoua* (1978).
—. *La Zerda ou Les Chants de l'oubli* [1980].
Fadika, Kramo Lanciné. *Djeli* (1980).
Faye, Safi. *Peasant Letter* (1975).
Folly, Anne-Laure. *Femmes aux yeux ouverts* (1993)
—. *Femmes du Niger* (1993).
Gerima, Haile. *Harvest 3000* (1974).
—. *Sankofa* (1993).
Gomes, Flora. *Mortu Nega* (1988).
Hondo, Med. *Sarraounia* (1987).
Kabore, Gaston. *Wend Kuuni* (1982).
—. *Zan Boko* (1988).
Maldoror, Sarah. *Sambizanga* (1972).
Mambéty, Djibril Diop. *Le Franc* (1995).
—. *Hyènes* (1992).
—. *Touki Bouki* (1973).
Mawuru, Godwin. *Neria* (1992).
Mekuria, Salem. *Deluge* (1996).
M'mbugu-Schelling, Flora. *These Hands* (1992).
Nikiema, Boureima. *Ma fille ne sera pas excisée* (1990).
Parmar, Pratibha. *Women Warriors* (1994).
Peck, Raoul. *Lumumba* (1992).
Pontecorvo, Gillo. *The Battle of Algiers* (1966).
Rouch, Jean. *Moi, un noir* (1958).
Sarr, Mamadou and Paulin Vieyra. *Afrique sur Seine* (1955).
Schmidt, Nancy. *Sub-Saharan African Films and Filmmakers*. London: Hans Zell, 1988.
—. *Sub-Saharan African Films and Filmmakers*, 1987-1992. London: Hans Zell, 1994.
Sembène Ousmane. *Borom Sarrett* (1963).
—. *Camp de Thiaroye* (1987).
—. *Emitaï* (1971).
—. *Guelwaar* (1995).
—. *Mandabi* (1968).
—. *La Noire de...*(1966).
—. *Tauw* (1974).
—. *Xala* (1974).
Sissoko, Cheikh Oumar. *Finzan* (1986).
Teno, Jean-Marie. *Afrique, Je te plumerai* (1992).
Traore, Mahama Johnson. *Njangaan* (1975).

Trinh T. Minh-ha. *Reassemblage* (1982).

Vieira, Luandino. *The Real Life of Domingos Xavier* (1971). Trans. Michael Wolfers. London: Heinemann, 1978.

PART ONE

THEORIZING AFRICAN CINEMA: POSTCOLONIAL PERSPECTIVES

THE THEORETICAL
CONSTRUCTION OF AFRICAN CINEMA

IN HIS INVESTIGATIONS INTO THE POSSIBILITY of an
African philosophy, V.Y. Mudimbe interrogates the various intellectual movements that have influenced the development of
Africanist discourse: Negritude, Sartrean existentialism, missionary writings, ethnophilosophy, anthropological structuralism, and
Fanonian neo-Marxist nationalism. A thorough study along the
lines that I am proposing for the investigation of ideological cur-
rents in African cinema and criticism should, ideally, address all
of these influences. For now I intend to make a few generalizations
in reviewing some of the recent critical works on African cinema,
the publication of which has highlighted the need for a systematic
study of the theoretical foundations of the discourse on African
cinema.

The contentious operative question underlying Mudimbe's
work concerns how African philosophy might be positioned so as
to avoid being confined by the Western discourses that were initially introduced into African culture through colonialism, and
which originally defined philosophy as a field of knowledge and
a disciplinary practice as such. It may be useful to recall how Hegel
presented the problem in relation to the African tradition in his
Philosophy of History:

> The peculiarly African character is difficult to comprehend, for
> the very reason that in reference to it, we must quite give up
> the principle, which naturally accompanies all our ideas—the
> category of Universality. (Hegel, 93)

On the basis of this logic, and by force of the institutions generated in its tradition, it became impossible to conceptualize such a thing as African history except as a sub-category of that of Europe; African thought, insofar as it was acknowledged at all, would nec - essarily be articulated in terms that extended out of the Enlightenment.

It would be hard to avoid the implication that any African dis - course making philosophical claims would have to be inherently a hybrid intellectual product, its very effort to link itself to the philosophical tradition having as a precondition some reconcilia - tion with Western culture. Thus, unsurprisingly, given the politi - cal relationship that has obtained between Africa and the West, the question of what "African philosophy" might consist of has been traditionally characterized by a struggle to distill the pure, authentic, original, traditional, or indigenous characteristics from what have generally been considered perverse external influences. Mudimbe's historicizations lead us to suspect that, articulated in this form, such an activity may not be very useful, and that the concept of authenticity may itself be implicated in formulations of intellectual originality, cultural appropriation, and mimesis that elide the very historical and cultural specificity that it is supposed to animate:

> The fact of the matter is that, up to now, Western interpreters as well as African analysts have been using categories and conceptual systems dependent on a Western epistemological order, and even in the most explicit "Afrocentric" descrip- tions, models of analysis, explicitly or implicitly, knowingly or unknowingly, refer to the same order. Does this mean that African Weltanschauungen and African traditional systems of thought are unthinkable and cannot be made explicit within the framework of their own rationality? (150)

The question grasps the fundamental philosophical problem invoked by the politics of authenticity as practiced by Africanists (both Western Marxists and African nationalists) and holds the possibility of redefining the theoretical grounds on which the Africanist project may be established.

I would like to consider how African film criticism and African films as objects of criticism contribute to and mirror this discus - sion of the possibility for an African philosophy. The same essen -

tial problem presents itself: what can be properly defined as African, and is it possible to separate this pure object from the pre-sumably unclean Western influences? By evaluating four major theorists of Third World and African cinema in the context of their critical positions, I hope to suggest how the question of authenticity can confine contemporary readings of African cinema, and how, in the very process of constituting African cinema as a tradition, its critics may contribute to its reduction

It may be assumed that Africa as an entity is an ideological product, that its unity and identity are constructed rather than hav-ing an a priori historical or material existence—an assumption that bears importantly upon the three main critical positions employed to discuss African cinema, all of which take for granted that African cinema should be essentially distinct, although they have difficulty identifying its unique characteristics. Without denying that African cinema may have unique qualities, or invalidating the positions of directors who see themselves as establishing a dis-tinctive African tradition with its own techniques of representation, I shall try to demonstrate how the misleading issues of authentic-ity and appropriation limit the ideological power of African cin-ema. From among the many rich theoretical possibilities available in interpreting African cinematic texts, these three relatively dis-crete theoretical positions repeatedly reemerge neo-Marxism, neo-structuralism, and modernism.

Neo-Marxism, the most common and fundamental of the post-colonial discourses, places the highest value and authority on oppo-sition or resistance, emphasizing the value of subverting dominant forms, methods, genres, and institutions. It is based upon a cri-tique of production and representation that could be traced most directly to the Frankfurt school; typically it seeks to define how cul-tural products can subvert, or exist independently of, a capitalist superstructure. This critical position evaluates texts according to their relation to dominant systems of production and dominant ideologies; it characterizes texts deriving from dominant ideology and capitalist systems of production as less authentic or less valu-able than those often speciously understood as rooted in an ideol-ogy and practice of resistance.[1]

A second critical position, neo-structuralism, assumes an almost scientifically objective stance, in contrast to the neo-Marxist one, which is usually overtly polemical; its goal is to describe or translate cultural products for different audiences rather than to prescribe or proscribe cinematic practices. The typical method involves the employment of binary categories to characterize ele - ments within the text and to mediate between the Western readers' presumptions and the text's historical, artistic, or cultural context. Neo-structuralist readings, like neo-Marxist ones, are grounded upon the differentiation of African films from Western films; but whereas the neo-Marxist seeks to valorize and heighten the dif - ference, the neo-structuralist sees the difference as already in place within the text or in reality, and merely wishes to demonstrate the differences through which meaning can take place. [2]

Modernism, the third major position, is closely related to the second in its absence of overt polemical intent; it emphasizes its own subjectivity in ascribing value to a text, attempting to relativize descriptions, level categorical differences, and move toward uni - versalistic interpretation and critique by means of a more detailed, particular, contextualized discussion. This sort of criticism is over - whelmingly practiced in its popular form by newspaper reviewers and biographers; it typically presumes the author's independence and dwells on the director or auteur as the center of the text, de- emphasizing the power relations in which the texts are embedded and the political situation of the work. The critical modernist tra - dition usually focuses on the text as an aesthetic event, and glori - fies the author as a consequence of having elevated the text to the status of high culture. [3]

Ferid Boughedir, one of the earliest critics of African film, is somewhat paradigmatic as a theorist who has insisted on impos - ing classification systems on the texts. He categorizes African films "according to the theoretical positions of their auteurs and their effect on the public...their ultimate function" (Boughedir, 79): the political tendency is a consciousness-raising exercise designed to mobilize the people in common resistance; the moral - ist tendency represents a shortsighted political analysis that indi - vidualizes the problems of African society; the commercial ten - dency attempts to entertain by selling emotions; the cultural tendency reevaluates contemporary African culture in relation to folk traditions; the "self-expression" tendency expresses the per - sonal views of an alienated author; and the "narcissistic intellec - tual" tendency, a sub-category of the previous one, is characterized by the naive idealization of traditional African culture and per - petuation of myths about Africa. Such categories would enable us to identify the liberatory and distinguish it from the regressive.

Within his construct there is a leap of faith where alliance with "the people" is seen as a transparent, positive position. The direc-tor has the possibility of being either for or against the people, regressive or liberal.

Teshome Gabriel, a leading advocate of the critical theory of Third World cinema, takes a similarly explicit and unapologeti-cally neo-Marxist approach, but with slightly more subtlety. Following the critical stance adopted by Franz Fanon and the Latin American advocates of a Third, or Imperfect Cinema, Gabriel's work is based on an attempt to formulate this other, essentially different cinema, as a subversive movement from domination to liberation. His system of classification identifies texts that fail to promote this movement, a tool toward the imposition of the tradi-tional Marxist distinction between authenticity (true conscious-ness) and inauthenticity (false consciousness) on films.

Gabriel reduces the tendencies of Third Cinema to three phases that represent a schematic evolution from oppression to liberation; only the third category can be properly called Third Cinema. The first phase, described as one of "unqualified assimilation," is con-stituted by its close relationship to the "Western Hollywood film industry" and its technical and thematic tendencies. Such films are disparaged, seen as "aping Hollywood stylistically" (Gabriel, 32), but Gabriel fails to cite examples; presumably films of this cate-gory are either easily recognized as such or not of much concern.

In *Third Cinema in the Third World: The Aesthetics of Liberation* (1982), Gabriel distinguishes between the typical Western treatment of race in South Africa as exemplified by a South African tourist film, *Journey to the Sun*, and its non-Western revolutionary counterpart, a film produced by South African exiles in Britain, *Last Grave at Dimbaza*. He argues that the film styles are essential to the effectiveness of the films: the tourist film is necessarily technically seamless, since it depends on an exoti-cization that must induce pleasure and excitement, while the lat-ter need not be finely constructed technically to succeed, but must make a persuasive argument. The examples are slightly specious however, as they seem to draw the line too unambiguously. We would want to know, in this regard, how to treat a film like Euzhan Palcy's *A Dry White Season* (1988) made through the Hollywood industry, very traditional and seamless stylistically; it is at the same time politically committed to exposing the injustices of apartheid and rooted in the formulation of political analogies through diaspora culture. Another film we might use to displace Gabriel's first category might be *Warrior Marks* (1993), which adheres to clearly committed anti-oppression pan-Africanist political positions, but is widely regarded as offensive and paternalistic toward Africans even by viewers sympathetic to the underlying motivation of the text to criticize the practice of female circumcision. As we begin to cite other ambiguous examples we come to suspect that as many examples of films standing between the boundaries can be found as ones standing within them, leading us to wonder what purpose the categories themselves serve.

Gabriel provides a somewhat more careful textual analysis of the difference between Western representation and authentic African representation in his comparison of anthropologist Jean Rouch and Senegalese filmmaker Sembène Ousmane. Jean Rouch is accused of treating Africans like insects, of studying them with an alienating objectivity, and above all, of tending to analyze them in voice-over narration rather than allowing them to speak for themselves. Sembène Ousmane is read as a folk hero, a modern griot, who utilizes oral traditions within cinematic texts. This point regarding oral narrative methods is emphasized, if somewhat forced, as it is one of the primary ideological reasons to ascribe authenticity to Sembène, the connection to folk cultural traditions in Africanist discourse having become essential to claims of Africanness. The choice of authors, again, seems specious, effec - tively drawing an unambiguous distinction between the authentic and the inauthentic.

The second phase, the "remembrance phase," seems to be more obviously contentious for Gabriel. It involves a qualified move from domination to liberation, which carries certain dangers. Films in this phase may fall into a reactionary "uncritical acceptance or undue romanticism of ways of the past" (Gabriel, 32). Gaston Kaboré's *Wend Kuuni* (1982) is placed in this category because of its thematic grounding in folklore; however, presumably because it represents traditional society as complex and inscribes the prob - lem of female power within the text, the film is vindicated. Third World film, Gabriel warns, must approach the medium as a tool for social transformation, "stamping out the regressive elements" (Gabriel, 32) otherwise the result is a "blind alley." The second phase is characterized by an indigenization, which will be impor - tant to the development of an authentic Third World film in the third phase.

The third phase represents the stage of liberation in Third World film. The system of production is uncoupled from capital - ist institutions and the ideological concerns are firmly embedded in themes of resistance; the third phase recognizes film "as an ide - ological tool" (Gabriel, 34). An avalanche of Sembène Ousmane's films are generally used to illustrate this third category as texts which are motivated by ideological intentions, although some - times it is acknowledged that there is some ambiguity with regard to their consistency with Western themes and styles. But such "grey areas" are acceptable because they demonstrate the "process of becoming" and the "multi-faceted nature" (Gabriel, 35) of Third World cinema rather than suggesting that the construct itself is problematic.

Gabriel elaborates his construct as an ideological tool directed toward the "development" of "new critical canons," (Gabriel, 35) and therefore situates himself as a part of this committed movement for liberation. The construct is not intended to provide an under - standing of the film texts themselves, valorizing them or their directors, so much as the imposition a revolutionary mandate on Third World film in general. It is not, however, feasible to totalize existing texts—these grey areas suggest that films can simultane - ously belong to all three phases—nor is it necessary to fix films within certain political categories; according to Gabriel, critical theory should serve to generate films which stimulate develop - ment and liberation of Third World peoples.

The goal of liberation becomes more problematic when Western and African film, along with Western theoretical con - structs, are viewed with greater complexity, so that Third World film viewed as liberatory solely in opposition to Western cine - matic paradigms becomes impossible. The charge of inauthentic - ity can easily be directed toward any film whatsoever if it fails to conform to certain revolutionary standards. That Gabriel avoids this accusation except in the most obvious cases (as in a film made by the South African government, or by a French anthropologist) merely conceals the dangers of Gabriel's strategy, which has con - sistently served the dominant forces of political repression in post - colonial Africa. The liberatory and "revolutionary" substitutes its own classificatory system for the repressive colonial ones, until the two begin to look dangerously similar.

Roy Armes and Lizbeth Malkmus, in *Arab and African Filmmaking* (1991) direct their criticism toward understanding the content of the films themselves as texts originating from different social and cultural traditions: the films are presumed to require supplementation to be understood across cultural differences. Although they discuss political implications in the introduction and insist on the importance of political ideology both in provid - ing background understanding and in mediating the symbolic play of meaning, they avoid becoming involved in polemical arguments with regard to the appropriate form of African film. Instead Armes and Malkmus position themselves, fairly self-consciously, as out - siders, looking in and reflecting from a distance on the political sit - uation of the texts. They employ binary distinctions to describe characteristic elements of African and Arab cinema, assuming an essential difference between non-Western and European cinemas and cultures. For Armes the oppositions of voice to voicelessness, narrativity to orality, space to time, and individuals to groups are formal tools to frame the description of the artistic, political, cul - tural, and social differences between African and Western films. The emphasis on structural methodology depoliticizes and deper - sonalizes, ultimately providing an ethnographic understanding of the texts, which emerge in his readings as authentic expressions of the African other.

Armes's discussion of *Wend Kuuni* provides a fair example of the benefits and limitations of the neo-structural approach. The film is viewed as turning upon Wend Kuuni's loss and dramatic reacquisition of voice: "The key event in this virtually wordless film is Wend Kuuni's acquisition of a voice" (Armes, 183). While we could argue that the function of voice in *Wend Kuuni* is some- what more ambiguous than Armes suggests, and that one could read Wend Kuuni as capable of being integrated within society and of functioning perfectly well within his given role without a voice, nonetheless Armes's work has shifted the discussion to an engagement with formal elements of the text, which is the great - est advantage of Armes's approach.

According to Armes, *Wend Kuuni* is structured so as to "set two spaces in opposition" (Armes, 193), the negative space of the "intolerant village of Wend Kuuni's early childhood" and "the sup - portive community into which he is adopted after being found in the bush" (Armes, 193). Again, Armes uses structural methodol- ogy to generate a fruitful discussion of formal elements of the text. He renders the film broadly accessible, in accordance with the uni - versalist assumptions, in contrast to the neo-Marxist assumption that would limit critical appropriation according to a dichotomy of authentic interpreters (those whose identities and politics allow them to understand the film properly) and inauthentic interpreters (outsiders whose critical appropriation is a regressive product of neo-colonialism), and views the difference in the subjective positions of readers as fixed and determined by the political context. As a generative tool to engage creative textual interpretation and to supplant the moralistic neo-Marxist prohibition against critical appropriation, Armes's approach is extremely fertile. The oppositions allow one entry into the narrative structure and the system of meaning inscribed in formal elements of films, in effect drawing them toward critical appropriation even where they are supposed to militate against such humanist, universalist readings. As Sembène once said: "In a word, Europeans often have a conception of Africa that is not ours." (Diawara, 32).

When analyzed more rigorously, however, the structural binarisms that Armes employs, such as the presumption of a Western concept of space as essentially different from African space, or the dominance of time as a narrative technique in Hollywood as opposed to the use of space in African films, appear to be very schematic. Although there is little doubt that the oppositions Armes constructs that are useful to Western interpreters, they can be seen as flawed or questionable as distinctive categories, and point to the very tendentious theoretical presuppositions upon which his work is grounded. The function of the individual in relation to the group, for example, as it is taken up in Armes' discussion of *Camp de Thiaroye* (1988), *Wend Kuuni*, and *Yaaba* (1989) rests upon a rather mythical comparison between Africa and the West. He argues that in each of these films a central character's position as marginal or as an outsider becomes important in the narrative only to emphasize the primacy of the group. Even where an individual is clearly central to the narrative, as in *Yaaba* where the film almost turns on a boy's individual stance set against the community, Armes claims that the individual merely functions as a symbol of a characteristic role in the culture or a mythological position in oral tales that has a general rather than an individualized importance. We might note that the same could as easily be said of Rambo or Dirty Harry, for instance, in that they could be interpreted as merely animating aspects of certain historical, cultural, or mythical narratives relating to Vietnam and the Old West. The individual/group index again turns upon an understanding of real ity in terms of a fundamental difference between the West and the Third World: in Hollywood films, "the personal and the social are all internalized within the individual protagonist" (Armes, 211), whereas in African films "space, set, and group structure ... oper - ate at a collective level" (Armes, 210-211). Although Armes avoids privileging certain films or making prescriptions, underlying the neo-structuralist approach is the same principle of difference, dis - guised, despite a more self-consciously theoretically grounded dis - cussion. His fundamental move, to interpret the other for a Western audience, carries presuppositions, which, perhaps inevitably, "invent" the colonized.

Manthia Diawara's *African Cinema* (1992) is probably the most difficult text to locate within the three critical positions that I have outlined, partially because of its inconsistency—especially the inconsistency of the final chapter on "African Cinema Today" with respect to the modes of criticism operating in the rest of the book. Overall *African Cinema* provides an extremely valuable his - torical perspective on African cinema. Diawara emphasizes the importance of local and regional political factors, especially those produced by colonialism, in understanding the background of African film production, and seems to follow Teshome Gabriel's call for an evaluation of non-Western cinemas according to their specific histories, contexts, and systems of production. He carefully examines the systematic restraints imposed on different regions within the colonial, missionary, and anthropological traditions of filmmaking, and the establishment of federations, organizations, festivals, and national production systems to promote African pro - duction.

His construction of Africa does not reinforce the understand - ing of the history of African film as the site of an essential politi - cal opposition between the West and Africa, but rather, relativizes the various colonialisms and their specific practices and products according to effects of particular regimes and spheres of influence. The approach could be described as modernist historicist to the extent that it participates in this relativization of the historical nar - rative, depolarizing political aspects in favor of the engagement, not of the scene of anti-colonial struggle, but of the historical con - text as a valuable point of the entry into a meaningful under - standing of texts and the constraints imposed by underdevelop - ment. By the time the narrative arrives at contemporary film it becomes clear that Diawara has rendered the films appropriable as texts whose meanings can be approached with less anthropologi - cally grounded tools then the neo-structuralist presumes, and less emphatically politically-motivated ones than those of the neo- Marxist.

A major shortfall of his approach, however, is that his detailed account of production and institutions fails to provide the reader expecting a general knowledge of African texts with a sense of the content of the films themselves. Although Diawara moves from the generalizations of Gabriel's Third Cinema to a more nuanced study of specific African regions, he fails to evaluate the texts themselves within the historical context that he presents, so that one is left with the mistaken impression that African texts themselves are underdeveloped. The last chapter on "African Cinema Today" attempts to provisionally address this matter. In this chapter he uncouples the films from their institutional context, addressing them in relation to three thematic groupings.

Diawara points toward a "thematic diversification," but instead of characterizing these themes within a metatheoretical schema and granting authenticity to certain themes, he considers the films historically, using the general narrative themes to indicate pre - vailing tendencies. His description becomes especially apolitical as the discourses of colonialism, and the historical analysis of insti - tutions, give way to discussions of individual, indigenous, and national film productions:

Clearly there are many African images, and it seems trivial to expect filmmakers of different generations, different countries, and different ideological tendencies to see the same Africa every - where. It is therefore not my intention to sort out which modes of representation are right and which are wrong. (Diawara, 141)

He observes the political motivations of the filmmakers but evaluates "each narrative movement in the context of its own modes of production" (Diawara, 141). Diawara does not dispense, however, with the traditional tripartite construct used by the pro - ponents of a Third Cinema, Solanas and Getino, and following them Gabriel, who constituted Third Cinema as the third of three progressively more liberatory phases of world cinema. Diawara's three categories sensitively modify the political implications that Gabriel assigns to the three phases of Third World Film, evaluat - ing the texts according to their "coherence in the particular dis - course they choose to deploy" (Diawara, 166). Certain similarities appear, nonetheless, within the tripartite divisions, pointing to an essentially unchanged theoretical construct.

Diawara's category of social realism, like Gabriel's phase of unqualified assimilation, is characterized by films, which employ music, romance, and comedy to entertain the audience. Diawara describes this category as a popular form because of its ability to identify with working class audiences, while Gabriel disparages the form as regressive, capitalist, Western-identified cinema. This is a significant move by Diawara, in effect resituating popular culture as valid in the African context where Gabriel rejects it out of hand.

Diawara's "return to the source" category, characterized by an absence of polemicism, includes films which review precolonial African conditions in relation to post-colonial problems and films which strive to develop a distinctive African film language. It is almost identical to Gabriel's "remembrance phase," described as an effort to indigenize the industry and film style, favoring the narrative conflict between the past and present. Gabriel gives this second category conditional praise, while Diawara neither privileges nor rejects this category of film.

Lastly the "Colonial Confrontation" category in *African Cinema* closely corresponds to Gabriel's "combative phase," both of which refer to a category of films playing on the initial opposition between the Third World/Africa and the West/Hollywood, although Diawara's category is somewhat narrower than Gabriel's; Gabriel includes in this phase not only the effort to combat neo-colonialism, but the attempt to make explicit anti-capitalist ideological representations.

More important than the similarities between the categories as Gabriel and Diawara have constructed them are the margins between the tripartite divisions. The contradiction between the neo-Marxist and modernist interpretation of social realist/popular/assimilationist cinema, typified by the problem of adequately understanding *La vie est belle* (1987) or *A Dry White Season* (1988), for example, as either strictly adhering to the social realist, unqualified assimilation, Western or African, categories, signals an essential problematic feature of the construction of categories to describe Third World and African film. What is at stake is more than the difference between two critics' positions with regard to the political and ideological purposes of cinema or criticism or the conflict between differently constructed categories. The question can again be traced back to the initial rupture com-

mon to the three critical techniques, all of which turn on the constitution of Africa or the Third World as a unity essentially in opposition to, or separable from, the West and its stylistic, thematic and
industrial characteristics.

The observation that the critical techniques taken up by the
three critics are embedded in Western constructs, tautologically
returns us to the same presumptuous—but historically founded
and culturally determined—opposition; more important is the
observation that the critics fail to rigorously ground their theoretical projects and as a result utilize prevailing assumptions without
evaluating their relation to dominant systems of interpretation.
Obviously it would be devastating to expect African and Third
World critics to apologize for appropriating Western modes of criticism, or for Western critics to apologize for appropriating African
and Third World film, as we will have lost in the atmosphere of
contention any true sense of the value of the texts themselves, and
ignored the emergent space in which an African world cinema is
being established. Sembène Ousmane, the great Senegalese filmmaker, has evidently struggled with the problem on his own terms:
We are not trying to define ourselves in relationship to any specific
cinema. We want to borrow from each one whatever we can and
transform it to make up our own cinema. We know that there is a
difference between America and Africa, but we don't want to spend
our time trying to define ourselves in relationship to America.
(Gabriel, 116).

Boughedir's contempt for intellectualism and individual
expression, Gabriel's call to purify Third World cinema of regressive, capitalist, Western influences, Armes and Malkmus's more
subtle appropriation of Arab and African cinema for the understanding of the West, and Diawara's still more unobtrusive evaluation of the history of African cinema in the context of particular
modes of production and thematic tendencies, all bear the unmistakable imprint of the Africanist imperative, like Said's Orientalists
who began with a mythological conception of the difference
between the Occident to the Orient: not to confuse Third World and
African cinema with Western, Hollywood, or capitalist cinema, to
maintain an essential distinction without bothering to reveal how
the difference was introduced into the criticism itself.

Julianne Burton is among the many critics who have emphasized the importance of foregrounding one's critical relation to the
text, attempting to resist the assumption of many of the categories

and oppositions confining critical practices. [4] Burton's suggestion is that a rejection of the small-minded logic by which Western theory is seen as antithetical to an authentic Third World practice, and a more conscious appropriation of Western theory would benefit Third World theorists and filmmakers by enlarging the possibilities for filmmakers and by enabling a more sophisticated film culture. Tomas Gutierrez Alea says something similar in his "The Viewer's Dialectic," albeit couched in very familiar Marxist constructs. It becomes increasingly apparent as African filmmakers continue to free themselves from the ideological constraints of Marxism and African essentialism, and incorporate more and more influences of indeterminate origins, that the critic, in turn, will require a different set of tools. Critics are bound to be stimulated in this direction by Djibril Diop Mambéty's *Hyenas* (1992), an adaptation of a Swiss modernist play (Friedrich Dürrenmatt's *The Visit*) transposed into contemporary Senegal. Indeed, the work of Djibril Diop Mambéty (*Touki-Bouki* [1973], *Le Franc*, *Hyenas*) frequently seems to work against the grain of the Africanist imperative, for the reason that his films are so intent on studying human relationships in all their complexity. His implicit subject, the African looking toward the West, is always represented with a caustic eye to the ideological complicity of social actors, who are nonetheless viewed sympathetically against the backdrop of their position in society. It is likely that with the right systems of distribution and proper modes of valorization such a body of work could be more fully appreciated in the world cultural system.

We might say that African texts exerting an influence on world culture already exist on some limited scale—limited more by the systems of distribution and production than by any ideological constraints or inherent technical incapabilities—and that the question of what is authentically African in film becomes increasingly anachronistic in light of this emerging moment. Cultural syncretism has always been present throughout Africa, but has apparently been covered over by the ahistorical dichotomies of modernity. [5] The divergent texts of African world cinema necessitate above all that we consider revising or rejecting the question "what is authentically African?" As critics, we have to approach texts with the idea of retrieving more than a correct representation of Africa, and to do so we must above all come to terms with how intellectual history has left its mark on our understanding of both African societies and the texts themselves. This becomes essential to evaluating the true originality of African cinema, as the inevitable charge that African cinema is grounded in constructs or styles suppos - edly derivative of a Western tradition still too often succeeds in reducing African cultural products; the encounter between Africa and Europe continues to be played out on the basis of the same rules in which Africa serves as a foil for the universalist claims of the West. What we identify as authentically African apparently must exclude the European and place itself in opposition to it so as to legitimate its authority. But this game of exclusion and oppo - sition, based on the premise—so omnipresent that even when rec - ognized as faulty it still exerts its influence—that Europe is the center and origin of all culture, in advance invalidates African texts as inauthentic; as post-structuralists like to say, even the reac - tion to the other is defined by the limits of the other's discourse. An investigation of the terms in which the problem of authentic - ity is posed may help us to understand the ways in which the con - structs used to evaluate African cultural products continue to return us to the site of colonial conflict, with its nearly exhausted colo - nial oppositions. We still await, however, the emergence of that Africanist discourse whose authority will be constructed such that it will no longer have the need to call itself African.

NOTES

1. See Teshome Gabriel, *Third Cinema in the Third World: The Aesthetics of Liberation*, 1982. Solanas and Gettino, "Toward a Third Cinema," 1976. Haile Gerima, On Independent Black Cinema, in *Black Cinema Aesthetics*, 1982. *Marxism in African Literature*. ed. George M. Gugelberger, 1988. Ferid Boughedir, *Le cinema Africain de A à Z*, 1987.
2. Also see Andre Gardies and Pierre Haffner, *Regards sur le cinema negro-africain*, 1987. Roy Armes, *Third World Filmmaking and the West*, 1988. Manthia Diawara, "Oral Literature and African Film: Narratology in *Wend Kuuni*," 1987.
3. Francoise Pfaff, *The Cinema of Ousmane Sembène: A Pioneer of African Film*, 1984. Francoise Pfaff, *Twenty-five Black African Filmmakers*, 1988. Mbye Cham, *Ex-Iles: Essays in Caribbean Cinema*, 1992. *Aesthetics of Spectatorship*, ed. Manthia Diawara, 1993.

4.	Trinh T. Minh-ha, both in her writings and cinematic exper-
iments, has demonstrated more concretely than anyone has
how the meeting of Africa and deconstructivist practices can
enrich and dynamize the emerging African world cinema.
Reassemblage (1982) as much as any indigenous African
film has effectively problematized the camera's objectifying
eye, the assumption that the camera can simply record some
existing truth about African culture, as well as the notion that
"correct" representation is possible. She initiates a genre of
critically reflective deconstructivist film that utilizes contemporary criticism in unexpected ways to rephrase the question regarding authenticity of representation.
5.	Youssef Chahine's *Alexandrie, encore et toujours* is another
example of this fourth or fifth cinema, the meeting ground for
an indefinite number of dialectical moments between cultures, oppositional without drawing the politics of identity
and modern binarisms too tightly around itself. *Alexandrie*
draws from Shakespeare and other texts of the Western tradition to discuss Egyptian identity, including a somewhat
affectionate parody of a Hollywood dance sequence that
might call to mind *Guys and Dolls*. In some ways *Alexandrie*
can be read as a response to theorists of national identity and
culture who are stuck on the opposition of the West to the
African, claiming a much wider scope of influence than that
of folk culture.

Works Cited

Alea, Tomas Guttierez. "The Viewer's Dialectic." *Jump Cut*. 30.
Armes, Roy, and Lisbeth Malkmus. *Arab and African Filmmaking*.
London: Zed Books Inc., 1991.
Armes, Roy. *Third World Filmmaking and the West*. Berkeley:
University of California Press, 1987.
Boughedir, Ferid. "L'image apprivoisee." *Jeune Afrique*. 914 (12
Juillet, 1978).
—. "The Principle Tendencies of African Cinema." *African Films:
The Context of Production*. Ed. Angela Martin. London: British
Film Institute, 1982.
Burton, Julianne. "Marginal Cinemas and Mainstream Critical
Theory." *Screen*. 26.3-4 (May-August 1985): 2-21.

Cham, Mbye B., *Ex-Iles: Essays on Caribbean Cinema*, Trenton: Africa World Press, 1992.
Chanon, Michael, ed. *Twenty-five Years of the New Latin American Cinema*. London: BFI and Channel Four, 1983.
Diawara, Manthia. *African Cinema*. Bloomington: Indiana University Press, 1992.
—. "Oral Literature and Film: Narratology in Wend Kuuni." *Presence Africaine*. (1987).
Gabriel Teshome, *Third Cinema in the Third World: The Aesthetics of Liberation*. Ann Arbor: UMI Research Press, 1982.
—. "Towards a critical theory of Third World films." *Third World Affairs*. (1985).
Hegel, G.W.F. *The Philosophy of History*. Dover: New York. 1956.
Mudimbe, V.Y. "African Gnosis." *African Studies Review*. 28.2-3 (June/September, 1985).
Pfaff, Francois. *The Cinema of Ousmane Sembene: A Pioneer of African Film*. Westport: Greenwood Press. 1984.
Pines, Jim and Paul Willeman, eds. *Questions of Third Cinema*. London: British Film Institute. 1989.
Solanas, Fernando E. and Octavio Gettino. "Towards a Third Cinema." In *Movies and Methods*, ed. Bill Nichols. Berkeley: University of California Press, 1976.
Trinh T. Minh-ha. *Woman, Native, Other: Writing Postcoloniality and Feminism*. Bloomington: Indiana University Press, 1989.

Films

Chahine, Youssef. *Alexandrie, encore et toujours*. 1985.
Kaboré, Gaston. *Wend Kuuni*. 1982.
Mambéty, Djibril Diop. *Hyenas*. 1992.
Mweze, Ngangura and Benoit Lamy. *La vie est belle*. 1987.
Ouedraogo, Idressa. *Yaaba*. 1989.
Palcy, Euzhan. *A Dry White Season*. 1988.
Parma, Pratibha and Alice Walker. *Warrior Marks*. 1993.
Sembène Ousmane. *Camp de Thioroye*. 1988.
—. *Guelwaar*, 1994.
Trinh T. Minh-ha. *Reassemblage*. 1982.
Walker, Alice. *Warrior Marks*. 1993.

AFRICAN FILMMAKING AND THE POSTCOLONIAL PREDICAMENT: *QUARTIER MOZART* AND *ARISTOTLE'S PLOT*

THE "POSTCOLONIAL" PREDICAMENT is the "Third World" predicament under another name: as Aijaz Ahmad puts it in a trenchant formulation on the subject of what "post-colonial - ism" means, "'Third World literature' gets rechristened as 'post - colonial literature' when the governing theoretical framework shifts from third world nationalism to post-modernism" ("The Politics of Literary Postcoloniality" 1). The change of name, and of para - digm, is a consequence of the historical defeat or stalling of the anti-colonial and anti-imperialist movements of the post-war era and of the relative failure of autonomous economic and cultural development which was to follow their attainment of state power (Ahmad, *In Theory*; Larsen, "Statement on Postcolonialism" and "DetermiNation").[1] The tendency of the African state and of African nationalism towards disintegration intersects a tendency in the Western academy towards the abandonment of grand narra - tives, including those involving the state and nationalism, in the cli - mate of a "post-colonialism" informed by post-structuralism, post - modernism, and post-Marxism. Africans have reason to be distrustful of post-modern post-colonialism as another foreign regime that tends to compromise crucial projects.[2] But those seek - ing progressive change in Africa must come to terms not only with the loss of Second World support for Third World liberation move - ments but also with the rapid evaporation of socialist ideology and practice throughout Africa (the transformation of the ANC once it rose to power being only one example) and the increasing difficulty of pointing to a socialist movement which would be the principal actor in a plausible revolutionary narrative. The main political demands of the 1990s–beyond sometimes insurrectionary expressions of the pains of structural adjustment–have been cast in terms of democracy and human rights, themes which, along with women's issues and the environment, open the purses of international patrons. It is not that neocolonialism and cultural imperialism have disappeared as basic structuring realities–they certainly have not—but that it has become difficult to imagine how to confront them directly. In this situation it becomes necessary and useful, practically as well as theoretically, to recognize the extent to which the political landscape has taken on a Foucauldian, postmodernist form, in which political resistance is far from dead but takes numerous dispersed forms, often at lower levels of political expression: in "the popular," the politics of everyday life, a "politique par le bas."

Economic collapse and the well-publicized failures of the African state have of course had massive, determining effects on African filmmaking, though mostly in the relatively undramatic form of failure to thrive, to develop from the original condition of what Sembène called *megotage* to a point past the current *bricolage*. Obvious problems include the general inability of local producers to control (or even reach) domestic screens anywhere in Africa, the demise of the pan-African cinema institutions established in Ouagadougou in the 1970s (with the notable exception of FESPACO), the dominance of co-production with European money and attendant compromises, the ghettoization of African film within the world market, and the unreadiness of African audiovisual producers to deal on reasonable terms with the "new world information order" created by the multinational corporations. Even the greatest successes of African filmmaking are beset by contradictions: Sembène's latest film, *Guelwaar* (1991), rails against foreign aid, but its credits reel off the usual list of European governmental and non-governmental funding sources.

Among cultural productions, filmmaking has been particularly vulnerable to the crises of economy and state. Because of its capital-intensive character, its unparalleled propaganda and cultural value, and the laws of neocolonial economics that make it impossible for a national cinema to exist anywhere in the Third World without state support (and, in Africa, without regional if not continental consortia), the arguments for the creation and support of African cinema have always been closely linked with nation building, cultural nationalism, and Pan-Africanism. The rhetoric of organizations like FEPACI has moderated considerably from its original militancy to a more commercial orientation and an accept - ance of "partnership" with European funding sources as a practi - cal necessity.[3]

But while cognizant of this development towards commer - cialization (Akudinobi), African film criticism, as represented for instance by the books by Manthia Diawara, Frank Ukadike, Teshome Gabriel, and Lizbeth Malkmus and Roy Armes, has for the most part continued to be dominated by Third Worldist terms of cultural nationalism, sometimes inflected by Marxism. The rea - sons for this must include the political motivations of most of those who become African film critics and the fact that the Third Worldist analysis has so much durable truth to it (whatever the fate of the projects of nation building). The cultural nationalist arguments are as necessary as they ever were in the battles that must be constantly fought in Africa to resist the flood of imported media and make domestic production possible (Larkin, personal communication). Yet there may be an element of inertia as well, in the slowness to come to grips fully with what has changed, and an element of nostalgia for a heroic, liberationist project in a post - modern world.

The post-modern post-colonialism which has fairly swamped literary studies in the Western academy has had strangely little influence on African film criticism. There has been no formal reck - oning with this fundamental shift in paradigm in terms of African cinema specifically, though in a broader context Paul Willemen's "The Third Cinema Question: Notes and Reflections," in the influ - ential volume *Questions of Third Cinema* (1989), addresses the issues with clarity and seriousness and is an exemplary attempt to bring the Third Worldist/ Third Cinema paradigm up to date and assess its continuing relevance.

Willemen begins with a quotation from the conference pro - gram of the 1986 Edinburgh International Film Festival, by way of admitting the need for a more sophisticated theory than that pro - vided in the revolutionary manifestoes: "'The complexity of the shifting dynamics between intra- and inter-national differences and power relations has shown simple models of class domina - tion at home and imperialism abroad to be totally inadequate'" (1). On the other hand, Willemen sees Third Cinema as a poten - tial antidote to the demobilizing effects of post-modernism:

[B]y turning to Third Cinema as a potential way forward, the conference implied that left cultural theory in the UK and in the US has become a serious handicap in that it has become hypo-critically opportunist (for instance, the proliferation of attempts to validate the most debilitating forms of consumerism, with academics cynically extolling the virtues of the stunted products of cultural as well as political defeat) or has degenerated into a comatose repetition of 70s deconstructive rituals. (2)

But the extent to which the ground has shifted under Third Cinema theory is revealed at several points in the essay. Trying to abstract a concept of Third Cinema from its (primarily Latin American) theoretical and practical elaborations in the 60s and 70s, he devel - ops a tripartite definition. First, Third Cinema is a cinema of lucid - ity rather than illusions. Second, it does not have any particular, prescribed aesthetic form. Third, it is a socially relevant discourse, which discusses things First and Second Cinema do not. This last is the weakest part of the definition: the second half is merely neg - ative, and the excessive flexibility of the first half ("a socially rel - evant discourse")—especially when coupled with the equally absolute flexibility of the preceding point about aesthetic form— is due to the fact that Willemen can no longer say what was obvi - ous in the 60s and 70s—that Third Cinema is cinema engaged in a world-wide socialist or at least anti-imperialist revolution. He will say at later points in the essay that Third Cinema is the work of socialist intellectuals in close dialogue with "a people itself engaged in bringing about social change" (27). One can and should remember African examples of such a cinema–the work of the revolutionary Film Institute in Mozambique up to 1991 (Andrade-Watkins) or the videos made and distributed by the South African union movement during the struggle against apartheid, for instance. But in spite of the valiant efforts of many directors, for African filmmaking in general it has been hard to come by the material conditions for a close dialogue with the people (given the problems of distribution), and, as I have been suggesting, at present it is not so easy to locate a cohesive, mobilized political movement with which to have the dialogue.

Another symptomatic moment in the essay comes as Willemen rehearses three basic options for creating a sense of national iden - tity (18-19). He seems to be tacitly following Fanon's famous three-stage progression of the consciousness of the colonized writer in *The Wretched of the Earth* (1961; 222-23). (This scheme is also a foundation for Teshome Gabriel's influential essay "Towards a Critical Theory of Third World Films" (31-35).) The first option is to identify with the dominant and dominating colonizing culture; the second is to reconnect with one's own people's traditions. The third option

> Refuse[s] both national chauvinism and identification with the aggressor in favor of a more complex view of social formations and their dynamics, including the fraught relationship with the West. As the Moroccan Zaghloul Morsy put it: "Whether we try to refute it, liberate ourselves from it or assent to it…the West is here with us as a prime fact, and ignorance or imperfect knowledge of it has a nullifying effect on all serious reflection and genuinely artistic expression." (19)

Fanon's third stage, of course, is the fighting phase, in which the intellectual connects with the people and shakes and leads them in their revolution. In its place Willemen offers "a more complex view of social formations and their dynamics" and the inevitable presence of the West as an element in the situation. We are now on the ground of "post-colonialism," with its characteristic shift from militant involvement with "real" politics and history to a readerly or writerly posture towards a complex, textualized reality heavily marked by hybridity and syncretism. (It is not at all accidental that Willemen's essay is preoccupied with Bakhtin, whose sociolin-guistic theory has provided post-colonial criticism with some of its most powerful tools.)

Even if we arrive at "post-colonialism" through painful his-torical defeats, and even if so much of what marches under its ban-ner is irresponsible and politically evasive, we do no service to African film by approaching it with a theoretical paradigm which has become in some ways antiquated: we need to be, if possible, ahead of the game. The textualizing turn is dangerous, but neces-sary in developing an adequate cultural theory. Theories of African post-coloniality offer alternative approaches to thinking about African film production which warrant investigation, not only to cheer ourselves up in the midst of Afro-pessimism but, more pos-itively, to suggest strategies for maneuver and methods of bring-ing new and altogether relevant phenomena into view. The post-colonialist deemphasis on the state and the national level, though politically dangerous, invites us to take a new look at supra- and sub-national and unofficial levels of organization which have indu - bitably gained in importance as history has moved on.

Syncretism becomes a crucial theme in all these domains of the supra- and sub-national and the unofficial. Syncretism is an old story in Africa, but the processes of globalization accelerate, deepen, and widen it. Postcolonial criticism in several disciplines has the virtue of having taken it up with the seriousness it deserves. African film criticism might do well to follow suit. African/European film coproductions are an instance of the supra- national processes of globalization, and it is common to bemoan the resulting, presumably hybridizing, effects; but as Elizabeth Mermin puts it, "The causal relation of aid to subject, though prob - ably significant, is not obvious" (123). Not obvious, but perhaps not unknowable either with an adequate critical-theoretical appa - ratus. At the other end of the socio-cultural scale, Karin Barber posits syncretism as having always been one of the essential char - acteristics of the unofficial African "popular arts" (23), including the (sub-national) example of the Yoruba travelling theater tradi - tion, which extended into television and filmmaking and most recently led the way in the video boom which has transformed the "film" environment in Nigeria and Ghana (Haynes, "Nigerian Cinema," Haynes and Okome, Larkin). Because of the technical and capital-intensive nature of filmmaking and the familiar prob - lems of distribution, African cinema has (with the Nigerian excep - tion) rarely been a "popular art" in Barber's sense of the term. But the widespread dissemination of video technology is bound to lead to the spread of grassroots video production everywhere in Africa, and its cultural dynamics will doubtless in large part be dominated by this sort of syncretic popular form rather than by the aesthetics or ideologies with which African film criticism is accustomed to dealing.

From the time of Jean Rouch's *Moi, un noir* (1958) there has been a history of resistance on the part of many critics to films which handle urban hybrid consciousness—the happy hunting ground for "post-colonial" phenomena. The reasons for this resist - ance have remained fundamentally the same: the formal preoccu - pation of African film criticism has been defining an "authentic" African style rather than handling hybrid forms, in spite of the manifest difficulties of this project given that the average African cinema-goer and cineaste have seen ten thousand foreign films and very few African ones; hybridity contradicts the essentialism of at least one kind of cultural nationalism; and a wounded sense of national identity may demand more dignity than the products of popular culture provide. An unhappy consequence of this is that African cinema and its criticism has not done terribly well at addressing what should be the heart of its audience: urban youth.

Enter Jean-Pierre Bekolo, a young (born 1966) Cameroonian. He is certainly not alone in making films about Africa's urban youth, but his two feature films, *Quartier Mozart* (1992) and *Aristotle's Plot* (1996), have been the most adventurous, not only in express - ing the consciousness and style of his generation, but also in recon - ceiving the current possibilities of African cinema in relation both to the popular (young) African cinema-going public and to the international situation of African film. Not at all a militant revo - lutionary in the manner of his cinematic ancestors, he is a cagy and attitudinous guerrilla roaming the post-modern globalized mediascape.

Quartier Mozart is marked simultaneously by globalization and the "micropolitical." It is about the lives of young people in a popular neighborhood in Yaoundé. Stylistically it is radically dif - ferent from almost all other African films: the director, then 26 years old, had experience making music videos, had studied screen - writing with Christian Metz, and claimed Spike Lee as an inspi- ration, whose *Do the Right Thing* he saw while a film student in Paris (Verschueren, 16). The style is very much in your face, fast, irreverent, and elliptical; jump cuts are the master gesture, though the technique is actually quite eclectic. Visually it is recognizably French post-modern (the director of photography and the costume and set designers are French), and on the soundtrack there is a good deal of American-influenced music, locally-made and com - missioned for the film: the songs are about the characters, and the final number, in rap style, samples bits of dialogue. The music may be a familiarizing element for foreign audiences, but in the first instance it is the soundtrack of the lives of the people in the film, ingrained in their sensibilities. As in Spike Lee, the Black vernacular arts of speech and dress are much of what the film is about, the film's own stylistic energies being continuous with those of its characters.

Jean-François Bayart may help to create a sympathetic view of such foreign influences. The following is part of his discussion of "extraversion":

> Everything points in the end to the fact that unequal entry into the international systems has been for several centuries a major and dynamic mode of the historicity of African societies, not the magical suspension of it. Their internal structure itself stems from this relationship with the world economy. Of course the concept of dependence still keeps its meaning, but it should not be dissociated from the concept of autonomy…

> …the concept of creolization is inherent in the historicity of African societies. A child of "total defeat," it derives precisely from the playful repertoire of the conquered…the young speakers of *Sheng* and *Nouchi*, the syncretic languages of Nairobi and Abidjan, lay claim in their humorous and provocative way to the exteriority on which the dominant class rests its power. These practices denote a projection of the social struggle into this area of relations with the outside world, which was historically so crucial, more than the "Europeanization," which offends contemporary ruling elites (as it did missionaries and colonial administrators) and is a source of chagrin for disappointed culturalists. Today, as at the time of the slave trade, what is really at stake is not the safeguarding of a problematical cultural veracity, but controlling the ideological and material resources resulting from integration into the world economy….Far from suggesting the withering of African societies, their marriage to overseas cultural influences shows their vigorous temperament. (27-28)

So one of the film's central characters, Saturday, declares that her independence from parental authority will commence as of 24:00 GMT—personal liberation to a global measure. She and her girl-friends use Michael Jackson as a sexual standard; Saturday prefers Denzel Washington. The girlfriend of Atango the tailor wants a skirt like Lady Di's, and so on.

Later Bayart talks of "popular modes of political action," which are not counter-hegemonic "strategies" but "mobile and changeable 'tactics'" (208-09)—a theme developed much further by David Hecht and Maliqalim Simone in their odd little book

Invisible Governance: The Art of African Micropolitics (1994). In this book, as in the film *Quartier Mozart*, the First World is always present as a source of technology, commodities, and styles, and as a place to go to, but it is not a controlling force and seems to have few intentions in the African world—the dynamic of colonization is really over. Agency is all with the Africans, mostly involving structures they make themselves. Hecht and Simone have a serious interest in the life of the poor and hit the right note when they talk of the mixture of despair and ebullience in the shantytowns and popular neighborhoods. They present the inhabitants as creatively polysemous, trickish, survivors with style, giving rise to wonderful anecdotes, and the literary values of the book, which are considerable, are those of magical realism, conveying a world of incommensurable varieties, jokes, strange destinies, unintended consequences, and wonder.

The framing tale of *Quartier Mozart* is magical as well: the Queen of the 'hood, a sassy school-girl, is transformed by a witch into a strapping young man, Myguy, so she can explore sex and gender relations from the other side: as the witch says, the best way to live is to be a woman in a man's body. (The witch, meanwhile, takes the form of a comic rural figure, Panka, who can steal men's genitals by shaking their hands.) Accepted by the guys who claim stylistic, social, and sexual dominion over the neighborhood, Myguy is egged on to prove himself by seducing Saturday, a hard target as she is the daughter of the police commissioner and consequently has been unattainable.

Something like conventional comic structure and themes emerge, underneath the post-modern visual assault. Saturday's father Mad Dog, the police commissioner, is a classic comic tyrannical father, to be gotten around and humiliated. In the midst of the farcical and unsentimental sexual comedy, Myguy/Queen of the 'hood develops genuine and therefore confusing feelings for Saturday. Changed back to her real shape, she draws a conventional moral: girls should be careful and certain of a guy's intentions and morals before they commit themselves.

Through the figure of the corrupt and tyrannical Mad Dog, official institutions become visible. He elides the distinction between family and state, talking on his police radio at the dinner table, calling for back-up to resolve a family dispute with his senior wife, pulling his service revolver on the new wife he has just married, and hiring the genital-stealing Panka, whom he has arrested in his official capacity, to guard his house. As champion of the family and the state he is on the most cordial terms with the church (rounding out the holy trinity) in the person of an accom - modating priest who is not in the slightest disturbed by Mad Dog's polygamy.

The political symbolism is resonant enough, even if one does not take into account the patriarchal form state domination often takes in Africa. Achille Mbembe has described the way the fam - ily is deployed as a symbol in hegemonic state discourse (14-16), thinking perhaps of Cameroon in the first place although the point applies elsewhere, albeit unevenly. Mbembe also says that since sexuality is one of the very few sectors of their lives that African young people have any control over, it gets invested with other values (141-42).

The political symbolism appears positively pointed since *Quartier Mozart* was made at more or less the time of the *villes mortes* ("ghost city") campaign in Cameroon (1990-91) to bring down the Biya dictatorship by a prolonged general strike. A national political allegory would seem to be intended as Mad Dog loses control of the government of his own household due to the rising power of the youth and (mostly) his own tyranny: Mad Dog has delegitimized himself by taking a new wife and driving his first wife out, and as the film ends he meddles increasingly in everybody's private business, enforcing his own curfew by order - ing the gossiping women at the public tap to go home and the local bar to shut off the music so he won't be disturbed, and forcing Atango, GoodFor and the rest of MyGuy's friends into conspiring against his relationship with Saturday. But finally his daughter brings Myguy home to her father's house to make love in her own bed, as it is now after 24:00 GMT, while Mad Dog's radio is once again announcing news of transfers, this time including his own. Blind with fury at being out of power he strikes out at his son and his new wife—for the last time, she tells him.

The culture of militancy is not visible in *Quartier Mozart*, but it turns out to be adjacent to it and perhaps latent within it. One would certainly not want to underestimate these potentials, as a post-modern political science may do when it is not "cynically extolling the virtues of the stunted products of cultural as well as political defeat" (Willemen, 2). Bayart, brilliant though his analy - sis of African politics is, failed utterly in his book of 1989 to fore - see the democratic upsurge of the early 1990s across Africa or to

provide any suggestion of where it came from, [4] though his analysis does help to account for the difficulties the democratic move -
ment has run into since. He writes confidently of the attractively
sardonic and satirical spirit of the rumor mills *Radio-Trottoir* and
Radio-Couloir:

> The research of C. M. Toulabor on the attitudes of young
> Lomeans shows that [*Radio-Trottoir*] has little potential for
> opposition or revolution. It can only add nuance to domination
> and seems essentially to be an indication of an amusing, but
> fatalist, culture of impotence. (252)

Four years later young Lomeans undertook one of the bravest,
most concerted and persistent campaigns of street demonstrations
that Africa has seen.

Still, in *Quartier Mozart* the personal/familial/sexual levels
are primary and are certainly not to be reduced to a national polit -
ical allegory. Bekolo's own statements suggest an overwhelmingly
personal motivation, due to his own family situation, and a sub-
"political" intention:

> My father is a police chief and also a polygamist so it was a bit
> tense. I was involved in that conflict for a long time, and it was
> very clear that I took my mother's side. Maybe that's why I
> made movies, because if I were on good terms with my father I
> could be an engineer making a good salary. But instead I went
> to work for TV.
>
> I was shocked by the way Africans speak French in the movies.
> It's like in books and not believable. Vulgar speech has a kind
> of strength, and the logic of people is in language….My film is
> not a political film, but I want to put this kind of freedom into
> people, this kind of strength. (Aufderheide, 36)

The politics of the film, then, are pitched at the level of "the
Popular"—the idioms, behaviors, values, sanctions and rituals that
derive from the street and embody coping mechanisms and resist -
ances to the banalization of power. The film's point of view stays
very close to that of its characters, who are learning to live in a
given world—an agonistic, confrontational, contentious world
where, from the first moments of the film, in which the characters

introduce themselves (or their constructed personae) directly to the camera, rough self-assertion is the dominant, indeed indispen - sable, style. Sex is the main game in town, and the young for the most part set their own rules: it is played competitively, men against women and vice versa, but also by men against each other and women against each other. The world beyond is so obviously cor - rupt that a satirical response is natural, but little energy is wasted on denouncing it. This film is not at all denunciatory in the man - ner of Bekolo's countryman Jean-Marie Teno's films *Africa, I will Fleece You* (1992), *Head in the Clouds* (1994), and *Clando* (1996), nor does it have the satirical distance of the Burkinabé Pierre Yameogo's film about the situation of Africa's youth, *Laafi* (1991).

The level terms on which the film meets its milieu are one of the most attractive and unusual things about it. The setting is taken as natural, without dressing it up or viewing it with scandalized hor - ror or sentimentality. There are many shots of Myguy (and others) against the background of this ordinary African neighborhood; the attention is on him, asserting his youth and vitality, but the sur - rounding reality is not hidden—bare earth, weathered wrecks of cars, tin roofs and walls whose crumbling plaster exposes mud and sticks underneath, and on the soundtrack roosters and crying babies and soukous music out of tinny radios.

Self-confidence and even glamour are to be found here: "I see it all here in Quartier Mozart," says a mysterious voice (Bekolo's own) on the soundtrack at the beginning of the film. Quartier Mozart is not given meaning primarily by any grand narratives running through it, nor are there any of the establishing shots, so often found in African films from *Borom Sarret* (1963) on, which contrast the high-rises of the colonial or neocolonial downtown with the surrounding slums (Malkmus and Armes 186-87), evok- ing a national context and history. But the neighborhood's self- sufficiency does not mean that it is isolated; in Bayart's terms, it is both autonomous and dependent. As has already been suggested, this locality is thoroughly irrigated by global media flows. Atango and his buddies GoodFor and Boss have a jocular conversation about the outside world, a copy of *Paris Match* in hand, which keeps them up to date on such issues as the menstruation of Princess Caroline of Monaco. They argue about their own place in this world, à propos of how African-Americans view Africans: one takes an Afrocentric point of view, claiming Nelson Mandela as the exemplary Black man and claiming a Pan-African kinship with American Blacks; another says African-Americans despise Africans because they are savages and generally out of the running on the world scene. Though in this conversation we are watching the sort of critical and creative appropriation of foreign materials which gives rise to the syncretic popular arts, the flow is over - whelmingly going one way, even if one of them is right that Michael Jackson borrowed from Manu Dibango.

The film is itself a counter-instance, a response: though in the first place it is speaking to and for the kind of people in the film, it is also talking back to the globalized world culture, using the common elements as a lingua franca. African influences help to produce rap music in the American ghettos; transnational corpo - rate capitalism sells the music back to Africa, which then reap - propriates it and tries to put it back, in this case via the soundtrack of the film, into international circulation.

And the genesis and circulation of the film itself? Seed money to make the film came from the usual French sources (the Centre National du Cinéma, the Ministry of Cooperation and Development, and ACCT), but shooting the film on the shoestring thus provided required the help of friends, and Bekolo reports des - perate plans were laid to develop the film stock in a bathtub in Cameroon (Verschueren, 14) before the film found backers and won a prize at the Cannes Film Festival, which allowed him to pay some of the bills for post-production work (Aufderheide, 36). During his moment of fame after Cannes, Bekolo talked about ambitious plans to market the film in Africa to its primary intended audience, but in Cameroon he encountered the usual problems: distributors were not interested because of their block-booking contracts, although a little theater in Douala did show it, and Bekolo worked out a special arrangement with the government which allowed it to be screened in the Yaoundé town hall for two weeks (Auderheide, 36). Programmers in Europe responded pos - itively to the film (Silla, 65). In the United States *Quartier Mozart* is included in California Newsreel's video Library of African Cinema, but has not broken out into the wider market. Audiences have found the film difficult: the foreignness of some of the film's cultural codes is compounded by its fast-paced and imperfectly controlled style (Cornelius Moore, personal communication, 1995).

Still, even if the film has not fulfilled hopes that it would break out of the limited, ghettoized circuits to which African cinema is condemned, it has enlarged the stylistic repertoire and demon -

strated an approach that is fresher and broader than most African films. It has shifted the ground beneath the old arguments about "authenticity" versus "universal themes" in African cinema by showing that a film can be authentic in the only sense that really matters, that is, by being true to its African subjects and audience and representing their lives without betraying them, at the same time that it is pitched to foreign viewers whose nervous systems are programmed to the rhythms of MTV.

Bekolo's second film, *Aristotle's Plot*, is even more jokey and obstreperous. It is also more theoretical, as a polemical film essay, which overtly addresses the situation of African cinema. Formally it is the most radical African film since *Soleil O* (1970) and *Touki Bouki* (1973), showing (apparently) the influence of Jean-Luc Godard's late-60s and early 70s radical examinations of cinematic representation. It shares with Godard's films a preoccupation with capitalist mass culture, and in particular American gangster imagery, but now the mood is post-modern and the position post - colonial. The topic is the alienation of African filmmakers from their African audience.

At the beginning of the voice-over commentary, which runs throughout the film, Bekolo describes the film's genesis:

> It started in the African bush, where I was with my grandfather chewing kolanut. I heard the drums telling me I had a phone call from London. The British Film Institute wanted me to make a film to celebrate the centenary of cinema. My grandfather wanted to know who else was on the list. Martin Scorsese, Stephen Frears, Jean-Luc Godard, George Miller. Huh. Then I started to wonder, why me? Was it Christian charity or political correctness? Was I accepting a challenge from someone already standing on the finish line?

Ceaselessly ironic towards African authenticity, Bekolo also approaches his international patrons with suspicion and a chip on his shoulder while nevertheless exploiting for maximum effect the prestigious association with illustrious figures of world cinema. The resulting film is intensely paradoxical and contradictory in its very being, an exaggerated example of the complex international circuits through which African films so often get made. In a "Statement by the Director" which appeared on the Internet (Internet Movie Data Base) he reports that, insulted by the com -

paratively small budget he was given for his film (compared to Scorsese, Bertolucci, and the other more famous filmmakers who participated in the project), he broke with the BFI, found a French producer (Jacques Bidou), and completed the film with money found elsewhere. The film's credits list, along with the BFI and the co-producer Framework International, the French Ministries of Culture and of Cooperation and Development, UNESCO, the Rockefeller Foundation, the Hubert Bals Fund, the EEC, and his own production company Kola Case. Though Bekolo is a fran- cophone Cameroonian, the film was shot in Zimbabwe with South African actors;[5] post-production work was done in Zimbabwe, France, and Canada.

The film is about the conflict between "Cineaste," represent- ing the whole tradition of idealistic, politically-motivated African filmmakers, and "Cinema," so-called because he has seen ten thou- sand movies, most of them American action films, who thinks "African films are shit." As the film begins both are handcuffed to a Policeman who has been assigned to write a report on how a person who dies in one film can reappear alive in another one, a problem which greatly puzzles and disturbs his superior officer (as if to suggest that the State may be a necessary intermediary between African cineaste and cinema audience, but it is liable to be a stupid one, oblivious to the nature of art). Cinema heads a gang whose members have taken the names of action heros: Schwarzennegger, Van Damme, Nikita, Bruce Lee. (This phe- nomenon has an old history in African popular culture: Oumarou Ganda has taken the name "Edgar G. Robinson," and his friends the names of other American stars, in Rouch's *Moi, un noir*.) Their hangout is "Cinema Africa," with a big sign advertising "Action Packed Movies." We will watch them watching such films and discussing *Terminator 2* (1991). When Cineaste goes there (appar- ently just to grumble about what he sees) he is roughed up and ejected by the gangsters. "You call yourself a Cineaste, but you're just a silly-ass" is a refrain throughout the film.

We watch Cineaste (otherwise known as Essomba Tourneur or ET, with the suggestion that he is an alien doubtless intended) pushing a shopping cart containing the reels of his film down a street with the abstracted, stiff-legged walk of a demented street person, obsessed and isolated from the world, while the voice- over tells us that when he graduated and came home from France the government put him in jail. When he was released he was taken for crazy, and it took him two years to begin to understand the local reality.

Now Cineaste (in line with the manifestoes of African film-makers) decides he has to enlist the support of the State to gain control of the local market, ejecting the gangsters from Cinema Africa. He is kept waiting at length in the tiny, funky Ministry of Culture while we listen to Bekolo sarcastically commenting, "ET was a powerful force. He was the lightning rod his country needed. He depended on contradictions within the system to achieve his goals." Finally he secures an official order for the police to evict the gangsters. The siege of Cinema Africa is shot as a parody of an action picture. Cineaste renames the theater Heritage Cinema, replacing the continental logo with a traditional mask. The gangsters, hiding out in the bush, plan to rob the cinema and show films in the rural areas. On the night of the robbery Heritage Cinema is empty, save for one Afrocentric African-American, looking for his roots. They kill him and slit the projectionist's throat.

Cineaste, discovering what has happened, metamorphoses into a shotgun-wielding avenger mounted on a Harley-Davidson, his booted foot on a poster of Schwarzennegger similarly mounted and armed in *Terminator 2*. He is suddenly glamorous, powerful, and sexy as he enters the realm of popular culture. The gang meanwhile has taken over an abandoned building and improvises a movie theater, using whatever comes to hand, their *bricolage* turning into an ideology: "We're building a new thing, a New Africa. [This is the name of the theater they are constructing.] We'll take what we can get. If it's old and it's good, fine. If it's new and it fits–action!" The films they have stolen turn out to be African, of the pious and dull sort, and during the screening Bekolo again keeps his camera trained on the audience. Their commentary is acid: "I can't watch this, there's no action. Wear rags, walk slowly and do nothing, it's an African film. These movies, you go out, take a piss, have a meal, they're still doing the same thing when you come back. And they call that culture, African culture. African action, chickens chasing dogs and goats chasing chickens, with traditional music."

This parable of African cinema is laced with numerous gags and drolleries of one kind or another (like a row of disreputable-looking white film distributors besieging the passing Cineaste in the manner of motor park touts), and it is accompanied by Bekolo's ruminative and often cracked voice-over commentary, one of the main themes of which is Aristotelian poetics, whose principles Bekolo claims to be following as he concocts his story, but which is also a symbol and central instance of European cultural domi - nation:

> A plot has a beginning, middle, and an end. But I still wasn't sure which chapter I occupied. I suspect the decision to invite me to celebrate the centenary of cinema could only be a subplot, 23 centuries old. Aristotle's plot. I was already trapped in the nar- rative my grandfather warned me to avoid. These days, Aristotle produces gangsters, illusionists, corrupt governments, and starv- ing artists. But it's not so bad. After the bitterness of the kolanut comes the sweetness.

The main point is the Aristotelian insistence on action as the heart of drama, which arouses pity and fear and results in catharsis, a principle with which the gangsters vociferously agree. They hijack ox and donkey carts, complaining about the lack of action in their country lives. "I'll show you some action!" says Cinema, skid - ding their van around in circles in a parody of the Hollywood redaction of Aristotle: the heart of a drama is a car chase. In a bar the gangsters continue: "We want African movies that kick ass! Hey we don't want fucking Jean-Pierre Bekolo here, okay!" They need narrative so badly that their desires summon up the appear - ance of Cineaste in leather as avenging hero; the gangsters are more than willing to pay the price of being cast as the bad guys, to be killed. A shoot-out in classic action style follows, in which everyone dies, but then–continuing the theme that has troubled the police from the beginning–they are alive again in the next scene, which restages their confrontation as a Sergio Leone-style face-off followed by a karate match. The police arrest them and we are back at the beginning of the film, with the bitterly quarreling Cineaste and Cinema both handcuffed to the Policeman. He releases them with a lecture about how the head and hands need each other. After a final scherzo reprise of the theme of death-and-resurrection through the miracle of cinema, the film ends with Cineaste riding off into the sunset with Cinema in the sidecar of his Harley.

What are we to conclude? Bekolo goes out of his way to be irresponsible, evading serious questions as furiously as he raises them. "Why are African filmmakers always asked political ques -

tions?" he asks. "Where is the Black man today? Are they all to be Nelson Mandelas? Can Nelson Mandela make a film?" Bekolo frequently takes refuge in the low social esteem accorded cin-ema–thought to be the training ground for rascals—and cineastes in Africa: "My grandfather told me a filmmaker is an outlaw who doesn't have enough personality to be a gangster." The song "ABC Cinema" (written and performed by Donny Elwood) which begins and ends the film suggests that filmmaker as well as film patron are just looking for a way to be a wiseguy, a showoff:

> You are scripting your life like a cineaste
> While you are only a silly ass.
> You want to do like in the movies
> And play the tough guy here and there
> You are showing off in the neighborhood.

Bekolo's verbal riffs on the soundtrack often follow a trajectory towards nonsense; so does the film as a whole, with its conclud-ing dumb jokes about life and death in cinema, as if seeking to shed responsibilities by plunging into the ludic.

Anxieties (perhaps) about the intellectual demands imposed by the British Film Institute and suspicions about the insertion of African cinema into world cinema find their ultimate horizon in deep paranoia about the ultimate plots of Western civilization, those of Aristotle and of the Bible which, Bekolo complains, con-demns everyone for original sin, lays a curse on the Black man, and promises salvation only in the hereafter. Escape is not easy. It would obviously be good to find an alternative to all this in African culture, but appeals to an "authentic" Africa always break down immediately and in fact are always framed by the foreign terms. Foreign validation is quickly trotted out at every turn. Often Bekolo seems to be parodying Afrocentric or Negritudinous arguments.

> My grandfather's words started to fill my mind. What is an ini-tiation ceremony? Crisis, confrontation, climax, and resolution. Sound, story, images, narration, rhythm. Is there anything in this cinema which is not African? Fantasy, myth, we got. Walt Disney, we got. Lion King, we got. Massacres, we got. Comed-ians, music, we got. Paul Simon, we got. Aristotle, catharsis, and kolanut, we got. What don't we got? Why don't we got an African Hollywood? Probably because we don't want to produce

our cinema outside of life, because when it is out of life, it is dead, like a difficult childhood. Which do you choose, the mother or the child? Life, or cinema? Because when cinema becomes your life, you are dead. It is dead. We are all dead.

The film hardly touches African ground and hardly attempts to do so. When Cineaste/ET returns home he fails to understand how overrun it has become by foreign culture, by Aristotle's plot. "ET had come home to his country, but he didn't understand it any more. The stories had replaced reality. His people identified more with Clint Eastwood" than with their own traditional religious beliefs. When the gangsters are forced out into the country their reaction is, "This place is prehistoric–Jurassic Park!" What we see of the country all looks remarkably and exclusively like the set of a Western.

This is of course a trick of the film's framing. Bekolo is film-ing in a country not his own and appears to have little specific interest in Southern Africa.[6] The film is set in a transnational men-tal space, the imaginary realm of cinema-in-Africa, where cinema wholly defines the identity of Cinema (the gangster) rather than being an element in the repertoire of a concrete historical human being in Africa, as in Rouch's *Moi, un noir*, or, for that matter, as in *Quartier Mozart*. For this reason, in *Aristotle's Plot* foreign influences are more apt to appear as alienation, rather than as healthy syncretism. During his song Donny Elwood plays dialog-ically with the African-American jive talking and obscenity to which the gangsters are addicted, but which is offensive to African sensibilities:

> What's up, what's up man? Hey, where is "what's up" coming from in our African neighborhood? First of all I'm not your man, I'm your *dara*. Fuck. Shit. Shut the fuck up. Who is fuck, man? Is it your cousin? Is it your sister, huh? *Dara*, who is shit?

But if the foreign cultural elements can be a maddening curse, they are also indelibly there, particularly in the form of Aristotle's plot and imported films, and the moral of the story is that Cineaste and Cinema must be reconciled. This requires Cineaste to learn to kick ass, to act, to move, to arouse pity and fear and produce catharsis in the actually existing African cinema audience. The solution comes through getting beyond the polarized opposition of popular/commercial formulas and intellectual/political purposes—that is the point at which the sparks fly and the fun begins, and a new African cinema might be created. Mermin points out that the Senegalese market—and this would be true of the Cameroonian and most other African markets—is too small to support an art cinema in addition to a mass commercial one (123). As in *Quartier Mozart*, Bekolo takes advantage of the post-modern breakdown between high and low art, finding the post-modern pleasures in playing with popular culture, picking up energies from it, and using it strategically. This is perhaps not entirely unlike Willemen's definition of Third Cinema as a lucid cinema, which works with the cultural materials at hand to produce a socially relevant discourse, though again the socialist aspect in both cineaste and audience has gone missing. Moreover, *Aristotle's Plot* does not escape from its own contradictions as a formally challenging, British Film Institute-funded polemic in favor of popular culture. Bekolo does not really address the material conditions which are doubtless more responsible for the divorce between African filmmakers and their audience than the slow pacing and rural settings of African films–conditions which have prevented his own films from reach - ing a mass popular audience in Africa. Still, he has given us a mor - dant and funny account of where things stand, and has pointed us in important directions: towards the popular audience which African film must reach, and towards the popular as a form of African culture with its own forms of participation in the global - ized media environment. This focus in itself is not a political pro - gram to replace the original revolutionary project of African film, but it is an indispensable part of any movement forward.

NOTES

1. I would like to acknowledge my debt to Neil Larsen for help- ing to clarify these issues for me through his remarks at the Rutgers-Newark conference and by steering me back to Aijaz Ahmad.
2. The special issue of *South Atlantic Quarterly* on "Postmodernism and the Periphery" has several articles addressing this theme, though usually not in an African con - text. See especially Richard and Yúdice.
3. This transformation is powerfully illustrated by the series of texts by filmmakers and their organizations collected in the

first two sections of Bakari and Cham's anthology *African Experiences of Cinema*.

4. This point is made by Colin Leys in "Confronting the African Tragedy," half of which is a review of Bayart's book.

5. Coincidentally, or perhaps not, at the same time two other films were being made in Southern Africa by francophone African directors: Souleymane Cissé's *Waati* and Idrissa Ouédraogo's *Kini and Adams*. The reasons for this rush to the south doubtless include a Pan-Africanist desire to reunite Southern Africa with the rest of the continent, artistically and imaginatively, and also the fact that, for historical reasons, Southern Africa boasts a highly developed technical infrastructure for making films and a number of superb actors but very few Blacks with experience as directors. Access to the worldwide anglophone market may also be a motivation, especially for a British Film Institute project. See Haynes, "The Pan-African Film Festival."

6. The old customized American cars which are an important if eccentric stylistic element in the landscape might be a reference to the role American culture played in the evolution of a detribalized township culture in South Africa, constructed against the policies of apartheid—but probably no such thing is intended.

WORKS CITED

Africa, I Will Fleece You. Dir. Jean-Marie Teno. Cameroon: 1992.

Ahmad, Aijaz. *In Theory: Classes, Nations, Literatures*. London and New York: Verso, 1992.

—. "The politics of literary post-coloniality." *Race & Class* 36.3 (1995): 1-20.

Akundinobi, Jude. "Survival Instincts: Resistance, Accommodation, and Contemporary African Cinema." *Social Identities* 3.1 (February 1997): 91-121.

Andrade-Watkins, Claire. "Portuguese African Cinema: Historical and Contemporary Perspectives 1969-1993." *Research in African Literatures* 26.3 (Fall 1995): 134-50. Rpt. this volume.

Aristotle's Plot. Dir. Jean-Pierre Bekolo. U.K./Zimbabwe: 1996.

Armes, Roy. *Third World Film Making and the West*. Berkeley: University of California Press, 1987.

Aufderheide, Pat. "De Maestro du Quartier Mozart." *Black Film Review* 8.1 (1994): 35-36.

Bakari, Imruh and Mbye Cham, eds. *African Experiences of Cinema*. London: British Film Institute, 1996.

Barber, Karin. "Popular Arts in Africa." *African Studies Review* 30.3 (1987): 1-78.

Borom Sarret. Dir. Ousmane Sembène. Senegal: 1963.

Bayart, Jean-François. *The State in Africa: The Politics of the Belly*. 1989; English trans. London and New York: Longman, 1993.

Clando. Dir. Jean-Marie Teno. Cameroon: 1996.

Diawara, Manthia. *African Cinema: Politics and Culture*. Bloomington: Indiana University Press, 1992.

Fanon, Frantz. *The Wretched of the Earth*. 1961; New York: Grove, 1968.

Gabriel, Teshome. "Towards a Critical Theory of Third World Films." 1985; rpt. in *Questions of Third Cinema*. Eds. Jim Pines and Paul Willemen. London: British Film Institute, 1991. 30-52.

—. *Third Cinema in the Third World: The Aesthetics of Liberation*. Ann Arbor: University of Michigan Research Press, 1982.

Guelwaar. Dir. Ousmane Sembène. Senegal: 1991.

Haynes, Jonathan and Onookome Okome. "Evolving Popular Media: Nigerian Video Films." *Nigerian Video Films*. Ed. Jonathan Haynes. Ibadan: Kraft Books for the Nigerian Film Corporation, 1997. 21-44.

Haynes, Jonathan. Rpt. *Research in African Literatures* 29:3 (Fall 1998): 106-28.

—. "The Pan-African Film Festival." *The Post Express*. March 26, 1997:27.

—. "Nigerian Cinema: Structural Adjustments." *Research in African Literatures* 26:3 (Fall 1995): 97-119. Rpt. this volume.

Head in the Clouds. Dir. Jean-Marie Teno. Cameroon: 1994.

Hecht, David and Maliqalim Simone. *Invisible Governance: The Art of African Micropolitics*. New York: Autonomedia, 1994.

Laafi. Dir. Pierre Yameogo. Burkina Faso: 1991.

Larkin, Brian. "Hausa Dramas and the Rise of Video Culture in Nigeria." *Nigerian Video Films*. Ed. Jonathan Haynes. Ibadan: Kraft Books for the Nigerian Film Corporation, 1997. 105-25.

Larsen, Neil. "DetermiNation: Postcolonialism, Poststructural-ism, and the Problem of Ideology." *Dimensions of Postcolonial Theory*. Eds. Fawzia Afzal-Khan and Kalpana Seshadri-Crooks. Durham: Duke University Press, 1995.

—. "Statement on Postcolonialism." Third World Studies in the 90s Conference, Rutgers University-Newark, March 1995.

Leys, Colin. "Confronting the African Tragedy." *New Left Review* 204 (March-April 1994): 33-47.

Malkmus, Lizbeth and Roy Armes. *Arab and African Filmmaking*. London and Atlantic Highlands, NY: Zed Books, 1991.

Mbembe, J. A. *Les jeunes et l'ordre politique en Afrique noire*. Paris: L'Harmattan, 1985.

Mermin, Elizabeth. "A Window on Whose Reality? The Emerging Industry of Senegalese Cinema." *Research in African Literatures* 26:3 (Fall 1995): 120-33. Rpt. this volume.

Moi, un noir. Dir. Jean Rouche. France/Côte d'Ivoire: 1958.

Pines, Jim and Paul Willemen. *Questions of Third Cinema*. London: British Film Institute, 1991.

Quartier Mozart. Dir. Jean-Pierre Bekolo. Cameroon: 1992.

Richard, Nelly. "The Latin American Problematic of Theoretical-Cultural Transference: Postmodern Appropriations and Counterappropriations." *South Atlantic Quarterly* 92:3 (Summer 1993): 453-59.

Silla, Mactar. "Africa, the North's poor relative." *Ecrans d'Afrique* 5-6 (3rd-4th quarter, 1993): 62-65.

Soleil O. Dir. Med Hondo. Mauritania: 1970.

Terminator 2: Judgment Day. Dir. James Cameron. United States: 1991.

Touki Bouki. Dir. Djibril Diop Mambéty. Senegal: 1973.

Ukadike, Nwachukwu Frank. *Black African Cinema*. Berkeley: University of California Press, 1994.

Verschueren, B., C. Tapsoba, and C.K. Maiga. "The Vision of a People Must Not Be Reduced to Reality: Interview with Jean-Pierre Bekolo." *Ecrans d'Afrique* 2 (Third quarter, 1992): 16-18.

Yúdice, George. "Postmodernism in the Periphery." *South Atlantic Quarterly* 92.3 (Summer 1993): 543-556.

TOWARDS A THEORY OF
ORALITY IN AFRICAN CINEMA

THE DIRECT IMPORTATION INTO AFRICA of methods, theories, ideas and psychoanalytical assumptions developed in the
First World and applied to African cinema is not without episte -
mological problems. Marxist, positivist, or liberal -humanist
approaches, amongst others, do not automatically apply in attempts
to understand African films and audiences.

The call on mainly Lacanian psychoanalysis as an interpre -
tive framework assumes that African viewers have essentially
white, Westernized subjectivities and that their readings are deter -
mined, as John Higgins (1992, p. 105) expresses it, in terms of
how "the film seeks to position the spectator so that the film can
be understood." This kind of film theory has little purchase
amongst audiences which evade the subjectivities and viewing
positions assumed or constructed for them by directors, and which
in turn are assumed by the critics to be themselves located within
the post-Freudian psyche. These kinds of "European deconstruc -
tivist rituals" (Willemen 1989, p. 1-29) assume particular sets of
modern and post-modern conditions and periodizations not nec -
essarily replicated in Africa in quite the same ways.

Oral cultures, as one example of cultural divergence, speak a
different world than those of written cultures. Ontologies shaped
by orality assume that the world consists of interacting forces of
cosmological scale and significance rather than of discrete secu -
larised concrete objects.[1] The kinds of storytelling strategies pos -
sible within the discourse of cosmologies which include the influ -
ence of para-normal agents, as described to an extent in Jean
Rouch's films, provide the grounding for divisions of existence

that differ from the dualism postulated by the dogma of the ghost in the machine.

The relationship of Africans as quintessentially the "Other" to the historical "Same" of Europe emerged from the respective experiences of colonialism and neo-colonialism. It is against this background of indeterminacy that we discuss the failure of Western film theory to understand the various comprehensions of existence, which inscribe the narratives and forms of many cinemas in Africa.

W.V.O. Quine's (1969) notion of the indeterminacy of radical translation proposes one way of approaching an understanding of such ontological difference: if the ontologies of African (the observed) and European (observing) languages differ, then such an indeterminacy can be seen to have existed at the historical root of the relationship between Europe and Africa. The relevant differences are ontological: the history constructed by an observer originating in one society will refer to existence in a world not quite the same as that constructed by someone from another part of the society or from a different society.

We follow the question of ontology by locating it in the interpretation of the realm of activity. Put differently, we draw on the kind of phenomenological interpretations carried out by, on the one hand, Martin Heidegger (1962), and, on the other, Hannah Arendt's (1958, p. 5) project to "think what we are doing." Specifically, we take that which exists to be culturally prior to that which is known, in the context of "culture" taken in its root sense of "nurture." Things are encountered as existents before we attain knowledge of them. Ontology is, therefore, involved with the interpretation of what we encounter in our maturation into this world during our lives.

Further, however, the fact that there is a "we" who are "here," implies that there are at least two generations present in the context of culture-as-nurture. In the African sphere, the ongoing disruption following the move to independence further implies, therefore, that experiences of the world differ from one generation to the next in a given context: the elders of a community can recall different "forms of life"—the whole context within one can speak about meaning and knowledge—in comparison with which they can pass judgement on their present condition (Wittgenstein, 1963). Younger generations frequently have no experience of these forms of life, and they become, in a special kind of sense, alienated from the possibilities subject to recollection among their elders (see Shepperson, 1995).

A final point before going ahead: the temptation does exist for this kind of work, whether by ourselves or others who engage criti-cally with Western-modern thought, to come across as if our position seeks to replace a "Euro-universalizing" paradigm with some or other "Ethno-universalizing" one. With some trepidation we suggest that if one adheres in part to Stephen Toulmin's (1991) analysis of the "hidden agenda of modernity," then the shift away from the univer-sal has become an accepted feature of the human sciences. We dif-fer slightly from Toulmin in our position (derived from Agnes Heller, 1983) that, in the realm of human affairs, the universal has to be replaced by the *general,* conceived as a global condition within which social and political action are possible. Where modernist discourse posited a dichotomy of the local with the general, we accept that the local can be seen as a specific realization of a concrete global poten-tial for the human condition, and not as the interpretation of an abstract axiom regarding some kind of "human essence" (see Toulmin 1991, p. 32-33; Heller 1983, p. 328-333).

ONTOLOGY

Previous work has pointed to the ontological encounter as being primarily pragmatic in nature. Heidegger, for example, locates that which is primordially interpretable in the "ready-to-hand." This, in turn, is a character of those "equipments" (*zeug*) which connect with our average everyday activity such that:

> [W]hen we deal with them by using them and manipulating them, this activity is not a blind one, it has its own kind of sight, by which our manipulation is guided and from which it acquires its specific Thingly character. Dealings with equip-ment subordinate themselves to the manifold assignments of the "in order to" (Heidegger 1962, p. 98).

This sight and manipulation can be compared to those things peo-ple do prior to there being any theory constructed about those things. Equipment (*das zeug*, in Heidegger's original) is a thing that becomes defined in relation to that which has to be done. Thus the character of "equipmentality" (*zeuglichkeit*) is at one remove from reality, because reality is more readily to be considered in the desired consequence of some or other intervention in the world (Heidegger 1962, p. 99). We return to this point later when discussing the ways in which African filmmakers differ from their Hollywood counterparts.

Circumspection is this very special kind of "sight," and it implies a pragmatic "looking-towards-use" that precedes the actual grasping of an entity in its being (Heidegger 1962, p. 98-99). In opposition to the ready-to-hand, Heidegger speaks of that which is "present-at-hand" (70-74): entities of this kind are not grasped in their equipmentality, but are encountered through what has been translated as "idle talk" (*gerede*; p. 168). They are; in other words, present to us through "interest" that does not incur any responsi-bility for the consequences of the use of things. [2] In this sense, the critique of film theory and practice has to account also for how film is exhibited and analyzed. These activities have consequences that are both desired and unintended: the "equipmentality" of film, in other words, precedes its exhibition because the filmmaker and/or exhibitors are doing what they do *for a purpose* (be this profit, resistance, pedagogy or whatever).

At a different level, C.S. Pierce, and later theorists like Ian Hacking (1983) and Clifford Geertz (1983) expand on a similar theme with regard to the existence of scientific entities and cultural imperatives, respectively. In all cases, the presence of a commu-nity, be it scientific or traditional, is central. Cultures/communities cannot exist in the absence of activity, a tradition of behaviour, or of doing something. In this context, their ontology is precisely that ready-to-handedness (so to speak) that precedes what they are taught or enculturated into knowing of the world. But this readi-ness-to-hand is never altogether a transcendental quality: it has a *temporality* that is related to the generational span specific to the generations present in a situation (Shepperson, 1995), and this, as indicated above, can have an alienating cultural character in situ-ations of change and/or disruption.

PSYCHOANALYSIS AND KNOWLEDGE OF AFRICA

Teshome Gabriel (1989a, p. 39), amongst others, has questioned the validity of psychoanalysis in terms of African and Third World Cinema:

Contemporary film theory and criticism is grounded in a conception of the "viewer" (subject or citizen) derived from psychoanalytic theory where the relation between the "viewer" and the "film" is determined by a particular dynamic of familial matrix. To the extent that Third World culture and familial relationships are not described through psychoanalytic theory, Third World filmic representation is open for an elaboration of the relation "viewer"/"film" on terms other than those grounded on psychoanalysis. The Third World relies more on appeal to social and political conflicts as the prime rhetorical strategy and less on the par-adigm of Oedipal conflict and resolution.

Lacan's psychoanalysis originates in the context of Freud's proj-ect of explaining the social and individual pathologies, which evolved along with industrial cultural (as in nurturing) practice. In this sense, then, the field is to an extent predicated on the idea (and the gaps in its formulation) of a paternalistic nuclear family, mir-ror phases, and clearly demarcated gender roles (Flitterman-Lewis, 1987).

The historical discourse within which these cultural norms and practices emerged is one that has been subject to critique many times (e.g. Toulmin 1991; Rorty 1980; Arendt 1958). In the con-text of this discussion, however, the historical dualism of the urban and the rural, which is part of the discourse, is relevant. Traditionally, Western industrial discourse has associated (rightly or wrongly) the rural with the illiterate. Urban industrial culture cannot consistently be conceived of in the absence of literacy. The consequence of this is a tacit association of the oral traditions of African society with the rural conditions against which capitalist production emerged in opposition to medieval agrarian practice.

In certain respects, the historical readiness-to-hand of writing in industrial communities places a limit on the ways in which the reality encountered by their members can be adapted as other con-ditions change. In the Western tradition, the idea of community in the sense of an ongoing intergenerational procession of average everyday contacts is becoming tenuous. Agnes Heller (1983, p. 303) points to the historical emergence of what she calls a "dis-satisfied society" in response to the classically modernist concep-tion of progress. In the context of this inquiry, we accept this "dis-satisfaction" as a feature, which is most strongly associated with the economics of Hollywood cinema, as it will also be found to be the case with other kinds of "commercial" media organization. The "ready-to-hand" has become relegated to the "merely present-at-hand," existents which are not grasped in their essential and complex readiness-to-hand.[3]

INDIGENIZING THEORY

European methods and theories often cannot account for ways in which African forms of expression have integrated with other forms, or for indigenous ways of knowing and making sense and interpreting films. Two entirely different ways of making sense—the literate and the oral (which often retains pre-modern cosmological elements) ensure differences in the encounter between them. In part, this is a consequence of the role that is played by religion in African communal life. As Pene Elungu (1992, p. 2) points out, religion in the African context:

> [I]s not seen as part of the rush of confessions which accompanied Western culture. In fact, our traditional religions placed that which is sacred—(the secret—*sacre*) things that cannot be discussed, things before which we bow—not in the individual person but in the link with parents and ancestors, community, the universe, and with God. This linking current is 'life.' Life is what is sacred, what is absolute: life is everything, everything is life, life overflows everything, even death, and life feels every-thing.

In this framework, reality in the ontological sense can be thought of as incorporating African kinship systems. As a context of nur-ture-culture, these are simply far too complicated, multi-layered, polysubjectival and multi-gendered to be easily subjected to the Lacanian categories upon which Screen Theory attempts to analyze representations of them. Screen Theorists coalesced in the late 1960s around the British journal *Screen* with the translation of Christian Metz's (1974a, 1974b) structuralist semiological propo-sitions into English. These were then read through Louis Althusser's (1971) Marxism and Lacanian psychoanalytical posi-tions (see, e.g. Higgins, 1992). Screen Theory privileges the Text and the critics' interpretation of it, irrespective of discrepant and different readings by others: it is a prescriptive rather than open-ended approach.

In the religious context of the colonial missionary project, it is not surprising therefore that among the first sympathetic attempts

50

to come to terms with African thought the focus was on the ontol -
ogy addressed by African languages (Tempels, 1959). If our inter -
pretation of this ontology is not quite the same as the being = force
orthodoxy that emerged from these interventions (Mudimbe, 1989)
we are not convinced that the oral tradition can be represented in
purely epistemological terms as in formal anthropology. What is
germane is that the reality of, for example, ancestral influence goes
beyond the mystification of the recognition of one's forebears as
"worship." The present necessarily contains the consequences of
previous generations' actions, as much as the future will be influ -
enced to some extent by what our generation gets right or wrong
when we act in our own lifetimes. In a different sense, the objec -
tivity of this kind of thought is rooted in *ubuntu*, the
having-been-there of some subjective agent who was always one
of *Bantu*, all the people who were there engaging the ready-to-
hand, the consequences of which are now *ours.*

While European theories offer explanation of how Western
audiences might interpret films which set out to portray such a
world, they simultaneously displace not only the subjectivities of
their directors, but also the reception strategies and interpretations
of their non-Westernised or partly acculturated African viewers.
The separation of the text from context—a limitation of Screen
Theory—is a "regime of signification" no matter the ideological
allegiance of those who apply this method.

Theories are needed to explain the various, often widely dif -
ferent and original, African applications of imaging and recording
technologies and their resulting aesthetics, which take into account
the subjectivities and cosmologies of particular sets of viewers.
Such theories need to examine the extent to which literate, semi -lit-
erate, and non-literate viewers interact through Western -African
and African cultures and gnoses. This is a crucial point as sight (i.e.
emphasis on the visual) fragments consciousness—the Subject -
Object relation—situating the observer outside of what s/he sees
or studies.

Such explanation cannot easily be accounted for by unrecon -
stituted Freudian or Lacanian psychoanalytic analysis. [4] An example of this kind of ignoring the obvious in the search for the abstract
can be found in Jeanne Prinsloo's (1992) challenging attempt to
understand African cinema through feminist perspectives. Citing
the examples of Elaine Procter's *On the Wire* (1992) and Mira
Nair's *Mississippi Masala* (1992), Prinsloo uses the explicitly

pro-patriarchal (Oedipal) categories of psychoanalysis to affirm anti-patriarchal arguments. This pre-supposes that one can generalize from an explicitly European mythology to the oral (and residual oral) traditions and gnoses rooted in entirely different cosmologies. We are not arguing that cultural or cinematic theories from other societies are inappropriate in the African context. Rather, our point is that they have a different purchase in these partly similar and partly different societies, which often exhibit in their generational-cultural temporality a simultaneity of the modern, post-modern and even pre-modern (Berman, 1988).

African interpretations of Western media, their rearticulation into different African contexts, and theoretical mixes, which acknowledge the impact on our analytical tools of the way theories, travel and mutate, similarly need explication and development. One route for such explanation is to study the way critical African filmmakers have tried to indigenize theoretical perspectives on film, video and cinema within the African continent (Achebe, 1990). With the exceptions of Teshome Gabriel (1989a, 1989b), Haile Gerima (1989), Francoise Pfaff (1984), A Gardies and Pierre Haffner (1987), Ferid Boughedhir (1987) and Mbye Cham (1982a), academic, and certainly reviewer, emphasis has tended to foreground discussions of national industrial structures and resources, production methods, the Ouagadougou Film Festival (FESPACO), and the difficulties of making films in Africa. Concerns with political economy have tended to overshadow questions of aesthetics and reception. The paradox of cinema made by Africans which is critical of neo-colonialism is that its makers act as cultural intermediaries germinating oral and visual styles and themes that are currently stored in exile. These films have to wait for appropriate conditions to break before returning 'home.' But even then, audience acculturation to Hollywood and conventional genres may have removed them even further from these cinematic memories of the readiness-to-hand, which the filmmakers are trying to access.

As intermediaries, critical African filmmakers are also travellers. They physically and psychically travel between the First, Second, Third and Fourth Worlds, cultures and ontologies. As global *griots* or bards they memorize and recite African legends and valiant deeds through story telling (Stoller, 1992). They are the storehouses of oral knowledge. The reach of these *griots* is global because they are often located outside Africa where they have sought safety from repression in their own countries. It is also here where they raise the bulk of their financial support. As *griots*, they represent and incubate the cultural ready-to-hand of the African societies from whence they derive. These films recover memo-ries, which have been partly destroyed by colonialism and neo-colonialism.

Most specifically, *griots* serve to recover and preserve for exhi-bition in film, that which has been alienated from the present gen-eration because of the disruption consequent to imposition of mod-ernization policies. In this sense, these filmmakers are also travellers between generations, and as *griots* they are the inter-generational counterparts of the medieval European troubadours who travelled in a more literally geographical sense. Peculiarly, the evolution of modernity has collapsed geographical space in a way that makes this kind of travelling one of the few ways open for exploration, with film being one of the vehicles wherein the explorer can voyage on quests, not of "new" discovery, but of *rediscovery*.[5]

The key to the task of developing film theories applicable in the African context requires a rethinking of the Western psycho-centric semiology, which informs a lot of this theory.[6] Reactivation of the silenced texts in African oral traditions still embedded in the residual surviving cultural traditions and popular memory seems to need another form of argument and theory. In broad terms, film theory is itself a form of metanarrative, in which categories of visual reception and filmic representation are arranged so as to provide for the analyst the framework of an argument with which to persuade others to understand films in one way rather than another (Nichols, 1991).

The problem with using the above kinds of categories is that they tend to be appropriated as having *apriori* status, instead of being understood as the negotiated outcomes of historical and intergenerational activity. For example, Prinsloo's (1992) use of Vladimir Propp's (1968) theory of narrative categories[7] in con-junction with Lacanian psychoanalysis gives rise to the following possible argument (narrative) when strictly applied in Western dis-course (even though Prinsloo is explicitly opposed to it):

1. Every film narrative is *apriori* preceded by Proppian nar-rative categories;

2. Every film spectator is *apriori* preceded by his or her Oedipal status; therefore

3 One can review a film by asking viewers to complete a suitably formulated Oedipal questionnaire, and not have to go to the trouble of watching the film for one's self.

These kinds of *apriori* assumptions highlight the extent to which film theories tend to minimize the potential for critical theory in the analysis of film in exhibition and reception.

The way in which the simultaneously public and enclosed space of film exhibition can be appropriated according to the public traditions of a given form of life, links what is shown into very different possible experiences from those anticipated by commercial and art film producers. A vivid example of this is Hamid Naficy's (1989) ethnography of spectatorship in Iranian cinemas, where he describes all the extraordinary activities, which occur while the film is showing. These range from buying and eating hot meals to urinating on the floor; those who had seen the film before would retell the story ahead of the screen action, calling forth shouts from others that they stop ruining the screening for viewers who objected to these impromptu performances.

What Naficy can be seen to be portraying is the relation of the activity and space of exhibition to the forms of life which prevail for those who attend such exhibits. Rather than seeking to connect such activity-in-exhibition with the logic of the categories of industrial production and consumption, the exhibition might also be seen as an index of the ways in which film is appropriated in the reproduction and reinforcement of the social and other relations present in the life of a community (Shepperson, 1994). In the African context, film frequently is exhibited in the presence of people alienated from their historical condition as a result of the cultural alienation between generations consequent upon the disruptions of modernization. Film theory, therefore, has to be cognizant of the context of these forms of alienation if it is to permit an understanding of what African filmmakers are attempting to portray as significant.

If Lacanian and Proppian theory is based in an assumed universality of psychological development and narrative forms respectively, then the way people encounter language and meaning in other parts of the world becomes problematic.

In the next section, we draw on Wittgenstein's (1963) con-ception of the encounter with language within a "form of life" to reconstruct the notion of what occurs when film is exhibited in contexts other than Western ones.[8] It is in relation to this imposition of the 'givenness' of the European 'form of life' that the notion of a Third Cinema can be conceived: such film begins from an understanding of the specificities of another form of life.

THIRD CINEMA

"Third Cinema" is a set of strategies developed by critical film-makers in South America and North Africa (Solanas and Gettino 1976). "First Cinema" describes commercially structured film industries, as in Hollywood entertainment; "Second Cinema" accounts for *avant garde,* personal, art or *auteur* movies. Third Cinema offers resistance to imperialism, to oppression. As a cin-ema of emancipation it articulates the codes of an essentially First World technology into indigenous aesthetics and mythologies. These aesthetics and mythologies respectively inform and explain the specific ready-to-hand nature of the world encompassed and encountered by the predominantly oral context of subjectivity within the so-called Third World.

Since the 1980s, Third Cinema has been redefined into other sites of resistance, including those in First World situations where class, gender and other kinds of social conflicts have taken on var-ious kinds of racial/ethnic character (Pines and Willemen, 1989). Third Cinema is a set of political strategies using film (and video) to articulate the experiences and hopes of the colonially oppressed (Solanas and Gettino, 1976; Salmane et al, 1976). Its purpose, according to the originators of the term, Solanas and Gettino, is to create a "liberated space" for emancipation.

Third Cinema engaged the positive aspects of Screen Theory in an emancipatory direction, but crucially introduced non - English and non-Western ethnocentric approaches to European cultural politics. In pursuing this framework the critic has to create situa-tionally adequate theories, which match the experiences of non-Western audiences rather than shoehorning viewers into a pre -exis-tent Grand Theory.

Much African cinema is Third Cinema in nature, if not in direct derivation. An example is Ethiopian Haile Gerima's *Sankofa* (1993). *Sankofa* is an Akan term meaning "to return to one's past, to rescue it from oblivion and to turn towards the future." The film tells the story of a vivacious contemporary Ghanaian photographic model called Mona, who through following her possession by spir- its, travels back to the brutal past where she lived as a slave on a North American sugar plantation. Through this less than pleasant recovery of the historical experience of slavery and rape via uncon- scious popular cultural memory (ready-to-handedness) induced by the spirit medium, named Sankofa, Mona recovers her African identity and rejects Western consumerism, exhibitionism and idol- atry.

Initially, African films, and much of Third Cinema, tended to be explicitly political, though this dimension has softened in the past decade or so. They start from the social premise that the Community is in the individual rather than that the Individual is in the community, as is the case with Western genre cinema. The 19-year-old Islamic peasant girl in *Ramparts of Clay*, for example, represents an emergent personal awakening, but within the context of an unshakeable allegiance to the freedom of her peasant com- munity. In the process of suppressing her individual subjectivity she knowingly commits metaphorical suicide in both her individual and feminist selves. She recognizes that she can be neither part of traditional culture nor of the corrupt new ruling class through which she is most likely to achieve her individualism and personal free- dom.

In *Sankofa*, the Community triumphs and Mona is reinserted into a pre-colonial romantic past as a slave girl, Shola. A white pho- tographer who represents contemporary commercial exploitation and the Western consumerist sexist gaze observes her. Mona returns from her historical journey dressed as Shola in traditional garb. She sullenly ignores the photographer who helplessly watches her walk away from him and all that he represents. Gerima gives no clues to how Mona, and those she stands for, should cope and interact with the present. In such narratives, the community, as a form of life, changes the individual rather than the individual changing the community. The structural relations of this process are acknowledged and made visible. This does not necessarily dis- empower the characters as individuals. Rather, it empowers them (and audiences) with knowledge as to the real nature of exploita- tion, both historically (the brutal stealing of labour) and contem- porarily (the pop-commercial appropriation of culture).

This reconstitution into a communal subjectivity may come across as paradoxical to Western film scholars and audiences, but it is hardly so to Third World audiences, which find their identities within communal relations. As forms of life, deliberately expressed in the plural, oral traditions rely on the contact between generations for the elaboration of individual subjectivities. The upshot of this is that where the ongoing existence of written language can occur in the encounter between an individual and a text in isolation from other persons, orally formed subjects need the presence of others in order to assert their identities.

In part, this paradox of identity is a function of the way in which the emergence of industrial social forms has transferred the realm of identity from the public sphere into the intimate (Arendt, 1958). It is sharpened when the form of film exhibition is taken into account, since this is always both public (especially in the case of cinema) and private, in that the venue of exhibition is sundered from other aspects of the public realm. As an explicitly modern art form, the cinema also works in exhibition in the peculiarly private way found in the case of the novel: the shrinking-away of the pub-lic realm in modern society is mirrored in the withdrawal of sub-jectivity from the communal into the solipsistic.

Critical African cinema is about the right of Africans to rep-resent to themselves the possibilities inherent in their past. The role of African filmmaker as *griot* becomes important when seen in the context of recent attempts by colonized people to recon-struct their histories and pasts against a predominantly European colonialist interpretation of those experiences. For instance, in his film, *Afrique Je Te Plumerai* (Africa, I will fleece you, 1991), Jean-Marie Teno's uses a combination of his reminiscence of childhood as cultural colonized person and a fable his grandfather told about a country of larks dominated by a race of hunters to comment on and re-examine Cameroon's colonial history and past. Not only does Teno present his own personal testimony as relevant for an understanding of Cameroon's cultural domination, but he also pres-ents his grandfather's interpretation of colonization.

Teno shows how writing has influenced the original oral cul-ture of Cameroon. The narrative is driven by the thorny question of how to steer Africa out of its cultural vulnerability—a vulner-ability that has led to its apparent helplessness and internal repres-sion by the local Black elite apparatchiks of global capital. In so doing, Teno fulfils one of the functions of the *griot* or oral historian, that of transmitting stories or history from one generation to another. This intergenerational transmission or testimony is one of the fundamental features of the oral tradition.

Writing brought with it a new form of oppression—that of sur‐ veillance and records regulated by the modern state bureaucracy. These cinema contests mediated images recirculated to Africa from the Western, and Islamic, neo‐colonial centres. Teno exposes this dependency through the words of his narration in Afrique: "colo‐ nialism perpetrated cultural genocide." The struggle of Africans is to overcome this genocide, and the feelings of inferiority that are its results. As one of his indignant, but humorous characters, com‐ plains: "Even when it comes to the number of seasons, we're sur‐ passed by Europe!" This cinema aims to transform the observer-observed relation where Africans are "Other" to the his‐ torical "Same" of Europe.

The title *Africa, I will fleece / pluck you*, is a lampoon of a children's nursery chant, "Alouette, gentille alouette, alouette, je te plumerai" (Lark, pretty lark, lark, I will pluck you). The song suggests the violence associated with the cultural colonization of Africa. Teno connects this song to the fable about the country of the larks. The plucking of "alouette" becomes a metaphor for the plucking or fleecing of Africa. The visual track reinforces this with scenes of Africans under forced labor, building roads for European penetration into the African hinterland, or harvesting cash crops for European markets. The message is blatantly communicated through the visual image, but is insidiously presented in this song.

Like Gaston Kaboré in *Wend Kuuni* (1983), Teno utilizes the oral performance genre as a significant part of his narrative tech‐ nique in Afrique. While Kaboré's film is a cinematic retelling of an oral tale, Teno rather exploits various aspects of oral narrative performance to communicate what becomes a tale of Cameroon's political, cultural, and economic colonization by Europe, and its continued exploitation and "humiliation" by its political leaders. *Wend Kuuni*'s episodic structure reflects that of the African folk narrative, also resembling European picaresque narratives. Various events are tied together only by virtue of their relationship to the theme or as the author/ narrator/ protagonist during the story encounters them.

In contrast, Teno undertakes his journey to understand how a country, which was "once composed of well‐structured, traditional societies," could fail to succeed as a state. As a journey/story, various stories run through *Afrique*. The film adopts the style of a journey/documentary of one person. But it ends up being poly - subjectival, including several Cameroonians as points of narrative subjectivity: Teno, Sultan Ngoya and a number of African politi - cal leaders.

The metaphor of the journey is a feature of folk narrative, tak - ing the form through a quest, a movement in search of something lost or yet to be found. *Afrique* is first and foremost Teno's quest for understanding of the political dilemma of his country/conti - nent. Teno uses documentary, re-enactments, news footage, humour, praise poetry, drama and music, and monochrome sec - tions in a colour film.

Direct and indirect narration, dialogue and sub -titles recreate the oral emphasis of African culture-as-nurture. This orality is fur - ther emphasized in that the storyline is advanced through a vari - ety of different characters—as opposed to the single meta -narra - tor of conventional First Cinema, and, for that matter, of the classical novel. Music (songs, performances, and lyrics), for exam - ple, is sometimes heavily foregrounded, operating as a narrative voice in its own right. The song is also used as a choral device, as in storytelling at various intervals of the film. It serves as a thematic and structural device, returning the audience to the central theme of the film and at the same time holds the various parts of the film together. The filmmaker examines various issues simultaneously. As such, this film appears very disjointed at times. The song is the structural thread that ties the disjointed parts to the central theme of "plucking Africa." The result, in the case of Afrique, is an entertaining post-modernist political protest film, which retains the depth and irony of the oral style.

The orality-visual combination is wider and potentially deeper than the codes of First Cinema, indicating therefore a need for a new film semiotics (grammar).

NEW VISUAL GRAMMARS

African directors rearticulate and localize Western -invented tech- nologies in the context of the forms of life, which ground African themes, stories, and forms of oral story -telling and cultural expres - sion. The intergenerational continuities and pragmatic encounter with reality suggested by these forms of life generate, we suggest, ontologies in which are to be found new visual grammars. In the way Elungu's evocation of a "linking current" calls forth the pos-sibility of a less atomized world of the ready-to-hand, so the ways in which people make sense of such a world might be understood as being governed by articulation strategies less rigid than the mod-ern forms of subject-predicate grammars. If these grammars are less precise in dealing with discrete objects, then they possibly have greater applicability when dealing with relations of culture-nurture which do not exclude non-equipmental influences which are ready-to-hand in the form of spirits and ancestral relationships.

African languages, unlike those which have emerged from industrial imperatives, describe a world consisting of more than objects. In a significant way, their grammar (especially when not subjected to the attentions of European educational specialists) has a place for qualifying an existent in terms of its relatedness to the other things, persons, and animals around it. Subject and Object remain interconnected and narratives retain spaces for the author-ity of the spirits, as in *Sankofa*. Yet, very little critical work on films made by Africans takes these kinds of spiritual and other-worldly dimensions into account. One of the few exceptions is the work of French anthropologist, Jean Rouch, who used his camera to try to understand the "scientifically unthinkable" occur-ring amongst his collaborators in Niger (Stoller, 1992).

Perhaps it is the more than essentially physical, or material, context of African ontologies and experiences represented in its cinemas that is unexplainable in terms of conventional Western film theories. This is one reason why academic analysis concen-trates on the material, the plots and the industrial structures, avoid-ing aesthetics, form and signification of interrelatedness, what Gerima calls "the central nervous system of what is at stake—African cinema language." He continues, "As long as critical the-ory in African cinema does not make the transition to critical analy-sis, (critical analysis deals with both content and form), the state of African cinema, now thirty years old, remains underdeveloped." The role of a critical African cinema theory, he concludes, will emerge only when an appropriate theory "fashions itself as a medi-ator between the African filmmaker and the African audience" (Gerima, 1993).

African Third Cinema directors are part of their societies in relation to the everyday activities of those societies; their profes-sion places them in a unique position with respect to the exploration of those activities in ways that can break the way in which the dependency cycle has influenced their viewers' everyday social activity. Editing and encoding in critical African films reflect this gnosis in which the world is interconnected through the specifici-ties of African languages. The writer in *Afrique*, for example, works at his typewriter in the middle of a street, not in seclusion, in the isolation of the Western artist or *litterateur*. He is part of the everyday life about which he is writing and which surrounds him. This image raises questions about the nature of Africanicity and its emphasis on being, on totality, on an integrated world not separated into dualisms—where the Western artist tends to hide away from 'life' in seclusion while "creating."

DREAMS AS PART OF LIFE

In African ontologies, the dream is in the realm of existence as part of the "linking current" in which contact is by nature estab-lished with the spirit world, the gods, ancestors, and unborn (the future) as well as the human essence, thus creating a sense of uni-versal unity and interrelation between the living and the dead. A revelation in a dream thus becomes very significant and spiritual. As important features of folk tales, dreams give the stories that "surrealistic quality" frequently ascribed to them by Western observers. They also provide a forum for communication between the protagonist and the spiritual world, and the sacred and the pro-fane realms of existence.

Dreams, definitively since Descartes, have been excluded from the reality of Western material waking experience. In earlier European forms of expression, for example, *A Midsummer Night's Dream* or some of the scenes in *Macbeth*, dreams and portents are integral to the comic or historical action of the works. After the seventeenth century, dreams become more the subject of fantasy, as in *Alice in Wonderland* or in Tolkein's sagas. In other aesthetic spheres such as painting and sculpture, the marginalization of dreams and other events of a non-material nature become realized in the very marginalization of the work of art into a "high-cul-tural" object. Indeed, the very need for there to be elaborate theo-ries of aesthetics relying on psychoanalysis has tended to divorce the dream-content of the work of art from the everyday ready-to-handedness of the uninitiated.

As "art," dreams become the object of specialist explanation, something displaced by their non-objective character into the realm of the merely present-at-hand: in art there is no certain knowledge in the sense demanded by Descartes. The question here is expressed as an epistemological one, precisely because for Descartes (and thus for subsequent paradigm philosophy) the question was one of certain knowledge as opposed to what people could assert on the basis of experience. As one of the most subjective of experiences, along with pain (Arendt, 1958), dreams in the Western philosophical tradition cannot be separated from the dreaming and therefore cannot be placed into an Archimedean point from which they can be displayed for examination. As part of this tradition, psychoanalysis understands film as having certain characteristics that make the encounter with it similar to a dream, primarily because of the exclusion of dreams from epistemological validity by paradigm thinking.

In the exchange between Western film production and non-Western film consumption, the ontological community of the producers is effaced during the exhibition of the film within the ontological community of the viewers. People, for whom the world exists in the religious sense described by Elungu, are also likely to have come to their knowledge of their world through a different route to that assumed by Western cognitive development theories (for example, Piaget). In their coming to know, they engage far more with the actual ready-to-hand equipment of their contexts. In the West, on the other hand, learning includes a greater emphasis on the deferred meanings of the written word, and in this context knowledge becomes directed more to the present-at-hand. Film theory generally has approached its topic as something present-at-hand, in the sense of being an "object of Knowledge," precisely because this is the manner in which knowledge is cast: it is always at one or more removes from the ready-to-hand.

However, in the context of film exhibition in communities for whom knowledge of the world is closer to the ready-to-hand, viewers do not necessarily become aware of the fact that what is shown in the film is assumed by the film's makers to exist in a way that is different (see Conquergood, 1986). By this we mean that for those in the post- or neo-colonial subaltern classes, there is a greater reliance than in the industrialized West on what is learned by doing. As a result, it is possible (even likely) that the kind of explanations and interpretations of this activity will be very different to those generated in a language which has been shaped by the exigencies of literacy. Language and action, that is to say, are more closely involved for these communities in the nurture of new generations than is the case of industrial societies where writing and labour define the historical relation between what-is and what-can-be-done.[9]

What seems to have occurred is that the conditions under which Western industrial society emerged have become defined on what Richard Rorty (1980, p. 6) has labelled the explanation of the world in terms of "philosophy as a theory of knowledge." As Stephen Toulmin (1991) indicates, however, the establishment of this culture in the West has its origins in a clearly articulated his - torical context of specific conflict between ways of doing things in the world. In the course of time there has been a devaluation of what Toulmin (1991, p. 30-5) calls the "oral, the particular, the local and the timely" in favour of grand theories based on the "writ - ten, the universal, the general and the timeless." Products proper to the world of the latter (e.g. film) are introduced into a world (or worlds) in which there remains to a greater or lesser extent the forms of life associated with the former.

Massive disruptions in the conditions under which African peoples experience their average everyday lives have occurred. As a result of the imposition of industrial orders of society (both market and state oriented), the effect has remained to a greater or lesser extent disruptions rather than revolutions. Put differently, African people outside of the elites associated with post -colonial (or, for many, neo-colonial) development still experience their lives in oral, timely, particular and very local ways, and they expe - rience the exhibition of film in much the same kind of ways. It is not the purpose of this article to judge whether these ways are authentic or debased or whatever, but rather to accentuate the dif - ficulties inherent to interpreting the experience of peoples for whom the separation of knowing from doing is foreign to their form of life. In the specific context of African film and its pro - ducers, there is the added burden of transferring the sense of this form (these forms) of life into a medium developed within and suited for variations on a single form of life in which to know (epistemology) is formally separated from a really existing realm of activity (the ontological).

The critique here is that of a tradition in which truth inheres in the Heideggerean present-at-hand in strict contrast with the Renaissance/ peasant/ savage/ working-class everyday engage - ment and consciousness of the ready-to-hand. There is, if we follow Charles Taylor's (1979, pp. 11-14) analysis of Hegel's antecedents, no doubt some Romantic influence in this, although there is no necessary hankering after some prelapsarian Golden Age so prevalent in the influences on much Continental thought. More to the point is that there is a tradition in the West that essen - tially states that "history is bunk" (pace Henry Ford), and that there is or ought to be one and only one true knowledge irrespective of what can or has to be done in the world. In contrast, we suggest that there is a possibility for equally valid knowledge to emerge from a context in which the continuity of human affairs does not exclude the consequences of human action.

IN SUMMARY

To recast the ideal of Marx's philosophy, the construction of African thought through Third Cinema interpretations can be seen rather simply and elegantly to efface the Western dichotomy of Subject and Object. It also restores some measure of the radical ideal of a collective consciousness, specifically in the way the present, as that which can be encountered by everyone there, is the consequence of what everybody has done (or of that which someone failed to do) among those who came before.

In contrast, a positivist approach to science, which derives from sets of dualisms driven by industrial imperatives calling them - selves "disciplines," cannot coherently come to grips with views of the world which have resisted fragmentation and which try to retain cosmological coherence through orality and contact with the spirit world. These Mind/ Body (ideal/ material; base/ super - structures, etc) separations are further sharpened by the move from orality to literacy. The result is to drastically reduce reliance by the young literate educated on their oral elders for information. This process of enculturation into the industrialised technological world results in the foregrounding of a solipsistic individualism over communalism, leading to a disruption of traditional intergenera - tional forms of deference and respect. Cultures and communities become fragmented, cultural memory fades into the cultural uncon - scious. This communal unconscious is recovered and brought to the surface by directors through appeals to the past as occurs in *Sankofa*.

Critiques of African films, which are inadequate to the task of reintegrating the Subject with the Object, can never meet Gerima's challenge for an African cinema language or appropriate kinds of criticism. This is because Western-based criticism tends to sepa - rate the visible world of actual behavior from the invisible spiri - tual realm. It can be hard for those from the West, in the absence of a sound understanding of the ontological referents in African languages, to establish whether non-Westernized Africans are in fact distinguishing the material from the spiritual. It is not an acci - dent, then, that much of early African philosophy was most sensi - tively recorded by a few sympathetic European missionaries and theologians such as Frans Placide Tempels. In visual terms, this task of recording and articulating African philosophies has now fallen to African filmmakers as they embrace the multiple and complex roles of traditional oral bards/historians.

The filmmaker's depend on their art for economic survival and thus function in a similar manner as the traditional "roving poets" who make their livelihood through their art. These poets/ *griots* often show no allegiance to anyone in particular and can vil - ify and praise an audience, politicians, rulers, or a lay person simul - taneously. Thus economics often determine the nature of the praise poetry performed. African filmmakers' art, however, is often not influenced by loyalty to established power, or faithfulness to an individual. Rather, the filmmakers' function is determined by a combination of artistic, economic, and political ideologies, as well as social vision.

The integration of the spiritual and the material is partly found in the oral tradition that many African societies have sustained through the centuries of colonization and Westernization. These filmmakers see their art as commentaries on their societies in order to enlighten people about the contexts of their experiences. Thus, seen in broader terms, the African filmmaker embodies the com - plex, yet multiple roles of *griots*/bards in their traditional contexts of origin. They are simultaneously social critics, historians, bards and seers; they criticize the present to encourage change; re-exam - ine and reconstruct the past to shed more light on its effects on the present; and they transmit cultures and histories from the past gen - eration to those who are present.

African directors, in decolonizing Western images of Africa presented to Africans, face the problem of Hollywood -hooked audiences and escapist entertainment seeking in their own coun - tries. Thus, while African governments mostly ban films made by their critical citizens, they become artistic fodder for First World film festival and conference circuits. As such, critical African films are sometimes subjected to alienating and misleading post -Freudian and Lacanian psychoanalytic critique. These theories are often inappropriately imported into African critical canons by travelling scholars trying to secure their First World relevance by recreating the neo-colonial bastions of Western psychocentric Screen Theory in a continent still resolving the tensions and problems of colo - nialism, let alone post-modernism.

NOTES

1. Our theory of orality is drawn mainly from Walter Ong (1982). Our approach to semiotics is detailed in Shepperson and Tomaselli (1993).
2. Heidegger's exposition of the ready-to-handedness of exis- tents closely matches Marx's analysis of the material reality of the products encountered in the context of alienated labor.
3. This point is made in different ways by Tomaselli and Smith (1990); Jane Gaines (1988); Teshome Gabriel (1989a, 1989b) and Hamid Naficy (1989).
4. Some Screen Theorists who have now seen the light have veered totally in the other direction—calling for reception studies, seemingly to the exclusion of other dimensions of cinema study. Eve Bertelsen (1991), for example, writes as if no one else in Africa or South Africa has dealt with these issues. In fact, it is not clear exactly which South African film theorists, if any, she has in mind. All her sources are European and North American.
5. The notion of *griots* in African cinema is subject to consid- erable debate. Manthia Diawara (1989, p.210) argues that while African filmmakers rest on the shoulders of traditional storytellers, the films point toward a new order, rather than the old and stagnating one in which griots are implicated. Diarwara's position is critiqued by Henry Overballe (1992, p.196) who argues that *griots* protect values not institutions and that they are the carriers of innovation and change.
6. This is not our task here. The reader is referred to Shepperson and Tomaselli (1993).
7. Propp presented a formalist analysis of Russian folk tales, concluding that folk narratives generally can be analyzed in terms of 31 categories of actions. These include the classical

notions of tasks assigned to characters; magic aids and objects donated and/or withheld, and so on.

8.   Ludwig Wittgenstein (1963) carried out an analytical critique of the 20th Century Anglo-Saxon tradition of linguistic philosophy. This work was aimed, albeit implicitly, at the way earlier works by, among others, G.E. Moore and Bertrand Russell had been received by the logical positivists. Indeed, Wittgenstein himself had started his philosophical career with a groundbreaking critical assessment of the early logical positivism of the Vienna Circle (1961).

In the former work, however, he takes what has been described by Agnes Heller (1983) as a "tragic" view of linguistic philosophy (not to be confused with philosophical work deriving from structural linguistics). References to "form(s) of life" are not frequent, but they are crucial in grasping Wittgenstein's position that meaning cannot be abstracted from the context of all the different kinds of activity possible for members of a community (1963, § 23). Similarly, he points out (§ 241) that the matter of consensual rule-following that is sometimes labeled as "conventionalism" cannot be reduced simply to "agreement in opinions," but to an agreement which stems from the whole active context shared by those who so agree. It is this context that Wittgenstein calls a "form of life." See also § 19, and 1963, pp. 174 & 226.

9.   The idea of "society" here is informed by the critique of the social sciences in Hannah Arendt (1958). The Social (note the capitalization) is for Arendt a consequence of the exclusion from human activity of the possibility of action, a condition brought about by the organization of human society as a consequence of the labor theories of value in early political economy (pp. 38-49; see also 126-135). In the world within which film as commodity emerged, there was an already-existing tradition in which the oral had been long made secondary to the written; film and what can be said of it became elaborated precisely within the consumption-reproductive form of life Arendt describes. In the absence of a comparable history of struggle regarding industrialization in the colonized world, the orality of nurture has never been completely marginalized by the imposition of the Social and its labor theories of (sur-

plus) value, as has been demonstrated of British life in the 1930s to the 1950s by Richard Hoggart (1956).

WORKS CITED

Achebe, Chinua. et al. *Library of African Cinema*. San Francisco: California Newsreel, 1990.

Althusser, L. *Lenin, Philosophy and Other Essays.* London: Verso, 1971.

Andrade-Watkins, Claire. *Francophone African Cinema: French Financial and Technical Assistance, 1961-1977*. UMI Dissertation Services.

Armes, Roy. *Third Cinema in the Third World*. Berkeley: California University Press, Armes, 1987.

Arendt, Hannah. *The Human Condition*; Chicago, University of Chicago Press, 1958.

Berman, R. "Rights and Writing in South Africa," *Telos*, 75 (1988): 161-172.

Bertelsen, Eve. "Radical Cheek: Film Theory and the Common Viewer," *South African Theatre Journal*, 5 (1991): 2-4.

Boughedir, Ferid. *Le Cinéma Africain de A a Z*. Bruxelles: OCIC, 1987.

Cham, Mbye Baboucar. "Ousmane Sembene and the Aesthetics of oral Traditions," *Africana Journal*, 13.1/4) (1982a): 24-40.

—. "Film Production in West Africa: 1979-1981," *Présence Africaine*, 4 (1982b): 168-187.

Conquergood, D. "'Is It Real': Watching Television with Laotian Refugees," *PCDS Directions*, 2(2) (1986): 1-5.

Diawara, Manthia. *African Cinema: Politics and Culture*. Bloomington: Indiana University Press, 1992.

—. "Oral Literature and African Film: Narratology in *Wend Kuuni*. Ed. Pines and Willemen, 199-212.

Elungu, P.E. "African Liberation and the Problem of Philosophy" (Trans. M. Mulumba). Mimeo. CCMS, University of Natal, Durban, 1992.

Flitterman-Lewis, S. "Psychoanalysis, Film and Television." Ed. R. Allen, *Channels of Discourse.* London: Methuen, 1987.

Gabriel, Teshome. "Towards a Critical Theory of Third World Films." Eds. Jim Pines and Paul Willemen, *Questions of Third Cinema*. London: British Films Institute, 1989a, 30-52.

—. "Third Cinema as Guardian of Popular Memory: Towards a Third Aesthetics." Pines and Willemen, 1989b, 53-64.

Gaines, Jane. "White Privilege and Looking Relations: Race and Gender in Feminist Film Theory," *Screen*, 29 (1988): 12-26.

Gardies, A. and Haffner, P. *Regards sur le Cinema Negro-Africain*. Bruxelles: Editions OCIC, 1987.

Geertz, Clifford. *Local Knowledge: Further Essays in Interpretive Anthropology*. New York, Basic Books, 1983.

Gerima, Haile. Notes. In "Appropriations: New Directions for African Cultural Studies: Conference Programme," University of Cape Town, 1993.

—. "Triangular Cinema, Breaking Toys, and Dinkish vs Lucy." In Pines and Willemen, 1989, 65-89.

Hacking, Ian. *Representing and Intervening*; Cambridge. Cambridge University Press, 1983.

Heidegger, M. *Being and Time*. Oxford, Basil Blackwell, 1962.

Heller, Agnes. *A Theory of History*. London, RKP, 1983.

— and Feher, F. *The Postmodern Political Condition*. Oxford, Polity Press, 1991. Chapters 2 and 3.

Higgins, John. "Documentary Realism and Film Pleasure: Two Moments From Euzhan Palcy's A Dry White Season," *Literator*, 13 (1992): 101-110.

Hoggart, Richard. *The Uses of Literacy*. Harmondsworth, Penguin, 1956.

Marx, Karl. *Capital*, Vol. I (G.D.H. Cole, ed.); London, J.M. Dent & Sons, 1972, 391-409.

Mudimbe, Valentin Y. *The Invention of Africa: Gnosis, Philosophy and the Order of Knowledge*. Bloomington and Indianapolis, Indiana University Press, 1979.

Metz, Christian. *Film Language: A Semiotics of the Cinema.* New York: Oxford University Press, 1974.

—. *Language and Cinema. The Hague: Mouton,* 1974.

Naficy, Hamid. "Autobiography, Film Spectatorship, and Cultural Negotiation," *Emergences*, 1 (1989): 29-54.

Nichols. Bill. *Representing Reality.* Bloomington: University of Indiana Press, 1991.

Ong, Walter. *Orality and Literacy: the Technologizing of the Word*. London: New York, 1982.

Overballe, Henrik. Narrative Traditions Among the Mandika of West Africa. Eds. Peter Crawford and Jan K Simonsen,

Ethnographic Film Aesthetics and Narrative Traditions. Aarhus: Intervention Press, 1992, 176-201.

Pfaff, Francoise. *The Cinema of Ousmane Sembene: A Pioneer of African Film.* Westport: Greenwood Press, 1984.

Pines, Jim and Willemen, Paul. *Questions of Third Cinema.* London: British Film Institute, 1989.

Prinsloo, Jeanne "Beyond Propp and Oedipus: Towards Expanding Narrative Theory," *Literator,* 13 (1992a): 65-82.

Propp, V. Morphology of the Folktale. Austin: University of Texas Press, 1968.

Quine, W.V.O. *Ontological Relativity and Other Essays.* New York, Columbia University Press, 1969.

Rorty, Richard. *Philosophy and the Mirror of Nature.* Oxford, Basil Blackwell, 1980.

Salmane, H., Hartog, S. and Wilson, D. *Algerian Cinema.* London: British Film Institute, 1976.

Shepperson, Arnold. "Tits 'n Bums: Film and the Disposal of Human Body," *Visual Anthropology,* 6 (1994): 395-400.

—. *On the Social Interpretation of Cultural Experience: Reflections on Raymond Williams' Early Cultural Writings, 1958.* MA thesis, University of Natal, Durban, 1995.

— and Tomaselli, Keyan. "Semiotics in an African Context: 'Science' vs 'Priest Craft,' 'Semiology' vs 'Semiotics,'" *Acta Fennica Semiotica, II* (1993): 159-176.

Solanas, Fernando and Gettino, Octavia. "Towards a Third Cinema." In Nichols, Bill. (ed.): *Movies and Methods.* Berkeley: California University Press, 1976, 44-64.

Stoller, Paul. *The Cinematic Griot: the Ethnography of Jean Rouch.* Chicago: Chicago University Press, 1992.

Taylor, C. *Hegel and Modern Society.* Cambridge, Cambridge University Press, 1979.

Tempels, Placide. *Bantu Philosophy.* Paris: Presence Africaine, 1959.

Tomaselli, Keyan. *'Appropriating Images': The Semiotics of Visual Anthropology.* Aarhus: Intervention Press, 1996.

— and Smith, Greg. "Sign Wars: The Battlegrounds of Semiotics of Cinema in Anglo-Saxiona," *Degres: Revue de Synthèse à Orientation Sémiologique,* 64 (1990): cc1-26.

Toulmin, Stephen. *Cosmopolis: The Hidden Agenda of Modernity.* New York: The Free Press, 1991.

Willemen, Paul. The Third Cinema Question: Notes and Reflections. In Pines and Willemen, 1-29.

Wittgenstein, L. *Philosophical Investigations*. Oxford: Blackwell, 1963.

Filmography

Afrique, Je te plumerai (Africa, I will Fleece You) Producer/director: Jean Marie Teno. Cameroon, 1992. French with English subtitles. 88 minutes, video & 16mm film

Mississippi Masala. (1990). Directed by Mira Nair. USA/Africa.

On the Wire (1992). Directed by Elaine Procter. South Africa.

Ramparts of Clay. (1970). Directed by Jean-Louis Bertuccelli. France/Algeria. 85 minutes.

Sankofa. Haile Gerima (1993). Ghana. Directed by Haile Gerima, Negod Gwad Productions. 125 minutes, 35mm.

PART TWO

STUDIES IN
POSTCOLONIAL FILMS

A PROBLEMATIC SIGN OF AFRICAN DIFFERENCE IN TRINH T. MINH-HA'S *REASSEMBLAGE*

T HE NOVELTY OF TRINH T. MINH-HA'S *Reassemblage,* if I can casually invoke the difficult notion of the new for a moment, lies in its ability to function as a meditation, through the medium of film, on the great structural problematic of difference in the context of Dioula, Sereer, Manding, Bassari, Fulani, and Sarakhole villages in Senegal. Through pictures and sounds of different dances, architectures, industries, and songs, as well as through Trinh's elusive narration, the structural problematic itself is eluci-dated. Taking on the presumption that the camera is an instrument capable of simply recording truth, along with the classical subjec-tifying conceptions of inside and outside that generate hierarchies of knowledge, Trinh subverts and objectifies the pretensions of both cinema and anthropology, initiating a genre of critically reflec-tive deconstructionist ethnographic film.

Although many of her techniques, even her least conventional ones, are similar to those used by "great auteurs"— Godard's New Wave jump cuts and sound discontinuities (*A Woman is a Woman*), Bergman's philosophical reflections on objectification and identity (*Persona*), Woody Allen's fusion of documentary form with confes-sional narrative (*Husbands and Wives*)—Trinh's film surpasses all of these in establishing a truly theoretical cinematic form, opening up a broad range of possibilities for abstract cinematic thought discon-nected from conventional plots and subjects: "A film about what? My friends ask. A film about Senegal; but what in Senegal?" (Trinh, 83).

According to Trinh the ethnographic documentary filmmaker, like the anthropological observer, is dominated by a voracious "will to knowledge," which even when tempered by acknowledgment of the subjective position of the observer, cannot seem to help appropriating and linguistically objectifying of the "other." The desire to create sense surpasses doubts regarding one's political relationship to the "natives"; moreover, an implicit construction of the other within the structure of language has always already performed the inevitable objectification. Jean Rouch inadvertently demonstrates this phenomenon in his article "On the Vicissitudes of the Self" where his self-conscious efforts to reflect on the "self" of the observer/anthropological filmmaker are bracketed off from the objectively framed discussion of the activities of his subjects (Rouch, 106). Rouch's *Les Maîtres-Fous* (1954) presents its ethnographic information in even more profound isolation. The voice-over narration, disembodied and superimposed over the images, takes on the transcendental quality of a deity; the native is positioned as an analysand, his actions scrutinized to reveal the neurosis and unconscious motivations underlying his irrational behavior; the camera and the anthropologist collaborate to fashion the subject into a readable text. The curious eye of the camera condescends to frame the subject, turning him into an image-sign, while the narrational subjectivity is disguised by conventions of documentary film: stable medium shots cut to capture the significant details, "the a, b, c's of photography" (Trinh, 86). A particular shot has often been commented upon by African critics whose sense of identification with the documentary subject has elicited anger and shame: a flashlight is shined in the face of a convulsing, foaming African, enabling the voyeuristic camera to capture the image. Indeed, the conventions of cinéma vérité suggest that the truth-value of the images is inherent: evidence to be used later, facts to be studied, interpreted, explained, but possessing an incontrovertible truth value. Trinh's work asks the question: is it not the anthropologist/filmmaker/analyst who constructs the text, rather than the historical, cultural or social fact that has metaphysical priority? The question returns us to the continental dispute between idealist and materialist metaphysics; we can see how Trinh's approach is rooted in the structuralist emphasis on the primacy of the signifier: we cannot know the truth about the other, only the omnipresent mediation of signs. "I do not intend to speak about, just speak nearby," she says. (105)

Drawing upon mystical eastern philosophical traditions and European post-Marxist structuralism, *Reassemblage* simultaneously points to its own constructedness and denies the validity of labeling what is seen. To claim understanding and interpret images is, for Trinh, inherently problematic, but also impossible to avoid, since processes of signification themselves are always implicit in human activity. Shots of various activities and technologies—rope-making, weaving, rice-sifting, cooking, and dancing—seem to refer specifically to the protolinguistic quality Levi-Strauss attributes to "sciences of the concrete." For Trinh, however, explaining the meaning of the activities, more than being superfluous, is viewed as only a preliminary step to establishing one's own supe - riority and reifying one's hegemony over the "other," the subject-objects viewed. Thus *Reassemblage* is about representing and reflecting upon visual images and objects even less than it is about the Senegalese people; it is a metadiscourse on the act of viewing itself. The viewer, confronted with purposefully disrupted images, sounds, and voices, slowly begins to become conscious of him or herself piecing together arbitrary information and reconstructing it into a meaningful system of signs. At the same time one is made aware of the presence of the filmmaker herself, whose subjectiv - ity is made more poignant by her disjunctive absence, which repli - cates the position of the viewer's self, simultaneously present and incapable of attaining a position outside of itself to understand the meaning of its own presence. *Reassemblage* is a reflection upon reflection: "Entering into the only reality of signs where I myself am a sign" (Trinh, 85).

Trinh creates this critically deconstructive effect in several ways. Gratuitous jump-cuts, excessive shifts in perspective, and an abundance of moments when images are either transparently posed or explicitly and uncomfortably voyeuristic (close-ups of breasts, disconnected body parts, faces looking curiously back at the cam - era) signal the narrator's subjective presence. Any sense of the perspective being "real" in any conventional sense or of the cam - era replicating the natural position of the eye is interrupted.

The use of sound, which in cinéma vérité was thought of as a means of capturing reality in its purest form, in *Reassemblage* serves to disconcert the viewer, punctuating the constructedness of the narrative, defamiliarizing the images, and subverting easy recognition and assimilation. Voices are either profoundly silent or disjointed, and always untranslated. The background sounds appear in contrast to the rhythm of the activities on the screen: the rice-sifting, corn pounding, dancing and jumping comes into corre - spondence only to move back into disconnection. The gross dis -

connection of sounds and voices points not only to the narrator's subjectivity but also to the voyeurism of the spectator, while the meticulous, methodical reassemblage of the sounds in a semi-coherent, semi-realist manner suggests the boundary between knowledge and incomprehension. In Trinh's narration, meaning comes ecstatically, fleetingly corresponding to the "reality," which is merely constituted by our preconceptions, only to again become pointedly meaningless. The paradigmatic anthropological effort toward reconciliation of the representation with the reality, of "our" understanding with "theirs," is thus presented as not just impossi-bly problematic, but not even desirable. (In any case, the formu-lation presupposes a division in the first place.) *Reassemblage* aims for irresolution, non-closure, the place Luce Irigaray pro-poses to reappropriate a properly female ethic.

Most importantly, however, is the manner in which *Reassemblage* gives rise to meaningful reflections that serve to justify the incoherence of the sounds and images and explain the underlying documentary construction. The reflections, together with the crafted film language, form an intelligible code that elab-orates the narrator's position, without, theoretically, rationalizing the activities of the Senegalese people or superimposing hermeneu-ticism upon the worldview of the subjects. A critical deconstruc-tion of film, subjectivity, and anthropology, the narration operates by suggestion instead of systematically, with the aim of prob-lematizing not only the analytic discourse of neocolonial anthro-pological film but also the narrator's own position, insofar as, within her own process of signification, she produces a pleasura-ble object, gratifying herself and others for whom theorizing is a meaningful and fulfilling narrative process. If the voice-over nar-ration, like the sound in general, is purposively fragmented, leav-ing the impression that the author is either unable or unwilling to posture herself as the universal intellectual pointing the way to truth and justice, it does, notwithstanding Trinh's hesitation to determine meaning, go beyond a vacant relativism or a "reassem-blage" of objectivity. Rather than asking what is the truth about these people, or what is the true meaning of their words and activ-ities, Trinh shifts the question to: how is truth constituted; how do power imbalances effect the production of meaning; what is the sta-tus of a critique of the production of meaning that is inherently a part of the problem it seeks to explain; is it possible to critique presumptions of subjectivity when the narrator is herself embed-

ded in a certain sort of subjectivity; would one really want to aban -
don the production of meaning, even if it were possible; and, would
the result not be a reconstruction of a presumptuous objectivity?
In other words, the film requires that we ask a series of questions
bearing upon the status of the search for knowledge in relation to
post-colonial Africa, rather than confirming a sense of a latent,
linear truth existing in a stable, monolithic reality.

Given the explicitly deconstructionist project of *Reassemblage*,
Nwachukwu Frank Ukadike's treatment of the text in *Black African
Cinema* (1994) is surprising in its unfairness and lack of concern
for the particular mechanisms at work in the text. Even if one
acknowledges the neo-Marxist approach that he adopts, one is
thrown off guard by the vehemence with which he attacks the film:

> Minh-ha's filmmaking is amateurish, bracketed by opportunism.
> Some of the major flaws of her films are lack of continuity ema -
> nating from unclear structure, incorrect exposure, out-of-focus
> shots, bad editing, and disconcerting voice-overs, which make
> one wonder if anybody would have looked at these films, let
> alone distribute them, if Minh-ha had made them outside of
> Africa. Although she argues that these flaws are deliberate (and
> some of her admirers agree with her), *Reassemblage* is struc-
> turally and aesthetically sloppy and is a failed experiment, which
> should not be commercialized. (Ukadike, 56)

Ukadike takes a typical neo-Marxist aesthetic position, presuming
a common, suprahistorical notion of correct representation: "From
the beginning the major concern of African filmmakers has been
to provide a more realistic image of Africa as opposed to the dis -
torted artistic and ideological expressions of the dominant film
medium..." (3). In its absence of regard for avant-garde technical
practices, Ukadike's critique appears strikingly provincial and anti -
quated. Even supposing Trinh's techniques turned out to be unmo -
tivated by avant-garde traditions, which also saw themselves as
revolting against stagnant cinematic conventions that were believed
to reinforce the passivity of the viewer, the major tradition in polit -
ically-committed, Marxist, and Third World cinematic traditions
has been a valorization of "imperfect cinema" as a mode of defa -
miliarization, destabilization, and realignment with non-domi -
neering systems of production. While *Black African Cinema*, in its
encyclopedic scope and attention to particular films, fruitfully

builds upon and broadens the work begun by Manthia Diawara in *African Cinema* (1990), ideologically Ukadike tends to return us to the point where African film is held up as the site of a pre-sumptuous mystico-primordial unity, one that *Reassemblage* was designed to critique.

Ukadike goes on to discuss the common intentions of African filmmakers to promote "new" modes of representation:

> Black African filmmakers contend that traditional ways of filmic representation—old ideas and attitudes—must give way to new ones, especially in portraying African cultures. The interest, participation, and collaboration of the people must be secured, stimulated, and maintained. Toward this goal, the majority of Black African filmmakers are united by their art and ideology. (3)

Ukadike's disregard for the reevaluation of the terms of intellec-tual debate are partially responsible for his hasty condemnation of Trinh's work, the rejection of it out-of-hand as neocolonialist, while neglecting to consider the ways in which it sets out to thoughtfully address the very questions he raises. The tone in which he describes Trinh as "a Third World feminist of Vietnamese ori-gin and a naturalized American" (54) is disheartening; there is an eerie sense in which this fact is just another proof of the impurity and inauthenticity of her work. This is consistent with the patron-izing recourse to essentialism implicit in his conception of the unity of African film. We should be reminded in this context of the way in which V.Y. Mudimbe showed how the "invention of tradi-tion" has tended to serve colonialist ends. Even Sembène Ousmane, who has come to epitomize neo-Marxist revolutionary cinema, said in a 1994 interview in reference to linguistic diversity in *Guelwaar*: "As far as I am concerned, I no longer support notions of purity. Purity has become a thing of the past." (Niang and Gadjigo, 174) A more thoughtful question to pose for Trinh, and one respecting the boundaries of the text itself, might have been to what extent *Reassemblage* has merely produced the African as a post-structural object, and whether the power relations inherent in such a project are not equivalent to the process by which Jean Rouch, in a different moment, constructed his own African subject between another set of parentheses.

Reassemblage never really resolves the conundrum opened up by its rhetoric, and the film has as an advantage over Trinh's writings a great deal of poetry in its composition, whereas in such essays as "The Language of Nativism" the argument is confounded by a stylized melange of post-structural feminist jargon. Where the film succeeds in convincing a careful reader that there is some - thing substantial behind the rhetoric, the less methodically con - structed essays fall flat. Perhaps the unfairness with which Ukadike responds to *Reassemblage* is balanced in some way by the heavy-handedness of Trinh's treatment of the discipline of anthropology, of which she nevertheless has made extensive use in her own cri - tique of representation, especially structural anthropology, to which her work is deeply indebted. This contradiction is particularly in evi - dence in *Woman, Native, Other: Writing Postcoloniality and Feminism* (1989), in which she repeatedly refers to Malinowski sar-castically as "the Great Master" and issues a critique of anthropo - logical nativist discourse initiated by anthropology itself. As she approvingly quotes Geertz, Levi-Strauss, and Barthes (who becomes the equivalent of "The Good Male" in her attempt to reverse the codes of the patronizing discourse of White Male power), she con - tinues to rebuke a dehistoricized "anthropology" for its complicity with colonialism as if it were a great unspoken secret, in spite of decades of anthropological scholarship that has taken its colonial history as an object. If in *Reassemblage* the text substantiates its position with very powerful images and assiduous editing, the writings in *Woman, Native, Other* bring out the superficiality of the basic premises of her critique of Western interpretation—a cri - tique seen by the end to embrace the rather puritan idea of Third World Womanism. It is invaluable to recognize that those who claimed to be demystifying African culture through the medium of anthropology were both complicit with colonial power and unable to escape from the semiotic system in which they were grounded, thus accomplishing a merely more sophisticated reduction and degrada - tion of African culture. But it is a triviality to call Malinowski a racist and anthropology a neocolonialist discipline without discussing the discourses in the context of their historical moments.

In a certain respect Malinowski's racism has a greater signif-icance than her comments would suggest; it is, among other things, evidence of that racial ideology is a function operating in a vari - ety of complex ways, and not always consistently. Further, it is easy to forget that Malinowski's contributions to anthropology, if they did not directly combat racial ideology, were instrumental to a body of scholarship whose effect was to delegitimate its premises and to so expand a sense of the complexity of human culture that it is a wonder the opposition between "Western" and "non-Western" could have ever come into being during the same historical period, if not for the corresponding, but also frequently conflicting, effects of power.

Trinh's real contribution in *Reassemblage* has not been in stating anything new regarding representation or post-coloniality, but in connecting avant-garde cinematic practices to the French intellectual traditions in which they are grounded by way of her own personal relationship to world culture and, by an extension of colonial politics, to West African societies. The intellectual experience that emerges is fresh, unconfined, expansive, and other, precisely because it is impure, implicated, formed out of dynamic cultural polyglossia.

One could find in this disagreement between the "African Male" and the "American Female" (however metissée culturally) an ideal representation of the structural problematic itself. The boundaries are drawn between two fundamental positions in academic culture, in accordance with a well-established schism between "neo-Marxist ethnic scholarship" and "Western postmodern theory." It might be appropriate to place the representation of the African female body between the two positions as a sort of mock battlefront, where the arguments are the most vociferous on both sides, and where the line itself begins to absorb both "sides" into a messy, implicated problematic. Trinh's position is already established fairly well in the preceding discussion. She is at once an outsider to African culture, an outsider in American culture, and an insider in American culture—to the extent that alterity is one of the definitive functions in American culture. Thus, as "Third World Woman" she can position herself as an accuser in relation to Malinowski on a pure ethical ground, while her Americanness leaves her vulnerable to the same charge of racism from Ukadike. Nevertheless, she is in an opportune "post-structural/post-modern" position, in which an unproblematic, indigenous identity is disturbed and the post-modern theoretical effect establishes another sort of subjective authority.

Ukadike, on the other hand, comes to stand for all Africans through the essentialist reduction and for the idea of authentic or pure representation; it is clear that his charges against Trinh are tied to the insertion of ethnicity into a morally grounded aesthetic judgement:

> Interweaving exoticism with nudity in a semipornographic blend, Minh-ha reaches Western audiences in a facile manner, a measure which also has *sacrificed* her *Third World values* for First World capitalistic taste...I have never seen so many close-ups of breasts in any other film, fifty-one shots in a forty-one minute film. Perhaps *Reassemblage* is admired by its promoters for its pornography rather than ethnography....Needless to say, the reviews are based on Eurocentric assumptions rather than African sensibility. (Ukadike, 55-6, *my emphasis*)

One striking feature of this critique is his reprimand of Trinh in a sort of "Uncle Tom of Third World Marxism" polemic; she has sacrificed her Third World values for money, Ukadike insinuates. (Ironically, one of the common features of both positions is that there is no significant money or commercial interest.) However, Ukadike himself never convinces us that this "pornographic" rep - resentation, simply because it contains close-ups of breasts, is par - ticularly un-African; in fact, the idea of what constitutes an African sensibility is never considered: it is simply assumed. In his pejo - rative use of the word "pornography" he, like Trinh when she accuses Malinowski of being a racist, acts parasitically in relation to an existing discourse in which the question of pornography is already articulated within a vapid, ultimately rightist construction of representation, rather than directly evaluating the image, how it is used, and what it signifies. Trinh's narration clearly indicates her intention of calling attention to the semiotic function of nudity in ethnographic film and Western cultural codes:

> Filming in Africa means for many of us
> Colorful images, naked breast women, exotic dances, and fear -
> ful rites.
> The unusual.
> Nudity does not reveal
> The hidden
> It is its absence
> A man attending a slide show on Africa turns to his wife and says with guilt in his voice: "I have seen some pornography tonight." (107-8)

Even in *Reassemblage*, however, a rigorous structuralist evaluation will reveal certain flaws in Trinh's formulation of the process of signification. One could find in *Reassemblage* a contradiction between her structuralist revision of the idea of representation and the post-structurally-grounded critique of power relations. When Trinh makes the subjectless statement, "the habit of imposing a meaning to every sign," (Trinh, 105), she suggests that the signifying process is invested with questions of hegemony, but the statement becomes paradoxical when made any more explicit. What would it mean to "impose a meaning to every sign," if we understand that a sign is a thing inherently signifying, for which reason we call it a sign? One could hypothesize such an "empty sign" on the level of the signified, which refers to that part of the signifying equation that might be considered prior to a specific meaning, but already we are implicating such an object by naming it according to its dependency on the signifier. (Jameson, 149) Admittedly this paradox is a product of a particular form of analytic logic that Trinh's more mystical influences would also reject, but if we were to challenge Trinh concerning, for instance, the image of the breast, it would be difficult to avoid conceding that the breast has an important meaning which she cannot dissociate from her own viewing eye within the "circle of looks" that constitutes meaning.

Her response is a typically enigmatic one, but if we suppose the idea of "imposing a meaning upon a sign" to be an intelligible one, the only way we can justify it is by reference a Buddhist conception of the signifying process, or to the point at which structuralism and post-structuralism become distinct; the point at which the scientific presuppositions of structuralism and its dependence on language are questioned by, in the former case, a pluck of the nose[1], or in the latter, by emphasizing the active construction of knowledge, rather than its embeddedness in something a priori.

The image of the African breast functions as a sign in relation to which neither Trinh nor Ukadike remains unimplicated or pure, precisely because, as subjects they inevitably engage in the process of objectification, whether as viewers or as critics. One of the disturbing things about viewing a breast in the context of the film itself is how it is inseparable from the conspicuous pleasure of being a spectator (even if, as some critics have pointed out, the image is not a particularly glamorized one), something which contemporary debate has usually condemned as voyeurism. When Trinh comments on the pleasure of capturing images and constructing a narrative out of them, she does so in a way which importantly discloses the emotions of a Malinowski; she is ambivalent, experiencing first fascination and excitement at the images she is capturing, and then revulsion, if not with the African subject, than with the system of signs and how it has implicated her as colonialist: "Watching her through the lens. I look at her becoming me becoming mine" (108).

Ukadike too, in calling the image pornographic reveals his discomfort with the image; something natural rendered violently, defamiliarized, and removed from its native context. His revulsion is also instructive, because what happens in the process may in fact be violent to the African sensibility (if we can rhetorically accept his use of the phrase), for which "nakedness" is not experienced as it is in the West (to round out the structural opposition). It would not be surprising if the image were generally considered offensive in its native context, in the same way, Trinh and Ukadike would agree, that Rouch's presentation of the foaming Maîtres Fous is offensive; the offensiveness defines the boundary between the different cultural conceptions: in the structural problematic this offensiveness illustrates difference itself, the real subject of *Reassemblage*.

Reassemblage does not present a correct representation of African culture. The film is neither value neutral, nor, unlike Ukadike's critiques, moralistic. It is positioned as a challenge to facile classifications, dualistic thought, and in particular to typical dichotomies in which an unproblematic distinction is maintained between the subject/object, viewer/viewed, traditional/ modern, and insider/outsider. Most prolific, possibly, are the silences, the moments of darkness, which speak to the lack of necessity to speak, or maybe the necessity at certain moments not to speak. The movie is both anti-didactic, refusing to make ethnographic claims and criticizing those who do (Peace Corps volunteers, anthropologists, filmmakers), and dogmatic to the extent that explicit (defamiliarizing, contextually new) manipulation replaces coersions inherent in cinematic conventions. The result is an intellectual experiment, which is striking, severe, and prolific. In the end, *Reassemblage* is much more about cinematic language and its capacity to function in the same way as anthropological discourse (or any other discourse for that matter) so as to define and confine, than it is about the people themselves. Is this representation objectifying?

Certainly, the images found in *Reassemblage* are no less disturbing or alienating than those found in traditional representations of Africa, since neither those viewed nor the audience control the construction of meaning. One is tempted to say that, to the extent that we recognize that "the people" are not the real subjects of the film, they fail to become signified in any totalizing way, but perhaps the terms themselves and our way of viewing have totalized them in advance. In any case, the true novelty of *Reassemblage* lies in the way it uses film to create the deconstructionist narrative illusion that interpretation is being wrenched from all of the expert and popular discourses in which it has been formed, and thrust upon a newly enlightened audience placed in the center of contemporary intellectual debate, although we are no longer naive enough to believe that the terms of this latest new hermeneutic moment have not already situated us in the exact same structural problematic, where narrative performs that dangerous and invaluable service of gratifying us by telling us what we already know.

NOTES

1. This parable comes to mind as a way of understanding Trinh's notion of a sign prior to specific meaning: "One day Pai Chang walked with Ma Tsu down the road when they heard the cries of wild geese in the sky. Ma Tsu asked, 'What is this sound?' Pai Chang replied, 'The cries of wild geese.' A long while later Ma Tsu asked, 'Where have they gone?' Pai Chang replied, 'Flown away.' Ma Tsu turned back and twisted Pai Chang's nose. Pai Chang cried with pain and Ma Tsu said, 'Yet you spoke of flying away.'" In short, the pinch triggers the student's awareness of the presence of the enunciating self and suggests the arrogance of the human tendency to appropriate by assuming knowledge of the external world. The suggestion is that language is somehow excessive or vain in relationship to the more fundamental experience of the self or the more fundamental reality of the object.

WORKS CITED

Diawara, Manthia. *African Cinema*. Indiana University Press: Bloomington, 1992.

Jameson, Fredric. *The Prison House of Language: A Critical Account of Structuralism and Russian Formalism* . Princeton University Press: Princeton, 1972.

Irigaray, Luce. *This Sex Which Is Not One*. Cornell University Press: Ithaca, 1985.

Levi-Strauss, Claude. *The Savage Mind.* University of Chicago Press: Chicago, 1966.

Niang, Sada and Samba Gadjigo. "Interview with Sembène Ousmane." *Research in African Literatures*. 26.3 (1995): 174-178.

Paul Rabinow, ed. *The Foucault Reader.* Pantheon Books: New York, 1984.

Rouch, Jean. *Les Maitres Fous*. 1954.

—. "On the Vicissitudes of the Self: the Possessed Dancer, the Magician, the Sorcerer, the Filmmaker, and the Ethnographer." *Studies in the Anthropology of Visual Communication* 5.1 (1974): 2-8.

Trinh T. Minh-Ha. *Framer Framed*. Indiana University Press: Bloomington, 1992.

—. *Woman, Native, Other: Writing Postcoloniality and Feminism* . Indiana University Press: Bloomington, 1989.

—. *Reassemblage.* 1982. (dist. Women Make Movies)

Ukadike, Nwachukwu Frank. *Black African Cinema*. University of California Press: Berkeley, 1994.

Look Homeward, Angel. Maroons and Mulattos in Haile Gerima's *Sankofa*

pourquoi retourner à thèbes ou tassili
pourquoi reprendre tombouctou ou ouadaghost
même l'oiseau sankoffa guidait mes pas sur les marches
escarpées te souviens-tu du mec despote qui traînait
son escarcelle et sa gibecière dans les couloirs du siècle
celui-là qui nous donnait des leçons de morale sans rire
—N.X. Ebony *Déjà vu*

VULTURE, EAGLE, OWL, DOVE, ALBATROSS: there is certainly more than one bird riding our storms, haunting our political and historical vistas. To this vast collection of wingèd emblems can now be added the Sankofa bird that Haile Gerima's recent film has brought to the attention of his public. *Sankofa* (1993) traces the metaphysical adventure of Mona, a young Black American model who has come to Elmina Castle in Ghana for a photo-shoot. Mona is unaware of the castle's former function as a warehouse for slaves, in the era of the Atlantic slave trade. Suddenly transported in space and time, she assumes the new guise of a plantation house slave named Shola. After a series of trials she is metamorphosed once again—returned to the present and to a new consciousness of her African identity.

Gerima begins the film by establishing an ingenious chain of correspondence between an icon (a staff crowned with the Akan symbol known as the "Sankofa bird"); an ageless priest, also named Sankofa, who serves as the self-appointed guardian of Elmina Castle; and a bird of prey that circles above, scrutinizing the play of the sea and the people below. Gliding above the castle like the souls of those deported Africans who sought a way back to Guinea and alluding to those birds that followed the bloody wakes of the slave ships, the bird of prey also evokes Kevin Carter's Pulitzer-prize winning photograph of the Sudanese child and the vulture. [1] In Gerima's *Sankofa*, both the bird of prey and the guardian send us back to the carrion of the past in an effort to impose on us an attitude of reverence towards ancestral Africa and towards the Middle Passage conceived as the foundational moment of Black history. Together, the words of the old man and the Sankofa icon (a bird perched on a pedestal with its legs extended and its beak and eyes turned backwards) command us to "return to the past."

The Akan symbol "Sankofa" was used frequently as a figure in the system of goldweights known as *abrammoo*, and also as a pattern in weaving (Kolb, 18). One of the most interesting repre-sentations of the Sankofa bird appears on the bowl of a pipe acquired by the collector Bowdich in 1817. [2] The symbol can be found as well among royal paraphernalia, particularly on the staffs carried by the spokesmen or "linguists" of the sovereign. [3] Whatever its form, the Sankofa bird plays an important role in the Akan sys-tem of symbolic relations. It functions as a kind of visual 'clue' that calls to mind a series of proverbs: *the king sees all; one must not be afraid to redeem one's past mistakes; turn back and fetch it,* etc. Drawing on this visual-semantic complex, Gerima privileges a single translation: *one must return to the past in order to move forward*. It is this version that Gerima, throughout the film and in the course of many interviews, has transformed into a virtual slo-gan. Curiously, his translation has acquired a degree of authority, to judge by the quasi-literal use made of it as a caption in the cat-alog (144) of a 1995 exhibition called "Animals in African Art" at the Museum for African Art in New York. Reducing the multiple meanings of the Sankofa bird to a simple formula, and indicating the obligatory direction and necessary steps of an "authentic" per-sonal and political awakening, Gerima brings to the screen an inno-vative, seductive, and disquieting Afrocentric meta-narrative. [4] In the film, the aesthetic variations on the theme of slavery and the necessary and happy return to sources adroitly fictionalize one of the deepest wounds in human history. By successfully equating, in interview after interview, his cinematic fiction of an imaginary slave rebellion with the actual history of the Atlantic slave trade and plantation slavery as well as with the diasporic memory of the deportation of ten million Africans, Gerima sacralizes his text. Somewhat skeptical of all this, I propose to investigate the historical content, the governing assumptions and the stakes at issue in this project.

In an interview recently published in *Transition*, Gerima proposed that "culture, a true culture, a democratic culture might heal society by juxtaposing two histories of a people" (Woolford, 94). Gerima is rather explicit in presenting *Sankofa* as a contribution to the elaboration of that democratic culture in the form of a histori - cal reinscription of Black resistance to slavery—a subject long censured in the cinema. With the film, Gerima takes upon himself the task of extracting "the stories" that people in the Diaspora "have stored in the marrow of their bones" (Woolford, 94). At the same time, the therapeutic (?) violence of his images is apparently intended to stir the anguish of Western societies secretly haunted by the specter of slavery. Presenting himself as the victim of the mission he has undertaken—that is, to provide the "African race" with the "weapon of history" (Woolford, 100), to counter the myths of official history by convoking the spirits of the deported—the filmmaker has repeatedly alluded to the difficulties he encoun - tered in raising money and finding distributors for this "epic drama of the African holocaust and of the battle for liberty," as the Mypheduh Films Inc. publicity release defines *Sankofa*. As a crowning misfortune, a fire in a Washington warehouse destroyed ten thousand copies of the film and much of the production mate - rial, as reported in the Nation of Islam newspaper *Final Call* (April 30, 1996:5).

In point of fact, however, *Sankofa* was partially financed by the Rockefeller Foundation, the MacArthur Foundation, DiProCi Television of Burkina Faso, the Commission du Ghana pour la Culture, and Neue Deutsche Rundfunk Television. After receiving two important prizes (the 1993 Agip Grand Prize at the African Cinema Festival in Milan, Italy and the 1993 Award for Best Cinematography at the FESPACO Pan-African Film Festival in Ouagadougou, Burkina Faso), the film quickly became a hit in the United States and elsewhere,[5] and is even currently available on video-cassette. Reviews in the press have been, in general, extremely positive, and tend to approach *Sankofa* as an historical or even documentary film that "retells the story of slavery from Pan-African subject positions" (Cham, 23), that depicts the daily life of slaves on a plantation (James, 8), and that celebrates the slaves' autonomous resistance to oppression without outside sup - port. The reviews underline the etiological value of Gerima's story for understanding both the loss of memory/identity on the part of a segment of the Diaspora as well as the internecine divisions that face it today.

Does the film then owe its popularity to the audacity of an African filmmaker engaged in rectifying (in the spirit of the Third Cinema) Hollywood's bucolic version of slavery? And does this success reward Gerima's labor to recount the struggles of the African Diaspora—struggles encapsulated in a sort of epic poem that traces the triumph of Rebellion over Alienation through the two figures who respectively incarnate them: the Maroon (Shango) and the Mulatto (Joe)?

In *Sankofa*, it is of some importance that nothing permits us to sit- uate the plot in space or time. If the vegetation—fields of sugar- cane and palm trees—invites us to place the plantation in the Caribbean, this hypothesis is weakened by the film's emphasis on the singularity of Shango's Creole language and dreadlocks. The language and gestures of the women working on the Lafayette plantation, as well as the clothing of the overseers, evoke, rather, the southern states of North America, where sugarcane was rela- tively unknown except in Louisiana. The film, however, makes no reference to the Creole culture that developed in that area dur- ing the century of French control between 1699 and 1803.

This "dislocation" would pose no special problem were it not for the fact that geography and economics in large measure gov- erned the forms of resistance to slavery. Thus, the dense forests of Brazil or the mountainous terrain of Jamaica favored the growth of large Maroon communities. Connections have been drawn as well between the frequency of slave rebellions and the develop- ment of the sugar economy. While Haiti, the "pearl of the Antilles," was the theater of a revolution brought to term, the Bahamas, which were not a sugar-producing colony, continued relatively free of social unrest until the 1830's. It is worth noting that *Sankofa* was filmed in Jamaica, Louisiana and Ghana.

Similarly, it is impossible to locate *Sankofa* in any historical era. Slave rebellions began with the institutionalization of slavery in the Americas (less than 20 years after the "discovery" of the New World by Columbus) and continued without pause until the eradication of the slavery in the 19th century, to which they significantly contributed. The events and circumstances described in the film, consequently, could stretch across a period of over three hundred years, from the first African revolts in the New World (1519 in Haiti[6]; 1526 in what is now South Carolina[7]) to the many blows struck in order to hasten final abolition. Many of these rebel - lions also faced the challenges of success—the formation of an enduring community and state. Such was the case of the Republic of Palmarès (circa 1600-1694), most famous of the *quilombos* and *mocambos* in Brazil, or the Maroon communities in Jamaica (around Nanny Town and Trelawny Town[8]), or for that matter, the Haitian Republic (1804-). The historical material is considerable and far from being exhausted, and has given rise to a number of lit - erary and cinematic masterpieces, including *Tamango*, by Prosper Mérimée, *The Tragedy of King Christophe*, by Aimé Césaire, *A Woman named Solitude*, by André Schwarz-Bart, *The Kingdom of This World*, by Alejo Carpentier, *Black Thunder*, by Arna Bontemps, *Quilombo*, by Carlos Diegues.

Does *Sankofa* derive its historicity, then, from the abrupt plunge into the past to which it subjects the viewer—following Mona as she is dragged kicking and screaming into her orphic quest for her "authentic" identity? The old priest's unremitting exhortation to return to the source, with the parallel and progres - sive elimination from the screen of all signs of the West—its faces, its technology and its associated values—indicates that for Gerima knowledge of the past is neither an end in itself, nor a step towards a better understanding of the present, nor even a series of frag - ments that an occurrence in the present might draw from memory. Rather, the past is a place where Gerima projects a definition of racial categories that differs little from the contemporary concep - tual norm, particularly that of the United States. In particular, he presupposes that a racial solidarity—innate, transversal, and supra historic—exists by definition between all persons of African ori - gin, defined as a homogeneous group. Paradoxically, his chosen theme—slavery and the slave trade—shows this vision of solidar - ity to be an anachronism: had it existed, the deportation of slaves could never have achieved the scale that it ultimately did. If such solidarity exists, it is the result rather than the underlying cause of the various social and political movements that inform it. For example, for the civil rights movements of the 50's and 60's, sol - idarity can be seen as emerging from a struggle for broader dem - ocratic representation, whereas for such figures as the Rastafarians,

Louis Farrakhan, and Haile Gerima,[9] among others, solidarity can only be achieved through separatism. The transformation of the "group name" (Negro, Black, Afro-American, African-American) is itself evidence that the historical conditions of this solidarity shift over time, creating new definitions and identities.

What Gerima proposes to that segment of the Black liberal bourgeoisie indifferent or recalcitrant to Africa—a group symbol - ized by Mona in the film—is in substance a three-step plan: first, a return to the period of slavery, then to the deeper past and a more profound encounter with Africa, and finally a resurfacing in the present and a joining into a Black community proudly conscious of its African origins. The therapy he envisions for all the Monas of the world (Woolford, 96) is a kind of re-education through work on the plantation—a tropical Gulag, so to speak. The reform of those who have strayed will show itself by public adhesion to what the Ghanaian novelist Ayi Kwei Armah calls in *Two Thousand Seasons* "our way":

> Slavery—do you know what it is? Ah you will know it. Two thousand seasons, a thousand going into it, a second thousand crawling maimed from it, will teach you everything about enslavement, the destruction of the souls, the killing of bodies, the infusion of violence into every breath, every drop, every morsel of your sustaining air, your water, your food. Till you come again upon the way. (26-27)

In *Sankofa*, Mona alias Shola returns from her hell by a narrow cor - ridor. She emerges into the light, naked as a newborn, to be cradled by a woman who covers her in a cloth and calms her cries. A "born again African," Mona is saved, and can thereby take her place among those who, in full consciousness of their history, are now reconciled with themselves and with Africa.

Africa in *Sankofa* is represented by two synecdoches: the past and Ghana, two parts of an absolutely pure whole. For Gerima, as for the collector of authentic African art, the goal is to recover a past uncontaminated by the European presence. In its effort to dis - mantle Eurocentric assumptions about Africa (among which the notion of teleological development from primitive to [post-] mod- ern culture figures centrally), Afrocentrism merely changes the direction of the vector. It draws us, with its Hegelian grip, away from the West or from the sites of the Diaspora and back towards

Africa, away from the present and back to the past, away from lib -
eralism and back to gerontocracy. Does *Sankofa* intend to com-
fort the viewer with the idea that the only true African culture and
identity belong to the period predating slavery, and that they can
only be recovered by means of a journey backwards, under the
firm guidance of the prophetic voice of the Elders? Doesn't the
"genius" of the peoples of the Diaspora—one thinks immediately
of jazz—define itself precisely through a triple movement of reten -
tion/rejection of the past, and creation of the new? The nostalgia
in *Sankofa* for a sacralized past derives not from the pressing prob -
lems of today but from an ideological straitjacket which leaves
unthought precisely the question of the transition from the past to
the present and from the old to the new. It may be useful to remem -
ber Fanon's *rappel à l'ordre*, even though it springs from a period
of faith in proletarian solidarity and is marked by its Francophone
context:

> For the Negro who works on a sugar plantation in le Robert,
> there is only one solution: to fight. He will embark on this
> struggle, and he will pursue it, not as the result of a Marxist or
> idealistic analysis but quite simply because he cannot conceive
> of life otherwise than in the form of a battle against exploitation,
> misery, and hunger.
>
> It would never occur to me to ask these Negroes to change
> their conception of history. I am convinced, however, that
> without even knowing it they share my views, accustomed as
> they are to speaking and thinking in terms of the present. The
> few working-class people whom I had the chance to know in
> Paris never took it on themselves to pose the problem of the
> discovery of a Negro past. They knew they were Black, but they
> told me, that hardly changed anything. And they were damn
> right too. (my translation)
>
> [Pour le Nègre qui travaille dans les plantations de canne du
> Robert, il n'y a qu'une solution: la lutte. Et cette lutte, il
> l'entreprendra et la mènera non pas après une analyse marxiste
> ou idéaliste, mais parce que tout simplement, il ne pourra con -
> cevoir son existence que sous les espèces d'un combat mené
> contre l'exploitation, la misère et la faim.
>
> Il ne nous viendrait pas à l'idée de demander à ces nègres
> de corriger la conception qu'ils se font de l'histoire. D'ailleurs,
> nous sommes persuadé que, sans le savoir, ils entrent dans nos

vues, habitués qu'ils sont à parler et penser en termes de présent. Les quelques camarades ouvriers que j'ai eu l'occasion de rencontrer à Paris ne se sont jamais posé le problème de la découverte d'un passé nègre. Ils savaient qu'ils étaient noirs, mais, me disaient-ils, cela ne change rien à rien.
En quoi ils avaient fichtrement raison. (181-2)]

In *Sankofa*, Ghana is re-imagined as the source of African culture from which the Diaspora renaissance must draw its strength. We know that when dealing with African origins and a possible "return," the Pan-African imaginary has usually preferred Ethiopia, or Guinea, or the Congo, neglecting those regions that have his- torically welcomed those who have returned to Africa—notably Sierra Leone, Liberia and Nigeria. Ethiopia has long served as a powerful metonymy for Africa, from its early appearances in the Bible[10] and the texts of Antiquity to Rastafarian iconography. Hence the term "Ethiopianism," which designates the nationalist aspirations of the local clergy that had come in contact with the African-American missionaries in 19th century Africa. Guinea, whose name is associated with an English coin[11] and with the cot- ton trade, was imagined in oral literature[12] and in the Spirituals as the Promised Land to which the dead returned. The association of the Congo with Africa appears in the taxonomy of skin color in the francophone Antilles, where the name refers to the darkest of skin pigmentations. In the poetry of Negritude and of Césaire in par- ticular,[13] the Congo, through its vegetal and fluvial power, serves as a metaphor for Black identity and speech:

> From brooding so long on the Congo
> I have become a Congo resounding with
> forest and rivers. (*Notebook*, stanza 52)
> [A force de penser au Congo/je suis devenu un Congo
> bruissant de forêts et de fleuves]

But the construction of Ghana as a symbolic anchor for the African Diaspora has little to do with either "the stories that people have preserved in the marrow of their bones" or poetry. The Portuguese visited this part of the West African coast, occupied by the Akan, in the 1470's. Soon after, it was visited by the Danish and the English, who rebaptized it the Gold Coast. Commercial alliances relating to the slave trade developed almost immediately between

the coastal populations and European merchants: in the 15th century, the Portuguese purchased Akan gold with slaves imported
from Benin. The Akan put these slaves to work in their mines. In
the 16th century, this market began to decline in favor of the
Atlantic slave trade, which would reach its peak in the 18th century. Commercial relations between Europeans and Africans led to
the development of fortified towns, which in turn generated
employment for a substantial fringe of the population. Powerful
families involved in brokerage, sometimes the products of Euro-
African marriages, also emerged from this commercial order.
Elmina Castle (St. George de la Mine), built in 1482 by the
Portuguese and later ceded to Holland in 1637, was the first of 60
forts established along a 300-mile section of the coast. The fort
served as a barracks for soldiers as well as a residence and store-
house for civilians. It also served as a warehouse for slaves. It was
in the vicinity of such castles that the first missionary schools were
opened, with the intent to create an assimilated local elite, often
drawn from the *métis* population. This elite found a role mediating between the Europeans and local leaders, at times intervening
in the latter's favor and even assuming those positions of leadership. Immanuel Geiss underscores the fact that it is from this middle class, educated along Western models and sometimes in
Europe, that the first Ghanaian nationalists emerged—notably J.R.
Ghartey (19) and Joseph Casely Hayford. He also emphasizes that,
through a kind of boomerang-effect due to the intensity of the slave
trade in the region, the Gold Coast was a veritable hothouse of
Pan-Africanist thought and activism, producing such figures as
Ottobah Cuguano, Marcus Garvey (of Coromante, i.e. Ashanti origin), and Kwame Nkrumah. Nkrumah, inspired by Garvey's
thought and an admirer of W.E.B. Du Bois, made Ghana, upon his
ascension to power and the organization of the Accra Conference
in 1958, the rallying point of Pan-Africanism. The participation of
African-Americans in this coalescing movement resonated in the
United States (where signs of Ghanaian culture, for example
"kente-cloth," have acquired a certain amount of mass cultural and
even academic appeal). As a consequence, Ghana has served less
as a locus of memory than as a political construction by means of
which the relationship of the Diaspora to Africa is theorized and
elaborated. This role is, in turn, inseparable from the fact that
Ghana is the site of so many contradictory experiments involving
the return to Africa. It is unfortunate that *Sankofa* reduces the

socio-political complexities that inform the history of slave trade in Ghana in general and at Elmina in particular, to a binary dis-course whose essentialism vies with its tautology. For racial fac-tors can neither completely explain the deportation of the Africans, nor guarantee the happy return of their descendants.

Of course, there are numerous and in some cases illustrious examples of successful returns to Africa. Du Bois, who was invited to Ghana by Nkrumah in 1961 to direct the *Encyclopaedia Africana*, opted for Ghanaian nationality and finished his days at Accra (Geiss, 234); Dolores Sheen, whose life and pedagogical project at Sasekofe were reported in detail in the *Los Angeles Times* (January 22, 1995. E, I *et seq.*) clearly found in Ghana the spiritual wellspring that she had come looking for. But we should take note as well of Richard Wright's account in *Black Power* of his visit to Ghana on the eve of independence. Elmina occupies a prominent place in Wright's African itinerary, and acquires a figurative role as a shield that he brandishes in order to ward off the irritating questions about his presumed origins and his intentions to return that follow him from the moment of his arrival in Ghana (*Black Power* 39-50). Wright's account ends, however, with a different and much more lyrical evocation of the castle (383-4). As if embar-rassed by his partial metamorphosis, Wright offers, in closure, a let-ter advising Nkrumah on a more rational direction for his affairs. In *Black Power*, Wright moves us by his constant efforts to rene-gotiate his distance from Africa—a distance he nonetheless feels obliged to maintain, and which allows him to deal ironically with a range of subjects, [14] including himself. Here, for example, is his account of his participation at a public meeting with Nkrumah:

> My turn came to greet the audience and I rose and spoke somewhat as follows: "Men of Ghana, I'm one of the lost sons of Africa who has come back to look upon the land of his forefathers. In a superficial sense it may be said that I'm a stranger to most of you, but, in terms of a common heritage of suffering and hunger for freedom, your heart and my heart beat as one. From the 30,000,000 sons and daughters of African descent in the New World, both in North and South America, and in the many islands of the Atlantic, I bring you deep felt greetings. I am an American and therefore cannot participate in your political affairs. But I wish you victory in your bid for freedom! Ghana, show us the way!" The handclapping was

weak and scattered. Perhaps they were not used to hearing speakers who did not raise their voices, or maybe they had not understood? (85)

Kwame Anthony Appiah also describes the complexities of the return to his "Father's House." To his remarks on his parentage, he adds a reflection on biology and race in Pan-Africanist ideology, proposing an alternative type of alliance—deracialized and dena - tionalized—that might free Africa and the Diaspora from their mutual tutelage. Having received from his father a "house," in the noble sense of the term— "Africa in general; Ghana in particular; Ashante and Kumasi, more particularly yet"—and the certitude that "in [his] father's house...there are many mansions...for all sorts and conditions of men and women" (vii-ix), Appiah shows that his return nonetheless alters the social fabric in two respects:

> [My father's] funeral was an occasion for strengthening and reaffirming the ties that bind me to Ghana and "my father's house," and at the same time, for straining my allegiances to my king and my father's matriclan—perhaps, even tearing them beyond repair. (181)

By choosing another possible translation of the Sankofa emblem— *one must not be afraid to redeem one's past mistakes* —Gerima might have taught us much about these complexities and ambiva - lences as well as their unspoken implications. Kwapo Opoku Agyemang has adroitly reflected on the disproportion in African literature between the exploitation of the colonial thematic and the silence concerning the Atlantic slave trade.[15] On topics as sensi- tive as the slave trade, when mentioned, and sometimes even col- onization, few writers have rejected fatalism or self-righteousness. One exception is the Congolese poet Tchicaya U Tam'si, who ques- tions: "The destiny of ancient divinities is in my way / Is that rea - son to always dance the song backwards" [my translation] [Le destin des divinités anciennes en travers du mien est-ce raison de danser toujours à rebours la chanson?] (*Le Mauvais Sang,* 45); another is Rachid Boudjedra, who has noted in more prosaic terms that [the ancestors] "were had and thus are responsible for the colonial disaster" [les ancêtres qui se sont fait avoir et qui sont donc responsables du désastre colonial" (Gafaïti, 37)]. Nevertheless, the question of "Black" participation in the slave trade has been debated on the occasions of such festivals as the Accra Panafest and the discovery of the African Burial Ground in New York—events followed by ceremonies of purification and penitence (*New York Times*, December 27, 1994, A4; *Washington Post*, August 3, 1995, B1; *Essence Magazine*, October, 1995, 60). If there remains, undoubtedly, much to be said, written, and filmed about this genocide, *Sankofa*'s Manichean representation of European barbarism, African fraternity, and mulatto duplicity does not sensibly differ, *mutatis mutandis*, from silence or omission.

Certainly, as an artist Haile Gerima gives himself a space of freedom for his cinematic text, which he makes use of according to his own ethical and aesthetic norms. One could claim that Gerima is under no obligation to be a historian, and that *Sankofa* is "an artistic expression of historical realities not often portrayed in film" (Woolford, 90). Similarly, the success of Boudjedra's work depends, it has been claimed, on introducing between the histori-cal novel and the history of historians something Hafid Gafaïti calls "le roman de l'histoire":

> History burst open and rendered through writing: details, small facts apparently without importance, pieces, fragments, packets of memory, elements of reality that upset the ideological model on which history rests, and where only great events are taken into account. [my translation]

> [Histoire éclatée, rendue par le mode de l'écriture: détails, petits faits apparemment sans importance, morceaux, fragments, parcelles de mémoire, éléments de realité qui renversent le modele idéologique sur lequel repose l'histoire et où ne sont pris en compte que les grands événements. (37-38)]

But these splinters of history only acquire sense if reading restores them to a spatial, temporal, and human frame suggested beforehand or constructed along the way by the author. Since this frame is not offered in *Sankofa*, should one then read the film as an epic? Epics, which elevate a series of battles to a titanic combat between good and evil, are interesting not only for their aesthetic specificities, but also as discourses which attempt to found a new politico-linguis-tic order. The demonization of the Other (the Saracen in *The Song of Roland* or Sumaoro Kante in *Sunjata*, for example) is never convincing in itself, except as a means of glorifying the epic hero and the new values he incarnates—Christian France or Mali uni - fied under a Muslim ruler. This is to say that a work that describes psychological or social tensions in binary terms without giving rise to new social constructions or identities and without casting into question the very polarities on which it is founded, unwill - ingly reproduces the Hollywood paradigm. The critic Ed Guerrero has observed that Hollywood, by limiting the roles of Black men to two antithetical types—failures or successes—is blinkered when it comes to representing them. He continues:

> [What is missing is] the intellectual, cultural, and political depth and humanity of Black men, as well as their very significant contribution to the culture and progress of this nation.... What is now needed is an expanded heterogeneous range of complex portrayals of Black men that transcends the one-dimensional, positive-negative characters usually contained within Hollywood's formulaic narratives and its most common strategy for representing blackness, that is, channeling most Black talent and film production into the genres of comedy or the ghetto-action-adventure. (397)

It seems that *Sankofa*, without rising to the level of the epic, cleaves to the discourse of legitimization, and do not go beyond this kind of one-dimensionality. The plantation site of Gerima's "ghetto-action-adventure" film, is divided by Du Bois "color line"—no longer a specific characteristic of the 20th century America, but presented by the filmmaker as the *sine qua non* of race relations in general. As a consequence, the diversity and the specificity of plantation life—for example, the contradictions and alliances within its various constitutive units of economic and cultural pro - duction—are erased. Gone is the concept of survival—that capac - ity to negotiate an existence among the numerous adverse forces of the slave economy and around which, significantly, the slave narratives are constructed. On the screen, the opposition between the Whites—sketchy caricatures responsible for malign cruelty— and a group of field and house slaves united with the foremen in combat, loses its strategic efficacy through its wrong-headed sim - plification. It's immediately clear that such a scheme cannot account for the trajectory of, say, a Toussaint Louverture: Creole, coachman on the Breda plantation, freed in 1776, owner of 13 slaves, in short, "a man of the colonial system" (Pluchon, 61) who was nonetheless leader of the Haitian Revolution and post-humous founder of the first Black republic. Without doubt, the insistence on the centrality of collective history in pan/African arts and let-ters is proof of the abolition of an exclusive western discourse on Africa and its Diaspora. To insist on this centrality also confers a stamp of quality, even more so if it is undertaken in the subversive mode. It is as if the "great" literary texts—*Notebook of a Return to the Native Land*, *Two Thousand Seasons*, *Bound to Violence, A Grain of Wheat, God's Bits of Wood*, etc.—are those freighted with the heaviest historical load and at the same time the most critical in their historical perspective. The comments of Abiola Irele on this subject are valid for the cinema as well:

> An important factor therefore which explains the present prominence of literature in Africa is that it has become the area of an active and focused self-consciousness which extends in its implications into both a sustained interrogation of history and a determined engagement with language. (255)

The main characters in *Sankofa*—Joe and Shola—are similarly one-dimensioned and too often gagged by the didacticism of the dialogue. Together with Shango they form a triad of symmetrical and predictable relationships. The hero, Shango (Mutabaruka), takes his name from the Yoruba god of war and thunder and wears his color, red. By all appearances, Shango incarnates the spirit of rebellion. He draws his strength from his knowledge of plants and poisons, like Macandal, and from his memory of the past, metaphorically contained in an amulet in the shape of the Sankofa bird. At that threshold moment when he decides to break free from his yoke, to flee to the hills, or to organize the slaves on the plan-tation, Shango represents how the slave transcends himself to become a Maroon. Having fully assumed his freedom, he exposes the depth of alienation among some of the slaves and thereby cat-alyzes their revolt. It is he who convinces scrupulous Shola of the necessity of violent action (she kills a planter in the canefields). It is also he who precipitates the conflict between Nunu, the symbol of Mother Africa, and Joe, the incarnation of hybridity: the burn-ing of the church where they meet prefigures the fire that will later ravage the whole plantation. Through an association of images, sounds, and ideas, we are invited to read Shango's identity, with his dreadlocks and the Jamaican Creole he speaks, as shading from

Maroon into Rastafarian—a modulation made all the easier inso-far as the myth of the Maroon "Freedom Fighter" has long been a staple of reggae music. It is nonetheless worth remembering that not all escaped slaves were Maroons, whence the distinction between *petit* and *grand marronnage*, as well as that between refugees and Maroons in their fortified camps (Kopytoff, 48 & 81). Additionally, Maroon identity was based on an oligarchic rather than revolutionary concept of liberty—a distinction which explains the fact that Maroons sometimes worked as bounty hunters in the pursuit of escaped slaves. In the insular colonial set-ting of Jamaica, moreover, Maroon identity depended on the pos-session of highly contested territory. After the first and second Anglo-Maroon wars in the 18th century, the rights of Maroons (and thus their identity) were only guaranteed on assigned reser-vations. Once the English had established control over the whole island, Maroon identity, deprived of territorial support, dissolved over time.

This brief account should make it clear that the Maroon, who is often presented as the essence of resistance to slavery and to the plantocracy, has also a history of his own. Gersham A. Nelson, in an article entitled "Rastafarians and Ethiopianism," makes a case for this ideological filiation between Maroons and Rastafarians. He shows that the quasi-repetitive socio-economic conditions of Jamaica—slavery followed by pauperism and discrimination—form a nexus in which one can situate the messianism of Jamaican Marcus Garvey (notably the theme of the religious return to "Ethiopia") and the subsequent rise to power in Ethiopia of Ras Tafari in 1930. The Jamaican Rastafarians, drawing from the impoverished margins of a Caribbean society stratified by nuances of pigmentation, gathered together this diverse heritage of resist-ance, religious separatism, Garveyite politics, and faith in the redemptive power of a return to Africa, not to mention the Judeo-Christian elements they incorporated into their doctrine. Nelson proposes that, although Rastafarians discovered the importance of their roots for mental liberation, "yet mental and spiritual freedom and a positive self-image may not be enough to release one from economic deprivation." (83) In short, for Maroons and Rastafarians alike, radical political change is not the ultimate concern. It remains that Shango, who conveys this dense range of associations, is by far the most successful characterization of the trio, and escapes, through his discursive autonomy, the wooden dialogue of the rest of the script: his frequently gnomic, Creole speech, is subtitled in English. Mutabaruka plays Mutabaruka.

The mulatto Joe—blond, blue-eyed, and light-skinned—is the perfect antithesis of Shango. Although Gerima claims to decon-struct stereotypes (Woolford, 98), the physical traits of this char-acter are intended to make his loyalties immediately obvious. [16] In the service of the planter and the Catholic Church (representative of Western colonialism, in Gerima's hasty Ethiopianist reading), Joe is the only one of the foremen who will not redeem himself through the rebellion. He is described by his mother as the rotten fruit of her womb, and he fails, appropriately, to establish any bounds of love with a Black woman. Joe's sexual impotence exploits a stereotype in the discourse of racial classification that would have it that the mulatto, like the mule or any other "unnat-ural" product of the mixture of races, is sterile. Living in fear of contamination and in search of a mythical white father, Joe is a kind of spineless Ariel, lacking the poetic and humanistic vision of the mulatto slave in Césaire's *A Tempest*. In his disarray, he commits a double parricide—against Nunu, his mother and, figuratively, Mother Africa, and then against his spiritual guide, the Spanish priest, whose inquisitorial trappings make allusion to the respon-sibility of the Church in the conquest of the Caribbean and the genocide of the Indian. The burning church is Gerima's own *auto-da-fé*, in which he consigns Joe and his ontological angst to the flames.

One can deduce from Joe's fate that interracial relations only yield a hybridity that castrates the African spirit of rebellion, and that the least possibility of contact between Black and White, be it conflictual or ambiguous, is excluded. The victory of one means the elimination of the other from the conquered space and with *Sankofa* Gerima has shown that the screen, too, is such an arena. Thus the tourists visiting Elmina Castle disappear by the end of the film, as does, of course, the photographer, Shango's rival for the possession of the body of Shola/ Mona. The latter is finally rejected by Mona who has in the meantime discovered her African iden-tity—with all its privileges, limits, and taboos. In her former incar-nation, her alienation makes her a foil for the figure of Joe; indeed, commentators have described her as a "foxy mulatto girl..." " frol-icking in her western abandon on the now sacred steps of Ghana's Cape Coast Castle" (Bakyono, 26, Mypheduh Press book). Whereas Joe pays with his death for his long duplicity, Mona, in order to obtain redemption, passes through several stages of puri-fying agony. In addition to the frightening visions that haunt her at the outset (the castle guardian's harangue, the slaves that surround her in the dungeon), she is made to suffer a series of ritual and public violations. She is marked by the red-hot iron of the slave-brokers, sexually exploited by the planter, whipped by the priest, and submitted to the double technological violation of the pho-tographer's lens and Gerima's camera-phallus, which brutalizes and strips bare this young Black woman, initially oblivious to her duties towards Africa.

Gerima's coercive teleological model of Black emancipation brings to the screen a new Afrocentric meta-narrative. He seems convinced that the production of a historical narrative that aspires to describe the totality of the Diasporic experience and that con-tradicts a supposedly monolithic and Eurocentric Western account of slavery, will help what he calls the "African race" to liberate itself. The film thus participates in the construction of a new African universalism. The nostalgia for an organic past, the search for essences, and the separatist ideology that animate *Sankofa* has predictably found an enthusiastic public in this period of militant Afrocentrism.[17] The characters in the film are neither more or less than thinly incarnated racial categories and the Sankofa bird is used as a totalizing symbol that fixes the meaning of the socio-his-torical material of the text—the passage into slavery, the return to Africa. The film accomplishes this symbolization at the expense of an allegorical opening that might simultaneously show the Sankofa bird as a fragment of the history of the Diaspora or else as an emblem that might reveal its multiple meanings. Moreover, in Gerima's hands the Sankofa becomes a fetish, that is, an object credited with autonomous power that protects its possessor(s) from the castrating loss of origins. This is of course not without irony, given that the concept of the fetish was invented by Portuguese merchants and then taken up by the Dutch in an attempt to stig-matize religious objects venerated by the Africans of the Gold Coast, who were allegedly ignorant of the nature of true religious faith and of its appropriate symbols. As for the Elmina Castle, it is promoted in *Sankofa* as a sacred monument: a collective tomb to victims without names or faces, the keystone on which the his-tory of the Diaspora is built. To the degree that the castle is allowed to become a cult object, however, it loses its connection to time. Its enormous symbolic presence is no longer permitted to take on the slow face of a ruin nor is its meaning granted the possibility of periodic renewal. Thus, for example, the lively debate between the Ghanaian government and certain African-American pressure groups concerning Elmina Castle was completely erased in a film that could have gained considerable complexity from it. While the Ghanaian government would like to restore the castle as a tourist attraction capable of generating revenues in a cash-strapped econ-omy, African-American pilgrims have tried to conserve it in its current state. The *Washington Post* echoed the frustrations of the two parties:

> African-Americans accuse Ghanaians of trampling on their past for profits. They say Ghanaians are handcuffed because "white" institutions such as the U.S. Agency for International Development and the Smithsonian Institution have pledged major financial backing and technical aid for the 5.6 million [dollar, sic] project. Ghanaians charge Black Americans with being overly sensitive and contend they should bear more of the financial burden for the project if they do not like the current donors. (A 10)

The question touches on the management of the foundational tragedy: will the commercial exploitation of the fort banalize the warning that it represents? Will the expansive maintenance of the castle in its current state shield it from change? By choosing Elmina as the point of origin and return of the Diaspora, *Sankofa* suggests a possible remedy to an intolerable *caesura* that separates Africa from its Diaspora. It identifies a plenitude that can be recovered. The commentary of Dolores Sheen on the meaning of her turn towards Ghana is significant in this regard:

> I needed to trace my origin tribe, and when I found out I had an Ewe origin, I wanted to make the circle complete. I wanted to give back what was taken when the strong and the creative were taken from Africa and displaced.
>
> (*L.A. Times*, E6, 1/22/95)

Gerima counts on the "horizon of expectations" of that part of the African-American community, which sees its relationship to Africa in terms of a loss, or deficit of identity. That group is vulnerable to anyone who can assert, as does the Ethiopian filmmaker, his unmistakable African roots. Thus, the rebellious Shango conspic-uously reflects Gerima's own descriptions of his revolt against Hollywood, "the plantation school of cinema" (Woolford, 92). Through the same *mise en abyme*, *Sankofa* comes to occupy the place of Elmina Castle as a monument to the history of the slave trade. The bastion remains nearly impregnable.

This being the case, can I, a Euro-African *métisse*, cast a suspicious eye on *Sankofa* without my being branded a Joe or Mona—with-out my discourse seeming to be stained with the same duplicity and a similar neurosis? The terms of the reader's contract established by Gerima mark me as a "non-implied viewer," or as a subject to be re-educated. That is the danger of having recourse to racial cat-egories in an attempt to define both the target audience [18] and the "correct" relationship of that audience with Africa. My own posi-tion is largely defined by my refusal of these reductive deter-minisms.

As a critic, I am interested as well in the conditions of the pro-duction of the film. I have watched, in interview after interview, the meta-film that Gerima has constructed around his rather prosaic story of fundraising and channels of distribution, and his skillful effort to superimpose these travails on the history of the massive crime perpetrated against Africa for three centuries and the con-comitant exploitation of the forced labor of Africans/Blacks in the Americas. Because I took seriously Gerima's promise to rewrite the history of Black resistance to slavery and to contribute to the emer-gence of a democratic culture, I wanted to examine the historical content of *Sankofa* before taking it at face value. The covert oscil-lation between two approaches to history, one materialist, the other tinged with mysticism (Woolford, 103) in order to compensate for attacks on Christianity that might offend the religious convictions of the target public[19] as well as the frequent recourse in *Sankofa* to stereotypes and to facile Africanisms that try to "revive the throbbing sound of drums, bathed in tropical mysteries," to borrow the expression of David Diop ("'faire revivre les grands mythes africains'/à coups de tam-tam abusifs et de mystères tropicaux" [13]), seem to me far from the demands of the praxis of history and close to what is called ethnophilosophy. As for art, I see it con-stantly occupied with subverting or surpassing or disappointing our preconceived notions, rather than with comforting dogmas or instituting counter-dogmas, as is the case with *Sankofa*. Now, is democracy guaranteed by simply juxtaposing versions of history or substituting one myth for another? [20] Or is it in the ethical confrontation of different interpretations that democracy best realizes itself, above all in regards to those questions in which the past and the present collide? Given that people have already begun to "act out" *Sankofa*—I am thinking of the group headed by Kohain Halevi, a Black Hebrew from New York, who locked himself in the Elmina dungeon for two days of fasting, in order that "this sacred ground be protected" (*Washington Post,* April 17, 1995, A10)—it is high time that the history of this fortress be accurately written or filmed.

The almost unbearable tension, which inhabits the historian, facing a past that is revealed at the moment of imminent danger, back turned to the present in order to better foresee it, is allegorized in Walter Benjamin's Angelus Novus:

> A Klee painting named "Angelus Novus" shows an angel looking as though he is about to move away from something he is fixedly contemplating. His eyes are staring, his mouth is open, and his wings are spread. This is how one pictures the angel of history. His face is turned towards the past. Where we perceive a chain of events, he sees one single catastrophe, which keeps piling wreckage upon wreckage and hurls it in front of his feet. The angel would like to stay, awaken the dead, and make whole what has been smashed. But a storm is blowing from Paradise; it has got caught in his wings with such violence that the angel can no longer close them. This storm irresistibly propels him into the future to which his back is turned, while the pile of debris before him grows skyward. This storm is what we call progress. (257-8)

I looked in *Sankofa* for a trace of prophecy but I found only an injunction—*one must return to the past in order to move forward.* I looked for a trace of that formidable tension between the past and the present and found only faith in the storm. I looked once more for the high pedestal from which the Sankofa bird *sees all*: I found only the "cra":

Cra, says Gerima, is a belief in spirits, a belief that people who have died but are not yet settled roam the village, trying to find a living body to enter, to go back into the living world to repent their crimes or avenge the injustices done to them. All of this was on my mind while working on the story for *Sankofa*. (Woolford, 103)

But I also looked for a written trace on the stone text that is the Elmina Castle. I found, on a plaque at its entrance, these words, unfortunately absent from the film:

"In everlasting memory of the anguish of our ancestors. May those who died rest in peace. May those who return find their roots. May humanity never again perpetrate such injustice against humanity. We the living vow to uphold this."

Translated by Joe Karaganis

NOTES

1. For a commentary on this photograph, see E. Roskis, "Images et vautours," *Le Monde Diplomatique* 485 (August, 1994): 32.
2. A sketch of the pipe by Mrs. Lee, his wife, was published in M.D. MacLeod "T.E. Bowditch: an Early Collector in West Africa" 100. See also "Verbal Elements in West African Art" 93.
3. For a discussion on the "linguist" or *okyeame*, see Yankah, 334-6.
4. See the fine developments on that topic in Gilroy's *Black Atlantic*, 185-201.
5. "Now in limited national release and 10 months into self-distribution by Mypheduh Films, *Sankofa* has confounded the industry by consistently producing large grosses on sin - gle four-walled screens in several cities. International box offices receipts have reached $2 million, with *Sankofa* tapping only a fraction of its international market." Mypheduh Press Release, October 3, 1994.
6. See "List of slave resistances and revolts between the 16th and the 19th centuries" in Thompson 315-317 & Rogozinski 158-160.

7. See "Chronologie" in Fabre 267-281.
8. See Kopitoff's *Maroons of Jamaica.*
9. Haile Gerima declared: "It seems to me very normal to develop separate, independent institutions in a very racist society like this one. But secretly, I think Hollywood has colonized most of us and we want to be part of that planet. Whatever subjugates us, we're not part of it, we seem to feel we're left out, and so we always destroy everything we build separately." See Tate "Africa Vision."
10. Psalm 68, XXXII: "Ethiopia shall soon stretch her hand unto God." See also Geiss 133-134.
11. Made of gold from Guinea, the Guinee circulated until 1817 and was worth 21 shillings (Dictionnaire *Le Petit Robert,* Paris: Robert, 1992).
12. Joseph Zobel provides a literary account of this connection in *La Rue Cases-Nègres* 57-58.
13. See also L.S. Senghor's "Congo." *Oeuvre poétique* 101-103.
14. See, for example, his response to the question of a lost origin (40), or his evocation of the incarceration by the English of the Ashanti King Prempah I (384).
15. I refer to his unpublished paper, "A Crisis of Balance: The (Mis)representation of Colonial History and the Slave Experience as Themes in Modern African Literature." See also Mildred A. Hill-Lubin's "The Relationship of African-Americans and Africans: A Recurring Theme in the Works of Ata Aidoo."
16. See Sander L. Gilman: "And [the ideologically charged iconographic nature of the representation] dominates in a very specific manner, for the representation of individuals implies the creation of some greater class or classes to which the individual is seen to belong. These classes in turn are characterized by the use of a model, which synthesizes our perception of the uniformity of the groups into a convincingly homogeneous image... [The stereotypes] serve to focus the viewer's attention on the relationship between the portrayed individual and the general qualities ascribed to the class." ("Black Bodies, White Bodies." 223).
17. See Carrie Rickey, "Labor of Love." *Philadelphia Inquirer,* August 25, 1994, E1. "The ancestors have decreed that this film would be made!" pronounces a young woman in the audience, voicing the spirit suffusing the room. "We don't

need Hollywood. We need him and others like him!" booms a mature male voice from the rear of the room. Inspired by this call-and-response, Gerima charges his converts to act: "This isn't my movie. It's your movie. If you want people to see *Sankofa*, hijack the airwaves" he says "Call the Mayor. Have him proclaim Sankofa Day."

18. "[Sankofa] does not tender to a white audience—as evidenced by distributors' collective reluctance to touch it. Essentially it is a film for all African people, the only people who could ever really feel the depth of emotions and connection it evokes" (Mypheduh Press book "The Spirit of Rebellion").

19. Armond White's article in *City Sun* examines the vision of religion in *Sankofa*. White emphasizes that the depiction of the alienating effects of Christianity cannot palliate the absence of economic analysis, given the relation of the African-American public to religion. Rather, it serves as a springboard into the Afrocentric credo.

20. Woolford 92-94 "Now what I did was flip this... Instead of feeding them the myth of Lincoln, just bring Nat Turner."

Works Cited

Agyemang, Kwapo Opoku "A Crisis of Balance : The (Mis)representation of Colonial History and the Slave Experience as Themes in Modern African Literature." (unpublished paper).

Appiah, Peggy "Akan Symbolism." *African Arts* 1 (1979): 64-67.

Appiah, Kwame Anthony. *In my Father's House: Africa in the Philosophy of Culture.* New York: Oxford University Press, 1992.

Armah, Ayi Kwei. *Two Thousand Seasons*. London: Heinemann, 1979.

Bakyono, Jean Servais "Voyage dans la mémoire." *Ecrans d'Afrique* 4 (2d quarter 1993): 20-27.

Benjamin, Walter. *Illuminations*. Trad. Harry Zohn. New York: Shocken, 1969.

Bontemps, Arna. *Black Thunder*. Boston: Beacon, 1992.

Buckley, Stephen "U.S., African Blacks Differ on Turning Slave Dungeons into Tourists Attractions." *Washington Post* (April 17, 1995): A 10.

Carpentier, Alejo. *Le Royaume de ce monde*. Trad. René L.F. Durand. Paris: Gallimard, 1954.

Césaire, Aimé. *Cahier d'un retour au pays natal*. Paris: Présence Africaine, 1956.

——. *Notebook of a Return to the Native Land.* Trad. Emile Snyders. Paris: Présence Africaine, 1968.

——. *La Tragédie du Roi Christophe.* Paris: Présence Africaine, 1963.

——. *Une Tempête.* Paris: Seuil, 1969.

Cham, Mbye "Le passé, le présent et l'avenir." *Ecrans d'Afrique* 4 (2d quarter 1993): 20-27.

Diegues, Carlos, (dir.). *Quilombo*, New York: New Yorker Films, 1984.

Diop, David. *Coups de pilon*. Paris: Présence Africaine 1973.

Ebony, Noël X. *Déjà vu* suivi de Chutes. Paris: Ouskokata, 1983.

Fabre, Michel (ed.). *Esclaves et planteurs dans le Sud américain au XIX'e siècle,* Paris: Julliard, 1970.

Fanon, Frantz. *Peau noire, masques blancs*. Paris: Seuil, 1952.

Foster, Hal. "The Art of Fetishism: Notes on Dutch Still Life." *Fetishism as Cultural Discourse*, ed. E. Apter, E. & W. Pietz. Ithaca: Cornell University Press, 1993. 251-263.

French, Howard W. "On Slavery, Africans Say the Guilt Is Theirs, Too." *New York Times* (December 27, 1994): A4.

Gaines, Patrice. "Bones of Forebears." *Washington Post* (August 3, 1995) B1 & B11.

Gafaïti, Hafid. *Boudjedra ou la passion de la modernité*. Paris: Denoël, 1987.

Geiss, Immanuel. *The Pan-African Movement: A History of Pan-Africanism in America, Europe, and Africa*. New York: Africana Publishing Co, 1974.

Gerima, Haile (director). *Sankofa*, Washington: Mypheduh Films, Inc., 1993.

Gilman, Sander L. "Black Bodies, White Bodies." *"Race," Writing and Difference.* Ed. Henry Louis Gates, Jr. University of Chicago Press, 1986. 223-261.

Gilroy, Paul. *Black Atlantic. Modernity and Double Consciousness.* Cambridge MA & London: Havard University Press, 1993.

Guerrero, Ed "The Black Man on our Screens and the Empty Space in Representation." *Callaloo* 18.2 (1995): 395-400.

Hill-Lubin, Mildred "The Relationship of African-Americans and Africans: A Recurring Theme in the Works of Ata Aidoo." *Présence Africaine* 124 (1992): 189-201.

Irele, Abiola. "Orality, Literacy and the African Literature." *Semper aliquid novi. Littérature comparée et littératures d'Afrique*. Ed. János Riesz & Alain Ricard. Tübingen: Gunter Narr Verlag, 1990. 251-263.

James, Caryn. "Reliving a Past of Slavery." *New York Times* (April 8, 1994): 8.

Kemp, Renée. "An Apology in Ghana." *Essence* (October 1995): 60.

Kolb, Eric de. *Ashanti Goldweights*. New York: Gallery de Hautbarr, 1968.

Kopytoff, Barbara Klamon. *The Maroons of Jamaica: An Ethnohistorical Study of Incomplete Polities, 1655-1905*. Unpublished dissertation. University of Pennsylvania, 1973.

Lemelle, Sidney. "The Politics of Cultural Existence: Pan-Africanism, Historical Materialism, and Afrocentricity." *Imagining Home. Class, Culture and Nationalism in the African Diaspora*. Ed. Sid Lemelle, & Robin D.G. Kelley. New York: Verso, 1994, 331-350.

Lyotard, Jean François. *La Condition postmoderne*. Paris: Editions de Minuit, 1979.

McLeod, M.D. "Asante Gold-weights: Images and Words." *Word & Image* 3,3 (July -September 1987): 295.

—. "T.E. Bowditch, an Early Collector." *Collectors and Collectibles*. British Museum Yearbook 2. London: British Museum Publications, 1977.

—. "Verbal Elements in West African Art." *Quaderni Poro* (1976):85-105.

Mérimée, Prosper. "Tamango." *Mateo Falcone et autres nouvelles*. Paris: Larousse, 1966.

Mypheduh Films, Inc. Release, *Press Book*, no date.

see in particular "The Spirit of Rebellion" no author, no date, no periodical title.

Mypheduh Films, Inc. Release, October 3, 1994.

Muhammad, Lyle. "Fire Destroys Films that Depicted Slavery," *Final Call (*April 30, 1996): 5.

Nelson, Gersham. "Rastafarians and Ethiopianism." *Imagining Home. Class, Culture and Nationalism in the African*

Diaspora. Ed. Sid Lemelle, & Robin D.G. Kelley. New York: Verso, 1994. 66-84.

Noriyuki, Duane. "Going to the Source." *Los Angeles Times* (January 22, 1995): E1-6.

Ngugi wa Thiong'o. *A Grain of Wheat*. London: Heinemann, 1988.

Ouologuem, Yambo. *Le Devoir de violence*. Paris: Seuil, 1968.

Pluchon, Pierre. *Toussaint Louverture. Un révolutionnaire noir d'Ancien Régime*. Paris: Fayard, 1989.

Research in African Literatures 26, 3 (1995). Special Issue on African Cinema.

Rickey, Carrie, "Labor of Love." *Philadelphia Inquirer* (August 25, 1994): E1

Roberts, Allen. F. *Animals in African Art. From the Familiar to the Marvelous*. The Museum for African Art. New York. Munich: Prestel 1995.

Rogozinski, Jan. *A Brief History of the Caribbean. From the Arawak and the Carib to the Present*. New York: Meridian, 1994.

Roskis, Edgar. "Images et vautours," *Le Monde Diplomatique* 485 (August 94): 32.

Schwarz-Bart, André. *La Mulâtresse Solitude*. Paris: Seuil, 1972.

Schwarz-Bart, André. *A Woman named Solitude*. Trad. Ralph Manheim. San Francisco, Berkeley: Creative Arts Book, 1985.

Sembene, Ousmane. *Les Bouts de bois de Dieu*. Paris: Presses Pockett, 1960.

Senghor, Leopold Sédar. *Oeuvre poétique*. Paris: Seuil, 1990.

Tate, Greg. "Africa Vision." *Vibe* (September 19, 1994): 40.

Tchicaya U Tam'si, *Le mauvais sang*. Paris: Editions Jean-Pierre Oswald, 1970.

Thompson, Vincent Bakpetu. *Africa and Unity: the Evolution of Pan-Africanism*. London: Longman, 1969.

White, Armond. "Haile Gerima Puts Faith in *Sankofa*." *The City Sun* (April 13-19, 1994): 21 & 40.

Woolford, Pamela "Filming Slavery: A Conversation with Haile Gerima." *Transition* 64, (New Series 1994): 90-104.

Wright, Richard. *Black Power. A Record of Reactions in a Land of Pathos*. New York: Harper, 1995.

Yankah, Kwesi. "Proverbs: the Aesthetics of Traditional Communication." *Research in African Literatures* 20. 3 (Fall 1989): 325-346.

Zobel, Joseph. *La Rue Cases-Nègres*. Paris: Présence Africaine, 1974.

THE MISSING NARRATIVE
IN *WEND KUUNI* (Time and Space)

"TIME AND SPACE CONSTITUTE dimensions within which any narrative evolves," stresses Madeleine Borgomano in regard to the African novel. She adds: "That is not surprising if we con - sider the narrative as a figuration or a representation of the funda - mental designs of social life, or yet, even more generally, of the meaning of life." Haig Khatchadourian, referring to cinema as a whole, specifies that those two entities "are organizing principles of all art, just as they provide the basic framework of the world and of subjective reality" (169). The list of critics could go on, since all agree upon the use of time and space as fundamental principles of a vision of the world, whether that vision be subjective or objec - tive, continuous or discontinuous, real or imaginary. Yet, what would become of the spatiotemporal organization, from which we draw a meaning or a vision, if that organization depended pre - cisely on a missing narrative that were to surface only at the end of the film? Such is the actual composition in Gaston Kaboré's *Wend Kuuni* (1982).

This consideration leads me to begin by presenting a brief summary of *Wend Kuuni* in a spatiotemporal perspective, as it appears *a priori* to the viewer watching the movie for the first time. *Wend Kuuni*'s first shot depicts the interior of a hut with a kneeling mother crying over her half-asleep son. We learn then, through the intrusion of one of the village men, that this young woman is being forced to remarry because of the extended absence of her spouse. The mother thereupon unveils to her son her plans to escape. The following sequence shows the child in the bush taken in by a merchant who shortly afterwards entrusts him to the care of a family in a distant village. Sheltered, then adopted, this young boy, who came from nowhere and who moreover has become mute, will bear the name of "Wend Kuuni," signifying *gift of God*. The movie then returns to Wend Kuuni's daily life among the members of his new family as well as within his new village. We subsequently discover, through the introduction of this *gift of God*, the traditional world of a small village of Burkina Faso. Only with the next-to-last sequence of the movie, thanks to a flashback, does the viewer piece together the missing narrative that separated the maternal scene in the hut from that of the discovery of the child abandoned in the bush. This sequence allows the viewer not only to re-establish the chronological order, but also to recover the significance of all of the sequences.

Thus, the film can only end when the missing narrative is recounted and the spatiotemporal ellipsis is fulfilled. That ellipsis, brought about by Wend Kuuni's mutism,[1] could be analyzed from an intrinsic perspective as the cause for the young boy's loss of speech (his mutism originates from his experience in the bush), as well as from an extrinsic perspective as the effect that generates the search for the missing narrative (his mutism produces a cinematic wandering until his speech is recovered). I will concentrate mainly on the second parameter, that is, more particularly on the character and the implications of this missing narrative, insofar as the cinematic narrative transforms itself into a true quest for Wend Kuuni's organizing speech. The episode that is omitted from the beginning of the movie will only be enunciated in images and speech at the end of the film, when Wend Kuuni, the principal witness of the missing story, recovers his speech. The viewer and the critic are therefore invited to discover how, despite everything, the movie sets up a semantic field, or a *signifiance,*[2] until they become a signified in Wend Kuuni's regained speech, and until the narration regains the recovered spatiotemporal chronology.

Insofar as the missing segment leaves in suspense a narration for which Wend Kuuni alone holds the mnemonic images that will give him back his speech, the cinematic narrative is condemned to wander through a continuum of scenes marked by captions (which double the signification of the images); yet, the film remains deprived of a unifying discourse until several scenes initiate the first shots, or morphemes, of Wend Kuuni's regained language. This could be explained as a deliberate choice on the part of Kaboré to establish a *new film language* using descriptive images based on the documentary,[3] until these images are able to recover their organizing speech (or, in other words, Wend Kuuni's return to his *new identification* relative to time and space).

This study follows a perspective parallel to that of Manthia Diawara who, while recognizing *Wend Kuuni*'s source in oral tradition, shows "the manner in which it [the film] transforms events and characters from their original representation" (41). He indeed illustrates how this film uses "the material of oral tradition to reflect the ideology of the time and not that of the oral tradition" (38), and he adds: "A return to the inner-self or to African culture does not therefore mean a subordination to tradition for the director who uses oral literature. It is a questioning of tradition, a creative process which enables him to make contemporary choices while resting on the shoulders of tradition" (39). While Diawara bases his comments on principles of the logic of narration that draw on the notions of function, order, and voice, we will use those of time and space, to the extent that those two entities may appropriately illustrate the new film language so sought after by African moviemakers, one which combines, as Diawara notes, the heritage of an oral tradition with a new contemporary African voice.

From this perspective, when we look into the nature and the order of the descriptive scenes, we realize that although they belong to a larger design, these scenes are easily recognizable since, as Lizbeth Malkmus and Roy Armes point out, they conform to a design of "repetition and variation" (183). However, if Malkmus and Armes most often recognize only spaces in binary opposition in the African cinema,[4] we have been able to determine three types of scenes in *Wend Kuuni* corresponding to as many "disconnected spaces" (Deleuze, 17): domestic scenes, scenes of exchange, and scenes in the bush.[5]

The domestic scenes comprise the scenes of the daily life of individual members of Wend Kuuni's foster family: the father weaving, the mother taking care of the household chores (sweeping, preparing butter and bread cakes), the daughter Pongnéré assisting her mother (in preparing the fire, setting up the millet, getting water, and delivering orders), and Wend Kuuni tending to the watering and pasturing of the goats, as well as helping his foster father in his chores as a weaver. The domestic space is thus that of daily repetition and of material cooperation among the family group. It corresponds in some ways to the *badenya* of the Mande, with the only difference being that it applies merely to the restricted circle of the family in this instance, and not to the village group or the ethnic community.[6] It represents the active account of a cultural and social heritage transmitted orally through a voice *perceived* by all, since it represents the voice of tradition.

The second space, which I will define as the space of exchanges, is distinguished from the domestic space by its focus on crowds or individuals whose actions stand out. This space is created by the presence of two groups or two individuals of the opposite sex within the same shot.[7] It appears in scenes that we may define as *bargainings* involving men and women. In the market scene, we remember the bargaining (for a piece of cloth) between Wend Kuuni[8] and a young woman, and in the scene of the village, we recall Timpoko's less honorable bargaining (a sexual bargaining) where she rejects her husband, whom she judges to be too old and impotent. These scenes of exchange, compared to the well balanced organization of the pre-ceding space with its focus on daily routines, act like a *contretemps*, and are located in an intermediary space between the domestic space and the space of the bush.

The space of the bush symbolizes the place of return, assimi-lated throughout the film to the infinite quest: it is illustrated by Wend Kuuni's real father's endless quest to find his way back, the horse-riders' quest and return to search for the young boy's fam-ily, and Wend Kuuni's trips to and from the fields until he recov-ers his voice and his way.[9] This space could be compared to the *fadenya* of the Mande insofar as it symbolizes the hero's site of searching.[10] Yet it is also the place where the quest for the miss-ing narrative or the missing sequences is initiated, since Wend Kuuni tells his story to Pongnéré when they are in the bush, and since it is in that very space that he has visions of his father and his deceased mother. It is likewise in that boundless space that Wend Kuuni's unconscious can be reported through a narrative voice.[11] Indeed, an omniscient voice unites the destiny of Wend Kuuni with that of characters of African mythical literature, where the quest presupposes the suffering of the main agent: "Although Wend Kuuni has a new family, he must still bear his grief alone. He thinks of all he's lived through. As a mute, he has no one to con-fide in" (film subtitles). Finally, the bush is the place of reconcil-iation between time and space, a place where the narrator can set this episode in the timelessness[12] of a distant era:

This was long ago, long before the white man. The Mossi Empire was in its days of splendor. There was much grain.

Rivers and wells were overflowing. No one was hungry. All
lived in peace and in good health. (film subtitles)

Furthermore, once the missing story is recovered by Wend Kuuni
during the last scene in the bush, time recovers its place in a completed chronology, and the sun can now set upon this ultimate reconciliation between time and space. This explains why the open
space of the bush is the space of Wend Kuuni's *longing* voice.

As long as the presented sequences are deprived of a struc-
turation or a temporality, for which Wend Kuuni alone holds the
key, another discourse drawing on film techniques must be instituted, which at the same time would account for the young boy's
wandering until he recovers his speech. The alternation of the various spaces is the very fundamental principle of this cinematic
discourse that is caught in a continuous present as if the hand of a
clock continuously advanced to ever mark the same hour. [13] Indeed,
in a very regular manner, the domestic scenes alternate with the
scenes in the bush, marking Wend Kuuni's wandering[14] between
the space of the *perceived* speech, or of the established speech
(domestic space), and that of the *longing* speech, or of the speech
to come, a space of infinite absence, of the possibilities of the
image or morpheme (the space of the bush). [15]

But aside from this cinematic discourse founded on the principles of alternation between the domestic space and that of the
bush, a dissymmetry occurs in three instances through the insertion
of shots originating from the space of exchanges. Indeed, every
time a scene of exchange appears on the screen, it either follows
or precedes a domestic scene, thus interrupting the expected alternation with a scene in the bush. This rupture to the rhythm ensures
a pivotal role for the space of exchanges in the cinematic construction. This space may therefore be defined as a mediatory space
between the family and the bush, that is to say between the *perceived* speech (the traditional narrative) and the *longing* speech of
an infinite space (the missing narrative). Henceforth, a domestic
scene comes after the market scene (space of exchanges →domes-
tic space) and the scene of conflict in the village follows a domestic scene (domestic space→space of exchanges). That space of
exchanges, a space manifesting an unusual occurrence, thereby
distinguishes itself from the repetitive temporality. This is why the
narrative in that space alone can escape both from the constraints
of an already established language (one giving the account of the

traditional narrative) and from a language suspended in a symbolic state (one relating an incomplete narrative in the bush). [16]

In a similar manner, the missing narrative could only be delivered by a being who would characterize that extraordinary trait: that
is, a being for whom the recovery of speech would lie between a
traditional language and a language suspended in the symbolic
state, and whose presence could be assimilated to the *contretemps*
previously evoked with regard to the space of exchanges. Now, is
this not precisely what Wend Kuuni represents, a *gift of God*, both
outside of time and outside of space?

Thus, once the enunciation is uttered by Wend Kuuni, the missing narrative gives a retrospective signification to the cinematic discourse, just as it also allows its principal speaker to unveil the
diegetic content of the film in its entirety. This signification, which
comes about during the narration of the missing segment (through
spoken words and images), allows the transition from a redundant
present, combined with a redundant spatiality (based on the principles of alternation and rupture), to a narrative present echoed by
a spatiality in motion (*diegetic* discourse). However, if Wend
Kuuni's making his voice heard corresponds to a repossession of
the story that allows him to emancipate himself from his state of
object in a temporality and spatiality that are not his, it is less the
repossession of his own missing story, since he is its only holder, [17]
than of that which unites him to others and which they freely speak.
Indeed, until Wend Kuuni recovers his speech, his individuality is
ruined by a speech that overrules him. He is the object of
Pongnéré's premonitory words that announce to him not only that
he spoke in her dream, but also that his recovery of speech will
soon occur. Likewise, his experience is surpassed by a voice spoken over him, a voice-over: "That day, Wend Kuuni awoke with a
strange foreboding. All day long the feeling never left him. What
was going to happen?"

Two shots relative to Wend Kuuni's past account for this emancipation insofar as they break once more the ordered rhythm of
the various spaces previously studied by being inserted in the space
of the bush, the territory of the quest. The first shot, that is to say
Wend Kuuni's first repossession of the spatial dimension, is a refu-
tation of the voice that dominates him: while that voice had
announced that he had no memory of his father, a blurred dissolve
following Wend Kuuni's aimless gaze reveals, if not a direct recollection of his father, at least a vision that is Wend Kuuni's own.

This becomes all the more pertinent when comparing that shot to another in which we discern a shape with a bow behind a tree, which can only represent Wend Kuuni's father, based on the facts given during the first sequence of the movie (the father is a hunter) as well as on the recollection of Wend Kuuni's mother during the flashback. However, in the latter case, no character or voice-over succeeded in giving a clearly uttered image of the father's presence, as was previously the case with the dissolve projecting Wend Kuuni's vision. The nature of the first shot thus symbolizes Wend Kuuni's control of the utterance, since he is the only one able to recover and bring back the image of the father.

After this first shot on the father, the second one brings to the screen Wend Kuuni's mother. That shot, corresponding to Wend Kuuni's vision of his mother lying dead at the base of a tree, cuts in like a flash in the middle of the scene when Wend Kuuni, returning to the bush to get his misplaced knife, finds, hanging from a tree, the man who was mocked in the village. Recovering his speech through a shriek, which later in the missing segment is associated with the discovery of the dead mother, Wend Kuuni reports that new episode of the village life. It is therefore he alone who tells the story, by repossessing both his story (his relation to his parents) and the story of the others (his vision of the world). This dual movement allows him not only to recover his identity but also to gain his place within the village.

Thus, only when Wend Kuuni recovers his autonomy with respect to the parental images—by symbolically killing the father (we remember that he returned to the bush to get his knife and that he found a lifeless male figure) and by dissociating himself from his mother (he recognizes his dead mother against a tree during a vision)—can he finally tell his story and restore a spatiotemporal structure to the cinematic narration. These two shots, that of the father and that of the mother, constitute the first two phonemes, "daddy" and "mommy," of Wend Kuuni's language and of the recovery of his speech, his identity, and his power.

Freed from his condition of being narrated by the Other, Wend Kuuni liberates himself from the timeless status of an unfulfilled character by placing himself within a past origin, tied to that of his parents, and by going beyond the story of the Other, that is to say, by fully assuming his role of enunciator. In the sequence that includes the missing narrative, this enunciation is initiated by the sudden awareness of an identity: "I remember," then by a delim-

itation in time: "one day...," and finally by the evocation of a spatiality visible to the viewer through a return to the maternal hut,
specifically where we had left it after the first sequence of the film.
Remembrance, time, and space—the unity is recovered in this
ultimate reconciliation supplied by the missing narrative. The
mother speaks-in the flashback, and then the missing sequence
appears on the screen: from the escape across the bush until the
awakening of the child who, with a scream of horror, discovers
his dead mother under the tree where the two had stopped. The
story told by Wend Kuuni continues; he recounts his flight across
the bush, his loss of consciousness, and the care given by the trader.
The cycle is thus closed, the spatiotemporal chronology re-estab-
lished, and the film can end on the image of a distant point (Wend
Kuuni) in the bush, perhaps, in other words, a fixed shot marked
by a period, the transcription in cinematic language of the final
period of the story.

By concentrating on effects of redundancy and of alternation,
Kaboré has managed to take advantage of the spatiotemporal structures so that they would determine the film's narrative structure and
not the opposite. Similar to the voice of the mute Wend Kuuni,
wandering until it finds its mooring and its *raison d'être*, Kaboré's
film reveals itself to the rhythm of alternating spaces until it
becomes a true spatiotemporal discourse, which in its own manner
traces a possible avenue for African cinema in quest of an authentic and personal becoming.

NOTES

1. Michel Chion, in his chapter entitled "Le dernier mot du
    muet," makes a distinction between "*muteness*, a physical
    condition of the subject that precludes him from spoken lan-
    guage (lesion or destruction of a nervous center or of an
    organ), and *mutism* which is the refusal to speak, for reasons
    qualified as 'psychological,' without the nervous centers and
    phonation organs being affected" (82).
2. Julia Kristeva, in *Sèméiotiké Recherch pour une sémanalyse*,
    defines *signifiance* as "that *effort* of differentiation, stratifi-
    cation and confrontation that is practiced in language, and
    deposits onto the line of the speaking subject a grammati-
    cally structured and communicative signifying chain" (11).
    In an article published in the *Cahiers du Cinéma*, Roland

Barthes applies those principles of semiotics of the text to cinema and defines *signifiance* as a *third meaning* or an *obtuse meaning*, located "outside of the (articulated) lan-guage, but however within the interlocution" (16).

3. Malkmus and Armes mention that "the film-makers' shared background and the pressure of the context in which they are compelled to work have led them to a common way of see-ing African reality and telling African stories. In adopting methods of documentary production developed in the West, they have devised ways of giving a direct voice to the African people" (216).

4. See in particular Chapter 10, entitled "Space," in *Arab and African Film Making,* in which the authors enumerate many plots of African films within which space is constituted in binary oppositions. For *Wend Kuuni*, Malkmus and Armes distinguish two spaces in opposition: "The first is the intol-erant village of Wend Kuuni's early childhood, the village from which his mother was expelled. The second is the sup-portive community into which he is adopted after being found in the bush" (193). My distinction of space is not founded on a distinction relative to positive or negative events, but rather on the cinematic construction of each of the scenes. Furthermore, it would seem that Kaboré had intended to reject any opposition implying a system of values (see note 12).

5. Although Diawara does not explore the function or the organ-ization of the three types of scenes, I am indebted to him for recognizing these scenes, which he calls scenes in "the home, the field and the market place" (40). I have replaced what Diawara names "scene in the market place" by the more gen-eral title of "scenes of exchanges" so as to include the scene of conflict in the village, which otherwise would not fit into any other scene category.

6. Charles S. Bird and Martha B. Kendall distinguish two axes in the Mande ideology: the axis of group affiliation, *badenya,* meaning "mother-childness" from *baden* meaning "group," and the axis of individuality, *fadenya,* meaning "father-child-ness" and connected to the notion of hero. In the first axis, the child must submit to authority, to stability and cooperation, thus to the social mass, and his/her interests are subordinated to the group's interests. That axis is associated with the cen-

tripetal force of society. In the second axis, the child must define himself/herself from the collectivity in order to then go beyond it and distinguish himself/herself from it. That axis is associated with the centrifugal force of society. Although these definitions relate to the Mande ideology of the Mali Empire in the thirteenth century, and although the More tribe is not considered to be of Mande descent, Bird and Kendall specify that this ideology originated in Western Africa. That is why it is used as a reference here.

7.	It is very unusual to see men and women presented within the same shot. Pongnéré and Wend Kuuni sometimes have that privilege, but in those instances, they are perceived as sub-ordinate characters in the adult world. In the last sequence of the film, the presence of those two characters in the same shot reveals an emancipation from their status of children inside the adult world; yet this time, it is in a harmonious fashion insofar as the new exchange that comes about blends the sexual roles (they both see themselves as ready to take on the masculine or feminine role of the other).

8.	In that scene, Wend Kuuni for the first time takes on a mas-culine adult role, since he replaces the father of his foster family.

9.	This is particularly apparent during the last scene when Wend Kuuni not only tells his story, but also finds his way back or perhaps even a new opening in life. Let us also note, albeit anecdotally, that "to wend" in English means "to journey on."

10.	See note 6 on the distinction between *badenya* and *fadenya*. Bird and Kendall add: "*Fadenya* may thus be seen as a tem-poral axis measuring the worth of individuals against the actual accomplishments of their predecessors and the antic-ipated challenges of their descendants. A person's starting point in the social system, then, automatically constrains his chances to make his mark, and simultaneously shapes his assessment of these chances" (15).

11.	Diawara associates that narrative voice with that of the *griot* when it summarizes or resumes Wend Kuuni's story.

12.	Françoise Pfaff in *Twenty-Five Black Filmmakers* reproduces parts of an interview granted by Gaston Kaboré on May 3, 1985, that sheds light on that timelessness intended by the author:

> *Wend Kuuni* takes place in pre-colonial times... [but] its
> exact time frame is not important. It could be 1420 or 1850
> because the sociocultural reality which I depict remained
> unchanged for years. Besides, the colonial and post-colonial
> eras have been amply illustrated by African cinema.
> Moreover, I did not want *Wend Kuuni* to be labeled a film
> on the emancipation of women, the conflict between tradi-
> tion and modernity, traditional hospitality or other tradi-
> tional values. Tradition is often contrasted with modernity,
> but for people with an autonomous culture...there is no such
> opposition. All of this brought me to choose a past and
> autonomous society with its own oppressive forces and
> inner contradictions, a community, which I did not regard
> as an ideal African society. (177)

13. This applies only to the character of Wend Kuuni and not to
    that of Pongnéré. Although the two stories, that of Pongnéré
    and that of Wend Kuuni, are intertwined, we consider this
    cinematic narrative only through Wend Kuuni's perspective
    since the film bears the name of the young boy and not that
    of its other main character.

14. This wandering gives the impression of an everlasting pres-
    ent when seen from Wend Kuuni's vantage point, since, from
    a temporal point of view, Wend Kuuni's story line stalls
    between the two polar spaces mentioned above.

15. This situation of the subject between the *perceived* speech (in
    other words, speech spoken or transmitted through tradition
    or customs) and a *longing* speech (that is to say, somehow a
    speech not yet spoken) evokes several Lacanian principles
    regarding the child's quest for language that we find in "The
    Seminar on Poe's *Purloined Letter*" ("Le Séminaire sur *La
    lettre volée*"): "Ce jeu par où l'enfant s'exerce à faire dis-
    paraître de sa vue, pour l'y ramener, puis l'oblitérer à nou-
    veau, un objet, au reste différent de sa nature, cependant qu'il
    module cette alternance de syllabes distinctes,—ce jeu,
    dirons-nous, manifeste en ses traits radicaux la détermina-
    tion que l'animal reçoit de l'ordre symbolique" (59) "That
    game where the child strives to conceal from his sight, to
    bring it back, then to obliterate once more, an object, other-
    wise different from his nature, while he modulates that alter-
    nation of distinctive syllables,—that game, we shall say, man-

ifests in its radical traits the determination which the human animal receives from the symbolic order" (trans. my own).
16. That language remains in the symbolic state insofar it has not yet been interpreted or transcribed in words by Wend Kuuni.
17. This is the case, whether this story is in Wend Kuuni's unconscious or conscious mind. Likewise, despite his loss of speech, Wend Kuuni may never have lost his memory.

WORKS CITED

Barthes, Roland. "Le troisième sens: Notes de recherch sur quelques photogrammes de S. M. Eisenstein." *Cahiers du Cinéma* 222 (1970): 12-19.

Borgomano, Madeleine. "Temps et espace dans le roman africain: Quelques directions de recherch." *Revue de littérature et d'esthéthique négro-africaine* 8 (1988): 5-13.

Bird, Charles S. and Martha B. Kendall. "The Mande Hero: Text and Context." *Explorations in African Systems of Thought*. Ed. Ivan Karp and Charles S. Bird. Bloomington: Indiana University Press, 1980. 13-26.

Chion, Michel. "Le dernier mot du muet." *La Voix au cinéma*. Paris: Etoile, 1982. 80-89.

Deleuze, Gilles. *Cinéma 2—L'image-temps*. Paris: Editions de Minuit,1985.

Diawara, Manthia. "Oral Literature and African Film: Narratology in 'Wend Kuuni.'" *Présence Africaine* 142 (1987): 36-49.

Khatchadourian, Haig. "Space and Time in Film." *British Journal of Aesthetics* 27.2 (1987): 169-177.

Kristeva, Julia. *Sèméiotiké: Recherchs pour une sémanalyse*. Paris: Seuil, 1969.

Lacan, Jacques. *Ecrits I*. Paris: Seuil, 1968.

Malkmus, Lizbeth, and Roy Armes. "African Film." *Arab and African Film Making*. London: Zed, 1991. 167-216.

Pfaff, Françoise. *Twenty-Five Black African Filmmakers*. New York: Greenwood, 1988.

YEELEN: A POLITICAL FABLE OF THE *KOMO* BLACKSMITHS / SORCERERS

SOULEYMANE CISSÉ'S 1987 FILM *Yeelen* ("Brightness") from Mali has been widely acclaimed in the West and garnered a Cannes Film Festival Jury Prize the year it was released. Commendation of its universal themes and gorgeous cinematog - raphy published in brief journalistic reviews is well deserved (Biloa; Carbonnier; Caron; Chevrie; Heyman; James; Lavigne). Tesson's praise of *Yeelen's* technical excellence refutes a com - mon perception of African film as naive and extols the film's breakthrough achievement in the grounding of science fiction in reality. Although his judgment of *Yeelen*'s beauty and sophistica - tion of technique is accurate, he overemphasizes the "fantas - tique" in deeming it a fairy tale (10). The mythic story set in an unspecified past before the advent of Christianity or Islam is comprehensible to international audiences. However, African audiences recognize serious contemporary issues in the narrative and perceive the direct relationship of the film to their own social and political problems. They refute Clyde Taylor's assertion that *Yeelen* "puts aside parables of contemporary social crises for an allegorical tale...." (57) and applaud James Leahy's observation that *Yeelen* is not "the product of any spurious attempt at a uni - versality, but grows out of a profound belief system, one which has been carefully explored and researched" (344).

Yeelen is so firmly rooted in West African Mande culture that the full resonance of the plot, characterization, artistic intent, and social / political significance can not be understood outside the cultural and historical context. *Yeelen is* a profoundly West African film, an epic *bildungsroman* centered on a dynastic struggle within the distinguished Diarra family of the Bambara

branch of the Mande people. This family ruled the Segou kingdom from the 17th through the 19th centuries. N'Golo Diarra,
having conquered the Peul people and the city of Timbuctoo,
reigned as Segou's most eminent king from 1760-82 and founded the family dynasty, which lasted until 1862 (Imperato, 15).
The glory of the Diarra family has been celebrated in oral epic
poetry, and its political prominence thrives today in Mali
(McNaughton, *Mande,* 2). *Yeelen* reflects the point of view of
Mali's dominant ethnic group, the Bambara, and uses the
Bambara language. However, its pan-Malian vision also incorporates the values and leadership of the two other major groups, the
Peul (or Fulani) and the Dogon.

The major male characters in the film belong to the powerful
secret *Komo* society, an ancient association of blacksmith/sorcer-
ers, which forms the central Mande social institution. Without
reference to the cosmology, anthropology, and ethics of the
Komo, Cissé's social and cinematic purpose remains elusive. The
film begins with a brief prologue explaining Bambara symbols
and cosmological issues essential to the *Komo* or divine knowledge. "Heat makes fire and the two worlds—earth and sky—exist
through light." The process of creation and destruction through
light *(Yeelen)* underlies the meaning of the entire film, and
imagery of light and fire unifies the cinematography. Through
sorcery, members of the *Komo* administer the cosmic power of
Korè, which is the seventh and final stage of initiation into divine
knowledge.

The lore and practices of the *Komo* are extremely complicated and occupy long technical treatises such as those by
Dominique Zahan *(Bambara)* and Germaine Dieterlen and
Youssouf Cissé *(Les fondements).* However, for clarity, emphasis, and the brevity required for a feature length film, Cissé sim-
plifies and condenses this complex material. He uses its basic
principles metaphorically to indict abuse of power by the current
rulers of Mali. Subtly but clearly *Yeelen* demands a return to the
traditional ideals of beneficent governance. Cissé hopes that his
film will arouse the conscience of his audience to cleanse government corruption and restore the ethical integrity of the ancestral Mali commonwealth.

The story of *Yeelen is* simple and straightforward. A young
Bambara man named Nianancoro Diarra comes of age, having
been raised from infancy by his mother after his father Soma

deserted and repudiated them. Soma is a famous sorcerer and member of the *Komo* fellowship, which for many generations has abused its control of the supernatural *Korè* to sustain tyrannical power. Soma now seeks to kill his adult son, fearing that Nianancoro is destined to terminate the corrupt *Komo* hegemony. Nianancoro leaves home to face his father, and during his apprenticeship journey through the territories of the Peul and Dogon he confirms his own considerable magic powers, acquires a wife, and is mentored by his Uncle Djigui. Father and son meet in an apocalyptic confrontation; both die as they unleash the full force of their sorcery. The voice of *Korè* condemns the malfea-sance of the old regime and announces the withdrawal of its power. The film ends a few years later as Nianancoro's young son accepts his father's legacy, implying that he will fulfill his own prophesied destiny: to restore virtuous stewardship of the *Korè* and ethical governance of all the Mande.

The cultural significance of the *Komo* invests the struggle for control of the organization with high metaphorical valence. The *Komo* fellowship forms a central social institution of the Bambara, a "glue" that binds many aspects of that culture and which is familiar to other ethnic groups in Mali. Patrick McNaughton comments in his excellent study *The Mande Blacksmiths* that the services of such associations are "so perva-sive in Mande society and so embedded in the Mande world view that they literally infuse the culture with much of its character" (5).

McNaughton lived for over a year in Mali during the 1970s and trained with several famous blacksmiths; his research docu-ments the continuing vitality of the blacksmith lore and practice today. The *Komo* traditionally has held the supreme position among the various secret societies, and despite attempts of Islam to extinguish its influence it still exercises great authority in con-temporary Mali, according to McNaughton (*Mande,* 131). The origin of the secret society probably antedates the advent of Islam into West Africa; the *Komo* existed before 1230 CE when the great epic hero Sunjata founded the Mali Empire (McNaughton, *Secret,* 19). Sunjata's main emissary and agent was the blacksmith Fakoli, who helped defeat the enemy Sosu and, according to oral tradition, organized *Komo* societies wher-ever he conducted military campaigns. Sunjata also included other smiths as political advisors. Smiths ruled the Soso kingdom in the late 11th century after the Ghanaian Empire fell apart (McNaughton, *Secret,* 19, 22). Thus from its beginning the *Komo* has been inextricably involved in Mande political life, but its professional activities extend far beyond the sphere of gover-nance into religious, technological, judicial, medical, education-al, and magical functions.

The *Komo* exerts broad influence through its base of power in the *Korè,* the universal, occult source of knowledge that medi-ates between the spiritual and material realms, which are tightly integrated in African cosmology. The society holds to the animist belief that all objects are invested with an inherent spiritual force called *nyama*, which animates all living beings, including plants and animals, and controls the powers of nature itself, governing crop production and rainfall. This psychic force impels all human thinking, will, and action, and in turn is released by all actions. It generates the underlying pattern or coherence of the entire world. Because it executes the operations of cause and effect, it could be termed African karma. Tapping its power is not only difficult but also quite dangerous, and *nyama* in concentrated form is deadly (McNaughton, *Mande,* 15-17). Customarily only special people like the members of the *Komo* dare confront it.

Komo members are identified with the blacksmith clan, which, along with several specialized professions like hunters, leathermakers, and bards, is termed *nyamakola* or "force-han-dler" because it administers *nyama* power using arcane ritual and knowledge exclusive to the group. The smiths employ the for-bidden power of fire to transform matter from one form to anoth-er by smelting and forging; they use their occult knowledge to inform their ceremonies and their professional activities. Blacksmiths are born into the group and inherit from their parents some degree of their native ability to "negotiate treaties with a complex of spirits through ritual" (McNaughton, *Mande,* 3,18). However, they also learn from each other trade secrets *(gundow).* In addition, smiths purchase the materials and the protocols *(daliluw)* that execute all their operations *(Mande,* 43, 150). Their overall mission is to harmonize and balance the occult and mate-rial worlds, to nurture the entire physical and spiritual life of the community.

People outside the clan fear and shun blacksmiths as strange, even alien beings and associate with them at their own peril. Smiths segregate themselves and jealously guard their professional monopoly and occult powers. Secretive and endogamous, they ordinarily do not even take lovers outside their group. They fear the dilution of their power and the loss of their particular knowledge (McNaughton, *Mande,* 4). Professional training is limited to the offspring (and sometimes slaves) of blacksmiths, and smiths must not reveal their secrets to outsiders.

On the other hand, blacksmiths receive great respect and are frequently consulted because of their special powers. Their var- ied functions make them indispensable to society. They forge the tools used by farmers, hunters, and warriors; they make the wooden and iron sculptures used in the rituals of the secret asso- ciations; they construct masks, fetishes, and amulets used by all the Mande. As paragons of sorcery they both practice the occult art and also protect others from its effects. Through divination, blacksmiths diagnose physical and emotional illnesses and treat them with herbs, powders, and amulets in addition to dances and other rituals. They witness in legal proceedings and arbitrate legal, political, and personal disputes; they advise rulers on poli- cy (McNaughton, *Mande,* 64-66); they exercise judicial power to search out and punish various malefactors *(Yeelen).*

But their most significant activity is to initiate and educate the young Mande. Their rites of passage are considered quite frightening and rigorous. Only skilled blacksmiths can perform the dangerous, delicate operations of circumcision and excision (McNaughton, *Mande,* 3). According to oral tradition, the leg- endary blacksmith Ndomajiri founded the *N'tomo* society to train young boys and transform the initiates from unformed young creatures into mature, civilized men who apply their knowledge for the benefit of the entire community *(Mande,* 146). Apprentice smiths begin their training before the age of 10 and undergo a painful, difficult, tedious seven to eight year curriculum of both practical experience and theoretical wisdom. Boys often are instructed by their fathers *(Mande,* 23).

Because the smiths exercise such extensive power in all vital areas of Mande life, it is imperative that they practice the highest ethical standards (McNaughton, *Mande,* 11-17) and renounce tyranny, vengeance, and self-aggrandizement. When they do not, injustice and suffering reign. Cissé measures the performance of the *Komo* association in the film against this ancient moral benchmark. The struggle between those who exercise ethical stewardship of the *Korè* and those who abuse their occult knowledge is the central conflict of *Yeelen*.

Sequences dramatizing a wide range of *Komo* activities—blacksmith work protocols, secret rites, ritual sorcery using occult paraphernalia—are central to the film. Cissé punctuates the story with shots of the sacred grove used for *Komo* ceremonies where a small boy ties up a white goat to a wooden fetish statue of a seated man blazoned with white spots [cf. similar decoration, Anderson 47] and holding the carved board called the Wing of *Korè*. Ritual gourds near the statue symbolize the *Komo* rituals. A young apprentice blacksmith massages the bellows while an old smith rhythmically hammers glowing tools into shape. Heated iron hisses when tempered by water in a stone cauldron. Nianancoro's mother seeks the help of the Mande blacksmiths to protect her son from Soma's magic. The Peul king solicits Nianancoro's magic power to repel invading warriors and to cure his wife's infertility.

The *Komo* fellowship meets in an isolated sacred grove under a kapok tree with magic inscriptions on its trunk. This sanctuary precludes intrusion by the uninitiated. The members of the *Komo* honor their leader, the elderly Master Blacksmith, who offers a "sacrifice" of millet beer, carefully pouring some on the ground as they imbibe the ritual drink. In Bambara religious belief, trees symbolize the *Korè* powers in nature (Anderson, 67) as they integrate the spiritual aspiration of branches lifting into the sky with the material foundation of roots buried in the earth, all growing according to the seasonal rhythm (Zahan, *Religion,* 27). Trees provide ritual access to divine forces such as the invisible spirits (jinn) residing in the groves (McNaughton, *Secret* 5). They also represent knowledge itself (Zahan, *Religion* 8-29).

The *Komo* cantor, Nianancoro's father Soma—whose name designates an especially powerful and competitive sorcerer who does not tolerate rival sorcerers (McNaughton, *Mande,* 49)—perverts his powers to wreak personal vengeance on his son. His dramatic chants invoke a panoply of supernatural forces: nature deities, sacred animals, and the power of hallowed sites such as the sacred crossroads. Like an African King Lear, he conjures cosmic havoc as he implores occult forces to dry up lakes, demolish buildings, break and destroy the very earth and sky for retribution on his son. Soma quotes traditional proverbs and axioms designed to justify his cause, rally the other *Komo* members—who grunt in affirmation—and elicit an effective course of action. For example, he calls his son a knife blade but himself the knife handle, which can never be harmed by the blade. This proverb alludes to the traditional designations *nya-makola* ("force handlers") for the blacksmiths and to *muru-kala-tigiw* ("masters of the knife handle") for those who perform sacrifices during rituals (McNaughton, *Secret,* 19). Soma boasts of his own invulnerability, ranting in the loud, bel - lowing voice used by sorcerers to intimidate *(Secret,* 33). He also performs vindictive private sorcery employing his magic post *(kolonkalanni)* to immolate chickens, a red dog, and an albino man.

In contrast, Nianancoro uses his magic powers with calm dignity for self protection and social benefit. Although technical - ly still a novice, he wields a rich repertoire of magic, a paternal legacy. By peering into a cauldron of water, a method used in Southern Mali (McNaughton, *Mande,* 55), he divines that his father is approaching to kill him. Later he prepares ingestible - powders that transmit the invisible *nyama*, which can both cause and counteract bad luck and illness. Nianancoro cures the infer - tility of the Peul king's young wife Attu with such a powder. Some infertility medicines appropriately increase the subject's sexual attractiveness (McNaughton, *Secret,* 14), precisely what happens to the woman after she swallows the bitter concoction. Her sad face lights up with desire and she begins to remove her clothing. Nianancoro also eats the medicine, and he impregnates her himself, fulfilling his medical mission in an effective but eth - ically questionable manner. To save the Peul people from an enemy raiding party, Nianancoro hammers a horse leg bone into a termite mound, unleashing angry bees and a brush fire to tor - ment and banish the warriors. Termite mound clay has special magic properties and is sometimes used to mold Mande figurines of great mythical power (Anderson, 64).

The most common sorcery technique in *Yeelen* is spitting, which fulfills many functions: to activate the bone in the termite mound, to conjure the images in the cauldron, and to effect and release spells that paralyze people. Saliva embodies strong *nyama* (McNaughton, *Mande,* 43) blending the material moisture of spit with the incorporeal breath or soul. Ritual speech also actualizes the sorcerer's command; one sorcerer releases a frozen arm by announcing, "The spell is broken." Even simple emission of *nyama* energy without words or overt action can execute the magician's will. Soma, Nianancoro, and his uncle Bafing all con - trol matter in this manner.

Sorcerers also use divination materials, which they carry in a bag. Commonly used are the fly whisk, a variety of amulets and fetishes, and wooden posts and boards. The whisk symbolizes authority and status in dances and ceremonies and activates occult power. It can become a weapon to flick poison onto vic - tims (McNaughton, *Secret,* 12). Amulets filled with herbs, ani - mal or human parts, and written texts are used for protection and customarily worn around the neck or on the wrist. Nianancoro wears a special amulet from his mother to protect him from Soma's power. Jewel-like fetishes also activate *Korè* power when placed on the sacred boards and post. Sorcerers employ a magic pylon or post *(kolonkalanni)* as a judicial divining rod to search out thieves, traitors, perjurers, and other malefactors. Both Soma and Bafing engage these to search for Nianancoro.

The climactic confrontation of Soma and Nianancoro unleashes the sorcerer's ultimate expenditure of divine energy: Soma uses his magic pylon and Nianancoro, his carved wooden board called the Wing of *Korè* . The Bambara boards, *korè kara,* represent divine knowledge by highly stylized geometric designs (Zahan, *Bambara* Plate XXXVII, No. 1; plate legend, p. 31). They resemble and may be similar in function to the plank masks encoded with moral instruction and mythical family lore worn in Burkina Faso for various ceremonies, especially initiation (Anderson illustrations, pp. 10, 68, 116, 117, 119). The two men activate the full *Korè* power in the blinding, apocalyptic flash that obliterates both of them and transforms the area into a Sahara-like wasteland. The voice of *Korè* rebukes the selfish and vengeful motives of the *Komo* rulers and withdraws itself from them after generations of partnership.

This episode draws on the traditionally fierce and often dead - ly competition among sorcerers to attain fame and prestige, settle grudges, or eliminate antagonists by harming or killing their rivals. The sorcerers' release of *nyama* can occur at any time but is particularly likely during ceremonial performances and dances to display power before small or large audiences. Master sorcer - ers are frequently targeted by other magicians yearning for ascendancy (McNaughton, *Secret,* 12-13).

The *Yeelen* confrontation, however, varies from the usual surreptitious ambush in being *open* conflict between *family* members. Soma has feared his son from the time of the boy's birth and disavowed his paternity because he knew that the boy was destined to challenge his own power. After Nianancoro is initiated, Soma becomes desperate to kill his innocent son, track - ing him by means of the magic post and invoking the full arsenal of nature's powers to assist him. Soma believes (correctly as the story unfolds) that his son will destroy him, but he distorts the truth about their conflict to the *Komo* assembly, charging Nianancoro with betrayal of the *Komo* by stealing fetishes and leaving his home area. Soma's indictment has a certain technical validity, but he willfully twists the context. Nianancoro has fled his village only to escape Soma, and his mother commands him to return the sacred fetish to the Wing of *Korè* where it belongs. Nianancoro hopes to pacify his father's wrath and reconcile with him. He seeks public affirmation of Soma's paternity to confirm his own identity as an honorable Bambara man and to terminate his and his mother's refugee existence. Although he expects to be overwhelmed by his father's power, nevertheless, he willingly risks death in the quest.

This father-son conflict violates the Bambara tradition that requires a father to foster his novice son in the discipline and secrets of the smith-sorcerers. Soma's perversion of his paternal duty exemplifies the Mande concept of *fadenya*, "*father* child-ness," a term , which usually designates the excessive aggression exercised by half brothers with the same father and different mothers (McNaughton, *Mande,* 14). Greed, vindictiveness, and egocentrism fuel their competitive zeal. Such willfulness under - mines social stability and fails the test of virtuous moderation. Members of the *nyamakala* clans with their secrecy, endogamy, and extensive powers are particularly susceptible to this negative aggression *(Mande,* 14). Soma's cruelty and obsessive invoca - tion of the powers of nature and the deities to assist his destruc - tive agendum brand him as a social menace. Furthermore, his success in gaining the support of the *Komo* for personal vengeance indicates that his behavior is not merely individual pathology but instead a sign of the entire group's moral decay.

The Bambara antidote for *fadenya* is *badenya* or "mother childness," the respect and loyalty that *full* brothers properly feel for each other. Such kindness restrains competitive violence and

sustains social harmony (McNaughton, *Mande,* 14*)*. Such qualities are displayed by Nianancoro, who tempers his paternal
inheritance of sorcery by virtue of his mother's proper and moral
Bambara education. Nianancoro has also learned from the example and tutelage of virtuous male mentors—the Peul king, the
Dogon keepers of the sacred Bongo spring, and his uncle Djigui,
Soma's identical twin, who has become the blind sage of the
Dogon people. The Peul king exercises mature, thoughtful leadership as he consults his council, particularly the elders, before
making any decision and heeds their advice. He allows the prisoner Nianancoro, whom he thinks is a cattle thief, to make his
case and then wisely enlists Nianancoro to rout invading warriors
with his magic and save the village. He intends to adopt
Nianancoro as son and heir, but his plans are shattered when
Nianancoro cures the king's youngest wife Attu's infertility by
impregnating her himself. Now he must make a private decision
about punishing the pair with no council to guide him, and he
chooses mercy even though Nianancoro has asked to be executed to salvage both men's honor. The king banishes the pair,
unwittingly orchestrating the decree of destiny that Nianancoro
and Attu's son will be the future leader. Generosity, reason, and
the subjugation of personal pride distinguish this king as a foil to
the men of the *Komo.*

The Dogon priest and the keepers of the perpetual waters of
the sacred Bongo spring graciously provide ritual cleansing for
Nianancoro and Attu even though they are strangers. Their
spring, like the *Korè* itself is "bottomless" and "inexhaustible,"
for it has no known source; it purifies the couple of their sexual
trespass before the final duel with Soma. These courteous, digni-
fied men openly reveal their methods of stimulating rain from the
clouds without concern for either keeping their knowledge secret
or augmenting their own prestige and power. As stewards of
communal welfare rather than exploiters of occult power, they
exemplify for Nianancoro what leadership should be.

Nianancoro's final mentor is his Uncle Djigui Diarra,
Soma's identical twin, who became blinded when he dared to
suggest to his father that the Komo secrets be shared for the benefit of all people. Like Nianancoro and his mother, Djigui was
exiled because of his integrity; now he radiates spiritual wisdom
among the Dogon. He keeps the Wing of *Korè* in a cave await-
ing the arrival of his nephew, who brings the missing fetish to

activate the wing's potency. The restored wing will arm Nianancoro sufficiently to match his father's power. Djigui teaches the young couple the history of the Diarra family and the cause of his blindness; he prophesies a glorious future for Attu's unborn son yet foretells great suffering and treachery among the Bambara people. Djigui proclaims the continued eminence of their family, the "placenta" and "umbilical cord" of the Bambara, which will survive future calamites as the conduit of *Korè* power.

Djigui's vision of tribulation materializes through the apocalyptic explosion of "light " *(Yeelen),* which destroys the old regime as well as the sacrificial young hero. The voice of *Korè* denounces the *Komo's* greed and selfishness and withdraws its sponsorship. But Djigui's hope also materializes in Nianancoro's young son, who at the end of the film digs from the sand two large white eggs and carries one to his mother. She exchanges the egg for his father's cloak and the Wing of *Korè,* and the film concludes as the boy carries them up a sand dune bathed in glorious sunlight. The egg embodies his father's reborn Korè power. The continuation of Nianancoro's spirit after death exemplifies a central Bambara doctrine expressed earlier by Djigui: "I believe that one can die without ceasing to exist; life and death are like scales laid one upon another."

Nianancoro's bittersweet destiny generates the next stage of history of the Diarra family, which, though cursed for generations, holds the vexed future of the Bambara in its hands. But this future also includes other major ethnic groups of Mali. The young boy carries the Peul lineage through his mother and the Dogon heritage through both the land adopted by his Uncle Djigui and the site where his father's and grandfather's spirits remain eternally crystallized in the giant eggs.

Likewise, the timeless work of the traditional blacksmiths/ sorcerers remains a vital reality in contemporary Mali as McNaughton's research during the 1970s documents. In *Yeelen* Cissé uses the ancient *Komo* heritage metaphorically to imply that Malians of all ethnic groups can discover unity as stewards of the *Korè,* exercise its power for the benefit of all, and ponder the eventual retribution for violating this sacred trust.

Cissé further intends a specific, immediate political point. He indicts the corrupt and violent regime of President Moussa Traoré, who came to power through the 1968 military coup that ousted the first president of independent Mali, Modibo Keita,

whose socialist economic policies had failed. But Traoré's promised reforms succumbed to problems similar to those that had
vexed Keita's administration—the nepotistic appointments made
by his wife Mariam and his own indifference to the severe economical and political suffering his policies caused the Malian
people (Andriamirado; Bourgi; Sada). His state-run economy
reaped generous income for government officials, particularly
from high food prices exacerbated by a Sahelian drought in the
early 1970s. Cotton produced for hard currency export replaced
many edible crops and resulted in scarcity of food and higher
retail prices.

Rural farmers were ruined by the low wholesale prices they
received for their produce while luxury villas financed by illegal
profits from food aid sprang up in Bamako. Desperate peasants
who fled to the cities ended up in urban ghetto squalor. Students
lost many of their government scholarships, and public sector
jobs for graduates were suspended. Civil servants endured lower
wages and higher food prices (Schissel). The lack of democratic
rights drove many Malians to believe they could not expect even
a fair audience from their government, much less economic
reform.

Cissé's protest of such conditions in *Yeelen* indicated a new
cinematic strategy for him. He commented in an interview with
Manthia Diawara that he deliberately shifted the style he had
used for two earlier socialist realism films, *Baara* (1978) and
Finye ("The Wind," 1982), both of which advocated the struggles of African trade unions against military regimes. The political tension these films elicited in Mali partially accounted for
Cissé's decision to employ a less confrontational style, which he
hoped would allow him to continue making films in Mali with
reasonable artistic freedom (Diawara, 160). I believe that he was
also motivated by the desire to explore another cinematic mode
to celebrate the values of traditional West African culture as a
model for contemporary Mali. The search for contemporary
inspiration in the roots of African culture is a major thrust in
African filmmaking exemplified in such films as Ousmane
Sembene's *Ceddo* (1976), Gaston Kaboré's *Wend Kunni* (1982),
and Idrissa Oeudraogo's *Yaaba* (1989).

Yeelen can be judged as premonitory about the vulnerability
of corrupt governments in light of events that occurred about four
years after its release. In March 1991, peaceful strikes and

A POLITICAL FABLE OF THE *KOMO* BLACKSMITHS / SORCERERS

protests against the Traoré government were violently suppressed, and as many as 200 unarmed protesters died at the hands
of government troops (Bourgi; Diallo; *Manifeste*). Shortly thereafter, Traoré was arrested and jailed, and some of his officials
were killed. A popular transition leader was chosen, and then in
June 1992 Alpha Oumar Konaré, a former member of the Traoré
cabinet, was elected president (Adriamirado). He continues to
hold that office today. Currently Traoré remains in custody technically under sentence of death.

Yeelen, like *Finye*, praises the sacrifice of young Africans to
restore justice to their society when most of their elders either
complied with the corrupt government or else despaired of ever
altering the structures of authority. It is significant that during the
Traoré regime students were among those most victimized bv
government policies, among those who played a signal role in the
revolt, and among those whose blood was shed during the rebellion. Only time will reveal whether Konaré's rule will heal the
wounds and nourish justice and unity in Mali.

Or will Cissé need to produce yet another alarum to conscience? Will he be called on again as a cinematic diviner and
prophet?

Works Cited

Andriamirado, Sennen. "De la mediocrité a la boucherie." *Jeune
Afrique* April 3-9, 1991: 6-9.
Anderson, Martha G., and Christine Mullen Kreamer. *Wild
Spirits: Strong* Medicine: *African Art and* the *Wilderness.* Ed.
Enid Schildkrout. Seattle and New York: University of
Washington Press; New York Center for African Art, 1989.
Biloa, Marie-Roger. "Lumières d'Afrique à Cannes." *Jeune
Afrique* June 3, 1987: 46-49.
Bourgi, Albert. "Les raisons de la colére." *Jeune Afrique* April 3-
9, 1991: 10-11.
Carbonnier, Alain. "La l umière." *Cinema 87,* May 22, 1987: 6.
Caron, Alain. *"Yeelen."* *Jeune Cinema,* March 1988: 36-37.
Chevrie, Marc. "Il ètait une fois" *Cahiers du Cinema* 397 (1987):
35-38.
Diallo, Siradiou. "Les leçons de Bamako." *Jeune Afrique* April 3-
9, 1991: 12-13.

Diawara, Manthia. *African Cinema: Politics and Culture*. Bloomington and Indianapolis: Indiana University Press, 1992.

Dieterlen, Germaine, and Youssouf Cissé. *Les fondements de la société du Komo*. Paris: Mouton, 1972.

Heyman, Daniele. "Dans la lumière de *Yeelen*." *Le Monde* November 29-30, 1987: 10.

Imperato, Pascal James. *Buffoons, Queens, and Wooden Horsemen*: The Dyo and Gouan Societies of the Bambara of *Mali*. New York: Kilima House Publishers, 1983.

James, Caryn. "*Yeelen*, based on Myths from Mali." *New York Times* October 8, 1987: C37.

Lavigne, Nicole. "*Yeelen*." *Sequences* September 1988: 91-92.

Leahy, James. "*Yeelen* (The Light)." *Monthly Film Bulletin* 55.658 (1988): 343-44.

"Manifeste africain pour le Mali," *Jeune Afrique* April 3-9, 1991: 16.

McNaughton, Patrick R. *The Mande Blacksmiths: Knowledge, Power, and Art in West Africa*. Bloomington and Indianapolis: Indiana University Press, 1988.

—. *Secret Sculptures* of *Komo: Art and Power in Bamana (Bambara) Initiation Associations*. Philadelphia: Institute for the Study of Human Issues, 1979.

Sada, Hugo. "A bon entendeur salut!" *Jeune Afrique* April 3-9, 1991: 14-15.

Schissel, Howard. "No More Room for Maneuver." *Africa Report* 29.5 (1984): 63-68.

Taylor, Clyde. "Light from Darkness." *Arete* 2.5 (1990): 55-57.

Tesson, Charles. "Genèse." *Cahiers du Cinema* 397 June 1987: 10.

Yeelen. Dir. Souleymane Cissé. Cissé Films. American distr. Cinecom, 1987.

Zahan, Dominique. *The Bambara*. Leiden: E. J. Brill, 1974.

—. *The Religion, Spirituality, and Thought of Traditional Africa*. Trans. Kate Ezra and Lawrence M. Martin. Chicago: University of Chicago Press, 1979.

PART THREE

THE QUESTION OF NATIONAL CINEMAS

NIGERIAN CINEMA: STRUCTURAL ADJUSTMENTS[1]

BASIC CONDITIONS

NIGERIAN CINEMA PRESENTS AN INTERESTING, even striking contrast to the situation of cinema in other West African countries. To be sure, there are broad, structural similarities: Nigerian feature film production began in 1970, just a few years after the beginning of cinema in the francophone countries; the distribution system continues to be largely closed to indigenous filmmakers, supplying instead a diet of American, Indian, and Chinese films; local production is therefore starved for money and equipment, so that one cannot really talk of a film industry—production is artisanal, informal and sporadic.

The rate of production in Nigeria is at best about four 16 mm feature films in a year—that is, films shot on negative film stock. More work is being made using cheaper technologies, such as reversal film stock (from which no prints can be made), or video, which is then blown up to 16 mm. Including such films, something more than one hundred features have been produced in Nigeria (Ekwuazi 16-18; Adesanya, *Index,* 116-18). The material infrastructure for making films is about the same as in francophone West Africa, though the financial infrastructure is probably even less developed. The disastrous decline of the Nigerian Naira has made importation of materials and equipment, and foreign processing, astronomically expensive. Production in 35 mm has ceased almost entirely since the seventies, and is unlikely to resume on any scale until the economic situation improves.[2] But 16-mm equipment (not always in the best repair) and experienced profession-

als to run it are available locally, and there is easy access to equipment from abroad. It is now possible to produce a 16 mm film of
good technical quality entirely in Nigeria, importing only the film
stock, and to do most of the post-production work there as well
(Adesanya, "Production Infrastructure"). Facilities for processing
black and white film have been in place for a long time; a new
color processing facility (with a sound dubbing studio) belonging
to the Nigerian Film Corporation has recently (May 1992) been
opened in Jos. As long as the Jos facility remains fully functional
(there is some skepticism about its commercial viability), it will be
possible to make a film in Nigeria from start to finish. The video
resources in Lagos are considerable, with about twenty video production houses, and since a feature can be produced on video (for
distribution by videocassette) for about a tenth the price of a celluloid film, there has been a pervasive structural adjustment
towards video production.

One crucial difference between Nigerian and other West
African cinema is the autonomy, or isolation, of Nigerian cinema:
it has developed with very little influence or participation from
outside, and exporting of films is an insignificant aspect. The
British had a Colonial Film Unit which produced documentaries
and propaganda, thereby introducing some cinematic technology
and skills into the country, but neither before nor after
Independence did they give any encouragement to Nigerians to
make fictional feature films. This of course is in great contrast to
the role of the French Ministry of Cooperation and Development
in the development of African film in France's ex-colonies. And
this historical difference remains true to date. A major theme of the
1991 FESPACO film festival was "Partnership," between African
filmmakers and foreign, mainly European co-producers and distributors, who (with attendant journalists) were present in large
numbers. But the screenings of the First Nigerian National Film
Festival (in Lagos, December 1992) were, by my informal survey,
attended by approximately one foreigner.

In the early days of Nigerian film there was some connection
with African-Americans, notably Ossie Davis, who directed several films in Nigeria in the 1970s, including the first Nigerian feature, *Kongi's Harvest* (1970)[3], which was made with American
money (Ekwuazi, 24-6). The film's producer, Francis Oladele, an
important pioneer of Nigerian cinema, was trained in the US.
Another of the founders of Nigerian cinema, Chief Eddie

Ugbomah, continues to have American connections, and a number of other filmmakers have been trained abroad. Recently, at the end of his life, Chief Hubert Ogunde coproduced *Mr. Johnson* (1990) with the director Bruce Beresford and an American company. But such support and influence has really been very limited. From the beginning, Nigerian films have been produced almost exclusively with Nigerian money.

Relations with other African countries and the Pan-African filmmaking community have also been extremely attenuated—practically embodied in the person of Ola Balogun, Nigeria's leading director, who speaks French, was trained in Paris at the Institut des Hautes Etudes Cinématographiques (IDHEC), and has regularly appeared at FESPACO. Otherwise, few Nigerians have come to the Festival, although this situation seemed to be changing in 1993. Because it does not have a national organization of filmmakers, Nigeria does not participate in FEPACI (the Federation of Pan-African Filmmakers). Films from elsewhere in Africa are virtually never shown in Nigeria. Nigerian films penetrate the market in neighboring countries in a modest way, particularly where there are Yoruba speakers, but are generally unknown to filmmakers or film audiences elsewhere on the continent.

The positive side of the isolation of Nigerian cinema is that insofar as it exists it is truly independent and autonomous: there are no questions about what effect foreign money may be having on the artistic imagination. At the Workshop on Film Policy held by the Nigerian Film Corporation in Jos in May 1992, the director Ladi Ladebo was virtually alone in talking of the foreign market as an integral part of Nigerian filmmaking, to be taken into account from the beginning in the financial, technical, aesthetic, and thematic dimensions. Nigeria's sheer size and its cultural vibrancy are factors in this autonomy. Still, film is an international as well as national industry: always and everywhere film industries count on the export market as part of their economic strategy. The isolation of Nigerian film stunts it.

The initiatives undertaken by the government to foster an indigenous film industry are a history of failures.[4] A color-processing lab in Port Harcourt was never completed. The distribution system, which had been in the hands of Lebanese and Indians, was indigenized by decree in 1972, but this resulted merely in the acquisition of Nigerian fronts. Investors rushed into the new business of production in the mid '70s, and then rushed out again. The need for a legal environment of copyright and contract law is just beginning to be addressed (see Oladitan and Ekpo in Ekwuazi and Nasidi). Grandiose plans for facilities in Jos, including a cinema village, are motivated more by political and bureaucratic interests than by a calculation of what filmmakers really need. Ola and Françoise Balogun have argued cogently from the beginning that what the government should be doing, instead of launching huge state-run projects, is to establish economic conditions that would encourage independent production (Françoise Balogun, *Cinema*).

Economic motivations still encourage distributors to take for-eign films being dumped at very low prices rather than Nigerian films whose producers are trying to recover their whole costs on the local market: imported films cost the exhibitor around a fifth to a tenth of the daily rental Nigerian films must demand. The measures needed include waiving taxes on Nigerian films,[5] using monies derived from entertainment taxes to support a fund for film production, requiring that a quota of films shown in theaters be locally made, and so on.

THE SHAPE OF NIGERIAN FILM PRODUCTION

The first Nigerian fictional feature film, *Kongi's Harvest* (1970), was adapted from a play by Wole Soyinka, who played the lead character. The cast included a number of people who were or would become central figures in the Nigerian theater, cinema, and even academic life (Pa Orlando Martins, Wale Ogunyemi, Femi Johnson, and Dapo Adelugba). Politically committed (it is an allegory of African despotism) and drawing on a wealth of intellectual and artistic talent, the film seemed—whatever its faults—to augur the development of a sophisticated and engaged national cinema.

This kind of cinema has failed almost completely to materialize. From the beginning there were attempts to create a less intellectual cinema, which would appeal to a mass audience. Eddie Ugbomah's approach was to make movies influenced by American action or Blaxsploitation films, urban in setting and dealing with crime or political violence: *The Rise and Fall of Dr. Oyenusi* (1976), *The Mask* (1979), *Oil Doom* (1981), *Bolus '80* (1982), *The Boy is Good* (1982), *The Death of the Black President* (1983). Ola Balogun moved in another direction, working with artists from the Yoruba Travelling Theater.

Film production in English, never more than a trickle, has become sporadic indeed. There have been only a few films in Igbo or Hausa, the latter sometimes made with heavy government sponsorship, perhaps reflecting the Northern influence in Nigerian pol - itics, though there has been no real policy of government support for Hausa films. (Adamu Halilu's *Shehu Umar* [1976] was made from a novel by the first Prime Minister of Nigeria, Tafewa Balewa, and was produced by the National Government as Nigeria's offi - cial entry for FESTAC '77; Halilu's *Kanta of Kebbi* [1978] was co-produced by the Sokoto State Government. Neither of Halilu's epics were screened commercially [F. Balogun, *Cinema* 70-71].) It has been pointed out that all the films sponsored by the Federal Government have been in English or Hausa, and that none of them has ever recovered its production costs (Ekwuazi, 57, 70). The sponsorship by the Babangida Presidency of a big-budget film by Sule Umar on the coup against Murtala Mohammed is the latest example of this sort of project.

Meanwhile, while all other kinds of filmmaking sputtered out for lack of an economic base, there have been more than a hundred films made in Yoruba, a completely independent phenomenon, whose basis—including distribution, which has always been the heart of the problem for African film—is carried over from the theater.

The Yoruba films[6] grew straight out of the Yoruba Travelling Theater. This form of popular drama was created by the late Hubert Ogunde out of the traditional Alarinjo theater, with the addition of elements from the Ghanaian Concert Party and elsewhere. Its for - mal structure includes substantial elements of music and dance and even acrobatics, as well as drama, and it incorporates tradi - tional Yoruba metaphysical and religious beliefs. This form of drama was wildly popular with Yoruba audiences and drew crowds even in non-Yoruba areas. It is known as the Yoruba Travelling Theater because none of the troupes had a fixed home: they trav - eled constantly, performing in rented halls or wherever they could. Often the troupes were composed largely of members of the fam - ily of the principal actor/manager, who might marry his actresses. At one time (around 1980) there were about 100 such troupes (Jeyifo, *Yoruba,* 1).

Now it is difficult to see a performance of the Travelling Theater troupes, as all the major companies and many of the minor ones have switched over to making films. Some of the leading

troupes (e.g. Moses Olaiya's Alawada Theatre) became accustomed to working with cameras through television appearances
(Lakoju 39-40; Okome, *Rise,* 276, 297). As Karin Barber has
pointed out, television also "was a catalyst in the process of shed-
ding the older operatic format and replacing it with a streamlined
tightly articulated comedy style carried almost entirely by straight
dialogue" (*Radical Conservatism,* 8).

The midwife of the transition from stage to film was Ola
Balogun, who made the first Yoruba film, *Ajani Ogun*, in 1977,
with Duro Ladipo and his troupe, and starring Adeyemi Folayan
(known as Ade Love); Balogun also worked with Hubert Ogunde
and the other principal star of this tradition, the comic Moses
Olaiya Adejumo (known as Baba Sala). All of Ogunde's films—
Aiye (1979), *Jaiyesimi* (1980), *Aropin N' Tenia* (1982), and *Ayanmo*
(1988)—began life as stage plays (though they were sometimes
extensively transformed and rewritten, as *Aiye* was by Ola
Balogun); so have most of Moses Olaiya's (Okome, *Rise,* 290,
302-3; Ola Balogun, personal communication).

Soon there were a host of imitators. The companies discovered
that there was more money to be made from films. Now reduced
in size, but associating themselves with other companies to produce
the films, the troupes continue to travel with their films, as they are
still excluded from the normal film distribution system, though
they do sometimes rent cinema halls. The National Theatre in
Iganmu, Lagos, now shows Yoruba films on a regular basis, and
Moses Olaiya owns a theater in Ibadan, which shows other Yoruba
films besides his own. But for the most part they screen the films
elsewhere: in hotels, schools, town halls, and so on. The company,
or some part of it, has to travel with the film because if they are not
there in person they will be cheated out of their share of ticket
sales. For similar reasons they generally put their work on film
rather than on videocassettes, for showing in the legion video par-
lors. Widespread piracy means the films are kept in the jealous
possession of the theater companies, whose presence at the screenings in any case makes for good publicity. The films are advertised
on television and radio, as well as by posters and sound trucks
making their way through popular neighborhoods.

Alain Ricard has pointed out very well the advantages and lia-
bilities of this system of distribution. On the one hand, the
actor/manager has the name and perhaps already has the resources
to capitalize a production. The circuit of distribution is already in

148

place, and those from whom he rents halls are used to treating him with the respect his popularity commands. He does not need to trust them or any intermediaries to handle his business for him, because he is on hand to oversee everything. All he needs to do is load a projector onto his vehicle as he sets out on tour, and so "the producer becomes his own distributor and realizes at a more or less artisanal level the vertical integration typical of capitalist suc - cesses in the cinema industry" (Ricard, 163).[7]

But, Ricard goes on, this system does not work at all for exporting films, where it is necessary to make copies of the films, manage their distribution and exhibition at a distance, and thus

> Employ an industrial and commercial know-how that a family enterprise of the popular theater, however prosperous it may be, doesn't have at its disposal. The structures of local exhibition are in place and easy to control: the international market remains inaccessible.[8] (164)

The Yoruba Travelling Theater filmmakers have shown remarkable entrepreneurship in distributing their films as far away as the Benin Republic and the Côte d'Ivoire, but their system does reach its limit. They also run into a language barrier: unlike francophone filmmakers, who may get their films subtitled in French at the expense of the French Ministry of Cooperation and Development, thereby giving them access to a much larger market, the Yoruba filmmakers get no help with subtitling and find it prohibitively expensive.

The system carries with it an aesthetic problem as well, as Ricard says:

> The principal failure of such a system, beyond its unexportable character, is thus to place the cinema entirely under the dom - ination of theater people, to make of cinema the servant of the theater. Now the principal features of this type of theater, notably the star system, and the taste for actors' "numbers," are part of the dramatic style of the popular theater and cannot pass onto the screen without transposition. And if the star is at the same time producer and distributor, the film director has no chance to voice a critical point of view, supposing he has one, and that he is concerned with adaptation for the screen and not with filming theater. (164)

Françoise Balogun's account of Ola Balogun's work with the Yoruba Theater people in *The Cinema in Nigeria* is a running complaint along these lines. Because they are successful enough—in some cases, wildly successful—with filmed theater, the theater people see little reason to move towards a more truly cinematic film language. This aesthetic blockage reinforces and is reinforced by the commercial blockage that stops the films at (or not far beyond) Nigeria's borders: the Yoruba films are not exportable because in most cases they do not meet the world's minimum cinematic standards, technically or stylistically.

Nevertheless, the conjunction of Ola Balogun with Hubert Ogunde and the others was of great symbolic as well as practical importance: the intellectual director embraced a popular and indigenous form, and thereby gained access to an enormous, enthusiastic, and unalienated audience, which simply followed their beloved actors into the new medium of cinema. The problem of establishing rapport with the audience, which took time to resolve in the francophone countries, evaporated.

THE DESCENT FROM PA OGUNDE

A principal genre of the Yoruba films is the costume drama, which aims to recapture the vanished splendor of traditional Yoruba culture in all its metaphysical, social and aesthetic integrity. It relies heavily on dancing and music and recreated festivals to do so; the visual aspect of these films can be stunning. Both the theme and the multi-media treatment are extensions of the Travelling Theater, as pioneered by Ogunde.

The films of the late Hubert Ogunde have enormous symbolic status for their audience. They are shown on holidays, like Sallah; the films themselves have a quasi-religious status. Ogunde is entirely identified with the character he plays in the films, Osetura, a benign and powerful priest who leads and defends his community and communicates on its behalf with supernatural forces. His first film, *Aiye* (1979, directed by Ola Balogun), begins with him leading a procession to the sacred iroko tree, where his sacrifices on behalf of the community are accepted, and where he does a fertility dance, to their acclamation. His last film, *Ayanmo* (1988), is even more clearly metaphysical in its dimensions: it opens with scenes in a witches' hell and a heavenly supernatural realm. Both films tell essentially the same story: witches disrupt the happiness of the community, until Osetura intervenes to defeat them. They both have the same narrative structure as well: we follow many parallel stories, through rapid cross editing; in each situation the witches bring confusion and disaster. The fragmented narrative structure helps compensate for the simplicity of the story. The total effect is of a unified but various worlds, a sense of the collective life of the village.

This world is idyllic, at least before the witches—a basically external force come to disrupt it. The idyll is at once cultural, social, and religious, and it is conveyed through a continuous aes - thetic heightening. Ogunde built a cinema village in his home town, a recreation of a traditional village, with the normal inflation of film sets: the buildings are more spacious than one would expect, everything is perfectly clean, costumes are authentic, but nothing looks lived in. Lighting and camera angles are carefully designed for aesthetic effect. Much of the screen time is taken up with music and dancing, or ceremonies of one kind or another. There are scenes of ordinary daily life, but they seldom last long before they are taken over by something else: women going to a pond to fetch water are apt to start singing and dancing, for example.

The charismatic, gap-toothed, benevolent Ogunde/Osetura is the patriarchal embodiment of all values. He is always imper - turbable, and invincible once he has begun to act. The audience applauds when he consults his vision pool to discover what the witches are up to, because the matter is now as good as settled— once he knows, it is inconceivable that he will not triumph, and that without any haste that would break his composure.

The ideological meaning of Ogunde's films is clear. They are nostalgic, aiming at restoring a pre-existing stasis; their world-view claims to be whole and intact. This in itself marks them as an ideological construct for conservative purposes, and is in strong contrast with the dialogized, fragmented, and multiple con-sciousness that goes with modern urban life. The films deal with the crisis that modernity has brought to the traditional Yoruba world by denying it. This accounts for their psychosocial power and even necessity, but also for their limitations. Hyginus Ekwuazi attacks this kind of film in the following terms:

> On the African screen, especially in the African folklorist cin-ema, culture takes the form of dance, of festivals. These dances and festivals, held up to the audience as flash cards for pre-

dictable reactions, bear only a tangential relationship to the action. The African atmosphere, the African mind, to wit, the African personality or culture, becomes a battle cry, the motif for political sloganeering as art. The familiar cliches heap up till well nigh breaking point: the *joie de vivre* of the African, the comely beauty of African maidenhood, the idyll of village life— the cliches pile up in a series of contrived situations which stick out like a sore thumb. (79)

One can trace a line of descent from Ogunde's films to the present. *Fopomoyo/Chaos* (1991), directed and written by the veteran actor Jimoh Aliu, is also set in an elaborately rendered traditional setting, where the coronation of a king (played by King Sunny Ade) and the life of the town in general are disrupted by the wicked Fadeyi "The Terror" (played by Ojo Arowosafe), in alliance with witches and, ultimately, the god Esu. The king (who does almost nothing himself, beyond maintaining his tranquility in the face of calamities) has as his champion Orisabunmi, the priestess of the Mother of the Osun River. The goddess herself ultimately inter-venes to kill the wicked Fadeyi. Again we are in a world densely saturated with cultural meanings. Again the conflict is a simple Manichean struggle of good against evil, which is identified with chaos. The aesthetic and technical quality of this film is also high. The crosscutting is abundant and moves even faster than in Ogunde's films; the scenes are rapid and packed. There are signs of careful overall design: the actors are under firm control, and the film must have been tightly scripted, with little room for the improvisation which is normal in the Travelling Theater tradition and the films that spring from it.

Though the religious element in *Fopomoyo* is strong, it seems less hieratic in its intentions than Ogunde's films—less interested in revealing religious truths than in using the supernatural to add a dimension to an action plot. It has much more dramatic sub-stance as a depiction of a battle between contending forces, full of reversals and so on, organizing tension and suspense in the man-ner of action pictures. It also seems to have a revisionist political agenda: in contrast to the absolute patriarchalism of Ogunde, here it is women who play the most active and decisive roles, notably the heroic priestess Orisabunmi, and a band of warrior women who defeat the party of evil when the men have failed to do so.

The evil Fadeyi also appears in a more recent film, *Agbo Meji/ The Two Forces* (1992), directed by Dr. Ola Makinwa. His antagonist Abija is another character the audience recognizes from other films (just as Ogunde always played Osetura, and Moses Olaiya Adejumo is always Baba Sala).[9] In the film, a king praying before an annual sacrifice is given two injunctions: he must sacrifice the child of one of his chiefs, and no strangers are to be allowed to enter the town during this period. The chiefs, comically disconcerted, decide a cow should be substituted, and the king (another weak figure) goes along; he also orders hospitality be granted to Fadeyi, who has appeared first as a corpse lying in a field, and then as an ominous stalking presence who intrudes into the king's court. When the king's daughter suddenly dies, Fadeyi brings her back to life, and she is given to him as his reward. A dreadful spirit orders him to sacrifice the two children he has by the king's daughter, and he does so. His unhappy wife joins a witches' coven to seek revenge but he overpowers her. His evil becomes more and more rampant; finally he bewitches the whole village and leads them off with him. At this point the good magician Abija intervenes. As his reward for bringing back the villagers he is given a chief's daughter, whom Fadeyi has been chasing. Fadeyi appears and kills the girl; a duel of incantations between Fadeyi and Abija is interrupted by the apparition of the goddess, who orders both of them to go back to the supernatural realm they came from. She explains that the dead girl is the sacrifice she had demanded, but that henceforth there should be no more human sacrifice.

Agbo Meji is an example of the dramatic power a juju tale can have. The religious dimension has been reduced pretty much to a formula and a frame, which permits the displays of magic. *Agbo Meji* is also an example of the aesthetics of SAP (Nigeria's Structural Adjustment Program, which has wreaked havoc on the economy since the mid 1980s). The washed-out colors and grainy scintillation of the images are the result of having been shot on video and blown up to 16 mm. The traditional setting is merely an ordinary Yoruba village filmed very much as it was found—there is nothing fancy about the houses or the costumes, no aesthetic heightening of traditional culture. The film displays the weaknesses of the Travelling Theater style. The editing and continuity are rough, though some of the violations of the (Western) canons of film language may be the result of the influence of oral tradition (as when Fadeyi is married to the king's daughter in one scene, and in the next, without transition, they suddenly have two children). Many of the actors are well-known professionals with a great deal of presence on screen, though—as is typical of all the actors who have moved over from the stage—their style is broad and theatrical, which comes across as overstated and crude in the very different medium of cinema. And there is weak directing and some very poor acting as well, as for example the contrived bulging eyes and bared teeth of the dancing witches in their coven. This film's budget does not allow it to approach the production values of Ogunde's films, nor does it seem to be aiming at their aesthetic standard.

There is actually a great range in the professionalism of current Yoruba film production. In some the acting, camera work, and so on are sophisticated and completely professional—for instance *Eri Okan (Conscience)* (1990), directed by Tunde Oloyede, or Baba Balogun's *Orogun Orun*, which premiered at the end of 1992 at the National Theatre. In both cases, significantly, the director had considerable experience in television. But there is a large class of films more modest even than *Agbo Meji* in their artistic ambitions, the issue of the Travelling Theater methods of production, the dire economics of SAP, and the spirit of Nigerian capitalism, which is to make money fast on a small investment. The Travelling Theaters have always had the character of small, informal sector businesses, looking for rapid but small returns on a minimal investment in equipment and training (Barber, *Radical Conservatism,* 7). Many of the films being made now are shot as cheaply as possible, without properly trained technicians, with abysmal results. They are also shot as rapidly as possible, with minimal rehearsals or attention to script (which is usually sketchy or non-existent in the Travelling Theater tradition). They are blown up from video onto 16 mm, or they may well be shot on 16 mm reversal stock, which results in a single, unreproducible print; when this print wears out, it is time to make another film. Techniques like color balancing are impossible in the reversal process; outdated film stock or chemicals may further degrade the quality of the color. Other dramas are shot on video, in conjunction with a video production house, and are marketed as cassettes, on sale in video stores and stalls. Some of these videos are quite successful within their scope, particularly if a strong actor carries them—for example the comedies of Jagua (like *Commander,* Parts I and II, which are in Pidgin but otherwise are comparable to the Yoruba productions); others are very poor.

As an example of the most absolute modesty, let us take the video *Ija Ebi Bi Ojo Wahala/Wrongful Strife Cause [sic] Troublesome-Rain*. The actor/characters include Abija (from *Agbo Meji*) and Orisabunmi (from *Fopomoyo*). It tells a simple story, about juju. There is a land dispute in a village; the king's arbitra-tion fails; the villain and his wife attack their opponent and ulti-mately the whole village with their powerful juju charms, but are finally defeated by the good juju of the hero and heroine. The moral is equally simple: bad magic is bad, especially in the serv-ice of uncontrolled greed; good magic is good, and obviously nec-essary.

The tin roofs of the village houses are the only sign of the modern world; on the other hand we do not see any objects or institutions so identified with the historical past that they are not still ubiquitous in Nigeria. The point is that the setting is not par-ticularly "historical"; it is taken entirely for granted. It is not glam-orized in the slightest—in fact one might be tempted to make a crit-ical connection between the obsession with occult powers and the obvious poverty of the village, but this is clearly not intended either. The true interpretation of the setting is probably that it was the cheapest one possible. The total production costs of this video appear to be whatever the cast was paid and the rental of one video camera. The whole thing is shot outside village houses or in the bush, with no interior shots, no lighting (the automatic lighting adjustment on the video camera creates a halo around figures as they enter the darkness of their doors), no costumes the actors probably did not already own, no musical production numbers. The handling of the video camera and sound recording are ama-teurish.

Nevertheless, the setting must necessarily also illustrate a worldview, and its treatment a kind of cultural politics. The world-view is the traditional Yoruba one, although its dimensions are shrunken. The film does not register any sense of historical change. The magical universe is simply there, as the traditional social world is, as if they were the most natural thing in the world to find on screen at the end of the 20th century.

Things have shifted considerably from films like those Ola Balogun made with Ogunde and the others, which glorified and defended African culture and the African past in (unspoken) reaction to the crisis of the present, making the audience proud of where they come from and giving them something in which to believe. The very importation of foreign technicians and the employment of a highly trained director were ways of dignifying the subject matter, making sure it was presented in a way that could represent Africa on the world stage, or rather, world screens. In *Ija Ebi Bi Ojo Wahala* the element of cultural/political polemic indicated by Ekwuazi is entirely missing.

Afolabi Adesanya's *Ose Sango/Sango's Wand* (1991) is interesting in this context. The director was educated at the San Francisco Art Institute and is bright, young, practical, and ambitious. He has chosen to immerse himself in the ethos of the Yoruba films, and *Ose Sango* is entirely devoted to occult matters. But here there are signs if not of alienation at least of self-consciousness in the face of the relationship of juju and modernity. In the film the power of the occult is measured against that of the legal system and of a scientific laboratory in the National Museum, and a crucial episode takes place when Sango worshipers come to perform their rites at the statue of Sango in front of the Nigerian Electrical Power Authority offices in downtown Lagos. The filmmaker is perhaps trying to exorcise his own skepticism by staging repeated triumphs of the magical.

Many other Yoruba films have a modern setting—they are mostly domestic tales in a moralistic framework, with an important element of juju. Magical effects are easy to produce in film, and it is rare to find a Yoruba film, which does not exploit them. Magical duels are also an easy way of creating dramatic tension—easier and cheaper to stage than American-style car chases, or elaborately choreographed Chinese-style martial combats. On the evidence of the films one would conclude that the lives and imaginations of contemporary Yoruba are dominated by juju. It obviously strikes a chord with the audience, whose explanation involves more than their supposed backwardness.

The "tradition" of a film like *Ija Ebi Bi Ojo Wahala* is a narrowed and decayed version, in which religion is reduced to magic. This is a transformation typical of the culture of the newly urbanized or otherwise disoriented. Modernity has not brought with it a decline in "superstition"; magic, as a way of explaining and controlling the world, is turned to more than ever in a situation in which people feel powerless and psychologically threatened by a breakdown of the accustomed cultural order. Juju is also the spiritual least common denominator in the multi-ethnic cultural melange of the cities, where the full ritual expression of religious beliefs, as once elaborated in the villages, is not possible, but where everyone sees the point in a method of getting back a husband or revenging one's self against a wicked employer.

The Yoruba filmmakers generally are not alienated intellectu - als trying to recapture their roots—theirs is a truly popular (or at least, "people's") form, as is the Travelling Theater.[10] Their inten- tions are, above all, commercial. They want to please their audi - ence, and their audience likes music, dance, festivals, comely maidens, and, especially, juju. The demand is predictable, and such stuff is easy to package and deliver. In the process it may very well become alienated; but it is the alienation of a commer - cial commodity, not of a colonized intellectual.

There is a body of opinion in Nigeria that holds that the empha - sis on juju is decadent, culturally backward, and stale. Even Moses Olaiya (Baba Sala) agrees:

> Maybe they are trying to copy our stage production and because it is making very good market, many of us are trying to follow the footsteps of (late) Pa (Hubert) Ogunde. For this reason every filmmaker applies witchcraft and magic in his film. It is becoming monotonous. This must be minimized….(Olaiya 25)

So also Niyi Osundare: "One of the flaws from the problem of presenting the supernatural cinematographically…is (the) pan - dering to the clamorous but misguided call for the exotic in culture, a facile glamorization of our disappearing past. The Nigerian film has yet to catch-up with the dynamics of Nigerian life and estab- lish its relevance to the Nigerian condition" (826).

The comic films do better at this, if only because of the tradi - tional function of comedy to hold a mirror up to contemporary society.

BABA SALA SAPPED

In the career of Moses Olaiya Adejumo, known as Baba Sala, there is an evolution parallel to the descent from Ogunde I have just traced. For his first film, *Orun Mooru/Heaven is Hot* (1982), he enlisted (as had Ogunde and Ade Folayan) the help of Ola Balogun as director, co-producer and co-script writer. The film was made with a big budget and opened with lavish publicity. It begins with Baba Sala living in a fishing village as a basket-maker, amusing himself by chasing women. A visit from an old friend provides the occasion for a flashback to better days when he had a shop in town selling electrical appliances. A babalawo (herbalist) tricked him into believing he could fill oil drums with money; this led to an ecstasy of grief, ruin, and the move to the village. Now his visitor, Adisa, loans him -N-500. Baba Sala interrupts his dance of joy to close his door and worry about where to hide the money. In the event, he loses it all, half to a pickpocket in town, and the other half when his new wife unwittingly trades the old container where he has hidden the rest for some new plates. In despair, he throws himself off a bridge, and finds himself in the underworld.

The underworld is represented with the help of special-effects trickery and the striking neo-traditional sculpture and architecture of the Grove of Osun at Oshogbo. Death tells him he is not ready to take him, and Baba Sala ascends to meet the Queen of Joy at her shrine surrounded by dancers. She sends him off with two magical eggs, and two of her disciples meet him on the beach of this world when he is cast up upon it, escorting him to an extravagant mansion. He cavorts with the two girls in the bedroom (in his childish, roly-poly, sexless way), and breaks one of the eggs on the floor, whereupon it turns into a huge pile of money—the magical wealth the babalawo had falsely promised him. He joins a big party downstairs, where the Juju musician King Sunny Ade is entertaining the guests, and is generally the center of attention in a wild ego fantasy. He returns upstairs and breaks the second egg, in spite of an injunction not to do so, at which point Death appears. Then we find Baba Sala coming to in his shack in the fishing village, with a flashback of his having been fished out of the water under the bridge from which he had thrown himself.

The themes of over-reaching greed and wild swings from village life to lavish prosperity and back again are close to the heart of the Nigerian national experience during the oil boom years. The oil drums, which are to be magically filled with cash, are a clear enough figure for "Petro-Naira" (see Barber, *Popular Reactions*). Propelled by his feckless moral will, Baba Sala bounces among four sharply opposed realms. One is the village, a pretty traditional place; this is where he wakes up with a hangover after the mad story is over, and it is also where Baba Sala is at his most relaxed and attractive, though the film does not go in for a moralizing polemic in favor of rural values. The town is lively and entertain-ing, but a place where desire (for upward mobility) can slip on treacherous ground: it is where Baba Sala gets cheated—twice, first by the babalawo and then by the pickpocket. The fantasy villa is still more unstable, because fundamentally unreal, although it is perfectly attractive as far as it goes; the pleasures it affords (notably King Sunny Ade's performance and the party surrounding it) are pleasures for the audience too. The metaphysical dimension is not introduced with any great solemnity (Baba Sala clowns his way through the sacred grove with labile, childish curiosity), but it adds depth and scope to the film, culturally as well as morally. In spite of the unhappiness of Baba Sala's own adventures, the film feels expansive, and reflects the buoyant outlook of Nigeria before the crash: the modern world was full of possibilities, and the tradi-tional realms of religion and art were there to back up and guide one's posture in it, if only one could pause from a career of tear-ing greed.

This was an extremely successful film, but a copy of it was bootlegged. Olaiya himself produced, directed, and scripted his next film, *Aare Agbaiye* (1983). The result was a precipitous decline in technical quality. The story once again involves over-reaching greed: a poor man becomes king through magical means, tries to become equal to the gods, and ends up in hell.

Mosebolatan/Hopelessness (1986) was made with the assis-tance of the fine (and prolific) cinematographer Tunde Kelani—Olaiya's Alawada Movies produced, and Ade Folayan (Ade Love) directed very competently. Olaiya/Baba Sala plays his usual role as a lecherous miser. The plot is large and complex. The family of Mosebolatan, Baba Sala's friend, was split up in a boat wreck; Mosebolatan has become a wealthy businessman, and his son, Jide, is an officer on a ship, while (unknown to them) his wife has become a market woman in the same town, struggling to put her daughter Shade through school. Baba Sala's son is in love with Shade, though his father won't hear of the match with a poor woman's daughter. Meanwhile Mosebolatan's son, Jide, rescues Baba Sala's daughter, Sala, and, since Baba Sala will not allow her visitors, Jide takes a job in his household as driver/cook/stew-ard, pandering to the father's miserly fantasies so he can court the daughter. Eventually the two fathers discover the lovers; then fol-lows a "recognition" scene in which everyone's identity is established. Mosebolatan's family is reunited, and the two marriages are contracted.[11]

The setting of *Mosebolatan* is very modern. Baba Sala and Mosebolatan are nouveaux riches on a grand scale, living in spa-cious mansions: Mosebolatan has a huge warehouse, and Baba Sala a large appliance store, larger than the one in *Orun Mooru* (in both films, as in the later *Agba Man*, he casts himself as a busi-nessman—which is what Moses Olaiya Adejumo is in fact, as owner/manager of his company). Mosebolatan is wholly good, and is irresponsible towards half his family only through a trick of fate. But Baba Sala is irresponsibility itself. His business is built on sharp practices, as we see at the film's beginning, where we also get a taste of his ways of getting himself into trouble with women. Later, as Chief Launcher at a benefit concert, he is unwill-ing to shoulder the responsibilities that come with his status.

This film seems to be more consciously contemporaneous than *Orun Mooru* is. When his cash box is stolen, Baba Sala has motor park touts tie his son to a stake in front of a wall of oil drums, like the armed robbers who were executed on Bar Beach; he some-times wears a Nike T-shirt, while Jide wears a Manchester United cap, as signs of the changing times. Other foreign elements are absorbed into the sophisticated soup of this film: Jide and Sala have several love duets obviously inspired by Indian films, and an early chase scene, in which Baba Sala swivels a road sign to throw off the pursuing police, draws on the tradition of American silent films. There are other, characteristically Nigerian elements, which may owe something to the revue-like aspects of the Travelling Theater performances: as in *Orun Mooru*, there is a long scene at a lavish party, where famous musicians play (in this case, their names appear on screen as titles), and Baba Sala (as Chief Launcher) pastes money on their foreheads.

Orun Mooru and *Mosebolatan* represent, in retrospect, the high-water mark of Nigerian film comedy, and deserve their great popularity. Baba Sala's personality and excellent acting are at the center of things, but are set in a rich, various, and well-structured comic world. In spite of the theatrical derivation of many of their elements, the films are fully cinematic in design and execution, and their high production values (e.g. the performances by musi-cians who are major stars in their own right) would not have been possible on stage.

Two of Olaiya's recent productions on video, *Agba Man* (1992) and *Return Match* (1993) (both in Yoruba, despite their titles), illustrate a dire degradation of means, and a contraction of artistic imagination. Writing, directing, and producing himself, Olaiya employed a small cast composed essentially of his core troupe. The video work is crude: there is no attention to direction or cin-ematography, no crane shots or special effects beyond amateurish freeze frames and video keying between scenes. Rank commer-cialization obtrudes: the name and address of AMCO Video Films, the video production house, scroll up the screen throughout the films. In *Agba Man* there are various internal advertisements: the locations are paid for by advertising them (the camera dwelling on a restaurant's sign board, for instance); near the beginning when the conversation turns to invitations to a birthday party, Baba Sala rec-ommends a specific printer by name and gives his address; later there are advertisements for Betamalt and Mayor Beer.

Both these films are comedies of sexual intrigue, but in *Agba Man* Baba Sala is at the center of things; in *Return Match* he is peripheral, playing a comic servant in a household where the wife is having an affair with a man who turns out to be her husband's friend. The two films display different halves of Baba Sala's nor-mal character. In *Agba Man* his miserliness and lecherousness is given full play; in *Return Match* he grabs the housemaid when he can, but the emphasis is on his goofy costumes and his strain of absurdist humor—he sticks the baby in the refrigerator, reverses the terms of a prescription, tries to jump into Madam's arms, and so on. The setting and aesthetic of *Return Match*, and its moralistic plot, are very much like those of the Nigerian bourgeois TV seri-als, though without so much glamorization of wealth.

In *Agba Man* Baba Sala is a businessman who spends his time chasing girls, and jealously trying to prevent his son and daughter from having romantic relationships. As usual Baba Sala is both miser and lecher; all his relationships with women are based on hard-nosed negotiations over how much sexual favors will cost. As in *Mosebolatan* his daughter Sala's boyfriend must resort to dis-guises to get into her house, and Baba Sala is miserly about his son's entertaining his girlfriends. Lovers still sing Indian-style duets, of worse quality than ever. As in the other films there are party scenes, with Baba Sala circulating, spraying the musicians with money, though now they are on a much more modest scale: a birthday party at the Sonnyville Restaurant, with three break

dancers performing to Tina Turner's music on a fancy sound system; a dance at a beer parlor, with a live band. Baba Sala is still
moving with the times, the musical styles and clothing absolutely
contemporary. This film, in fact, seems more realistic than the others, in the sense of being closer to the quotidian life we see on the
streets, though this is probably just the effect of the low budget,
which does not permit the more spacious recreations of cinema. A
certain theatricality hangs around Baba Sala's own character—he
is always the performer, and always "on"—but not around anyone
else; the locations never feel like sets.

In comparison to the earlier films, *Agba Man* seems claustro-
phobic. Baba Sala is still wearing his crazy outfits, and he keeps
up an endless comic patter, but in an atmosphere of slapstick farce
and fabliau-style intrigue, the cruelest forms of comedy. The element of fantasy and imagination has contracted drastically—there
is nothing like the Oshogbo artistic element in *Orun Mooru*, or its
metaphysical dimension, or the aesthetic self-consciousness and
variety of *Mosebolatan*. His character has shrunk too—certainly
shrunk from the cheerful satyr of *Orun Mooru*, so full of genial-
ity and playfulness, whose lust for money and sex are the expressions of an untrammeled childish ego. Now there is a hard ball of
selfish greed inside him, and not much else. This film is pitiless
towards its own character.

In *Agba Man,* Baba Sala's desire is comic but degrading. The
multiple plots are always and directly about the joyless purchase of
sex. Most of all his desire is preternaturally persistent, leading to a
potentially infinite proliferation of plots, all of the same kind, as his
girlfriends multiply. These stories always come to a humiliating
denouement. The young whom he is exploiting have seamy imaginations and desires of their own, and are better masters of deception.
The plots involving his children are the most unsavory. It turns out
both father and son have been having affairs with and are engaged to
the same woman, Segi. In the end her father drives them both off. And
finally, in a brothel, Baba Sala is brought in to his own daughter. His
friend Adisa is on hand to tell him he has gotten what he deserves.
He has been a sugar daddy, and his daughter has chosen to be a sugar
baby. He has learned his lesson the hard way.

A nasty kind of comedy, but in its very nastiness it conveys a
strong satire on the Nigerian business class and its parasitic attendants. Baba Sala's accumulation of girlfriends is hardly an unre-
alistic element; his greed is the greed of a class, which leads mul-

tiple lives with multiple women, enjoying the advantages that irresponsible wealth brings. Baba Sala's caricatures of western dress, his symbolic Mercedes, his patronage of entertainment spots, all are references to the behavior of a specific class in a specific set - ting; always the comedian of impossible desire, his miser is no archetype floating through history.

How much of this critique is intended, and how much is it an accident of the low budget and a mood to suit the hard times? The challenge for criticism is to neither exaggerate nor minimize the critical potential of populist cinema.

POPULISM AND A NATIONAL CINEMA

The Nigerian Film Corporation Workshop on Film Policy in May 1992 revealed a marked division—indeed antagonism—between the Yoruba filmmakers on the one hand and the bureaucrats, aca - demics, and intellectual filmmakers on the other. The Yoruba film - makers were well aware that they had created a viable and even flourishing popular cinema, with absolutely no help from anyone, and resented having their deficiencies pointed out by people who had never made films, or made money. On the other side, embar - rassment and chagrin at finding that Nigerian cinema had come to mean atrociously made films about witchdoctors and adultery led to proposals for censorship, including one suggestion that films liable to convey a negative image of Nigeria abroad, through their technical quality and/or cultural content, be denied a license nec - essary for exporting the film.

This antagonism is unfortunate: one will not truly be able to speak of Nigerian Film until the rift between the Yoruba film - makers and the rest of the filmmaking community is overcome. Both sides clearly need one another in order to progress. For those who look to cinema to exercise a progressive political and social function, the sole redeeming feature of the Yoruba cinema may be simply the fact of its existence. If it suffers all the characteristic lim - itations of populism, it is at least cinema of the people, by the peo - ple, for the people, expressing their consciousness, and it bears the promise of a future industry. As the television director Lola Fani-Kayode said at the Jos Workshop, the most important thing now is simply that Nigerian films exist: all other questions are sec - ondary. True, but that does not mean the other questions are not important, and intractable.

The Yoruba filmmakers generally have limited formal education, and tend to be apolitical. I have already said something about
the conservativeness, or evasiveness, of the films on metaphysical
subjects. As in Indian or American films, the representation of the
contemporary bourgeoisie is largely uncritical—and, as in those
films, the world represented on screen is typically one of ostenta -
tious luxury, which serves as an advertisement for bourgeois val -
ues and an incentive to accumulation. What criticism there is of the
rapacious primitive accumulation and rampant corruption and
greed which have dominated the scene in Nigeria since
Independence tends to be either moralistic (and may well be mixed
up with juju—e.g., a wicked wife gets a babalawo to help her take
over her husband's property) or comic (Baba Sala's misers). There
is never anything like a systematic analysis of the situation, or the
suggestion of a political alternative. The filmmakers can express
the popular imagination, providing it with themes and symbols,
but cannot show the way forward.

The rhetoric of the Nigerian Film Corporation—for instance
in the draft for a Film Policy circulated at the Jos Workshop—is
full of nationalist concern for Nigeria's image abroad, countering
racist stereotypes, and so on. Then military President Babangida,
the Minister of Culture, and such people echoed these sentiments
in speeches to the Workshop, when they talked of the importance
of establishing a film industry in Nigeria. These points take on
added force in a situation where a new flood of images from
abroad, transmitted by satellite and videocassettes, threatens to
bury the self-created image of Africans altogether. Filmmakers
like Ladi Ladebo, Kunle Balogun, and others talked in the same
way. Ladebo writes,

> Everyone seems to be in agreement as to what commercial film
> content ought to be. We all agree that our locally made films
> should present the facts of life in Nigeria so that others may
> appreciate and understand those things that may appear strange
> or ridiculous. It is only natural for us to be uncompromising in
> our objective of using our films for positive self-projection.
> (153)

But this is essentially the only political role accorded to film, and
it is conceived of in very conservative terms. The adopted *Film
Policy for Nigeria* calls for the State, through legislation, to:

- Encourage the exploitation of our heroic past and cultural heritage in the production of films, designed for both local and external consumption;
- Encourage the adoption of themes which shall emphasize the desirable, rather than the negative aspects of our present social existence, including belief in the capacity of our people to overcome extreme adverse conditions of nature and socio-cultural arrangement....(6)

It continues in this vein. If one compares this with, say, the film policy enunciated by the Federation of Pan-African Filmmakers in the Charter of Algiers, which calls for film to be used as a means to teach the people to think critically and to mobilize them to polit - ical action for the liberation of the African continent, one sees how conservative this agenda is. The concerns are roughly those of the pre-independence Negritude movement: counter racist images, provide role models Africans can be proud of, dust off and dress up traditional values. Film is not supposed to *do* anything within society except make it generally better through the gentle suasion of noble examples. There is a recurrent, even obsessive, concern for producing a positive image for foreigners. The propaganda concerns of the government intersect here with the old-fashioned inferiority complexes of the Western-educated intellectuals.

This remarkable consensus about the political and cultural pur - poses of film production presents an extreme contrast to the rest of the Nigerian cultural scene—where Negritudinist ideas were never very influential. The emphasis of contemporary literature has shifted decisively away from recapturing the past or dealing with the colonial legacy to the description and analysis of the sorry state to which Nigeria's leaders have brought the nation. The leading playwrights of the second generation—Femi Osofisan, Bode Sowande—are overtly political, and their stance is (or was) revo - lutionary. The years of SAP have produced a new generation of artists whose bitterness and impoverishment have created a new aesthetic of hunger and rage, expressed most eloquently by their poets.

This radical position was entirely unrepresented at the Jos Workshop, where the absence of the politicized figures from the '70s era was noticeable: Balogun, Ugbomah, Soyinka, whose *Blues for a Prodigal* with its "underground" alienated aesthetic might have been (despite all its failings as a film) a model for the SAP generation. But it was a forerunner with no successors.

SOME OTHER FIGURES

In spite of all the difficulties, a few films do get made, outside of the Travelling Theater mode; the following profiles of four direc-tors show something of the conditions of possibility that currently exist.

Afolabi Adesanya has already been mentioned, as a (foreign) educated filmmaker who has attached himself to the Travelling Theater mode of filmmaking. His first film, *Vigilante* (1988), made with his brother Adedeji (who directed), was a different sort of thing: made in English and Pidgin, it addressed a topical social issue—the crime wave in Lagos, and vigilantism as a response to it—and did so with a light touch, compounded of elements of social comedy and action-picture drama. One would have supposed this would be a canny formula, exactly the sort of thing Nigeria needed, and that success would follow. But the film did not do terribly well. Adesanya points to several reasons for this. The middle class audience which the film targeted simply will not come out to see films anymore, partly because of the crime which is the film's theme—they are happier at home with their VCRs. The popular film-going audience was disconcerted that the film was in English: since all the names on the poster were Yoruba, they expected a Yoruba film in the familiar mode and did not know quite how to relate to what they were seeing.

Adesanya's conclusion was that there was no market for English language films in Nigeria—that an ethnic base was nec-essary.[12] *Ose Sango*, therefore, is in Yoruba, is all about the super-natural, and stars actors from the Travelling Theater. This is a new breed of Yoruba juju film, with a modernized thematic and sym-bolic structure. Adesanya distributes it in the old way, carrying it around in a vehicle with a projector and a crew, which is time-consuming, but viable. The rest of his time is spent in less artisanal pursuits, like directing pilots for TV, or working on his useful *Nigerian Film/TV Index*.

Ladi Ladebo was connected as a producer and/or scriptwriter with the early Nigerian films *Countdown at Kusini* and *Bisi, Daughter of the River*. He has since directed several films, notably the fictional features *Vendor* (1988) and *Eewo/Taboo* (1989). The former is an elaborate morality play, in English, about corruption in Nigeria; at the First Nigerian National Film Festival in Lagos (1992) it swept most of the prizes, showing how much the judges at least appreciated this sort of socially concerned film. *Eewo* is a melodrama about drug addiction, and in various ways is closer to Yoruba culture (the dialogue is sometimes in Yoruba, though mostly in English, and there are supernatural elements from Yoruba religion).

Neither of these films has been distributed in Nigeria, though bits of *Vendor* were used in government (MAMSER)-sponsored spots on TV, and bits of *Eewo* have also been on television as part of the anti-drug campaign. Ladebo is a businessman, trained in the US in marketing, and he is one of the people thinking most creatively and practically about how Nigerian films could be dis-tributed abroad; but he is unwilling to subject himself to the time-consuming system of distribution that exists in Nigeria. His most recent projects (a documentary, and short and feature-length fic-tional films, all on women's issues) are being made for international agencies, notably the United Nations. Ladebo has faults as a film-maker—his actors often turn in wooden performances, and his scripts tend to be excessively and flat-footedly moralistic—but aesthetically he is in some ways the most sophisticated and creative of all Nigerian directors (for instance, in the way he handles the interplay between image and soundtrack), and he is utterly dedi-cated to using film to address important social topics. It is tragic that his country does not have a system that supports his efforts.

Brendan Shehu has made a number of documentary films, and now a fictional feature, *Kulba Na Barna* (1992). In spite of the fact that Shehu is General Manager of the Nigerian Film Corporation, financing the picture was a struggle: finally it was arranged through a company associated with Ahmadu Bello University. This is that rare thing, a Hausa film. Shehu is a tal-ented director—the film is a pleasure to look at, and there is a fine quiet dramatic wit running through it. However, the film takes two hours to tell a simple tale of a schoolgirl seduced and abandoned by a rich alhaji, which could have been told easily in half an hour. The script is derived from a novel (of the same name) which is required reading in secondary schools. One supposes the fact that the film retells a well known and officially sanctioned story was counted upon to generate an audience. In any case, the film suffers from its reliance on this story, which is so simple and moralistic as to seem less than fit for adult viewers. Surely the budding Hausa film tradition needs more ambitious projects.

Saddiq Balewa's *Kasarmu Ce/ The Land is Ours* (1991) is such a film. It was made rather on the model that obtains in francophone Africa: Balewa was trained as a filmmaker in Britain, at the National Film and Television School, which supported the film by making facilities and equipment available. The crew and producer are European. The bulk of the funding came from the European Community; the rest from the National Council for Arts and Culture, the Bauchi State Government, and private individuals (Balewa, 26). It has made the rounds of the international film festivals. The film is nearly perfectly conceived. Visually its stunning landscapes, austere costumes, and attention to peasant folk ways will appeal to outside audiences, but it treats realistically, which is to say usefully, a story of a village struggling against its exploiters, who, having discovered that the land is littered with sapphires, are trying to defraud the peas - ants of their inheritance. The ending does not exaggerate the victory the peasants win: the snake has been stunned but not killed. The film combines a convincingly rendered local focus with a comprehensive and intelligent political vision.

"NIGERIA DESERVES A FILM INDUSTRY"

"Nigeria Deserves a Film Industry" is the title of one of Ola Balogun's manifestos, this one published in the *Daily Times* in 1974. Like Cassandra, Balogun has always been right, and has never been listened to.

Because of the iron laws of neo-colonial economics it is some - thing of a wonder if anything like a film industry appears in any African country. Still Nigeria, with its size and wealth, should have been able to manage it if anyone could. The reasons a national cinema does not exist correlate with the political failures of the Nigerian nation:

- On the official level there has been lack of interest, ideo- logical bankruptcy, incompetence, and misconceived proj- ects. The necessary economic structures have never been put in place. There has been no integration of television with film production, which would have been an obvious first step both in supporting a film industry and in improving the locally sourced television programming.

According to Ladi Ladebo, "Unfortunately for Nigeria, after three decades of television in Nigeria, and with nearly thirty nine stations all over the country, that industry has not even begun to search for a meaningful relationship with the local film industry" (151). Ekwuazi claims that "no Nigerian film has yet been programmed on television in Nigeria" (133).

- The national bourgeoisie has been equally irresponsible. They have been generally unwilling to invest in film production, preferring quicker and safer investments. Philistines, they are normally unwilling to support the arts, whether traditional or modern, unless their vanity is directly served. The petty bourgeoisie has deserted the cinemas in favor of television and VCRs.

- A consequence of the failure to establish a strong national center, in cultural projects as elsewhere, is disintegration into ethnicity, expressed in modes which encourage backward tendencies. TV serials—*Village Headmaster*, *Basi & Co.*, *New Masquerade*—have sometimes been powerful agents in the creation of a national Nigerian culture. Film has made no such contribution. There are strong arguments for making films in indigenous lan- guages. Still a situation in which one ethnic group is responsible for virtually the whole of Nigerian film production is inherently undesirable, and even dangerous in a polity that suffers from enormous centrifugal forces.

- The nation remains supine in the face of neo-colonialism: the cinema screens are dominated by foreign productions, a situation, which will only be intensified in the new world information order. The psycho-political consequences of this are so frequently bemoaned that there is no need to rehearse them here.

In Nigeria, amidst so many other disintegrations, the institution of "cinema" has disintegrated both socially and technically. Now the middle class never attends films, in cinema houses—the films do not suit their tastes, the places are too rowdy, and their cars are apt to be vandalized. Instead the elite live in a world of VCRs and satellite dishes, tuned to foreign programming. Patronage of film is left to the working class and lower middle class, who conjured their indigenous entertainers from the improvised theaters through television studios onto celluloid. But their patronage cannot any longer support real film—their -N-10 or 5 does not convert into enough foreign exchange to buy negative film stock, so they get a mixed bastard technology, determined by a logic of poverty and piracy. SAP has, across the board, collapsed industries and stim- ulated petty informal sector activities. Strategies of import substi- tution become impossible, let alone manufacturing for export. A real film industry is farther than ever from realization.

Is it time, then, to stop hoping for and talking about one? Has "a virile film industry," like the production of a Nigerian-made automobile, become a shibboleth of modern nationhood that is just no longer affordable? Perhaps, though the dream dies hard, and there is no reason to stop attempting what is still possible. But there is an argument to be made that—for the moment at least— it makes more sense to emphasize video production, in coordina- tion with television. This has the great advantage that it is already flourishing. The objective is to diversify production, and raise the quality. Private broadcasting should create a greater demand for indigenous programming. But above all, the virtue of video tech- nology is that it is so open to (modestly funded) initiatives from below.

At any rate, Nigeria has appropriated film, in its own style and according to its means. It may not have a proper film industry, but it certainly does have something that is alive and kicking, and that mirrors the paradoxical image of the country, expressing its ethnic divisions, its relative industrialization, its huge market, and its cur- rent poverty, which does not however prevent busy, inventive, informal activity. This takes strange shapes because there is no legal environment of copyright and contract law, a problem that in itself would impede a real industry from forming. Investors con- template a howling chaos, shudder, and withdraw; the white ele- phants of government intervention lumber by to rapid extinction. The dumping ground for Hollywood's toxic waste, Nigeria is also a notorious pirate, and producer of goods so shoddy no one would import them. If film distribution in Nigeria is as clear a case as one could want to see of continuing neo-colonialism, the Yoruba cinema is also an extraordinary example of popular cultural self- assertion, producing something modern out of an old tradition, speaking directly and effectively to a mass audience, without any concern for who else might be listening. The same country that imports junk vehicles and makes wondrous imitation spare parts adopts the reversal process and low-budget video: both produce lots of accidents but traffic does move, in rattletrap vehicles going at full speed. And so the country maintains a churning reproduction of itself, not surely in the form it deserves, but indomitably.

NOTES

1. Much has changed since this article was written in 1993-94: celluloid filmmaking in Nigeria (including reversal films and video blown up to 16 mm) has ceased almost entirely, while there has been a remarkable boom in video productions. See Jonathan Haynes and Onookome Okome, "Evolving Popular Media: Nigerian Video Films," in *Nigerian Video Films*, ed. Jonathan Haynes (Ibadan: Kraft Books for the Nigerian Film Corporation, 1997); forthcoming in *Research in African Literatures*.

    A part of the present article was presented as a paper at the "Media, Popular Culture and 'The Public'" conference, 29 April-1 May 1994, jointly sponsored by the Institute for Advanced Study and Research in the African Humanities at Northwestern University, the Chicago Humanities Institute, the Department of Anthropology and the College of the University of Chicago. It was published along with other conference proceedings in *Passages* 8 (1994) as "Structural Adjustments of Nigerian Comedy: Baba Sala." I want to thank Karin Barber and the other participants at that confer-ence for their valuable comments. I am also grateful to those who have read and responded to the whole of this manuscript in various stages of its composition: Ola Balogun, Steve Daniel, Kenneth Harrow, Jibrin Ibrahim, David Konstan, Brian Larkin, Yacubu Nasidi, and Onookome Okome. They are of course not responsible for my opinions or errors of fact. This essay also appeared in Onookome Okome and Jonathan Haynes, *Cinema and Social Change in West Africa* (Jos: Nigerian Film Corporation, revised edition, 1997).

2. Ladi Ladebo gives figures demonstrating the economic impossibility of making a profit on a 35-mm film; he says no Nigerian film in 35 mm has done it (145-49). But Ola Balogun disagrees; saying the early films did make a profit (personal communication, April 1994).

3.   The honor of having produced the first Nigerian feature is dis-
      puted: *Kongi's Harvest* was preceded (barely) by *Son of
      Africa*, produced by Fedfilm Ltd., which some would dis-
      qualify on the grounds that it was really Lebanese, though it
      was shot in Nigeria with a Nigerian actress and directed by
      Segun Olusola. See F. Balogun 49-50.

4.   On government policy see Ekwuazi *Film in Nigeria*, Ekwuazi
      and Nasidi, Okome "Rise," Diawara, F. Balogun *Cinema*, O.
      Balogun, Opubor and Nwuneli, and Shehu. The Baloguns
      and Adegboyega Arulogun (in Ekwuazi and Nasidi) are par-
      ticularly trenchant critics. Ekwuazi has written the fullest
      accounts of the history of government policies, *Film in
      Nigeria*.

5.   Some States in Nigeria levy an entertainment tax of up to
      40%, which makes it virtually impossible to turn a profit on
      a film. At the National Theatre in Lagos, the premier show-
      case for Nigerian films, 30% of the gate goes for tax, and
      another 35% goes to the management.

6.   I will sometimes be using, for the sake of convenience, the
      terms "Yoruba film" or "Yoruba filmmaker" to refer to the
      products and producers of this kind of cinema which grows
      out of the Travelling Theater. I recognize that the terms are
      extremely problematic. Figures like Ola Balogun or Ladi
      Ladebo or Afolabi Adesanya are Yorubas and filmmakers,
      but certainly do not fit the mold of the folk artist— Adesanya
      objects very strenuously to being referred to as a "Yoruba
      filmmaker" [See his letter in *The Guardian* (Lagos), 27
      March 1993: 16]. I certainly do not wish to encourage the eth-
      nicizing of Nigerian film or of discussions of culture in gen-
      eral. Still there is a tradition and generic category of films too
      useful to ignore, and "Yoruba" is the name generally attached
      to it. Alternative terms for it, like "ethnic" or "folkloric cin-
      ema" (used by Ekwuazi and Okome), are no less problematic.
      (Françoise Balogun objects to "folkloric," "Originality," 68.)

7.   All translations from French are my own.

8.   This peculiar method of distribution is of course not so good
      for the film scholar either, or anyone else interested in mon-
      itoring film production and exhibition. Hyginus Ekwuazi,
      dean of Nigerian film scholars, evidently speaks from exas-
      perating experience as he points to how secretive the whole
      business of Nigerian film is: "the industry very jealously

guards its facts and figures. Producers, like distributors and exhibitors, are all reticent beyond the limits of tolerance" (*Film in Nigeria,* 132). Any kind of reliable overall statistics are very hard to come by as there are so many unregistered exhibition locales, and so many films never pass by the censor for registration.

A new Film Archive building has recently (1992) been inaugurated by the Nigerian Film Corporation in Jos, where copies of all new Nigerian films are to be deposited, but it seems exceedingly unlikely that the filmmakers will actually give up copies of their films, given their paranoia about piracy.

9. Karin Barber has explained this tendency of actors in the Travelling Theatre tradition to play the same part in various plays or films as part of a strategy of self-promotion on the part of small-scale entrepreneurs trying to carve out a niche for themselves in the entertainment business; their consistent projections of a fictionalized version of their personalities will be recognizable to a loyal clientele. "Radical Conservatism" 8.

10. "Yoruba travelling theatre is a *people's* theatre in the sense of being both produced by and addressed to the lower layers of society: the worse paid, less educated majority who are furthest removed from power. But it has been accused of failing to be a *popular* theatre in the sense of serving the people's real interests. Instead of opening the people's eyes to their objective situation, the accusation runs, it distracts them with reactionary, escapist or plain vacuous rubbish." (Barber, *Radical Conservatism*, 5). See also Barber's *Popular Arts in Africa*.

11. This plot is in fact identical to that of Moliere's *The Miser.* Olaiya (who wrote the script) denies having had any knowledge of Moliere, until after the film was released and lecturers from the University of Ibadan came around asking him about it (personal communication, June 1993), but it seems impossible that such an elaborate and detailed resemblance could be pure coincidence.

12. Ade Love agrees (Fatunde, 74). One could point to the parallel difficulties in establishing a viable English-language theater, outside the auspices of the universities. Wale Adenuga's *Papa Ajasco* (1984) is an example of a popular English-language film; the fact that it was based on a famous

comic strip may have had something to do with its success. There is a market for (comic) video productions in Pidgin, exploited by Jagua and others; the potential of Pidgin deserves exploration.

WORKS CITED

Adesanya, Afolabi. *The Nigerian Film/TV Index*. Ikeja: A-Productions Nigeria Ltd., 1992.

—. "Production Infrastructure." In Ekwuazi and Nasidi, 218-27.

—. Letter to Editor. *The Guardian* [Lagos] 27 March 1993: 16.

Balewa, Saddiq. "Troubles of a Young Filmmaker: Interview with Onookome Okome." *Media Review* 7, No. 2 (July 1992): 26.

Balogun, Françoise. *The Cinema in Nigeria*. Enugu: Delta Publications, 1987.

—. "Originality and Mediocrity." *Ecrans d'Afrique* 2, third quarter (1992): 66-69.

Balogun, Ola. "Nigeria Deserves a Film Industry." *Daily Times*. 25 March 1974; rpt. in Françoise Balogun, *The Cinema in Nigeria*: 105-08.

Barber, Karin. "Popular Arts in Africa." *African Studies Review* 30, No. 3 (September 1987): 1-78.

—. "Popular Reactions to the Petro-Naira.," *Journal of Modern African Studies* 20, No. 3 (1982): 431-50.

—. "Radical Conservatism in Yoruba Popular Plays." *Bayreuth African Studies Series* 7 (1986): 5-12.

Clark, Ebun. *Hubert Ogunde: The Making of Nigerian Theatre*. Oxford: Oxford University Press, 1980.

Diawara, Manthia. *African Cinema: Politics and Culture*. Bloomington: Indiana Univ. Press, 1992.

Ekwuazi, Hyginus. *Film in Nigeria*, 2nd ed. Jos: Nigerian Film Corporation, 1991.

—. and Yakubu Nasidi. *Operative Principles of the Film Industry: Towards a Film Policy for Nigeria*. Jos: Nigerian Film Corporation, 1992.

Fatunde, Tunde. "Ade Love: 'I recognize the importance of mother.'" *Ecrans d'Afrique* 2, third quarter (1992): 74-75.

Film Policy for Nigeria. Nigerian Film Corporation. n.p./n.d.

Jeyifo, Biodun. *The Yoruba Popular Travelling Theatre of Nigeria*. Lagos: Nigeria Magazine, 1984.

—. *The Truthful Lie: Essays in a Sociology of African Drama*. London: New Beacon Books, 1985.

Ladebo, Ladi. "Film Production and Content: the Nigerian Experience." In Ekwuazi and Nasidi, 144-68.

Lakoju, Tunde. "Popular (Travelling) Theatre in Nigeria: The Example of Moses Olaiya Adejumo (alias Baba Sala)." *Nigeria Magazine* 149 (1984): 35-46.

Olaiya Adejumo, Moses. "Baba Sala on Magical Films: Interview with Onookome Okome." *Media Review* 7, No. 2 (July 1992): 25.

Okome, E. K. O. "The Rise of the Folkloric Cinema in Nigeria." Ph.D. Thesis, University of Ibadan, 1991.

Opubor, Alfred E. and Onuora E. Nwuneli. *The Development and Growth of the Film Industry in Nigeria*. Lagos: Third Press International, 1979.

Osundare, Niyi. "A Grand Escape into the Metaphysics." *West Africa*. May 12, 1980: 828.

Ricard, Alain. "Du théâtre au cinéma yoruba: le cas nigérian." *CinémAction* 26 (1983): 160-67.

Shehu, Brendan. *No...Not Hollywood: Essays and Speeches of Brendan Shehu*. Ed. Hyginus Ekwuazi and Yakubu Nasidi. Jos: National Film Corporation, 1992.

PORTUGUESE AFRICAN CINEMA: HISTORICAL AND CONTEMPORARY PERSPECTIVES—1969 TO 1993

THE HISTORY OF FILM PRODUCTIONS in sub-Saharan Africa, and of films by African filmmakers in general, must be considered in the context of an acute shortage of technical and financial resources, as well as a lack of viable circuits of distribution and exhibition. These difficulties, in turn, have been compounded by colonial and post-colonial traditions and policies regarding cinema: first, cinema targeted for Africans during the colonial period, where it existed, was integrally linked to administrative, military, religious, or educational objectives; second, post-colonial—either European or African—film policies, and filmmakers' initiatives aimed at ameliorating colonial conditions have not led to an economically viable and stable film industry in the region.

A major stumbling block continues to be the bottleneck created by European and American conglomerates whom own and operate the lucrative distribution mechanisms for cinema throughout Africa. For these companies, the continent is merely a commercial market, a dumping ground for foreign films of dubious merit. The continued lack of control by Africans and their governments over the distribution process means that revenues are being drained from the continent, rather than redirected to building and supporting cinema productions and its related industries. [1]

Given this scenario, the context of film production and distribution—specifically, the manner in which financial and technical structures of film production have had a major impact on the ideological perspective, form, content, and purpose of cinema in post-

colonial Africa—assumes added significance in the history of cin-
ema in Africa. Historically, the dominance of francophone Africa
in film productions was due in large measure to France's two-
pronged post-colonial film policy. Financial and technical assistance was provided to African governments for production of
newsreels and documentaries, and to aspiring African filmmakers
to explore and expand their "cultural expression in film" (see
Andrade-Watkins "France's Bureau").[2] Technical facilities, however, were not created within Africa, perpetrating the need for
African governments and filmmakers to go to Paris to complete the
film production process. This underdevelopment was arguably tied
to the primary purpose of France's post-colonial aid to their former
colonies: a continuation of cultural, linguistic, and economic
dependency on France.

Mozambique, on the other hand, insisted on merging ideology with form, content, and context, pioneering a successful model
of "guerrilla" cinema that embraced a Marxist conception of the
engagement between film and society. More importantly, the film
industry was nationalized, so that infrastructures of production,
distribution, and exhibition were created and supported by a government that viewed cinema as a vital force in post-colonial development and education. Mozambique and the other Portuguese
colonies spread around the continent—Angola, Cape Verde,
Guinea-Bissau, Sao Tome and Principe—shared the legacy of a
harsh and impoverished colonial reign. Galvanized by the revolutionary movement for independence, a distinguished vanguard of
senior African statesmen and revolutionaries—Agostinho Neto in
Angola, Eduardo Mondlane followed by Samora Machel in
Mozambique, and Amilcar Cabral in Cape Verde and Guinea
Bissau—provided the intellectual, political, and ideological leadership that challenged, fought, and overturned colonial rule
throughout Africa.

Conceived ideologically and thematically in the spirit of the
liberation struggle against the Portuguese during the 1960s and
1970s, films from lusophone countries—particularly Mozam-bique
and Angola—comprise an important chapter in the history of
African cinema in general and the genre of "guerrilla," or liberation, cinema in particular. For the purposes of this study, the period
of liberation cinema begins in 1969 with "Towards a Third
Cinema," a pivotal manifesto written by Argentinean filmmakers
Solanas and Gettino. The subsequent development of "guerrilla,"

or liberation, cinema in Mozambique during the 1960s and 1970s is examined in the context of film production in sub-Saharan Africa, and the study concludes with the transition in Mozambique in the late 1980s from state to private sector production, interna-tional coproductions, and financing. The discussion of change in Mozambique and Portuguese-speaking Africa is placed in the wider context of film production in sub-Saharan Africa, while the historic and contemporary participation of Cape Verde, Angola, and Guinea-Bissau is also highlighted.

THE ORIGINS AND DEVELOPMENT OF LIBERATION CINEMA 1969-1978

The decade of the 1960s witnessed an explosion in cinema that cut a swath through the "Third World." Fueled by Argentinean filmmakers Octavio Gettino and Fernando Solanas's pivotal 1969 manifesto, "Towards a Third Cinema," and further encouraged by leaders of African independence movements, waves of revolu-tionary ideology swept across Latin America and Africa, leaving in wake a cinema that confronted dominant historical, colonial, cultural, and ideological norms in society and cinema. Latin America, Cuba, North Africa, French-speaking and Portuguese-speaking Africa—especially Mozambique—became major cen-ters for the theoretical and practical development of cinema. Only Ghana in English-speaking Africa and Guinea Conakry in French-speaking Africa came close to the production potential of post-independent Mozambique. The government of Guinea Conakry shared Mozambique's commitment to a functional and educational "third cinema," going so far as to nationalize part of the distribu-tion and exhibition film sectors in the country.[3] However, the British had no interest in the post-colonial development of cin-ema, although a colonial legacy of documentary traditions in English-speaking Africa is visible in the strong television and gov-ernment networks in Ghana and Nigeria.[4] While Ghana inherited full 16mm and 35mm capabilities from John Grierson's Colonial Film Unit, the government unfortunately neither espoused the ide-ological significance of cinema nor entertained the vision of Ghana becoming a regional center for production.[5]

In contrast, vestiges of colonial cinema were extremely faint in Portuguese-speaking Africa. (See Taylor). In the decade pre-ceding independence from the Portuguese—1974 for Guinea-

Bissau and 1975 for the other colonies—film production was galvanized by two revolutionary forces. The first was an internal, newly awakened sense of unity, purpose, and collaboration among the colonies, and the second was external support from the international community for the revolutionary war efforts and governments that included FRELIMO (Frente de Libertacao de Mocambique, 1962); the MPLA (Movimento Popular de Libertacao de Angola, 1965); and the PAIGC (Partido Africano Pela Independencia de Guine e Cabo Verde, 1956). [6]

Both forces—the African liberation movements and their foreign supporters—viewed cinema as a powerful force in the liberation struggle and a vital component in the documentation, education, and dissemination of information about the war. Consequently, films produced both informed the international community of the armed struggle against the Portuguese and contributed internal information and educational and cultural programming for the African populations.

The revolutionary governments of Mozambique and Angola, the most active centers for film production, supported landmark films made by pioneering filmmakers in the nascent African cinema. Sarah Maldoror was a major contributor to both the cinemas emerging from within the lusophone region, and the revolutionary cinema of the era. A Guadeloupean by birth, Maldoror received her training in Moscow and became a longtime supporter of the independence struggle. *Sambizanga* (1972), her first feature-length film, was also the first and thus far only fiction film devoted to the liberation struggle in Angola (Hennebelle, 110). The film's story line was based on Angolan novelist Luandino Viera's *The Real Life of Domingos Xavier* and adapted to screen by Mario de Andrade. Set in the 1960s during the war for independence from the Portuguese, the narrative follows Maria in her search through the prisons of the capital for her husband, an organizer for the MPLA independence movement. [7] The film celebrates the comrade and his wife's sacrifice and loss while exhorting supporters to continue the struggle. The last line of dialogue is a call to arms for February 4, 1961; the day hundreds of Africans attacked the police and military in Luanda and launched the armed struggle in Angola. This ending clearly reflects the political tone, theme, and focus of films made during this period.

Prior to filming *Sambizanga*, Maldoror directed a short film of 18 minutes, entitled *Monangambee*. Filmed in 1970 and financed by the Comité de Coordination des Organisations nationalistes des Colonies Portugaises, *Monangambee* illustrates the total lack of understanding between Portuguese and Africans through a dra-matic confrontation between an African prisoner, whose comment about a national dish made during a visit by his wife, is totally misconstrued by the Portuguese officer, who orders the prisoner beaten. While not distinguished by its cinematic quality, this pro-duction reaffirms the themes of revolutionary struggle.

Films made by an eminent group of international filmmakers and activists from countries as diverse as France, Sweden, Yugoslavia, and Cuba comprise the second, congruent movement of revolutionary cinema. Efforts from the United States were spear-headed by African American, Robert Van Lierop, a lawyer turned filmmaker. These films chronicled the struggle against Portuguese domination, and were shown extensively abroad, resulting in a ground swell of international support for the liberation struggle (Hennebelle, 111).[8]

Neither Cape Verde nor Guinea-Bissau was engaged in pro-duction. Rather, growing political and revolutionary stirrings against Portuguese colonialism were felt in the Cape Verde islands, a tiny archipelago of drought-stricken islands lying 200 nautical miles off the coast of Senegal. A modest yet significant intellec-tual movement stimulated by the cinematic and revolutionary ideals of the period began as early as the late 1950s.

Cape Verdean intellectuals studying at the lycée on the island of Sao Vicente were profoundly affected by the fervor radiating from the intellectuals and young revolutionary leaders studying in Lisbon, as well as the Negritude writers like Léopold Senghor, and Aimé Césaire, Panafricanists like W.E.B. DuBois, Pan-Africanism, and by African American literary giants such as Richard Wright, author of *Native Son*. Imbued with the spirit of African nationalism through books clandestinely brought into Cape Verde from Senegal, the young intellectuals of the 1950s were closely attuned to the activities on mainland Africa and through-out the diaspora. Encouraged by the emergence of leftist protest in Lisbon against the fascist government of Antonio Oliveira Salazar, a small group of Cape Verdean intellectuals formed a cine-club in the capital city of Praia, on the island of Sao Tiago, following the example of the cine-clubs in Lisbon that served as forums for intel-lectual dialogue, debate, and artistic exhibitions (Filinto Correia e Silva, personal interview). The first meeting of the cine-club was held in 1960 at the Cine-teatro Municipal da Praia. Open to the public, this cultural program featured Cape Verdean poetry. Plans were made to develop and continue a range of cultural program-ming, including cinema, music, and poetry. A list of possible films was proposed for future exhibitions, although the only concrete activity in cinema was a regular radio commentary, presented by the president of the cine-club, on social and cultural issues raised in commercial films being shown at the theaters (Filinto Correira e Silva, personal interview). However, by April 1961, the PIDE (Policia Internacional de Defesa do Estado, the Portuguese polit-ical police), fearing collusion or support for anti-colonial revolu-tionary movements, brought the activities of the fledgling cine-club to a halt with the arrest and imprisonment of two leaders of the association, Anastacio Filinto Correia e Silva and Alcides Barros, and the deportation of others from Sao Tiago (Filinto Correia e Silva, personal interview). No further efforts were made to revitalize the cine-club until independence.

Immediately following the coup in Lisbon, Portugal, which overthrew the fascist government of Antonio de Oliveria Salazar, colonial rule ended in 1974 for Guinea-Bissau with a defiant, uni-lateral declaration of independence. Angola, Mozambique, Cape Verde, Sao Tome, and Principe followed suit in 1975. Independence coincided with the crowning moment of cinematic endeavor in lusophone Africa: the creation of the Institute of Cinema in Mozambique. The architect of that reality was a legend in the history of world cinema, Ruy Guerra. A Mozambican by birth, Guerra was the leading figure in Brazil's Cinema Novo movement. His return to Mozambique after independence to head the Institute of Cinema was a major factor in the cultural ascen-dance of Mozambique in southern Africa, sub-Saharan Africa, and the lusophone diaspora.

This early national period of cinematic activity was a time of experimentation in the form and direction taken for cinema and tel-evision in Africa—a harbinger of subsequent developments in lusophone Africa. In a rare convergence of ego and talent, pro-genitors of three major movements—Ruy Guerra, cinema novo, Jean Rouch, cinéma vérité, and Jean-Luc Godard of the new wave—converged on Mozambique in 1978. The Institute had invited Rouch to explore the possibilities of super 8mm film, and Godard had a contract with the government to do a study about the possibilities for television and video in Mozambique (Diawara,

97). The connection between the critical and even acrimonious interactions among these cinematic giants and the forces that shaped the formal, social, and technical development of Mozambique's cinema illuminates a dilemma intrinsic to African cinema in general, and merits a digression in the narrative of the region.

The experimental phase of Mozambique cinema was preceded by the post-colonial initiative in cinema launched by France. While lacking the revolutionary fervor of Portuguese-speaking Africa, the French shared a spirit of adventure and experimentation and were optimistic about the prospects for cinema within Africa. In 1961, France created the Ministry of Cooperation with the express purpose of providing financial and technical assistance to her for - mer colonies. The Bureau of Cinema, created within the Ministry in 1963 under the direction of Jean-René Debrix, provided tech- nical and financial assistance to Africans to foster cultural expres - sion through cinema, allowing Africans from francophone Africa to launch the embryonic movement of sub-Saharan African cin- ema.

In retrospect, African cinema as envisioned by Debrix through the Bureau of Cinema was flawed, if not doomed, from the outset. Government bureaucracy hampered rapid deployment of resources or technical support. Administrative and operational procedures imposed by the Ministry on the Bureau were unwieldy, impracti - cal, and ill suited for production. For example, instead of a lab order taking one call in a non-governmental production center, technicians at the Bureau had to wait days for the processing of a request for the same service through the Ministry (Daventure, per- sonal interview).

The French film professionals looked askance at the Bureau, viewing the whole operation as unprofessional and financially and technically inadequate. The inability of the Ministry to provide effective and appropriate administrative mechanisms for produc - tion exacerbated increasing tensions between the filmmakers and the Bureau, on one hand, and the upper echelons of the Ministry and African governments on the other hand, over a range of issues involving the films, their content, form, and distribution. [9]

Jean Rouch, a pioneering ethnographer and filmmaker, and a controversial figure in African cinema, clashed both with African filmmakers and with Debrix on technique and themes. Rouch and the African filmmakers had distinctly different philosophies: he

183

dreamed small, i.e., 8mm, or 16mm, and the Africans dreamed large, 35mm format, the standard for professional, commercial cinema.[10] Rouch was reproached by the filmmakers for trying to institutionalize a level of technical underdevelopment by advocating the use of the smaller formats. In Rouch's view, however, the 35mm format was neither pragmatic nor cost-efficient and the African's emphasis on it amounted to a mystification of technology, where "the tripod was the beginning of a temple, an altar" (Rouch, unpublished interview).[11] In Rouch's capacity as the Director of Research at the Centre National de Recherches Scientifiques in Paris, he was involved in innovative experiments with the super 8mm format, which he applied to the 1978 experimental pilot project in Mozambique, supported in part by France's Ministry of Cooperation. Rouch believed that super 8mm was an expedient; cost-efficient format that would help developing countries catch up to the more technologically advanced countries. Furthermore, Rouch felt that the super 8mm format demystified the process of filmmaking and was a format that was accessible for use by more people since the cameras and editing equipment were cheaper, lighter, and smaller than 16mm or 35mm (*CinemAction,* 20-36).

While Rouch argued for super 8mm, Godard, on the other hand, was fascinated with the possibilities of video and television, and the creation of the images for that medium. For both men, Mozambique was in some ways a laboratory—an opportunity to identify or select the tools of production to build and shape a national cinema and television. Neither Rouch nor Godard's experiments came to fruition. Both were perceived as too costly and were canceled.[12] Although unproductive, these efforts in Mozambique exposed the ideological and theoretical implications of production methods and technological choices. Had either Rouch or Godard's vision persevered, the unique convergence of Marxism with viable structures of production, distribution, and exhibition that took place under Guerra's direction might never have occurred. While Godard and Rouch were arguing the merits of their vision for Mozambique, Guerra was actually realizing his vision in the documentary, educational, and feature film projects launched at the Institute of Cinema. Closely modeled after Cuba's acclaimed ICAIC (The Cuban Institute of Cinematographic Art and Industry) where many of the Mozambican personnel were trained, Mozambique's Institute of Cinema became the most powerful center of politically engaged and economically innova-tive indigenous cinema on the continent of Africa.

These differing perceptions among the Europeans, on the one hand, and the Africans, on the other, also underscored a wider struggle in post-colonial Africa between indigenous cultural, polit-ical, and economic autonomy and neo-colonial control. In this instance, the locus of the struggle was the context of production. Guerra's success insured that the Institute of Cinema pro-duced a viable, prolific, engaged cinema—integrally con-nected to the issues and realities of achieving military, psycho-logical, educational, and cultural independence in Mozambique in particular and southern Africa in general. In short, the effective and triumphant creation of a functional "guerrilla" or liberation cinema.

TRADITION FROM REVOLUTIONARY TO FREE MARKET FILM PRODUCTION 1978-1991

Cinema production in Mozambique after 1976 was on the ascen-dant, due in large measure to the activity of the Institute of Cinema. Launched in 1975 and officially established in 1976 by the revo-lutionary government of Samora Machel, the Institute of Cinema was the first cultural institution to be set up after independence. By 1978, an ambitious and sustained vision was created in Mozambique that addressed the cultural, educational, and infor-mational needs of a people engaged in armed struggle and a social-ist reconstruction of society and government.

Despite the internal battles with the South African-backed opposition forces of RENAMO, the Mozambique government con-tinued to support the Institute and their efforts to articulate, docu-ment, educate, and disseminate cogent and germane films about the crisis in the region and the ongoing destabilization efforts by South Africa against the Marxist governments in Mozambique and Angola. In Angola, on the other hand, film production after inde-pendence dropped off markedly—the result of nonexistent pro-duction infrastructures and ongoing internecine warfare between the Marxist MPLA and the opposing FNLA and UNITA factions.

Angolan filmmaker Sarah Maldoror, a pioneering filmmaker of the previous decade, continued to produce within the intra-regional lusophone community, making two short films in 1979 for the government of Cape Verde, *Fogo, l'île de feu*, a profile of the environment and culture of the island of Fogo, and *Un carnaval dans le Sahel*, which includes feast day celebrations and a PAIGC rally (Pfaff, 212).

Unlike Mozambique, Angola, which lies parallel to Mozambique on Africa's West Coast, never developed a national center of infrastructure for cinema. However, television was established in 1975, and after independence, senior Angolan filmmakers including Ruy Duarte de Carvalho and Antonio Ole produced many documentaries for that medium. Portuguese by birth and Angolan by declaration, Duarte produced five sections of *Sou Angolano trabalho com forca*, a major eleven-part 1975 documentary series on the workforce. He collaborated on this series with Ole, who continued on to make *Apprendre pour mieux servir*, *Le rythme du N'Gola Ritmos* (1977), and *Pathway to the Stars* (1980). Although Duarte produced mostly for television, he also produced the feature film *Nelista* in 1982; an elegantly crafted film based on two tales from southeastern Angola. *Nelista* is the story of two families escaping from a great famine and their efforts to overcome their situation. Nelista, the hero of the film, fights against evil spirits, and, with the help of animals and his friends, delivers his people.[13]

Television (TNCV) came to Cape Verde after independence in 1974, including productions by local filmmakers on the stories and folklore of their islands. Independence also brought a revival of the cineclub movement and renewed participation in the dialogue of the nascent African cinema. On May 7, 1975, the Cineclub Popular da Praia was established, including many of the members of the earlier thwarted cine movement of the late 1950s and early 1960s. The objectives of the cine-club, as delineated in their formal charter, stressed the support of the cine-club for cinema and TV as vehicles for informing the population about current and foreign events through documentaries, encouraging active participation in national history, contributing to national arts, popular culture, the education of the population—politically and socially—as well as for creating a national cinema (*Estatuto*). Supported and encouraged by the PAIGC, the club resumed its exhibition of films, which were rented through the cine-clubs in Lisbon, and then shown on a weekly basis. Fortunately, the artistic films were much cheaper to rent than the commercial ones, giving the members of the cine-club exposure to many different genres ranging from Italian neo-realism and American classics to Cuban, Brazilian, and

Japanese films. Picking up the slack from the new revolutionary government, which was busy organizing the first elections and facilitating other critical transitions of independence, the cineclub organized the filming of the first elections and other independence activities (*Estatuto*).[14] This highly visible, informed, and engaged community of intellectuals was committed to the development of cinema and television in Cape Verde and helped disseminate a wider vision of cinematic development throughout mainland Africa.

A delegation from the cine-club in Cape Verde joined repre-sentatives from nine other revolutionary African countries for a historic meeting in Maputo, Mozambique, between February 21 and 24, 1977, when the Conferencia Africano de Cooperaco Cinematografica, or Association Africaine de Coopération Cinématographique (AACC) was formed. The primary objective was to displace the foreign distribution monopoly and create regional, intra-African circuits of distribution for cinema. This ini-tiative failed, due in large measure to a lack of political commit-ment by the majority of the participating countries (Pimenta, let-ter to author). During these halcyon days, the Institute in Mozambique was already recognized as the center for cinema, as evidenced by their convening and hosting this ambitious, but flawed attempt to address the distribution problems within the con-tinent. Fortunately, the internal successes of the Institute were more tangible and long-lived.

The Institute was empowered by its mission and mandate to restructure all sectors of cinema, including distribution, exhibi-tion, and production. The Institute grew to include a lab, cine-matheque, and training program. Additionally, the significance accorded to cinema in the revolutionary process was apparent in the Institute's allocation of resources and manpower. During the peak years of the Institute, 1976 to 1986, three shifts worked twenty-four hours a day to produce, process, and edit the newsreels, documentaries, and, eventually, dramatic productions distributed within Mozambique and abroad (Pimenta, interview). Films such as African-American filmmaker Robert Van Lierop's *O Povo Organizado* (1976), a documentary on the challenges facing the reconstruction and development of the newly independent coun-try, helped foster continued support for Mozambique and bolstered the high international visibility of the fledgling Institute. [15]

The jewel in the crown of the Institute was the Kuxa Kanema. Conceived in 1981, this project was created to answer specific needs of the population for information about the country, and it provided the first step in the technical training of the staff of the Institute. As the major center for documentary production, Kuxa Kanema produced 395 weekly editions, 119 short documentaries, and 13 long documentary and/or dramas before the decline and ultimate collapse of the Institute in 1990 (Pimenta, letter to author).

The military engagement with South Africa, the corrosive influence of the West, internal criticism of Mozambican political structure, the battles against illiteracy, disease, and poverty, his-torical and cultural self-determination—these were the themes that dominated the productions of the Institute. [16] As a result, Mozambique's ability to quickly respond, reflect, document, pro-duce, and disseminate documentaries and programs on current events established the country as the ombudsman of the region. Vertically integrated infrastructures of production, a cadre of trained personnel, and the Institute's innovative horizontal sys-tems of distribution and exhibition (which included mobile cin-ema units reaching out to rural areas and urban audiences with lit-tle or no previous exposure to cinema) were the marks of a self-sustaining, healthy national cinema, one capable of recouping its production costs through distribution and exhibition. In short, inspired by the vision of an ideologically engaged, alternative cin-ema, with appropriate vehicles of distribution and exhibition and the development of trained African technicians, the ultimate objec-tives of the Institute were achieved. Mozambique, already assured a leadership role in the cinematic development of the region, was poised to become the model for the future of African cinema. [17]

That vision, however, was not to be realized. The revolution-ary transformation of the 1960s and 1970s reversed direction in the 1980s. No longer were the ideological demands of liberation strug-gles the determining force in the form, content, and purpose of cinema. A series of external and internal crises accelerated the decline of the Institute and the future prospects of cinema from Portuguese-speaking Africa. First, the assassination of Amilcar Cabral in 1973 and the death of Samora Machel in 1986 weak-ened the ideological, intellectual, and political leadership of luso-phone Africa. Second, the unity of the lusophone community began to fray after the split in 1980 of the PAIGC (the political party under which Guinea Bissau and Cape Verde fought for independence) into two separate parties: the PAICV for Cape Verde, and the PAIGC remaining in Guinea-Bissau. Third, independence for Angola and Mozambique from the Portuguese provided a pyrrhic victory—a lull before the plunge into protracted, internal guerrilla warfare and the destabilizing maneuvers of what was then Rhodesia and South Africa.

Activity and production at the Institute began to taper off, especially after the death of Machel in 1986. However, before its demise, four major large-scale productions were realized between 1986 and 1991. Zdravko Velimrovic's *Time of the Leopards* (1987), a Yugoslavia/Mozambique/Zimbabwe 90-minute feature co- pro- duction, recounts a fictional episode in the armed struggle for the liberation of Mozambique. The primary action of the film takes place during the turbulent early 1970s when the war weariness of the Portuguese was apparent, and victory was imminent. The story unfolds in the northern plateau's rich and protective cover for guer - rilla fighters. A hunt is organized for Pedro, the commander for a FRELIMO detachment, whose courageous actions begin to worry the Portuguese military in the area. Pedro becomes the object of a manhunt, is captured, and killed. His memory inspires the new generation, which continues the struggle and attack the barracks where Pedro had been imprisoned.

Jose Cardoso's *O vento sobra do norte* (The Wind Blows from the North, 1987), a 16mm 90-minute feature, opens in the north of Mozambique in 1968 where the liberation war has been going on for four years. Colonial settlers, unable to comprehend the reality of the slaves' revolt, exhibit an arrogant boldness along with a sense of uncertainty. Rumors of the changes sweeping through the rest of the country create widespread terror and guilt among the colonialists, who fear the vengeance of the Blacks, "mainatos," coming to reclaim the land taken from them five centuries earlier.

The third film, *Borders of Blood* by Mario Borgneth, a 16mm color 90-minute documentary, was shot in 1985 and completed in 1986. This feature film examines the South Africa's destabilization tactics and subsequent impact on Mozambique's reconstruction. Finally, *Devil's Harvest*, a 1988 Institute of Cinema co-produc - tion with France, Belgium, Channel 4 in England, and Denmark, directed by Brazilian Licinio Azevedo and Brigitte Bagnol from France; it weaves fiction and fact to tell the story of a drought-stricken Mozambican village, which is defended by five veterans of the war for independence who struggle against the daily men -

ace of harassment by bandits hidden in the surrounding forest. These productions illustrate the capacity of the Institute to produce feature-length fiction and documentary films while incorporating the themes of armed struggle, regional destabilization, internal cultural and historical change and post-colonial turmoil. Ironically, the Institute halted at the peak of its financial and technical capability to produce, distribute, and exhibit politically and ideologically engaged cinema. Unfortunately, instead of being harbingers of a powerful voice within the region and of African cinema, in general, these films were public symbols of the end of an era.

The death knell for the Institute was an electrical fire on February 12, 1991. The Institute and its technical facilities were badly damaged: the film equipment depots, sound studio, editing rooms, and processing labs were destroyed. As a result, all documentary production halted, training of personnel ceased, and distribution ground to a halt, since all the prints were destroyed in the fire (Pimenta, fax). This devastating loss, compounded by the death of president Samora Machel, changes of leadership within the Institute, the economic toll of protracted internal guerrilla warfare, and the declining support and influence of Marxist regimes for Mozambique effectively brought a close to the fifteen-year history of the Film Institute.

PRIVATE SECTOR PRODUCTION 1991-1993

The crumbling of the Soviet and eastern bloc's ideological and financial support to Marxist governments accelerated the democratic changes sweeping through Africa in the late 1980s. The ascension of a conservative, Western-leaning government in 1990 in Cape Verde, and movements toward negotiated peace settlements within Angola and Mozambique in 1991 and 1992 presaged subsequent changes in cinema. In Mozambique the bureaucratic and administrative transition from state-controlled production to a free market was already underway, as evident in numerous seminars held on "the democratization of television" for film and television producers (Pimenta, telephone conversation). The changes became more concrete after the fire in 1991.

The subsequent shift in Mozambique was both geo-political and economic. Mozambique's geographical, political, and economic relationship within the southern African region superseded to a large degree the earlier cultural and political links with the wider lusophone community. The regional realignment of Mozambique with Angola, Botswana, Lesotho, Namibia, South Africa, Swaziland, Zambia, and Zimbabwe, however, creates new challenges, exacerbated by diverse historical, political, cultural experiences and differing expectations and traditions for cinema and television.[18]

Hypothetically, the financial and technical potential for regional film production, backed by the resources of a stable South Africa, is enormous. Producers from the region are collaborating on a range of ventures, including the production in 1992 of *The Southern Africa Film Television and Video Yearbook and Catalogue* that lists the regional production companies and films available for distribution. Economically, Mozambique is increas- ingly linked to the international, competitive, commercial film marketplace. Close on the heels of the "Partenariat" in 1989 and 1991, four privately owned production companies emerged in Mozambique. A leading force is Ebano Multimedia, Lda., an inde- pendent production and distribution company established in 1991 by experienced film professionals, including many senior produc- ers and administrators from the former Institute of Cinema. Ebano is the first of the private companies to venture into feature film production with *The Child from the South*, a 1991 co-production with Channel Four in England. Set in war-torn Maputo, Nadia, a South African woman journalist meets a committed but weary Mozambican doctor. This elegant, contemporary love story addresses Nadia's feelings of loss and alienation created by her forced exile as a child from South Africa. *Marracuene*, a 43- minute, 1991 Ebano co-production with German television (ZDF) Channel 4 in England, is a dramatic documentary about a village situated in a heavy war zone. Once a bustling stop on the railway lines, the village has become a veritable shadow. Every night, the remaining villagers flee to the other side of the river to avoid the terror of nightly raids, returning the next morning to the sight of devastated homes and businesses (Garcia and Helburg, 11-12).

Both films—*The Child from the South* and *Marracuene* mod- ify the treatment of the prevalent war theme of the earlier didac- tic/revolutionary films of the region, to stories that appeal to non- African television audiences. In *The Child from the South* especially, war becomes a backdrop for an intense personal drama. *Marracuene*, while actually set in the village, includes stylized visual cut-aways and dramatized personal accounts of the nightly sieges. Arguably, in both instances, forces of international financ - ing and marketing have resulted in shifts in content and form. A similar trend, to lighter, or stylized, touches, is also apparent in contemporary Angolan productions.

A north-to-south co-production between Belgium and Angola yielded Mopiopio a 52-minute documentary on music and every - day life in Angola made in 1990 by Angolan-born Zeze Gamboa, a veteran of Angolan television. Another recent Angolan co- pro - duction between Italian and Portuguese television is *Moia-O recado das Ilhas*, a 1989, 35mm feature film by veteran Angola producer Ruy Duarte de Carvalho. A poetic drama, taking place in both the present and an eighteenth-century set adapted from Shakespeare's *The Tempest*, *Moia* is the story of an Angolan woman of Cape Verdean descent whose return to Cape Verde forces her to confront and question her existence and identity as someone who is neither totally European nor African. Always strong in television, Angola remains relatively quiescent in film production. Unlike Mozambique, Angola did not develop pro - duction facilities. Furthermore, the uneasy peace in the country inhibits further television production or wider participation in regional activities. However, interest and hope remain strong among Angolan filmmakers for their future participation.

In West Africa, Guinea-Bissau, the tiny mainland neighbor of the Cape Verde islands has emerged as a major presence in African cinema. The 1989 film *Mortu nega* catapulted native-born direc - tor Flora Gomes and Guinea-Bissau to international acclaim. The narration is focused through the eyes of Dominga, the wife of a guerrilla fighter, and the viewer witnesses the commitment, tenac - ity, and will for independence that sustains the morale of the sol - diers. Dominga follows her husband through the bush as he and his unit engage the Portuguese in unequally matched warfare, pro - viding encouragement, love, and unswerving support to her hus - band and friends. Unparalleled in its drama and realism, *Mortu nega* offers an unprecedented and distinct dramatic and highly realistic portrayal of the high human cost of the war against the Portuguese.

Produced solely by the government of Guinea-Bissau, *Mortu nega* affirms the priority of cinema in the country's development plans. Although there are six filmmakers in the country at the moment, the National Center of Cinema is collaborating with the Ministry of Education and the government to:

- Improve commercial importation and exhibition in the country.
- Produce and co-produce films by Guinea-Bissau film-makers.
- Train personnel for all levels of film production. To reinforce these goals, filmmaker trainees are attached to all productions occurring in Guinea-Bissau.

Flora Gomes's second feature, *The Blue Eyes of Yonta* (1991), again brought critical acclaim to the director and his country. The government of Guinea-Bissau participated in the production, along with the Institute of Cinema in Portugal, Vermedia Productions, and Portuguese television. Set in the capital city of Bissau after the war, the film involves a beautiful girl, Yonta, who falls in love with a war hero. He never learns of her infatuation, nor in turn does Yonta recognize the passion that a young man from the water-front, Ze, harbors for her. More important, the film shows a post-war reality for Guinea-Bissau, its people, and their sense of loss, psychological displacement, love, conviction, and hope for the future.

The contemporary movement in Guinea-Bissau is similar to the former Institute of Cinema in Mozambique in the effort to develop stories germane to the historical and political reality of the people of Guinea-Bissau. Similarly, Guinea-Bissau's National Center for Cinema and the government are developing strong pro-duction, distribution, and exhibition structures. The key difference between the contemporary initiatives of Guinea-Bissau and the former Institute of Cinema in Mozambique is the shifting focus from Soviet bloc financing to free market economies, international financing, and/or collaborations.

International television is an increasingly important production partner in African cinema. The credits for *Blue Eyes of Yonta* include Portuguese and English Channel 4 television as well as the Institute of Cinema in Portugal. Experienced Lisbon-based producer Paulo de Sousa and his company, Vermedia, have been instrumental in securing international financing for filmmakers from the nascent lusophone sector. Vermedia produced *Yonta* and served in the same capacity for the 1993 production of *Ilheu de*

Contenda, Cape Verdean director Leao Lopes's feature debut. Based on a novel by noted Cape Verdean author Teixeira de Sousa, the story takes place in the 1960s on the island of Fogo. Two broth - ers united to settle a family estate, struggle with conflicting values and perspectives on emigration and Cape Verdean identity, domi - nant themes in Cape Verdean literature, history, and culture. Financing for the production was raised from advance television sales and the Institute of Cinema in Portugal. The experience gained in the location shooting of *Yonta* in Guinea-Bissau and now Cape Verde establishes Vermedia as a leading production partner in Portuguese-speaking Africa.

Cape Verde is an increasingly popular location for feature film productions, a development encouraged by the revitalized Cape Verdean Institute of Cinema. Founded in 1977, the primary func - tion of the Institute was the distribution and exhibition of foreign films. Since 1988, under the direction of Daniel Spencer Brito, the Institute has been successfully broadening its scope to attract for - eign productions and train local personnel. Prior to 1988, most productions in Cape Verde were documentaries produced or copro - duced for Cape Verdean television. Brito is cautiously optimistic about the future of cinema by and for Cape Verde. He hopes to bring more African films to the screens in Cape Verdean. Language, however, presents a daunting challenge for both pro - duction and distribution. Portuguese is the administrative language; Cape Verdean, however, is the spoken language of the people, the music, and the literature. Furthermore, it varies from island to island, creating difficulties for the local distribution of indige - nously produced films as well as imported films (Garcia, 24-25; Brito, personal interview).

It is clear that Portuguese-speaking Africa—Mozambique, Angola, Cape Verde, and Guinea-Bissau—is in step with chang - ing trends and influences in the production and distribution of cin - ema in sub-Saharan Africa. How their participation affects, mod - ifies, changes, or encourages the development of African cinema remains to be seen.

CONCLUSION

Mozambique in particular and lusophone Africa in general repre - sent a small but vital contribution to the extant history of sub-Saharan and world cinema. This unique purview contextualizes the instrumental if not pivotal role of Mozambique and lusophone Africa within historic movements and events that shaped these first decades of African cinema. More specifically, the strongest influences on cinema in Portuguese-speaking Africa between 1969 and 1975 were:

- the internal and external movements and productions in support of liberation struggles;
- the launching of the Institute of Cinema in Mozambique; and
- broad issues and debates within African cinema—as evinced by the experimental period with Rouch and Godard or the Bureau of Cinema.

Without question, the pinnacle of cinematic achievement for luso - phone Africa was the Institute of Cinema. Prior to its demise and destruction in 1991, the Institute had evolved into a mature, suc - cessful production center combining theory, practice, and imple - mentation: a monument, testament, and finally, solitary beacon of sub-Saharan Africa's revolutionary cinema. Historically, the Institute symbolized the optimism, euphoria, and expectations for cinema throughout the lusophone diaspora in the years immediately following independence where early initiatives such as internal and foreign lusophone collaborations or the cine-club movement in Cape Verde continued, or in the case of the Institute of Cinema, flourished. Those dreams died due in large measure to the con - stant instability of the film production and distribution in sub-Saharan Africa.

Lusophone filmmakers are today joined in a common, com - petitive pursuit of a global audience. As southern Africa begins to pull together under the aegis of democratization, the lusophone producers in the region, Mozambique, and Angola, prepare to re-enter the global film market on a new footing. The nascent com - mercial sector is expanding with private production companies developing projects and exploring co-production and collabora - tive ventures with other African countries and Europe. Cape Verde and Guinea-Bissau are also part of this scenario. In short, film - makers from the sector are employing increasingly sophisticated marketing and economic strategies to meet the growing demands of an increasingly appreciative international audience. Always sus - ceptible to shifting external and internal political and economic trends, sub-Saharan African cinema is a microcosm, or barometer, of the shifting priorities in socio-political, historical, ideological, and economic trends occurring within a broader, continent-wide context. As indicated in the three areas of this study—liberation cinema, the transition from state to freemarket production, and private sector productions—each shift brought new directions, trends, themes, and participants in African cinema.

Although the 1990s have brought increased visibility and acclaim to African cinema, the sector moves toward the future like the Sankofa bird from Akan mythology that flies ahead while look-ing to the past. African cinema marches backwards into the future, searching for an aesthetically, economically, and culturally "liber-ated" voice, while shackled to a past and present encumbered by perennial problems in distribution, exhibition, and financing.

NOTES

1. Some African countries have successfully nationalized their film sector completely or in part. However, the lack of inter- and intra-regional coordination impedes the possibility of cre-ating comprehensive, alternative, continent-wide distribution circuits, creating a void that exceeds the capabilities of indi-vidual African states in general or filmmakers in particular.
2. The argument advanced in my "France's Bureau of Cinema" is that the cinematic development supported by the French in the newly independent French speaking West African countries was undercapitalized, creating a neocolonial economic and technical dependence on France that reinforced colonial poli-cies of assimilation through French language, culture and finance.
3. While capable of 16mm production, the 35mm facilities were never completed, and the lack of laboratory processing facil-ities made them dependent on technical supports in Europe. Furthermore, the unmitigated anger unleashed by de Gaulle and France at Guinea Conakry's dramatic declaration of inde-pendence in 1958 resulted in a brutal economic and political backlash that hobbled Guinea Conakry's potential in all sec-tors.
4. Ghana has the most sophisticated 16mm and 35mm facilities and laboratories in West Africa, a legacy of William Grierson's Colonial Film Unit. Unfortunately, it has never been fully and

effectively used within Ghana or for the rest of sub-Saharan Africa. The Bantu Educational Kinema Experiment (1937 to 1939) and the British Film Unit (1939 to 1945) were, in the first instance, short-lived programs aimed at rural education of the Africans and, in the second, propaganda films to mobilize Africans to fight during WWII. Other noted ventures in colo-nial cinema include films made by Catholic missionaries in the Belgian Congo's Congolese Center for Catholic Action Cinema (CCAC). Finally, in French Conakry Guinea, Sily Cinema was created in 1958 and made documentary and edu-cational films and newsreels. Basic 16mm production was established, but 35mm facilities remained incomplete.

5. Anglophone Africa has pioneering filmmakers in African cin-ema, including Nigerian Ola Balogun, Ghanaians Kwaw Ansah, King Ampew, Kwate Ni Owee, and others. However, although they might receive some government assistance, most of the work is produced in the private sector. As noted earlier, dramatic and documentary television programming to date is the main activity in anglophone Africa.

6. See Rudebeck 7, 12, 21, 71; Anderson; Kempton; Munslow.

7. Maldoror also made two short films after independence for the government of the Republic of Cape Verde in 1979, *Fogo, l'île de feu* and *Un carnaval dans le Sahel*.

8. For Mozambique, films included: *Viva Frelimo* (1969, Dutch), a report on Frelimo and an interview with Samora Machel; *A luta continua* (1971, American), by Robert Van Lierop, on Frelimo with a historical analysis of the country; *Dans notre pays les balles commencent à fleurir* (Sweden); *Etudier, pro-duire, combattre*, a film on a Frelimo school in Tanzania; *No pincha* (1971, Guinea-Bissau), 70-minute documentary on PAIGC; *Madina Boe* (1968, Cuba), *Nossa terra* (1966), *Labanta negro* (1966, Italy), *Le cancer de la trahison, Une nation est née* (1974, Sweden), *Free People in Portuguese Guinea* (1970, Sweden).

9. For a fuller discussion of this issue see Andrade-Watkins, "Francophone African Cinema" 215-35.

10. This is despite the fact that the productions through the Bureau of Cinema were 16mm, an issue, which became a source of contention between the filmmakers and the Bureau.

11. For a fuller discussion of Rouch, see "Jean Rouch, un griot gaulois."

12. Television came to Mozambique in 1979 without any particular benefit of Godard's participation.
13. Duarte's films include, chronologically: *Sou Angolana, trabalho com forca* (1975), a five-part TV documentary; 1976's *Uma festa para viver*, TV: 1977—*Angola 76 e a vez da voz do povo*—three documentaries for TV; a 1977 feature film, *Faz la coragem, camarada*; 1979—*Presente angolano, tempo mumuila* (10-part documentary series, TV); 1982—*O balanco do tempo na cena de Angola* (documentary); 1982's *Nelista* feature *Moia-O recado das ilhas*.
14. In late 1976/1977 the cine-club of Praia suspended its activities. Lack of financial support and internal struggles over direction of the cine-club contributed to its demise.
15. For example, the first major benefit in the US for the Institute was an historic national tour in 1981, organized by Positive Productions, Inc. in Washington, DC, and spearheaded by Ethiopian filmmaker Haile Gerima. The success of that tour resulted in the purchase of an optical printer and other materials for the Institute of Cinema. Gerima, an early supporter of the Institute, contributed his films to the library and archives of the Institute and encouraged other filmmakers to do likewise (Haile Gerima, personal interview, January 21, 1993).
16. Early landmark films of the Institute include: *They Dare Cross Our Borders* (1981 BW 25 minute, 16 or 35mm), South Africa's attacks on Mozambique and the reaction of the government and people; *The Offensive* (1980, BW, 30 minute, 16mm), an internal offensive against efficiency and incompetence; and *Unity in Feast* (1980, color, 10 minute, 16mm), a film on Mozambique culture, with a particular objective of valorizing and preserving the rich traditions scorned by colonialism. A prime example of regional collaboration is the documentary *Let's Fight for Zimbabwe* (1981, 60 minute), a documentary, co-produced by Mozambique and Angola, dealing with Zimbabwe's independence and with questions about the political stability and future of the region.
    The first feature-length documentary was *These are the Weapons* (1979, BW, 50 minute 16mm), a chronicle of the fight for independence, the internal struggles facing the people of Mozambique, and South Africa's strategies of disruption. Bringing the touch of Cinema Novo to Mozambique, Ruy Guerra's *MUEDA: Memorial and Massacre* (1979, BW,

35mm), was the first feature by a Mozambican; it is a blend of theater and reality. A small village in northern Mozambique, Mueda, was decimated by a massacre by the Portuguese in 1960. The theater play, created in 1968, is an annual reenact-ment staged by the survivors to commemorate the massacre.

17. Although Angola had a National Film Institute and shared the commitment of Mozambique, their lack of infrastructures lim-ited their production capabilities to collaborations or co-pro-ductions. A growing cadre of trained African technicians and administrators such as Pedro Pimenta, who joined the Institute in 1976, found their way to the Institute. As the Assistant Director/General Production Manager of the Institute, Pimenta played a pivotal role in the emergence of Mozambique. Born in the Central African Republic, Pimenta studied Economics in Portugal and taught in Maputo before joining the National Film Institute.

18. Some films were caught in the transition from the Institute to the free market sector. Two young Mozambican filmmakers, Joao Riberio and Jose Passe, were finishing their film training in Cuba during the upheavals at the Institute. Riberio's *Fogata* (1992, 20 minute, 16mm) is a drama based on a novel by Mozambican writer Mia Couto in which a peasant couple struggles with assuring each other's proper burial. Passe's *Solidao* (1991, 30 minute, 16mm), is a drama set on the eve of independence and revolves around the despair of a white Portuguese settler over his marriage to a Black woman, and the subsequent inevitable changes coming with independence.

WORKS CITED

Anderson, Hilary, *Mozambique: A War against the People*. New York: St. Martin's, 1992.

Andrade-Watkins, Claire. "France's Bureau of Cinema: Financial and Technical Assistance between 1961 and 1977—Operations and Implications for African Cinema." *Society for Visual Anthropology Review* 6.2 (1990): 80-93.

—. *Francophone African Cinema: French Financial and Technical Assistance 1961-1977*. Diss. Boston University, 1989.

Brito, Daniel Spencer. Personal interview. August 12, 1993.

Daventure, Andrée. Personal interview. Paris, August 9 and 25, 1987.

Diawara, Manthia. *African Cinema*. Bloomington: Indiana University Press, 1992.

Estatuto. Unpublished document of the Cineclube Popular de Praia. May 1975. Published in "B.O." 19 (May 10, 1975).

Filinto Correia e Silva, Anastacio. Personal interview. Sao Tiago, August 22, 1993.

Garcia, Jean-Pierre. "Le cinéma au Cap-Vert." *Le Film Africain* 12 (1993): 24-25.

—, and Caroline Helburg. "Cinéma et télévision au Mozambique, Rencontre avec Pedro Pimenta." *Le Film Africain* 9 (November 22.): 11-12.

Gerima, Haile. Personal interview. January 21, 1993.

Hennebelle, Guy. *Guide des films anti-impérialistes*. Paris: Centre d'Information sur les Luttes Anti-Impérialistes [CILA], 1975.

"Jean Rouch, un griot gaulois." Ed. René Prédal. Special issue of *CinemAction* 17 (1981).

Kempton, Daniel. *Soviet Strategy toward Southern Africa: The National Liberation Movement*. New York: Praeger, 1989.

Munslow, Barry, *Mozambique: The Revolution and its Origins*. New York: Longman, 1983.

Pfaff, Françoise. *Twenty-Five Black African Filmmakers*. Westport, CT: Greenwood, 1988.

Pimenta, Pedro. Telephone conversation. August 1992.

—. Letter to Claire Andrade-Watkins. January 27, 1993.

—. Personal interview. New York, November 11, 1992.

—. Fax to Rod Stoneman, Channel Four Television. London, February 1991.

Rudebeck, Lars. *Guinea-Bissau: A Study of Political Mobilization*. Uppsala: Scandinavian Institute of African Studies, 1974.

Solanas, Fernando, and Octavio Gettino. "Hacia un Tercer Cine" (Towards a Third Cinema). *Tricontental* [Havana] 13 (1969). Also in *Afterimage* 3 (1971): 16-35.

Taylor, Clyde. "Film Reborn in Mozambique." *Jumpcut* 28 (1983): 30-31.

A WINDOW ON WHOSE REALITY?
THE EMERGING INDUSTRY
OF SENEGALESE CINEMA

As INTELLECTUAL AND COMMERCIAL INTEREST in films from Africa grows, critics and artists alike continue to debate what exactly makes a film African, and what African cin - ema should be. Manthia Diawara's comprehensive work *African Cinema* ends with a chapter on "African Cinema Today," which describes the films at the 1989 Pan-African Film Festival at Ougadougou (FESPACO) in terms of three "narrative move - ments—the return to the sources, the historical confrontation between Africa and Europe, and the social realist" (140). He goes on to contextualize these movements within the discourse that surrounds African cinema:

> Each one of the narrative movements...presents an image of Africa that *makes a claim to be fuller and more faithful to real - ity* than the others...many people interpreted the diversified styles of films as a sign of maturity in African cinema. Others...argued that it marked the end of "mégotage" (film - making on shoestrings that reflects the "miserable" African condition of life) and the end of an era that privileged polemi - cal and loosely constructed contents at the expense of cine - matic forms. And others expressed concern that some film - makers have *used this opportunity to turn their backs on poli - tics* and on a serious questioning of the oppression of women and the marginalized. This argument also put forth that film - makers, by emphasizing beautiful images over serious content

analysis, *had surrendered to European notions of what African cinema ought to be*. (148, emphasis mine)

We can see in this account the most common demands that are made upon African cinema in critical circles: a demonstration of "maturity," a valorization of realism, the incorporation of a polit - ical message, and liberation from "European notions" or aesthet - ic demands. Wedged between accusations of unaesthetic simplic - ity, didacticism, and capitulating to the demands of a foreign mar - ket, African filmmakers nevertheless continue to produce the films that the world will, if sometimes reluctantly, call African cinema.

Diawara opens his book with an illustrative anecdote in which he quotes the director of the 1935 Bantu Educational Cinema Experiment arguing against the distribution of commer - cial films in Africa:

> With backward peoples unable to distinguish between truth and falsehood, it is surely in our wisdom, if not our obvious duty, to prevent as far as possible the dissemination of wrong ideas. Should we stand by and see a distorted presentation of the white race's life accepted by millions of Africans when we have it in our power to show them the truth? (1)

Ironically, this fear has reemerged in the north, particularly on the western side of the Atlantic. The "backwards peoples" have been replaced by a European/American public who are seriously underinformed about Africa. Members of this public, the majori - ty of whom may, consciously or not, take the cinema as a window to reality, risk generalizing from the one or two African films to which they are exposed to Africa writ large. This fear is clearly more reasonable than those of the British experimenters, and thanks to racism and an international power imbalance the con - sequences of the misinterpretation of African cinema by a north - ern public are potentially far more grave than those the British worried about. Misinterpretations do not have to be limited to non-African audiences; a spectator in Dakar might see a film from Ghana and decide that the Asante are like this or that, or that same spectator, who has spent all 16 years of her life in Dakar, might see a film set in a village in eastern Senegal and take it as a representation of her country's history. The British were wor -

ried about misinterpretations because they wanted to introduce Europe to Africa in a manner that would instill a proper dose of fear and respect; African filmmakers today worry because they have taken on the burden of representing to a potentially mass audience cultures that have been consistently and unfavorably misrepresented, when they have been represented at all.

In African studies today there is widespread recognition that there is no single African "truth" to parallel the mythical white truth that the British sought to represent. Within Africa as else - where, there are many different truths, many different stories and theories of representation, and many different filmmakers and films. What I would like to do in this paper, beginning from the three moments with which Diawara leaves off, is to look at a very local phenomenon: the status of Senegalese cinema in Dakar as of spring, 1994.

One can't talk about Senegalese cinema without talking about problems of finance and production. Senegal has no shortage of aspiring filmmakers, but it does lack technicians, producers, materials, laboratory facilities, film schools, and finances for the arts. Much more often than not, the cameraperson, top techni - cians, and producers of Senegalese films are European. This dependence (usually on France) is intricately and persistently tied up with any attempt to define Senegalese cinema, and much writ - ing and discussion have been devoted to its complexities (Diawara; *Presence Africaine*).

Even in Senegal, Senegalese films are difficult to find. The theaters in Dakar are usually filled with films from the United States, India, China, and a few from France. [1] There is no nation- al film archive, and at any given time a large percentage of Senegalese filmmakers are in Paris. The most comprehensive collection of African films on video can be found at the Centre de Communication, de Culture, et de Formation Daniel Brottier, at the Catholic Mission in Saint-Louis, though even here African films make up only a small portion of the center's videos, and only a few of these (less than ten in 1994) are Senegalese. [2] Other than this valuable film library, Saint-Louis has little else to offer filmmakers. For production materials one must go at least as far as Dakar.

At the French Cultural Center in Dakar one can find a few more Senegalese films (all those funded by the French Ministry of Cooperation) shelved away in canisters. The only other way to see Senegalese films is to find filmmakers who have copies of their works on video. Made-for-TV movies from Senegal are broadcast on francophone television stations, but even these are difficult to find after the fact. Not only does this situation com-plicate things for the scholar, it also means that young Senegalese filmmakers trying to situate themselves within "Senegalese" (or even "African") "Cinema" may have difficulty finding out what this cinema is.

There are political and financial explanations for this situa-tion. The broadest is that Senegal is in the midst of a severe eco-nomic crisis, which makes it impossible for the government to give the arts the kind of support that it did under the former pres-ident, Léopold Senghor. Nevertheless, filmmakers in Dakar believe that things could be better than they are, and to this end there are two issues that they repeatedly raise: taxation, and a national ticket office. Diawara has explained the difficulties faced by an African film trying to break through distribution monopolies and be screened in Francophone Africa (104-115); in Senegal, if a film does make it to local screens it is struck by the 30% tax that the state applies to all movie revenues. This high tax rate means that only very successful movies can make a profit, and since Senegalese films haven't had a chance to build up an audience or a following, they usually lose money. A number of filmmakers have refused to let their films be shown in the Senegalese cinemas until this tax is lifted for African films. [3] For this reason many Senegalese films are never shown in Dakar.

Some suggest that the government should nationalize ticket-ing and create a fund whereby revenues from movie admissions would be channeled back into local filmmaking (such a system exists in Burkina Faso). But in 1994 the country was still reeling from the currency devaluation imposed by France and the IMF in January of that year, and supporting film was not a high priority. Few people were optimistic that any such measures would be taken. For the three previous years filmmakers at the RECIDAK festival (Rencontres Cinématographiques de Dakar) had request-ed these changes, but despite the presence of President Diouf at RECIDAK '92, and the government's declaration of the 1990s as "the decade of Senegalese cinema," little has changed.

So the money for the films must come from elsewhere. Since independence, the French have maintained very close ties to Senegal through the sponsorship of cultural productions and events. This has allowed French technical and production companies to maintain a firm grasp on west African film both as a market for technicians and materials and as a commercial product. Though Senegalese filmmakers do often look elsewhere for funding (Switzerland, The Netherlands, and increasingly other African countries), a glance at the cinema scene in Dakar makes it clear that the French are still in control.

French involvement in Senegal has never been disinterested, and the film industry is no exception. If a production company agrees to take on a Senegalese film, it is because they think that they can make money from it. This raises another major question: who is this cinema for? Filmmakers in Senegal generally feel that African films should be made foremost, though not exclusively, for African publics. A common response to this is that the African public doesn't like African films. But while some argue that people go to the movies to escape and don't want to see their daily problems reproduced on the big screen, others say that people naturally prefer films about their own problems and experiences to those from other cultures.[4] Whatever the case, for many filmmakers these arguments miss the point, which is that by the time their films make it to the theaters in Dakar, they have been altered to cater to the demands of their European producers. Diawara speaks of "a typology of narratives that compete for the spectator's attention" (140), but it is the producer's attention for which the narratives must compete first. And producers see the main markets for African films as festivals, arts theaters, specialized television, and universities.

There is disagreement over exactly how the pressures of production play themselves out. Some filmmakers say that Europe wants films about a romanticized rural Africa that is of no interest to modern urban Africans, some that Europe insists on funding films about the city when every African could tell or would like to hear a story about the village, and others that European producers play with and create false rural/urban, traditional/modern dichotomies. The causal relation of aid to subject, though probably significant, is not obvious: it is as difficult to talk about "the" Senegalese public, its tastes, demands, and needs, as it is to talk about "the" Senegalese filmmaker, and so speculating as to what a strictly by and for the Senegalese film would be like is probably not worthwhile.

The discussion of Senegalese versus European audiences is further complicated by the fact that the Senegalese film market and world are not large enough to support a high and a low culture industry. The success of African films in Europe and America is usually at festivals, art houses, and in academic or intellectual circles. American and European markets are large enough that a film can make a little money without being a blockbuster. In Senegal, perhaps even in Africa as a whole, this is not the case. Distinctions between high and low culture in Senegal are less obvious (to the European/American critic) than they are in Europe or America.[5] Abstract or experimental films that might make money in an arts circuit would have little chance in the Senegalese market. A Senegalese film must therefore either compete with the popular films in Dakar, or target an audience abroad. As a result, filmmakers who chose not to cater to popular formulae are accused of being Westernized—if a film seems an impossible bet for the Senegalese public it must, the reasoning goes, be aimed at Europe. Thus both of Djibril Diop Mambéty's beautiful feature length films, *Touki Bouki* and *Hyènes*, which are probably too obscure to appeal to a mass audience anywhere, have been accused of being too European. (The irony, of course, is that popular formulae are no less European.) Rather than freeing Senegalese film from culturally imperialist influences, external demands, even when they come from Africa, often essentialize and dictate boundaries that constrain the genre.

Many believe, therefore, that financial independence is a prerequisite to an independent cinema, a cinema free to express its own aesthetics and politics. At the 1983 FESPACO, which was held under the theme "Cinema and Liberty," Mahama Johnson Traoré described the process of cultural bribery and constraint imposed by the semi-involvement of African governments in cinema production:

> en tenant les cordons de la production, en refusant la mise en place de véritables enterprises audio-visuelles, en laissant la possibilité à d'autres sources de financement "d'aider" le cinéma africain à se faire, les pouvoirs politiques et financiers se réservent-ils toute possibilité de contrôler, en amont et en aval, la création cinématographique en Afrique. (30)

[by holding the strings of production, refusing the establishment of genuine audio-visual enterprises, leaving open to
other sources of funding the possibility of "aiding" the making
of African cinema, the political and financial powers reserve
for themselves all possibilities of controlling, from above and
below, cinematographic creation in Africa.][6]

The government has provided enough aid to impede the development of private local structures, but not enough to support a
national industry. Because this aid is incomplete, filmmakers find
themselves bound, if not to their own governments, to the interests of the northern countries that provide funding. Traoré makes
it clear that aid from the north is not charity: "En retour, cette
même démarche a permis à ces pays du Nord...de créer des
vocations de producteurs exclusivement branchés sur les films
africains" (31) [In return, this same course has allowed these
Northern countries...to create jobs for producers working exclusively on African films]. The lack of local structures for production and training assures the African filmmaker's dependence on
the north, and Traoré links thematic liberty to financial liberty:
"Qui dit bailleur, dit *décideur*...outre le fait qu'il [le réalisateur]
perd sa liberté de création, il devra souscrire, impuissant, à l'image que l'Europe veut imposer de l'Afrique" (31) [Those who
lend money are those who make decisions...beyond the fact that
he [the director] loses his creative freedom, he must subscribe,
powerless, to the image of Africa that Europe wants to impose].

Foreign aid and light government intervention have impeded
the creation of an independent inter-African film industry, allowing Europe to continue to represent (and, when possible, profit
from) the African films of its choice, as its discoveries. Many
Europeans have capitalized the most from the notion that the
future of cinema lies with Africa. In the following reading of
three recent Senegalese films, I hope to bring out traces of the
process of a cultural decolonization, both theoretical and practical, with which Senegalese cinema is struggling.

Three feature length Senegalese films have met with success over
the past few years on the international film-festival circuit:
Ousmane Sembène's *Guelwaar* (1992), Moussa Touré's *Toubab
Bi* (1991), and Djibril Diop Mambéty's *Hyènes* (1992). All three

have shown in Paris, but only briefly in Dakar. Sembène refuses to let his film show in Senegalese commercial cinemas until the tax is lifted. When Sembène was awarded the 1993 Grand Prix de la République du Sénégal pour les Lettres for the collection of his literary works, he publicly asked President Diouf to fix a date for a grand opening of *Guelwaar*. In December, the film was shown in the Foire, a huge and somewhat inaccessible theater, with tickets costing between 2000 and 5000 CFA ($8-$20). [7] About a month later it was shown in Thiès as the highlight of a Sembène film festival; but two years after its release it had yet to be made widely available to the Senegalese public. Moussa Touré insisted that *Toubab Bi* open simultaneously in Paris and Dakar (at the French Cultural Center), but only two years later did it appear in a commercial cinema in Dakar (in an elite theater, where it remained for a week). *Hyènes*, the only Senegalese film selected for Cannes 1992, did respectably on the French film market, but lost money when it showed in Dakar. Collectively, these films illustrate the problems faced even by the best-financed, most technically sophisticated, and most successful Senegalese films.

The difficulties and antagonisms surrounding his latest film serve to emphasize that the evolution of Sembène's cinematographic career is inseparable from that of African cinema. His films are the best distributed and, in Europe and the US at least, the best known of any African filmmaker. He began setting the course for the industry in the sixties with films like *Borom Sarret* (1963), the first film produced under the support of the French Ministry of Communication, and *Le Mandat* (1968), the first film in an African language (Wolof). His films are political and critical, attacking French colonial abuse of Africans (*Emitai* [1971], *Campe du Thiaroye* [1988]), religious imperialism on the part of both Christians and Moslems (*Ceddo* [1977]), and post-colonial bureaucracy and corruption (*Le Mandat*). *Guelwaar* continues on this track, mixing social critique, and political message.

The film opens with the announcement of the death of Guelwaar (an honorary title that associates the hero with the virtues of noble caste). His funeral is held up for lack of a corpse, because the hospital has confused two bodies and given Guelwaar, a Catholic, to a Muslim family. By the time the mistake is discovered, the Muslims have buried Guelwaar and refuse to believe that any mistake has been made. The Christians march out to the Muslim cemetery to reclaim the body; the Muslims march out to protect their sacred space. Their religious leaders negotiate, and the military holds the Muslims at bay while the Imam disinters the corpse (the troop of gendarmes provides as much comic relief as protection: when they descend from their truck and point their huge guns at the hot, angry people armed only with blunt objects it is clear whom any ensuing violence will claim). The Imam digs up the body and hands it over the fence to Guelwaar's family, who takes it away for a Christian burial.

We are introduced to Guelwaar himself through a series of flashbacks. We see that he is fiercely independent—he shouts to his wife that he would rather his daughter be a prostitute than a beggar—and in his grandest scene he gives a speech at a rice donation ceremony denouncing the mendacious mentality that has taken over the country. (During the speech, we see various government officials looking gravely at one another, and there is a hint that their decision to put an end to Guelwaar's preaching is not unrelated to his unexplained death.) The closing is didacti- cally symbolic: the funeral parade comes across a truck full of donated rice—presumably the rice promised to the Muslims by the round, suited National Assembly delegate who shows up in the midst of the crisis to assure the people of his hard work and devotion. The procession comes to a halt while the children stop the truck and dump the rice on the road, and then continues, crushing the donated rice beneath their feet and under the wheels of the cart that carries Guelwaar.

This film, circulating around a corpse, offers the audience no single hero to follow. The closest thing to a hero is Guelwaar himself, but since he is dead before the film begins the spectator is denied the easy pleasure of placing hopes and sympathies in a single character. In 1983 Jacques Binet cited the relative absence of heroes as characteristic of African film, and suggested that spectators of such films risk becoming voyeurs, detached from the spectacle. Binet describes this as a strategic error, but it could also be a tool: by refusing to offer a character through which to enter the story, *Guelwaar* shuts spectators out, making them feel themselves as observers rather than participants. The film opens with a dim back view of Guelwaar's lame son walking slowly into his house, bearing news of his father's death. Guelwaar's wife and daughter are introduced through partial shots, crossing very close to the camera; only after we've heard them wailing do we see their faces, and the son, whom we followed into the house, disappears from view. The dead man is an ideal driving the film, and the visual and narrative cross cutting from character to character illustrates and contextualizes this ideal.

Guelwaar's wife wails on and then reproaches the empty suit waiting on her bed, in one of many scenes, which suggests that the fate of the corpse cannot overshadow the fate of the living. In the Islamic village, the dead Muslim's two wives hide their magazines and put on their mourning dress as they hear their brother in law and a policeman approaching. A few scenes later the younger wife throws of her mourning clothes and tells her co-wife that she can't stand the boredom, she's had it with mourning, and she's going back to her family. Similarly, the mourners at Guelwaar's funeral tire of waiting for hours for the body to show up, and grumble about needing to get back to their lives. And when the body finally turns up, it smells: throughout the battles being waged on its behalf, it has been rotting. The story thus circulates around the corpse, but is never subordinated to it; a series of other stories emerge while we wait for the body.

We are clumsily led through the search for the corpse by Guelwaar's other son, who lives in France and has taken French citizenship. Appearing in a dark Western suit, expressing scorn for Senegal, and initially refusing to speak Wolof, this son serves as an unambiguous portrait of cultural alienation. The policeman with whom he is reluctantly paired in his search is the person through whom we first see Guelwaar in the form of a flashback to a confrontation between the two men about religious violence. Sembène plays with our loyalties, and so while the policeman was an enemy of the dead hero, he wins the audience's sympathy as he calmly deals with the son's whining about the heat, the slowness, and the formalities of negotiating with the Muslim family. The son tries to get his way by calling upon his French citizenship, but earns only scorn and jokes at his expense, and a small victory is won for Senegal when the son finally confronts an uncooperative officer and demands his rights as a Senegalese citizen. The message is hardly subtle: though there are no colonialists in the film, the son demonstrates that there are Africans who are willing to take the colonialists' place. Despite his educational success and tasteful French clothes, this son is part of the plight that Guelwaar's widow bemoans: her daughter is a prostitute, one son is lame, and the other is physically and psychologically lost to France. Through the widow's mourning and anxieties, we see that Guelwaar too is a complicated hero whose family suffers for his resolute insistence on financial independence.

If we were to file *Guelwaar* within Diawara's classifications, we would call it socialist realism. The colonial conflict is implicitly present in the film's three major themes: religious conflict, refusal of foreign aid, and false consciousness or cultural alienation. The juxtaposition of these three themes reminds the viewer that the religious conflict that serves as the film's central axis is no less of a disruptive importation or imposition as are the aid that Guelwaar refuses and the French nationality assumed by Guelwaar's son.

Such a take on religion is not new to Sembène. His film *Ceddo* (which Sembène translates as "un homme de refus" [Hennebelle 125]) is a story of resistance to three hostile foreign elements in the seventeenth century: Islam, Catholicism, and the trade of guns and alcohol for men to be sold as slaves. The battles of religious conversion are thus shown to be inseparable from the slave trade. Two hundred years later, Islam and Catholicism are still tearing people apart, but the exogenous leaders have disappeared; the slave trade has been abolished, the colonialist leaders have withdrawn, and subordination is now assured by a steady stream of aid that, according to Guelwaar, creates bonds of dependence. As Chris Miller puts it, "France promotes by impeding and impedes by promoting" (188), which is to say that decolonization is contingent upon the maintenance of economic relations with France (and also with the international monetary organizations) on France's terms (as the January 1994 devaluation of the CFA made painfully clear). In the film, foreign aid is used by the neocolonial political powers (the well-dressed delegate) to buy their subjects' political loyalty, much as the politicians themselves have presumably been bought off by the foreign donors whose aid they embezzle.

What kind of relationship does *Guelwaar* have to the kind of political and financial pressures it critiques? The film was a co-production between the French company Galatée Films and Sembène's company, Domireev. Financial support came from the French ministries of cooperation and culture, as well as several European television stations. But the producers claim to have minimized French involvement, and describe the production as 75% Senegalese, 25% French: "Notre savoir faire était utilisé à la demande des Sénégalais" (Garcia and Helburg, 1992:7) [our knowledge was used as requested by the Senegalese], they explain. The film received no aid from the Senegalese govern-ment. Is it possible to detect in *Guelwaar* traces of the restraints described by Traoré? The film is an unapologetic treatment of the manipulative relationship between religious and political powers in their battle for the loyalties of the people (which represent democracy, demanded by the North as a condition for aid). The political drama that takes place in the film mirrors those that Traoré describes in the film industry: democracy and filmmak-ing, both potentially powerful institutions, are manipulated for immediate political aims. It is possible, therefore, to recognize in the film a metaphor for the conditions of it's own production.

The film is filled with discouraged, wounded people (the Muslims, the Catholics, and the Gendarmes) who seem willing to kill each other to protect the ideologies they live for (Islam, Catholicism, and the State). But the thing that remains alive and independent throughout the film is the Wolof dialogue, which makes no concessions to French financiers. Non-Wolof speaking viewers are aligned with the Westernized son, who doesn't get the jokes (of course, his language and vitality come back to him when he reclaims his Senegalese citizenship, while foreigners have no such option). Also, the incorporation of the rituals that one sees every day in Senegal and the mocking of pious hypocrisy (religion is not wholly condemned—while many of the followers are made to seem petty and naive, the Imam and the Priest have a laudable spirit of dialogue and attempt to avert bloodshed) create a humor that is dependent upon an understand-ing of both the rules that are being broken and the realism of the caricatures. Offering a dead hero, digging up a corpse, mocking religion, the state, and the influence of France, *Guelwaar* asserts its freedom from French and Senegalese mores alike through its language and cultural jokes, while providing the foreign viewer with just the kind of exoticism that sells best as "African film." By using the language and beauty of his culture both to appeal to a foreign audience and to tell a story that this audience can't understand, Sembène simultaneously caters to and resists European demands.

Moussa Touré's *Toubab Bi* is structured around the kind of bina-ry oppositions that *Guelwaar* challenges. Touré does provide the spectator with a live hero to follow through the film—Soriba, a young filmmaker going to Paris for an internship. But the quest for cinematographic knowledge is subordinated to tasks given to him by his relatives and friends: primarily, to find his childhood friend Issa, who for many years has been sending home money without a word. As a hero, Soriba has little to be faulted for. In Dakar we see him getting along wonderfully with his family (mother, sister, wife, and child), joking with and charming people on the street, and respectfully following the counsel of old men. When he pairs up with a little boy whom he is given at the airport and told to reunite with his father in Paris, the two of them charm the audience and most of the people they meet (including the frail young woman he takes up as a lover, with no trace of tension or guilt about his wife and child at home). Issa, in turn, is a perfect antagonist: he runs a successful prostitution and drug business out of a porn-video shop, takes no interest in his family in Senegal, has two wives in Paris whom he treats as servants, and operates not by charm but by intimidation. To get Issa back to Dakar, a marabout sacrifices a rooster, wraps it in a Maggi Cube box, and sends it airfreight to Paris. We then see Soriba dreaming of chasing Issa through the baobab forest at home and through the streets of Paris, finally touching Issa's cheek with the rooster and inflicting a large gash. When he awakes, Soriba searches for Issa and finds him at the airport, being deported by the French police, with a gash on his cheek.

The film presents an opposition of caricatures: Soriba is the obedient son, loyal to his home but unafraid of exploration, faithful to his elders; Issa is the alienated cynic who sees no future for Africa and is seduced, from within his velvet-wallpapered office, by the seedy and criminal side of city life—drugs, sex, too much leather. The film opens in Dakar with Soriba searching through bales of used clothes for a winter coat, and is sprinkled with jokes about the dangers of the cold, a cold that chases Soriba and the boy back into the metal and glass of the Paris airport. Dakar and Paris are thus presented in terms of a set of opposites: Dakar is colorful, warm, friendly, and familial, with small open houses, beaches, spiritual leaders, and happy children; Paris is grey, cold, and laden with sin and madness, with tall buildings and automatic doors, irresponsible fathers, abandoned elderly mothers, and spoiled dogs. Dakar is a mixture of urban social sights (markets, street-barbers, *car-rapides*) and nature (the ocean, old men on the

213

sand, boys among baobabs); Paris is mechanized and isolating (the echoing airport, escalators, towering buildings, the metro), and the only nature on view is the snow. After a run through the pillars of a Paris building that parallels their childhood runs through the baob-abs, Soriba shouts at Issa that he must return to Senegal, "vivre dans la pure simplicité" [to live in pure simplicity]. Issa, high on heroin, laughs. This simple binary structure is the central axis of the film. Touré explains that his object was to awaken a part of the public that was alienated and cut off from their roots by a "false" culture: "L'image…ne signifie plus une idée, mais un choc. Ce qui est blanc, doit être blanc, ce qui est noir doit être noir" (Gnonlonfoun, 10) [The image…no longer signifies an idea, but a shock. That which is white, should be white, that which is black should be black]; "toubab bi" translates from Wolof as "the white person"—meaning Issa's false consciousness).

These caricatures produce an upbeat comedy with a simple moral in which good triumphs over evil. The character who sug-gests that the binary order can be questioned or escaped is pun-ished, and the order is reestablished. One can read the film, pro-duced by the French, as illustrating both African social criticisms and European desires. Africans can travel to France, but they should ultimately live in Africa—moving permanently to France (like Guelwaar's son) means sacrificing the family, denying African identity, and trying to turn oneself from black to white. The film lets us choose between the happy man who loves Africa and is scared of the cold and the pimp drug runner. It adds to the familiar interpretation of acculturation as destructive to Africa the comment that it is also destructive to France—which, given the rise of the racist right in France over the last few years, might be considered politically irresponsible. And yet why should an African film be required to provide an all-encompassing political answer to problems of racial prejudice and imperialism? Such a demand recalls the Bantu film experiment and the fear of repre-senting a culture to those who might mistake image for reality. So while the film's considerable merits (good acting, comic moments, slick production) deserve acknowledgment independ-ently from its politics, an examination of this politics can tell us about the culture—a French-Senegalese, post-colonial, late capi-talist, artistic culture—that produced it.

The rigid binary structures produced and reproduced in *Toubab Bi* reveal an anxiety about boundaries. The borders

between Senegal and France can be crossed with relative physi -
cal (if not political) ease in both directions, and the results are
unsettling. The film's highlighted French presence in Senegal—
the old clothes people fight over in the market and the aspirin
sold on the street as a formula against the cold—is relatively
unobtrusive, though French (neo) colonialism is implicit in every
urban shot. The Senegalese presence in Paris receives more atten -
tion. Soriba finds a small, friendly restaurant full of west
Africans, but also an upscale Senegalese restaurant with a white
clientele, including a whining woman with braided blond hair
whom Soriba coldly dismisses as she tries to show off her curso-
ry knowledge of Wolof. Issa brings Senegal to Paris with his
polygamy, the irony of which is represented by the boubou that
he pulls over his leather suit so that he can sit on a stool and eat
a Senegalese meal around a bowl in his luxurious house.

Food and clothing no more preserve Issa's cultural identity
than they make the French woman Senegalese. Nor do Issa's
slicked down hair, clothing, or other accessories make him
French. The work started by the marabout that sent the sacrificed
rooster across the ocean is completed by police who escort Issa
to the airport in handcuffs for deportation. The French forces of
legal order thus unite with the Senegalese forces of traditional
order to maintain identities and reestablish borders. Challenging
one's identity is translated in France into drugs and prostitution,
to challenging the law. Cooperation, like co-production, is possi -
ble only if boundaries between Senegal and France are respected
and affirmed. A film internship in Paris does not, the film insists,
weaken one's Senegalese identity, and as long as an exchange
remains simple and temporary, like a voyage or an affair (Soriba
won't let his French lover photograph them together—a relation -
ship without evidence, outside of but not against the law, will not
disturb identity if it is not frozen into permanence), it poses no
threat. When one tries to create a new life outside of the laws of
essentialized identity, when one suggests that things might be
more complicated than black and white, the law steps in to set
things straight. And one is left with a popular comedy.

Mambéty's *Hyènes* is an adaptation of Friedrich Dürrenmatt's
play *The Visit of the Old Lady*, set in the fictional Sahelien town
of Colobane. Linguère Ramatou, who left the town 30 years ear -

lier poor and pregnant, returns now old, crippled, and richer than the World Bank. She offers the impoverished town financial sal-vation in exchange for the death of Draman Drameh, her former lover who denied before a tribunal that he had gotten her preg-nant so that he would be free to marry a richer woman, forcing Linguère to leave Colobane in shame and become a prostitute. Linguère wants a trial, his life to pay for the loss of her youth. The town responds indignantly that their pride and humanity are not for sale. Thus begins what would be a beautiful tale of para-noia were it not based in truth. Draman, the town's shopkeeper, starts noticing luxury items among the poor townspeople, who suddenly demand huge credits from his store, which, though he knows they will never pay, he doesn't dare refuse. People con-stantly assure Draman of their loyalty, but tension and greed in the town grow until finally, in the name of justice, the people of Colobane decide to try and punish Draman for wronging Linguère.

The film sticks by the fantastic details of Dürrenmatt's play: Linguère's body is made up largely of artificial parts, the result of a plane crash years earlier of which she was the sole survivor, and she brings with her the two men whom Draman payed to bear false witness at her trial, whom she has castrated and turned into her personal slaves. Despite the entirely Senegalese cast, the Sahelien setting, and the use of Wolof, the film has a placeless quality—the costumes, for instance, not only of Linguère and her entourage but also of the villagers, come from no single tradition or people. And the magical and disorienting appearance of a car-nival in the middle of the desert suggests that money can make all places the same. The precision of the translation from play to film and from Switzerland to the Gambia suggests an implicit capitalist universalism—money corrupts in much the same way everywhere in the late-capitalist world of international consump-tion (the villagers are won over by imported cigarettes, liquors, and shoes from Burkina Faso).

The reception of *Hyènes* in the European press, as reported by Jean-Pierre Garcia in the French journal, *Le Film Africain*, is telling:

> Dialogues crus, froids, terriblements contemporains et… occi-dentaux. Djibril Diop Mambéty donne une nouvelle dimension au cinéma africain. Ses personnages s'inscrivent dans une

tragédie que la terre africaine amplifie et sublime... *Hyènes*, film emblême d'un pays aride et sauvage...(4)

[The dialogues are harsh, cold, terribly contemporary, and Western....Djibril Diop Mambéty gives a new dimension to African cinema. His characters inscribe themselves in a tragedy that the African land amplifies and sublimates... *Hyènes*, film emblematical of an arid and savage country...]

The dialogue, of course, is largely from Dürrenmatt, and "contemporary" and "Western" appear to go hand in hand, while Africa adds sublimely savage landscape. And again:

La mise en scène de Djibril Diop est particulièrement efficace dans la mesure où elle est trés occidentale dans son rythme soutenu et son découpage; elle conserve néanmoins une couleur profondément africaine par la musique de sa langue, la saveur de ses dialogues et l'interprétation de ses acteurs. (4)

[Djibril Diop's direction is particularly effective to the extent that it is very Western in its constant rhythm and its editing; it conserves, nonetheless, a profoundly African color with the music of the language, the flavor of the dialogue and the interpretation of the actors.]

These praises are based on the familiar binary structure of the technical versus the natural: the dialogue, the pacing, the editing are "Western," while the landscape, the language, and the actors make the film "African." The film is praised for being less African than most African films, for incorporating Africa's natural, exotic appeal into the technical rigor of the West. But why are technical skills automatically coded Western? Why and for whom is the African countryside tragic? In fact, the figure of Linguère challenges this coding: her reconstructed body blends the technical and the natural, Africa and Europe, cruelty and tragedy. She comes home to Colobane, but refuses to romanticize it. From within the framework of a German play, Mambéty's film plays with, and bends the boundaries and definitions that Touré's film rigidly enforce.[8]

Thematically, Dürrenmatt's play provides Mambéty with a subject particularly appropriate to the state of Senegalese film production. Like *Guelwaar*, *Hyènes* comments on the corrosive powers of money. As Linguère puts it, "C'est moi qui propose l'affaire. Et je dicte mes conditions" [It is I who propose the affair. And I dictate my conditions]. Is it possible to resist the demands of the people with the checkbook? Do filmmakers, like the people of Colobane, fool themselves into thinking that what the producer wants is what they had planned all along? Of course, we can't take the comparison between Linguère and French pro - ducers very far—Linguère suffered at the hands of Colobane and is coming back for revenge. She is both the hyena who waits for her prey to die before she descends and the omniscient bird described by a song in the film as "l'âme des morts" [the soul of the dead] who promises liberty. The Senegalese film industry at times seems almost as financially destitute as Colobane: is finan - cial support a promise of freedom or a death sentence? The answer depends on whether one identifies with the people of Colobane or with Draman. For Linguère these questions are irrel - evant; she is concerned only with the result. The film is a search not for identity, but for survival and revenge.

In these three films it is possible to read varying commentaries upon the condition of Senegalese cinema today. Where is this cinema going from here? "Il risque de mourir" [It is in danger of dying], says Mahama Johnson Traoré, former president of the Association des Cinéastes Sénégalais (interview). The financial difficulties are overwhelming, and filmmakers have yet to unite to create the inter-African production and distribution circuits that everyone agrees are essential to a competitive African film industry. Though there are many aspiring filmmakers, few films are being made, and there is a significant absence of well-trained young filmmakers (1994 Sembène is in his seventies, Mambéty passed away in 1998; Touré is one of Senegal's youngest film - makers, in his thirties). The excitement and motivation of the 1970s, when the industry was new and money was available for productions, film school abroad, and distribution, have vanished.

Most films being made today are short films for television, both documentary and fiction. They focus on very particular aspects of contemporary Senegalese life: Dakar nightlife (*Bandit Cinéma* [1993], Bouna Medoune Sèye), AIDS in the city (Saï Saï Bi [1995], Bouna Medoune Sèye), women's sexual secrets (*Dial-Diali* [1992], Ousmane William Mbaye), a train across the Sahel (*Dakar Bamako* [1992], Samba Félix N'Diaye), teenage aspirations and rivalries in a small town (*Les enfants du Popenguine* [1993], Moussa Sene Absa). One of the best shorts of the nineties is the late Amet Diallo's *Boxumaleen* (1991), a comic, and moving day-in-the life about a gang of boys in Dakar, which won the Prix de la Création at Cannes. The other recent major feature length film, Clarence Delgado's *Niiwam* (1992), is an effective and technically daring adaptation of a novel by Sembène about a village man taking a bus through Dakar with his dead child. These are beautiful, playful films with serious undertones, which prove that the major African filmmakers have no monopoly on technical skills, and that critics need to stop complimenting African films as being "mature." These films pay at least as much attention to form as to content (the films of photographer Bouna Sèye have a particularly impressive aesthetic), and are uninterested in political didacticism.[9] The films' subjects are treated with respect and intimacy, and in turn they allow the camera a glimpse into their lives. Many of the actors are amateurs, people whom the director finds already living in the film's setting. In these cases the relationships between the director and the actors determine the final product—especially when, as is often the case, the screenplay is written in French and the dialogue is in Wolof, adapted by the actors themselves.

Senegalese cinema must now confront the awakening of a capitalist consciousness among the people within and around their films. The extras collected at the train station, the man whose dried fruits artfully obscure the camera, and the owner of the taxi borrowed for the shoot all recognize cinema as an industry, and know that the camera, lights, and people in action represent money. When European directors came to Africa, the exploitative relationships were obvious; but when race and colonization are set aside, economic inequality remains. Mambéty puts himself into his films as an extra, performing a small subversion of hierarchy. In his short film *Le Franc* (1995) he sits through a scene on the fender of a *car-rapide*, with his head hidden in his arms, as the action files past. The foreground is occupied by extras found on he spot, momentarily taking center stage while the director hides his face in the background. The film, which tells of a poor man who dreams that he has won the national lottery, portrays a dream masquerading as reality in which the poor become rich, "extras" become central, and powerful people are obscured—obscured, but present, on both sides of the camera.

Within the short playful films that constitute much of Senegalese cinema today, the escapist fantasies that make cinema a powerful international industry are struggling, against daunting economic realities, to emerge.

NOTES:

1. For a comprehensive history of distribution politics, see Diawara, 104-115.
2. In addition to a substantial library that includes complete collections of over 40 film periodicals, the center has a file system with a folder for almost every African film, even if many are empty or contain only one article (this file is on computer, along with a 100 question African cinema trivia game). The library/cinematheque was created and was run for many years by the French Missionary, Père Vast.
3. The director of the Office of Cinema in Dakar told me that President Abdou Diouf signed an agreement to lift the tax in 1991. In 1994, he said that it had not yet passed the Ministry of Finance, but that the change was imminent. The information in this essay about laws and screening histories of individual films dates from late 1994.
4. In Pikine, a densely overcrowded Dakar suburb, teenagers in a Hindi club learn dances and songs from Hindi movies, dress in Saris, and study the language: whether or not this is evidence for movies as escapism, it indicates a sincere enthusiasm for foreign cinema.
5. In *In My Father's House* (Oxford: Oxford University Press, 1992), Kwame Anthony Appiah argues that in Africa "the distinction between high culture and mass culture, insofar as it makes sense at all, corresponds by and large to the dis-tinction between those with and those without Western style formal education as cultural consumers.... The opposition between high culture and mass culture is available only in domains where there is a significant body of Western for-mal training"(148). Though it certainly exists, the high-cul-ture market for Senegalese film is small and promises little profit.
6. This is my translation, as are all following.
7. In an interesting demonstration of the politics of cinema, Sembène changed the date of the opening twice in an

attempt to assure the presence of the President. Though security at the opening was heavy, after an hour of waiting Sembène had to make do with a selection of ministers and wives, Diouf having ostensibly stayed home to mourn the passing of Houphouët-Boigny, the President of the Ivory Coast.

8. The production and reception of *Hyènes* raise theoretical questions about cultural translation, universalism, and the definition of "African" cinema. Why can the adoption of a Swiss play by a Senegalese filmmaker be read as alienation, while the use of African materials as inspiration for European artists is rarely criticized on the same grounds (although debates over appropriation of cultural capital have been taking place at least since the 1984 "Primitivism in Twentieth Century Art" show at the Museum of Modern Art in New York). What if a Swiss had made the film? What if Mambéty had made the film in Switzerland? These questions indicate how entrapping attempts to define culture with essentialized identities can be. *Hyènes* might have benefited from a more ambitious departure from the original play, but this is a formal, not a cultural or theoretical critique.

9. "Moussa Sene Absa's feature *Tableau Feraille* came out while this article was being published and it represents an interesting hybrid of didactic politics and fantasy.

PART FOUR

FEMINIST APPROACHES
TO AFRICAN CINEMA

WOMEN WITH OPEN EYES, WOMEN OF STONE AND HAMMERS: WESTERN FEMINISM AND AFRICAN FEMINIST FILMMAKING PRACTICE

IN THE INTRODUCTION TO HER *Black Women Writing and Identity* (1994), Carole Boyce Davies defines the term "Black" provisionally and relationally, refusing to assign to it one fixed signified. Nonetheless, in all of its different nuances she finds a core of resistance, of oppositionality to the whiteness that would absorb it. "The term 'Black,' oppositional, resisting, necessarily emerges as whiteness seeks to depoliticize and normalize itself" (8).

A similar formulation might also be used to distinguish the approaches to feminism taken, in general, in the West—and more specifically in the theoretical writings of the French feminists of the 1970s, with their strong psychoanalytical approaches and dis - ruptive strategies—from those followed by the preponderance of African feminists, and more specifically those women producing films around feminist themes. For the Europeans such issues as the status of the subject, gender identity, gendered language, patri - archy, and above all oppositionality predominate; for the Africans, feminism is more a concern over gender equality and social or economic justice. One would overturn the club; the other would join it.

For French feminists like Cixous, Irigaray, and Kristeva, oppo- sition to patriarchal structures led to radical challenges to the ways in which the subject was constructed. Following Derrida's decon - structionist attacks upon logocentrism came feminist attacks upon the phallocentrist positions of a subject heir to Enlightenment val -

ues and to the Law of the Father. Barthes's (1953) description of realism as an essentially bourgeois project, with the foundations of the novel established in the rise of the 18th century bourgeoisie, led to conclusions that tended in the same general direction: the power relations underlying the social structures of Western society were manifested in cultural practices which disarmed any opposition by privileging representation, and by assuming a "natural" and "normal" point of view. Opposition came to be associated with deviancy, hysteria, or, as transvaluated by Kristeva, the feminine. It also was translated into literary madness, refusal marked by silence; marginal practices, marginal living; art without control, automatic writing giving way to bodily inscriptions, and finally, for cine-critics, the embrace of sound superseding the scopophilia of sight.

Undergirding the ideology of the realist novel, as well as that of mainstream commercial cinema, is the dominant position accorded representation. In the Lacanian analytic approach, devel-oped by Stephen Heath in *Difference* (1992), representation is associated with the illusory wholeness of the Symbolic order, the "scene of the phallus"—phallus here taken as signifier of signifiers. It is not on the imaginary, but on the Symbolic order that we func-tion to restore the lost sense of wholeness, for our sense of our-selves and for the world around us, disrupted in the mirror stage. That wholeness marks the gaze and its desire—desire not just to restore wholeness, but also to inform the object of sight with mean-ing. The scene of the phallus is thus integral to the pleasures of scopophilia, and is generated by the positioning of the subject as the one who looks, and thereby finds/produces wholeness and meaning. (The equivalent action occurs when the signifier is affixed to a signified, or, more broadly, when language emerges as the ground for the subject-position. The "wholeness" of the sub-ject then has its equivalency in the wholeness or meaningfulness of the object of sight.) If the mirror stage is marked by lack, by the castrating repressions of the Law of the Father, the sight of images organized into a wholeness restores the subject to a position of empowerment where its desires can be fulfilled. The subject is sit-uated through the look, in contrast to the subject position associ-ated with sound. The correspondence between sight and wholeness arises because sight naturally fixes on an object and endows it with the quality of undividedness—at the limit with a perfection, expressed in film as a *Ten*, a seamless torso that can be seen without itself having a subject-position from which to return the total-izing gaze. For conventional cinema that perfect object is the site/sight of the woman. And when she is not a *Ten*, when she turns interlocutor, or better, mirror reflection, it is not so as to upset the action of the lens—camera oscura or ocular—but to affiliate her gaze with that of her admirer. Katherine Hepburn and Spencer Tracey as the perfect couple who see so much alike.

This conventional totalizing gaze appears throughout virtu-ally every scene in *Warrior Marks* (1994) in which each image is turned into a representation with its meaning tagged on before-hand. Its meaning is always uncontaminated by division, and is returned so as to confirm the a priori significations attached by the filmmaker—the one who looks and whose look imposes order. The final order, like Katherine Hepburn's universe, is a pure reflec-tion of the conventional signifying film—a man's film in women's clothing. While Alice Walker recounts her own story of ocular mutilation, concluding with the defiant gesture of the warrior, what is reinforced is the phallic order of the Symbolic, an order whose regime is so imperative that even the old women circumcisors are reintegrated into an anti-circumcision order. The truth of the film is grounded in the notion of a neutral, natural order where there is no gendered speech, no "*écriture féminine*," but only the order of truth—phallic and Symbolic. Instead of disruption there is merely substitution; instead of silence, or a new language, it is the same old words with the same old meaning, with only the terms switched around.

The fears of Carole Boyce Davies that Black feminist criti-cism should be subverted or subordinated by mainstream Western or Western feminist criticism (Davies, 1994: 52) can be seen to have been well grounded when we consider Walker's dominant position in *Warrior Marks*, a position like that heavily critiqued by Trinh T. Minh-ha (1982, 1989) as belonging to the outsider who assigns to himself the authority to impose a meaning on every sig-nifier—the authority Walker translates into the woman warrior's stance. [Figure 1] The symmetries of the Symbolic are not dis-rupted, nor is there the silence of another order, but the accept-ance of the conventional patterns of meaning in which the only challenge to patriarchy—to those who inflicted the patriarchal wound on Walker's eye, or on the women's genitalia—is to do battle on their own terms.

Figure 1

Representation, in film, cannot avoid the implicit codes of mastery built into its own conventions, its anthropological posi-tioning. Oppositional filmmakers could only escape these traps by establishing a self-conscious structuralism that insisted first upon meta-textual analysis, and then the rejection of meta-textuality, and finally rejection of a grounded text altogether. The end result of this rejection is an assemblage, a re-piecing together of scenes, laid disjunctively side-by-side, with a sound track placed in approx-imate proximity. The dead end of this filmic practice could only take the form of Trinh T. Minh-Ha's question in *Reassemblage* (1982), "a film about what?," or more apropos, the lapidary asser-tion, "I find less and less the need to express myself." Julianne Burton has indicated the approach interpreters of Third Cinema, if not Third World cinema, must take to escape being trapped by Hollywood, mainstream cinematic values: "Since only bourgeois or colonized film-making endeavors to conceal the processes by which it produces meaning, the role of the interpreter of Third

World film is simply to place Third Cinema in its proper socio-aesthetic context and to appraise its achievements in terms of its own cultural/ideological outlook" (Burton, 8).

Such a simple formula occludes the problematic issue of representation and of the subject for the French feminists. A film about what? becomes, with many African women filmmakers, a film about women's problems; the open ended texts of Cixous and Irigaray, *l'écriture féminine*, its silences and resistances, become, for mainstream African feminist filmmakers, films about questions for which all the answers are provided. Open space closes down again, as the self-assured camera becomes the unseen, unobtrusive, invisible mechanism with which the real world is represented with its real world problems. In short, the revolution of western women feminists turns against the cinematic practices of Black women activists, and the metaphor employed by Cixous, that women are the dark continent, turns ironically around against itself.

Similarly, the neutral space of the mediator whose function is to place Third Cinema in its proper context can be likened to the neutral language of standard speech, to the neutrality of dominant theoretical propositions, to the neutral values with which main- stream culture has always affiliated itself. Neutral and neutered return as dominant and gendered, or, in any event, like the camera, as positional and relational. In analytical terms, the neutral order is the order of the Symbolic; conventionally the ground for patri- archal structures, for the order of the signifier, or the phallus, engaged in the struggle to overcome its division from the signified.

In her early work in *Ngambika*, Boyce Davies would seem to evoke an African feminist approach that moved in the direction of that same neutral, or universal, position when she writes, "An International Feminism to which various regional perspectives are contributed seems acceptable to African women while the European/American is not" (10). The propositions of this International Feminism are then enumerated in programmatic fashion, and include concerns over "[the] lack of choice in mother- hood and marriage, oppression of barren women, genital mutila- tion, enforced silence, [etc.]" (7), all of which Boyce Davies describes as lying at the crux of African feminist theory.

In her more recent study Boyce Davies would seem to eschew such an Internationalist approach, as we see in her warnings against assimilation or co-optation; we now find the resistance of

"Blackness" to a whiteness that seeks to depoliticize and to normalize, a resistance that resembles French feminism in its stance
against patriarchal culture, language and practices that represent
themselves, represent representation, as normal, neutral, and apolitical, and ultimately as the ground for goodness. And we find a
strong current of African feminist filmmaking practice, from Safi
Faye to Sarah Maldoror to Anne-Laure Folly, that reaffirms its
own mainstream cultural norms by adopting a cinema of *vérité*, of
truth, of one truthness, of representation. Further, this is a cinema
in which the solutions put forth take the form of women joining the
exclusive male club, not disrupting the established order. If we are
to look for Burton's placement of this cinema in its own cultural
context, we would have to ignore its considerable distance from
Third Cinema as disruptive, as *Imperfect Cinema*, as Garcia
Esposito (1970) would have it, and recognize its adopting of mainstream anthropological or realist film practices and presuppositions.

One finds in the writings of Assia Djebar, Werewere Liking,
or Calixthe Beyala a resonance with the call for an " *l'écriture
féminine*" issued by Irigaray in the 1970s. Djebar has attempted to
carry this project forward with her films, and it is important that
we begin to assess whether the work of other African women filmmakers cannot also be seen as concerning itself with more radical
feminist positions; whether, in other words, the act of seeing is not
problematized so that the resistance to patriarchy is extended to the
expressions of the body or to sound; whether the totalizing effects
of visual representation are not resisted in such a way as to call into
question the Symbolic order; whether film can be shot, edited, and
its images abused so as to evoke something of Kristeva's semiotic
or pre-Symbolic chora, a space in which the terms "morality,"
"equality," and "knowledge" are not yet posited as answers.
Whether there is an African cinematic practice that resembles
Heath's description of the feminine specificity in writing, defined
as

> [E]ither silence, she silenced in the discursive reality, the real-
> ity of discourse, or writing as silence, her silencing—Forrester's
> forgetting—of the orders of language, her practice of a language
> that is wild, on the body, unauthorized. (73)

The "unauthorized" question that occurs at the meeting of these two feminisms, is whether European feminists would regard African feminist filmmaking practices as inadvertently sustaining a patriarchal order, thus subverting their own goals. The question can also be turned in the opposite direction by asking whether the grounding of French feminism in western theoretical and analytical values doesn't automatically produce a disjunction with African feminist approaches committed to social agendas. Are we dealing with a fundamental incompatibility, or are there valid criticisms of each position to be made? To determine the answer, we will turn to two films, *Femmes aux yeux ouverts* (1993) by Anne-Laure Folly and *These Hands* (1992) by Flora M'mbugu-Schelling, whose approaches will be assessed in light of this dilemma.

Femmes aux yeux ouverts begins with Martine Ilboudo presenting three conventionally constructed positions that indirectly lend support to the above critique of African feminism. The assumptions she makes are that oppression of women stems from three proverbial beliefs, i.e., that:

- Women should follow all the instructions of their husbands;
- Women shouldn't be educated, shouldn't read;
- Women shouldn't open their eyes.

From these statements we can derive the propositions whose Enlightenment values automatically follow:

- All men are equal, meaning women like men should share in equality;
- Knowledge is power, meaning women should share power with men;
- Seeing is knowing, meaning women should seek understanding for themselves and not rely upon men to provide them with answers.

All these propositions rest upon the assumption that women's problems lie in an uneven distribution of power, and that that is entirely built into their relations with men. Once power is redistributed, like land, the problems will be solved. There is no questioning of the distribution system upon which power itself depends, certainly no challenge to an existent order. That would make little sense in a scenario in which women's goals are to adhere to that order.

Thus when we learn that women led the revolt against the government in Mali, it was not so as to create a new structure of power
relations in society, but so that women could be part of the government. If this was not the point of the protest by the women
themselves, it is implied in the film when we see that now there is
a woman stepping into the limousine, and occupying the position
of governor in the region of Bamako. Similarly, by the end, it is not
a challenge to the distribution of capital in society that is mounted,
but rather a celebration of the presence of women millionaires in
Benin. The subject-positions are reallocated without themselves
undergoing any transformation.

The highlighting of reading as a means of gaining access to
power is significant. It conforms to an understanding of the
Symbolic order as the basis for all claims to legitimacy, and identifies the basic demand of the women's movement in this film as
adherence to the established order. This is reinforced by the third
and most prominent proposition: that women be given sight. The
subject-position of the sighted is that of the one who looks through
the lens, whose seeing is recorded as testimonial to the truth
implied in the vision. The epistemological position of the images
of the women is that of passive objects recorded by the camera as
doubly feminized: they are *seen as women* because they are
engaged in typical feminine activities, and because they are seen:

> The woman is to be seen, completely, she is all seeing, satisfied
> in that, always there in the mirror, hidden and visible, behind the
> keyhole; which is to say that, omnivoyeur, spectacle of vision,
> she has no look, provokes only in image and not as subject in
> return. (Heath 79).

If we have women on both sides of the camera, looking at each
other, the images are no less totalized; no less undivided representations of those in need of opened eyes (*Femmes aux yeux
ouverts*).

The voice-over that assures us of the presence, meaning, and
needs of the women never turns back on itself, never sees the split
in the mirror of its own devisings. It turns us outward towards a
"condition" whose meaning is defined by the act of presentation:
"Voilà la condition de cette femme-là." "Voilà la condition de cette
femme-là" presents the real as certain and whole; establishes the
narrative space as equally undivided and authoritative; and even

Figure 2

establishes its authenticity in the accented speech that is recognizably that of an African woman. Authenticity is thus self-authenticated, while our attention is directed outward, towards the women on the other side of the bars, the women held in the frame of the tree and its branch. [452] The viewers' point of view is shared by the narrator, and is subordinated to the order of the narrator, which is established not only by the camera but by the distance marker *"là"* tagged onto the narrative *"cette femme-là."*

The bars suggested by the trees evoke a strange imprisonment, with Foucault's tower and panopticon as the site of knowledge and power joined to the camera's position. As the woman is defined as *"l'objet donné,"* we observe the woman observing the camera, looking back…at us; not challenging, but not ignoring the apparatus either. As the narrative voice continues to describe the women as passive and submissive, the images of the women seem to move in defiance of the bars, of the controlling space and frames, out into an openness. The dialectic is then established between the wonderfully aestheticized portraits, women held in perfect and perfectly natural frames, and those moving independently. *"La femme africaine,"* anonymous, defined, and compliant—the perfect image—contests the apparatus as she is fixed by it. [Figure 3]

Figure 3

There is little space in the film's narration for free movement. We are continually told about the African woman and her predica - ment: *"tout est à l'homme, vient de l'homme, doit finir à l'homme."* But in the end, it is the wealthy women merchants of Benin to whom everything belongs, and ironically it is not by the acquisi - tion of "book," not by the status of the educated, that their position is obtained. They are not literate and they carry on their computa - tions in their heads—without Bic or calculator. The irony is not accidental. After the list of oppressions is concluded—the excision, forced marriage, AIDS—what remains, despite the Enlightenment program of reform, is the reconstitution of the woman's image into a new identity, one so entirely removed from that Western ideal of enlightenment as to subvert the film's own scientific propositions in the process of articulating and exhibiting them. This is the read - ing I propose to the extraordinary footage of the woman wearing conventional Muslim scarf and sunglasses who presents the tech - niques of utilizing condoms before a bemused male audience. [Figure 4] The woman's public role as health worker and family

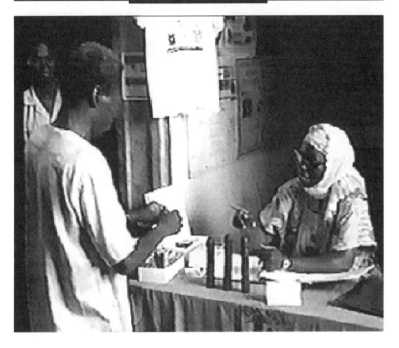

Figure 4

planner conveys the new attitude towards modernity, one underscored by her desk and "equipment," while the conventional dress
reaffirms her determination to shape her role within the space of
her own cultural definitions.

In contrast to the rational substratum and structuring of
Femmes aux yeux ouverts, we have the exquisitely understated
formulations of Flora M'mbugu-Schelling whose film, *These
Hands*, provides the images of women whose lives consist of
pounding rocks for a living. Here one finds much that might be
seen to be antithetical to *Femmes aux yeux ouverts,* despite their
common reformist intentions.

Unlike *Femmes aux yeux ouverts,* which begins with three
stated propositions to guide us along its trajectory, *These Hands*,
by Flora M'mbugu-Schelling, begins with silence, restraint, and a
rhythm that combines labor and detailing—physical labor and
meticulous cinematic detail [Figure 5]—and that ultimately succeeds in establishing a finely tuned rapport with the film's audience. The viewer is joined by a fastidious, slow panning of the

235

Figure 5

women's blows, to experience with them the endless task of reducing large stones to small ones, of transforming a hillside into gravel,
so that the trucks, driven by men, might cart it away. We don't
even know whether the women are doing this as some form of
penal labor, or whether they are working for a mining concern,
until the end of the film when we are informed that the mounds of
gravel they are heaping up, and that it takes a woman two months
to produce, earn her twelve dollars.

Patiently, the film seems to be telling us this is how to pound
a rock and break it into smaller and smaller pieces. And as we
watch, we are gradually forced to enter the rhythm of the tedious
work. We are, in fact, at a great distance from those films in which
visual pleasure is bought at the price of the woman's subject-position. In place of the erotic object, a new kind of cinematic woman
emerges here—the woman of stone and hammer, deglorified, de-
eroticized—full, not in the sense of possessing a wholeness of
meaning, but with the force of determination, of pedestrian persistence. This is one of the most wonderful of testimonial record-

Figure 6

ings of the African woman, one in which any superior sense of pity the viewer might feel is suppressed as the distance between "us" and "them" is gradually effaced, and we spontaneously enter into a sympathetic sharing of the women's lives.

At one point there is apparently a rock slide and a woman is hurt or killed—we don't know, can't see, aren't told what hap - pened. Shortly thereafter a mourning song is intoned by a circle of women whose voices are now heard as they sing, "We remain with silence," and, "In a strange jungle/ there is only silence." And carved out of the gravel pit, by their collective voices, their clap- ping of hands, is the dancing figure of a new grace who is suppli - cated, "Don't disappear into vanity." [Figure 6] Then the sound and sight of hammering return.

There are no millionaire women at the end of this film, no women warriors, no victims even. Just stone hard images of women who must persevere in what seems like a Sisyphisean effort at sur - vival, and who yet can find it in themselves to laugh and dance and sing a song about longing for home.

At the conclusion of the film a written text appears, informing us about the nature and payment for the women's work. But the cin - ematic experience reaches for something other than statistical fact about the hardship of women migrant laborers. That other dimen - sion we may also wish to include in our understanding of a newly shaped African feminism in which the instrumentality of the cam - era now figures along with the voices and gestures of working women. In this regard, *These Hands* is exemplary for its quiet expressiveness and restraint, which permit the cinematic experi - ence to unfold as an "other" form of film.

One way in which to define that "otherness" may be found in John Fiske's (1989, 1992) deployment of the concept of "distance" in cultural theory. Fiske demonstrates that markers of distance function so as to separate high and popular culture, so that a read - ing at a distance might be seen to yield universal, aestheticized meanings, whereas a reading in close proximity will foster histor - ically or socially specific meanings. The former depends upon a social authority that is inseparable from the institutional context that frames the reading; the latter upon a closeness to bodily sen - sations, "for it is our bodies that finally bind us to our historical and social specificities" (1992, 154). The "mundanities of our social condition" are set aside in favor of a transcendental appreciation of universal values.

The application of this opposition to our two African films is obvious. *Femmes aux yeux ouverts* strives to impart a set of val - ues that are universally valid for women. It cannot attach itself to any mundane experience in women's lives without simultaneously averring a principle that extends beyond the particularities of the moment. This is also true of *Warrior Marks* where the issue of distance is made all the more significant by Alice Walker's pres - ence, by her imbrication into the issue of excision in Senegalese culture and her refusal to acknowledge an indigenous justification for the practice. Fiske would employ the term "distance" to indi - cate a means of inhabiting a certain space, a "habitus," as he would have it, borrowing the term from Bourdieu. Fiske's elaboration of this manner of inhabiting a habitus describes the *Warrior Marks/ Femmes aux yeux ouverts* form of feminist practice perfectly:

> [It is] characterized by high educational levels, high cultural but low economic capital that has been acquired rather than inher- ited. And within this same habitus we may find the taste for

congruent social and academic theories, a taste expressed in the dispositions for macro-theories that transcend the mundanities of the everyday through distantiation, that move towards generalized, abstracted understandings rather than concrete specificities and that try to construct academic or political theories that are as distanced, detached, and self-contained as any idealized art object. (155)

It is no coincidence that *Ngambika* and *Femmes aux yeux ouverts* begin with lists that define the condition of oppressed African women *in general*, and that the film presents that list by employing the filmmaker, Martine Ilboudo, to provide the authoritative narrative voice. The "idealization" is clearly indicated by the truths we are invited to perceive, as is indicated by the *"yeux ouverts"* in the film title.

The habitus constructed in *These Hands* is infinitely more modest. The "habits" of those who inhabit the space are reduced largely to the action of pounding rocks. Yet it is ultimately seen as a social space, where all the main "axes" of the social order appear, i.e., economic capital, cultural capital, education, class, and historical trajectories (Fiske, 1992, 155). The camera's close-up, the repetition of shots of hands holding rocks, hitting them, taking up the pieces, hitting them again, taking up new pieces, hitting them again, brings us as close to the rhythms and physical experiences as can be done with film. The absence of narrative voice to guide us places us alongside, and not in front of, the women. It is a substitute habitus, whose substitution, through cinematic image, cannot be expunged, but whose distantiation can be minimized. And so, although we eventually learn who the women are—"we" not being Mozambican women living in exile, pounding rocks in Tanzania—and are also invited to form our opinions about the conditions that result in such labor being compensated at a rate of $12 per two months, the Symbolic significance does not overwhelm the Imaginary. More to the point, the matrix of semiotic elements, to use Kristeva's term for the presymbolic imaginary, is conveyed through the emphasis upon bodily signification at the expense of cognitive signification. The "message" is inscribed in the blows of the women of stone and hammer, in their fingers and arms, and in the repeated actions that lead to the production of mounds of gravel.

If it is through the body that "the mechanisms [work] that organize us into disciplined subjects required by capitalism" (Fiske, 1992, 161), then it will be through feminist theories of the body, and feminist films that approach the signifying practices of the body, that our appreciation of the disruptive potentialities of fem - inism can be realized. In our study of these two different African women filmmakers' endeavors we can see the possibilities for a meeting of French feminist thought and African feminist film practice, as well as for the well-known collisions between Euro-cen - tered theory and Afro-centered production.

WORKS CITED

Barthes, Roland. *Le degré zéro de l'écriture*. Paris: du Seuil, 1953.
Burton, Julianne. "Marginal Cinemas and Mainstream Critical Theory," *Screen*, 26, 3-4 (May-August 1985): 2-21.
Davies, Carole Boyce. *Black Women, Writing, and Identity*. New York: Routledge, 1994.
— and Anne Adams Graves. *Ngambika*. Trenton, New Jersey: Africa World Press, 1986.
Esposito, Julio Garcia. "For an Imperfect Cinema" (1970). In Michael Chanon (ed.), *Twenty-five Years of the New Latin American Cinema*. London: BFI and Channel Four, 1983.
Fiske, John. "Cultural Studies and the Culture of Everyday Life," in *Cultural Studies*, ed. Lawrence Grossberg, Cary Nelson, and Paula A. Treichler. New York and London: Routledge, 1992.
—. *Understanding Popular Culture*. Boston: Unwin Hyman, 1989.
Heath, Stephen. "Difference" in *The Sexual Subject: A Screen Reader in Sexuality*. London and New York: Routledge, 1992.
Minh-ha, Trinh T. *Woman, Native, Other: Writing Post-Coloniality and Feminism*. Bloomington: Indiana University Press, 1989.

Films

Femmes aux yeux ouverts (1993), dir. Anne-Laure Folly.
Reassemblage (1982), dir. Trinh T. Minh-ha.
These Hands (1992), dir. Flora M'mbugu-Schelling.
Women Warriors (1994), dir. Pratibha Parma.

THE MATURE AND OLDER WOMEN OF AFRICAN FILM

Everyone is in the hands of their [sic] mother.
—Postscript of *Ta Dona*

MATURE MATRONS AND ELDERLY WOMEN are frequently and eloquently presented in films produced in sub-Saharan Africa during the last thirty years. These films sharply focus on the struggle of African women to re-define their identity in the context of global turmoil in contemporary African culture. Because of their repertoire of experience and their relative freedom from the cycle of pregnancy and child rearing, mature and older women have developed greater personal autonomy and social sophistication than their younger counterparts. The painful tension between tra -dition and change affects these women dramatically because they, more than their younger sisters, are wedged between old and new social expectations. These women's lives mirror the tumult and the challenge of contemporary Africa.

I emphasize representative patterns in the characterization of women while acknowledging that there are exceptions that do not conform. Rather than discussing all the relevant examples exten -sively I concentrate on the richer, more complex illustrations drawn from these mostly recent films made in western, central, and south -ern Africa:

Country	Title	Director	Year
Senegal	*Xala*	Sembène	1974
	Guelwaar	Sembène	1991
	Touki Bouki	Mambéty	1973
	Hyènes	Mambéty	1991
Mali	*Yeelen*	Cissé	1987
	Finzan	Sissoko	1989
	Ta Dona	Drabó	1991
Burkina Faso	*Yaaba*	Ouedraogo	1989
Zaire	*La vie est belle*	Mweze & Lamy	1987
Cameroon	*Quartier Mozart*	Bekolo	1992
Zimbabwe	*Neria*	Mawuru	1992
South Africa	*Mapantsula*	Schmitz	1988
Madagascar	*Angano...Angano*	Paes & Blanc-Paes	1989

The cinematic portraits of women reflect African conventions about body types and distinguish among young, middle-aged, and elderly women. These images also express social assumptions about the distinct functions of the "three ages" of women. Nubile women tend to be svelte with a classic facial beauty compatible with western or—if you will—universal standards (e.g., Kabibi in *La vie*, Attu in *Yeelen*, and the bride in *Xala*). Young women tend to be tall and wear form-fitting clothes, either western or African, to compliment their willowy bodies. Their appearance radiates youthful beauty and sexual vitality rather than fecundity.

In contrast, the typical matron is heavier, more robust, and wears African clothing with matching head ties. Loose garments accommodate her amplitude. Matronly faces conform to the African preference for large features (e.g., Mamu and Mama Dingari in *La vie,* Sytsalla in *Quartier*, and the bride's mother and Oumi, in *Xala*). Their figures express the African association of fertility with fleshly magnitude. These women emanate the prosperity and confidence attained through their increased power and status in the family. Some matrons gain independence and wealth from losing a mate (whether to death, desertion, or divorce is not specified). By independently brokering advantageous matches for their marriageable daughters these women accrue profit and pres - tige for themselves and often maintain their control over these daughters.

Elderly women are thin, almost emaciated, with sparse hair and wrinkled features, etched by years of experience. They wear rough, homemade garments and subsist in rural poverty. They live alone or at least without husbands. They have ceased to be sexual objects or potential mothers and can no longer perform hard labor. Their inability to fulfill such crucial female roles places them in social limbo with paradoxical consequences. On the one hand, they may be respected for their special powers such as arcane knowledge of fetishes, proficiency in remedies for illness and injury, and insight into human behavior. But, on the other hand, they may evoke social ostracism or even persecution as dangerous witches, charges that continue to vex African societies today (Drogin).

Such double-edged stereotypes powerfully inform the cine-matic roles of elderly women. Nianancoro's mother in *Yeelen* exemplifies the virtuous, wise crone who comprehends secret Bambara knowledge and Diarra family history, which hold the key to her son's fate. She has become a refugee and exile to protect him against his violent father and to safeguard the powerful fetishes that Nianancoro requires to complete his mission. Although she can not act directly against her evil husband, still she manages alone to rear a strong and ethical hero. To aid him in his quest, she sac-rifices to the water goddess. She stands waist deep and bare breasted in a reedy lake, displaying a natural dignity untarnished by sexual self-consciousness. Cissé's choice for this role of an 83-year-old woman—much too old to be the mother of a young man about twenty—indicates that he intends her to be an icon of wis-dom rather than a realistic portrait of a biological mother. Her ema-ciated body displays the triumph of spirit over flesh.

Yaaba ("grandmother") illustrates the destructive attitude toward older women. Sana, an elderly crone, lives in poverty and isolation from other people. She has no family and is vilified and shunned by the village adults, who deem her a dangerous witch responsible for all misfortunes. The film condemns such cruelty and emphasizes the affection between two powerless groups within rural society—the very old and the very young—who band together against the prejudice and hostility of the other villagers. Two chil-dren befriend Sana, bring her needed food, and seek her guidance and affection. In return, she diagnoses the girl's deadly tetanus and obtains special medicine to save her life. Sana also teaches the children compassion and tolerance for people who, like her, do not conform to rigid, moralistic community values.

These examples indicate that even the elderly women respected for their special knowledge do not "fit" the conventional roles for women and pay the price of social isolation, which could develop into alienation or even persecution.

Life is problematic even for the matrons who have spouses and adhere to the traditional female roles—childbearing, domestic labor, and obedience to the husband. They pay a price for their conformity, particularly when polygamous marriages exist and the succeeding wife becomes the "trophy" spouse. In *Xala* El Hadji's first wife Adja, a traditional woman who wears the old fashioned Muslim robes, remains at home to care for her children and never complains about her husband's polygamy even when he neglects her in pursuit of a third, very young bride. Adja is not even aggres-sive like the other wives in requesting money. She exerts only passive resistance to the second wife, Oumi: Adja insists that Oumi must come to greet her, a prerogative of the first wife. And she alone stands by her husband in his financial and professional ruin. The film takes an ambivalent view of Adja—respect for her loy-alty and dignity but not for her passive suffering, which Sembène implies results from destructive Islamic custom.

Mad Dog's first wife, Sytsalla in *Quartier Mozart* does not openly rebel when her husband takes a younger second wife Kongassa. But Sytsalla competes with her rival by flaunting her superior cooking, and she commandeers the television set for her room. The director plays this domestic situation for comedy, yet the conflict darkens when Mad Dog threatens to shoot Sytsalla and then evicts her bodily from the house. She is separated from her children and forced to sell her food in the market to make a living.

Guelwaar's wife in *Guelwaar* combats a different rival—her husband's political activism—for which she pays a heavy emo-tional and financial price. He does not support his family, and they live on the earnings of their daughter, who is forced into prostitu-tion. He spends his time campaigning against Senegal's corrupt acceptance of western food aid. His wife complains bitterly to Guelwaar, throughout the marriage, and, after he dies, she addresses her anger to his burial suit laid out on the bed. The empty clothes symbolize Guelwaar's deafness to her feelings and his default of domestic responsibility.

Adherence to customs regarding the remarriage of widows inflicts great cruelty on Nanyuma in the fiercely feminist *Finzan*. Rejoicing in her new freedom from a brutal, unloved husband, she must then fend off her foolish brother-in-law Bala's obsessive love for her. The chief, most of the village women, and even her own relatives refuse to support her objection to him, citing the custom that the dead husband's brother must assume legal responsibility for the widow. Nanyuma is kidnapped, beaten, tied up, and brought by force to submit to the marriage. But she refuses any sexual rela - tionship with Bala and threatens him with a knife. At the end of the film, she leaves the village for an uncertain life away from the oppression she has experienced, asserting the feminist credo of *Finzan* that the future of Africa depends on justice for women.

In contrast to victims such as these, some mature women aggressively seek status and money. Matrons use their privilege as mothers of nubile daughters to achieve status through advanta- geous, usually polygamous matches. Both Kabibi's mother in *La vie* and the mother of the young bride in *Xala* "sell" their daugh- ters to rich, powerful older men without regard for the prospect of marital harmony. These mothers reap a harvest of gifts and public adulation by praise singers. Kabibi's mother, a successful and grasping landlady, dictates the rules governing her mini-fiefdom and constantly raises rents for her impoverished tenants. Although these women must support themselves and could justify their alle- giance to traditional practices, the films condemn their greed at the expense of others and their indifference to the personal happi - ness of their daughters.

The second wives of El Hadji in *Xala* and Mad Dog in *Quartier Mozart* compete with the first wives for sexual access to the husbands and/or control of domestic affairs. Both women are westernized in dress and manner and psychologically dominate their husbands by heaping on them a litany of abuse and demand. To support her taste in clothes and life style, El Hadji's wife Oumi drains him like an inexhaustible bank. Money seems the only source of power he retains in this marriage, and he substitutes it for personal responsibility. But neither marriage succeeds as both sec - ond wives desert their husbands when they lose their position and income. These women have adopted the economic rationale for marriage, which custom has taught them.

Mamu, the wife of Nvuandu in *La vie*, exercises the most comic and ruthless female dominance. She counters her husband's penchant for secondary school girls and his taunts about her infer - tility with constant verbal insults and commands. In addition, she belongs to a sorority of liberated matrons who band together to drink, party with handsome young men, and generally flaunt their insolent disregard for their spouses. Mamu has the advantages of a wealthy husband, a luxurious house, a car with chauffeur, her own lucrative textile business, and complete freedom; she will brook no rivals. She thwarts her husband's second marriage to a young girl by aiding the girl's access to her truelove, a penniless musician who works as Mamu's house servant.

Yet these quarreling spouses eventually reconcile and affirm their underlying love for each other. Mamu repents of her partici-pation in the women's group and asks his forgiveness; Nvuandu gives up his young bride and presumably terminates his quest for schoolgirls. The film's closure conforms to the comic requirement that the proper couples are matched in happy unions and that exces-sive behavior by all parties is purged. *La vie* could be termed an urban fairy tale, but its dark tones undercut its optimistic title or turn it ironic.

Even though some films like *Xala, Quartier Mozart*, and *La vie est belle* employ shrewish or manipulative wives as instru-ments of satire against husbands or instigators of comic disorder to upset conventional male control, there is more at stake than ful-fillment of a genre. The satire and comedy arise from sexual and economic inequality in real life, and the films reflect at least uneasiness and confusion about male-female relationships and at most a criticism of male dominance.

Many films indicate a serious moral/ethical dimension in women's defiance of social rules and concur in the women's revolt. Kabibi in *La vie* submits to the arranged but loveless marriage but continues to rendezvous with her lover, and, when the husband violently curtails her freedom, leaves him and his dazzling bribery gifts. Mad Dog's second wife Kongassa responds to his physical abuse of her and of his children by leaving him.

Female rebellion strikes not only at domestic injustices but also at larger social and global perversions of justice. Nianancoro's mother in *Yeelen* loses everything but her life and her son as she flees her vicious and politically powerful husband. She invests her energy in rearing a child who will destroy his father's corrupt male secret society and restore ethical Bambara governance.

An elderly woman named Ambaraziy in *Angano...Angano*, the Malagasy documentary about oral tradition, objects when her brother rationalizes the inequity for women in customary inheri-tance law. The folktale he tells concerning a shiftless husband with a hard-working wife justifies his two-thirds share and her one-third by invoking the difference in how much weight each could carry, men using a shoulder pole and women a basket on the head. Ambaraziy laughs but says that, if she had been in the story, she would have used a pole. He retorts that God ordered each sex to carry in its traditional way. She concludes that "We've been had." Ambaraziy's open opposition to custom is surprising and significant in several respects: she attacks not just a male but her brother, and she undermines the very foundation of Malagasy culture—the social and religious authority of oral tradition. In addition, her objection is not private but recorded on film for a public audience.

Traditions concerning widows, particularly in rural areas, pre - clude justice for the women. In *Neria*, when Neria's husband dies, her brother-in-law Phineas and her mother-in-law expect Neria to leave her city job and home to rejoin the rural relatives, marry Phineas, and relinquish control of her life, children, and property. Rural law considers women as tied to the husband's ancestral lands and family and as helpless without male guardianship. Neria rep - resents the "new" independent and employed African woman who must use European, urban law to regain her rights. Neria's mother-in-law comes to understand through this turmoil that she has per - verted rather than fulfilled traditional custom, and she then supports Neria's choice to remain a widow living in the city. Although this film suffers from a rather contrived "happy" ending and fits more comfortably in the category of educational/propagandistic rather than artistic film, its very didacticism qualifies it as a barometer of significant social issues.

Personal tragedy radicalizes a Soweto mother in *Mapantsula*. When her son Sam dies in police custody after being arrested at a political demonstration, she is no longer just an ordinary old woman trying to survive the daily hardships of poverty and corrupt township government. She marches in the vanguard of the student protests and falls a martyr to the police tear gas and gunfire assault. Her courage inspires even a selfish street hoodlum and police informer to refuse further cooperation with injustice.

Using the mode of social realism to document women's rights issues, African films forge a powerful social instrument to empower women in a more effective way than expository vehicles of persuasion. The emotionally compelling stories and characters of the films implicitly urge women to take responsibility for their own lives and to reject destructive traditions. But they refuse to gloss over or sentimentalize the price women may pay for their defiance of convention. *Finzan* expresses its message with explicit militance, concluding with these words of the persecuted Nanyuma as she leaves her village in search of a new life:

> The world comes from our wombs. It mistreats us. We give life, and we're not allowed to live. We produce the food crops, and others eat without us. We create wealth, and it is used against us. We women are like birds with no branch to perch on. There's no hope. All that's left is we must stand up and tie our belts. The progress of our society is linked to our emancipation.

But there is another, rarer dimension in the cinematic portraits of older women, which endows them with a mythic, sometimes archetypal, resonance that transcends ordinary social reality. Filmmakers such as Cissé, Drabo, and Bekolo create larger than life characters by exploiting the inherent surrealism of the film medium with its dream-like communication. They tap unconscious psy - chic resources to give their films a profound resonance. Their use of gesture and body language, ritualized actions, symbolic visual motifs, composition/rhythm of shots, and *mise-en-scéne* radiates mythic energy.

These directors' mythic characters are exclusively older women. The two most elderly—Nianancoro's mother in *Yeelen* and Mother Coumba in *Ta Dona*—are similar in significant ways. Both live in exile from their people and are so old and physically depleted that they exist on the cusp between life and death. Their special knowledge surpasses rational understanding and ordinary experience. Yet the two women are also individualized.

Nianancoro's mother is primarily an icon of pious, sacrificial motherhood. Numinous imagery animates powerful sequences such as her oblation to the goddess of waters. As she stands waist-deep in the river, she becomes a creature half flesh and half liquid. The flowing streams of milk she pours on her head consecrate her upper body, and unite the devotee with the deity. The milk sacri - fice mimics both the literal and metaphoric nurturing the mother has provided her son. The shots of her lifting bowls high above her head while intoning her prayer are slow, repetitive, and ceremonial. The empty bowls move on the water seemingly by their own power and nestle against the reeds. This imagery suggests the attempt by

Moses's mother to save her son's life by committing him to the Egyptian river.

A more complex and explicitly mystical woman, the elderly healer Mother Coumba, appears in *Ta Dona*. She lies solitary and dying in the desolate cliff area of Mali where sacred grave niches hold the bodies of ancestors. Magic fetishes—including female fertility objects—adorn her dwelling. She possesses lost, secret Bambara knowledge, the seventh *canari*, a sovereign remedy for childbirth and associated conditions. Mother Coumba remains alive, much like Simeon in the New Testament, only until Sidy, the one destined to receive her knowledge, arrives.

Mother Coumba, an archetypal wise crone, is associated with paradoxical symbolism. Her medicine, properly used, saves lives but is lethal in the wrong dosage. The actual medicine is never visualized and resides in a bottomless jar that magically transforms into a complete jar as Sidy handles it. Coumba's title is ironic in that she, a midwife who has delivered 119 babies, has no children of her own. She is an outsider who has not fulfilled the most basic female function—to give birth—but nevertheless attains occult knowledge through direct female transmission from her grandmother. Through Mother Coumba, Drabo honors elderly women as guardians of life's most profound mystery.

A different sexual myth animates Bekolo's erotic comedy *Quartier Mozart*, which invests several older female characters with preternatural powers. The sorceress Mama Thecla, a gender-bending African version of the femme fatale, teaches her lore to a young recruit, a pubescent schoolgirl called Queen of the 'Hood, introducing her to spooky scenes of witchcraft rituals and a mysterious yellow car with the power to kill and to transmogrify people. Since the Queen's main interest is prying into the sexual secrets of the neighborhood, Mama Thecla enables her to peer through walls. She then transforms Queen into a local stud, My Guy, intent on seducing Saturday, the most eligible virgin in the 'hood. Queen believes that she will gain control over her budding sexuality and evade male exploitation by discovering firsthand what young men are like. Mama Thecla transplants herself into the male body of Panka, who fractures masculine pride by shrinking men's genitals with a simple handshake. After the dynamic duo of sorcerer and apprentice disrupts life in the whole 'hood, the Queen concludes that she will have sex only with a man who loves her.

Bekolo includes in the film three heft, matrons wearing the same style African dress and head wrap who regularly meet in the town square to obtain water. The ritual appearances of these women, like those of the witches in *Macbeth*, punctuate impor-tant episodes in the film. The trio knows everything that goes on in the community and gleefully gossip about the latest sexual humiliation Mama Thecla has wreaked on the neighbors. Like a Greek chorus they articulate the point of view of the community at large. As they display the African penchant for laughing at pain and disorder, they resemble domesticated Olympians, validating the superiority of mature women by mocking the folly of men and younger females. The special powers of older women administer Bekolo's dark sexual comedy.

The most sustained and powerful use of myth occurs in Djibril Diop Mambéty's mordant satires of contemporary life in Senegal and Senegalese adulation of colonial culture. His surrealistic cin-ematic style creates a hyper-reality in which imagination and fan-tasy permeate mundane reality. Mambéty's use of strange and ambiguous montage juxtaposes symbolic elements with narration and creates symbolic parallels through repeated visual motifs. In *Touki Bouki* and *Hyenas* he characterizes older women as agents of divine vengeance. We first see Aunt Oumi in *Touki Bouki* as a butcher quietly and expertly slitting the throat of a sheep, then later as into a raging Fury or sorceress. With ceremonial gestures—arms upraised and knife brandished in one hand—she stands in the middle of the road imprecating the protagonist Mory for defaulting on his debts to her. In retrospect, the earlier scene of sheep killing is colored by the symbolism of the later scene, tak-ing on implications of ritual sacrifice rather than merely commer-cial butchering. We wonder if she would slit Mory's throat with the same dispatch as the sheep's and if her curses will be efficacious.

Oumi's mythical power is reiterated in a third scene where she appears as a traditional praise singer in Mory's fantasy of his own apotheosis. Instead of abuse she now confers honor and status on him through her ritually powerful language and gesture. Employing the same posture she used to curse, she raises her arms to draw spir-itual power down to an earthly being. Mory (like Mambéty him-self) recognizes Oumi's numinous, threatening energy but egotis-tically subverts it in his imagination to his own benefit.

Mambéty refines and perfects his use of mythical female char-acters in *Hyenas*, an adaptation of Friedrich Dürrenmatt's play *The*

Visit. In her youth the main character, Ramatou, rejected by her lover Dramen Drahmeh in favor of a rich fiancée, was expelled in shame from the village of Colobane because of her pregnancy. Dramen hired perjured witnesses who enabled him to evade legal responsibility for his paternity. Many years later Ramatou, now fabulously rich and powerful, returns to wreak vengeance on him and the town that drove her into prostitution. She offers the impov - erished townspeople huge sums of money if they kill her former lover, now a respected man and mayor-elect of Colobane. She suc- ceeds in turning the people's greed into self-righteous conviction, exposing the entire town as a metaphoric brothel.

Mambéty conceives of Ramatou as a preternatural being belonging to a different order than normal people. Uniformed marching drummers proclaim her arrival. Tall, stern, dressed in old-fashioned yet elegant robes and headdress of stark white or black, she keeps everything but her face covered. Old yet timeless, she radiates cold serenity. Ramatou carries herself regally, holding court, moving and speaking slowly, her every word and gesture expressing the imperative mood. She dispenses money as if it were common as paper. The townspeople convey their obeisance to her by bows, supplication, and extravagant praise.

Ramatou dominates each scene where she appears; the eye lines of other people all fix on her. She surveys the townspeople in the square from her throne-like chair in an upper story niche that frames her and her attendants like a formal portrait of royalty. Exalting her status, the camera takes the point of view of her sub - jects by shooting up to her with a low angle below.

A strange, surreal retinue accompanies her an oriental woman in modern police uniform with handcuffs on her belt; three beau - tiful, stylish young African women with elaborate, colorful dresses, jewels, and coiffures; a valet (played by Mambéty) in a black vel- vet suit and hat, supporting his crippled leg with a crutch.

Ramatou also is handicapped by an artificial leg and arm, the fruit of a plane crash, which killed the other passengers. She has symbolically returned from the dead as an alien and created arti - fice. Her anomalous appearance is emblematic of her inner self. Suffering and vengeance have wrung from her the last ounce of pity or reflection. She has become retribution itself, one of the Erinyes, ineluctably exposing and punishing hidden sin. As an agent of fate, she foresees and orchestrates each event and emotion, smil - ing with bitter satisfaction as she observes the townspeople pros -

titute themselves for her money and rationalize the murder of their most popular citizen as an act of dispassionate justice. Ramatou provokes complex and paradoxical emotions: she is strong and pitiable, magnificent and horrifying, admirable and ruthless.

Yet, as the film proceeds, we sense that she still loves her betrayer and that in executing his demise she both punishes and saves him. Drahmen changes significantly during the film. Having witnessed the treachery and self-righteousness of his fellow citizens and having affirmed his own guilt and cowardice, Drahmen now rekindles his buried love for Ramatou. He not only accepts his inevitable death but even yearns for it, expressing his relief and gratitude that his "meaningless life" will soon terminate. Mambéty creates Dramen as a tragically appealing character who is spiritually revitalized by his ordeal. His regeneration may have been integral to Ramatou's agendum.

At an underground desert bunker that resembles a tomb she waits for his death. She will bury him on her island guarded by the god of the sea where she alone will possess him. Ramatou eagerly anticipates her own imminent death, which will unite the two forever. Mambéty, by enriching with mythic dimensions what was merely a vengeful women in Dürrenmatt's play, has fashioned one of the supreme creations of African film. But does Ramatou have any social significance for Africa?

Important scholars of African film like Teshome Gabriel, Manthia Diawara, and perhaps even Nwachukwu Frank Ukadike might say that she does not. They believe that the mission of African directors is defined more or less in terms of cultural activism: to undermine the colonial mindset, to raise African consciousness about its traditional culture, and to revolutionize African society.

Certainly, most of the African directors present characters that exemplify urgent social and ethical problems for women—unhappy arranged marriages, polygamy, poverty, heavy domestic responsibility, deprivation of legal rights (especially for widows), physical brutality, and the indignity of second-class status. They imply that conditions for women are especially rigid and harsh in rural society but more open to change in cities. The films champion the cause of justice for women and reform of traditional sex roles.

Ramatou seems not to fit this paradigm. Even though male treachery and self-righteous moralism have victimized her, she has triumphed with great worldly success; furthermore, she deals with her pain in a very old-fashioned and some might judge evil way—more like Medea than Ibsen's Nora. What can a contemporary African audience learn from her? The question is a subtle one.

Perhaps the criteria for judging the worth of African film should include great art with or without an activist social agenda. The mythic power of the story and characters of *Hyenas*, its fable of greed, revenge, love, and salvation touches the unconscious as well as the conscious mind of its audience. We might find their most profound instruction in the ultimate source of social injus-tice—the labyrinthine human heart. Surely there is room in the cinematic pantheon for seductive, magnificent characters such as Ramatou. Perhaps with older women we can have it all.

WORKS CITED

Angano...Angano. Directed by Cesar Paes, Laterit Productions,. 1989.

Finzan: A Dance for the Heroes. Directed by Cheick Oumar Sissoko. 1989.

Diawara, Manthia. *African Cinema: Politics and Culture*. Bloomington: Indiana Univeristy Press, 1992.

Drogin, Bob. "S[outh] Africans Revive Burning of Witches." *LA Times*. Reprinted in the *Arkansas Democrat-Gazette* (Little Rock) January 1, 1995: A19, A22.

Gabriel, Teshome. *Third Cinema in the Third World: The Aesthetics of Liberation*. Ann Arbor: University of Michigan Research Press, 1982.

Guelwaar. Directed by Ousmane Sembéne. Domireew; Galatee Film; FR3 Film Production; Channel IV; WDR, 1991.

Hyènes. Directed by Djibril Diop Mambéty. ADR Productions, Thelma Films AG, Maag Daan, MK2 Productions S. A., 1991.

La vie est belle. Directed by Ngangura Mweze and Bernard Lamy. Lamy Films, 1987.

Mapantsula. Directed by Oliver Schmitz. Haverbeam and David Hannay, 1988.

Neria. Directed by Godwin Mawuru. Media for Development Trust, 1992.

Quartier Mozart. Directed by Jean-Pierre Bekolo. Kola Case, 1992.

Ta Dona. Directed by Adama Drabo. Kora Films and C. N. P. C-Mali, 1991.

Touki Bouki. Directed by Djibril Diop Mambéty. Cinegrit, 1973.

Ukadike, Nwachukwu Frank. *Black African Cinema*. Berkeley and Los Angeles: University of California Press, 1994.

Xala. Directed by Ousmane Sembène. Film Domireew; Societé nationale cinémaphoto-graphique, 1974.

Yaaba. Directed by Idrissa Ouédraogo, 1989.

Yeelen. Directed by Souleymane Cissé. Cissé Films. American distribution by Cinemon, 1987.

THE LOCUS OF TENSION:
GENDER IN ALGERIAN CINEMA

In memory of Kateb Yacine

THE TRAGIC EVENTS PRESENTLY OCCURRING in Algeria are creating a kind of historical amnesia, in the sense that the last decade almost seems to have invented and propagated its own explanations, as if it has no causes from the past. Analysts, indeed, target the NLF (National Liberation Front), which led the fight against France and, which, for three decades, was the only political party in post-colonial Algeria, as the principal cause of the Algerian crisis, be it economic or a sociological. Furthermore, most analysts focus on the political realm as if the State and its apparatuses could themselves shed light on the complexity of Algerian society. In so doing, they minimize the anthropological dimension of this very society.

Because this article deals with Algerian cinema of the seventies and the early eighties, I will focus on the political, the sociological, and the anthropological dimensions of Algerian society in relation to gender. More specifically, I will attempt to locate, through gender, the ruptures created by cultural practices (for example cinema in postcolonial societies) as well as the ways these practices put into question (or resist) dominant models of modernity, such as development. I will also show the impossibility of escaping models of modernity, which are themselves frequently seen as homogeneous and are governed by economic exigencies.

Cinema is a primary example of the societal ruptures mentioned above: it employs modes of expression, which show the relative autonomy of the cultural sphere as compared to the political or the economic. Furthermore, the role of cinema seems to me to be crucial, because of its ability to construct its own image and thereby to convey a sense of unity in place of what had been actually fractured, that is, an Algeria that had experienced 130 years of French colonialization. Of course, such "unification" is the essential function of the image, which is, one should add, always related to political and ideological dimensions. To be sure, the restitution of a proper image is not the prerogative of cinema alone. Television and other media also share this common function. Cinematographic fiction, however, introjects something else into the project of image-construction and into the projection of a uni-fied entity. Indeed, despite the fact that the cinematographical pro-duction is state controlled and despite its realistic *writing/écrit-ure,* it somehow displaces the dogmatism and orthodoxy presiding in other media such as the press, or in state-controlled broadcasts in Algeria. It was not until the youth rebellion of 1988 that the Algerian Press—and only the Press—was liberalized and priva-tized. Until today, cinema and national television remain under the state control and the films I will analyze here were all state-financed.

In order to analyze the construction of a "Nation-Image," I will limit my inquiry to the 1970s and the early eighties. It was over the course of this decade that Algeria not only proclaimed its modernity, endowing itself with state-of-the-art technology, but it also embraced strategies privileging heavy industry (the so called "industrializing industry") over light industry and agriculture. It was at this time that Algeria promoted a modernity of its own, affirming the possibility of a "specific socialism"—in the French sense of "socialisme spécifique." The adjective *specific* accounts here for the Islamic component in an economic model otherwise copied from the USSR.

This formula and the strategies it engenders are of the utmost importance for defining gender relations in Algeria. Although this link is regularly overlooked by political analysts, gender relations make clear the oscillations and contradictions in Algerian soci-ety.[1] Indeed, gender relations constitute a privileged vantagepoint that allows for a deeper comprehension of Algerian society. This is because gender relations constitute poles of tension, which man-ifest, in turn, the specificity of Algerian modernity promoted under the auspices of the NLF.

The Algerian model of development privileged aspects of pro-duction and productivity, and considered women to be productive individuals in the general pursuit of the nation's welfare. Women were conceptualized as agents whose "promotion" and "emanci - pation" was directly linked to those of the Algerian people. Given this ideology, Algerian women did not need to imitate the struggle of Western women; they were supposedly already « *des citoyennes à part entière»,* "full citizens" endowed with all the fundamental democratic rights and privileges to which they might aspire. This reference, among others, to "the people" as a whole served as a pre - text to halt specific demands made by women *as women,* i.e. as sexed individuals. It furthermore neutralized any reference to sexed individuals, namely women, in new modern spaces such as schools, factories, and offices. If women are subsumed under the aegis of "the people" (allowing them access to public space), it is only at the price of the negation of their "being-woman." Women are not only considered to be productive agents, but more importantly, they are also the guardians of deeper Arab-Islamic values (*"valeurs profondes arabo-musulmanes"*).[2] In this respect one may conclude that it is the duty of women to uphold the "specificity" of Algerian socialism.

This complex discursive construction accounts for a crucial anthropological fact with respect to gender relations: the spatial separation of gender follows the dichotomies of exterior/interior, public/private, which subtend the logic of honor.[3] This logic is fundamental, for the spaces allotted to men and women are clearly defined. The integrity of women's space goes along with the integrity of their bodies. This space is called the "*harem,"* that is, forbidden or "inviolable" space. In this perspective, the female body (encumbered by a tremendous number of rules and pre - scriptions) acts as a metonymy for the community—every attack on its integrity is an attack on the community. Contrary to the gen- eral belief held in occidental societies, the Islamic conception of female sexuality is very active, which effectively turns women into a potential threat to the integrity of their group.[4] While the female body poses an integral threat, it carries, at the same time, positive values. In a word, this positive value is motherhood, which in turn privileges the procreation of males. Men, for their part, have to face the exterior world, to protect their land and their chil - dren as well as the women of their family.[5]

The spatial separation of gender is a structuralizing element, since it permeates the practices of social agents—a phenomenon not unique to Algerian society. Its traces can be found at all levels of discourse—including the official and the normative. Furthermore, this separation is not simply implicit, but constantly reworked and foregrounded in all social discourses. Cinema is but one example.

The duality of the female role in Algerian modernity has been thoroughly analyzed and is indeed paradoxical. Indeed, the tradi-tional logics of honor as well as Islam coexist with the modern one. Radia Abdelkrim-Chikh has accurately diagnosed this para-doxical co-existence as an "institutional schizophrenia," [6] as is the case in law where the equality of women is recognized by the Constitution but undone or even negated by a Family Code inspired by the *charia*.

While most analysts stop at this aporia, it seems to me more important to trace the effects and interrelations of the logic of honor and of the logic of modernity in order to understand what is at stake in the issues they raise. The structural separation of gen-der relations, which is grounded in a spatial separation as I have indicated, goes far beyond the strict frame of the relations of social agents, and contaminates official discourses by giving a particular connotation to women's right to leave the domestic sphere. If Algerian women gained a certain equality thanks to their involve-ment in the battle for political independence—an argument repeat-edly used in official discourse—their demands based on their spe-cific status as women have constantly been denied and denounced as bourgeois and anti-revolutionary. [7] The use of popular notions such as "the people," "the state," and "the revolution," served to silence women's demands. Also, in their interpellation of women, these very notions present themselves as neutral and sexually undif-ferentiated. The political discourse of Algerian modernity could thus speak to women without interfering with their integrity, and without awaking the distrust of men.

Having said this, what may one say about Algerian cinema? How does cinematographical discourse position itself with respect to these issues? How does cinema, itself an instrument of moder-nity, deal with gender relations, and how does it produce them in turn? To answer these questions, I will draw upon a corpus of Algerian films of the 70s and the early 80s: *Le Charbonnier* by Mohamed Bouamari (1972); *Le Vent du Sud* by S.M. Riad (1975); *Leïla et les autres* by S.A. Mazif (1978); *Omar Gatlato* by M. Allouache (1976); *Le Vent de sable* by M. Lakdhar-Hamina (1982);

Premier pas by M. Bouamari (1982) *Une femme pour mon fils* by A. Ghanem (1983).[8]

While films of the 1960s focused only on the War of Independence, in the 1970s and 1980s Algerian cinema started dealing with social issues such as the housing shortage, unem-ployment, and problems, which faced the youth and women. More importantly, it was in the 1970s and 1980s that the first images of Algerian post-colonial identities were constructed. Cinema was a major player in the process of re-appropriation of the collective and individual subjectivities as presented in terms of interpersonal rela-tions, especially between men and women.

I am concerned here with the main elements of the represen-tation of gender relations: the filmic treatment of *history*, because specific historical references characterize social objects, which have been selected (this explains the reasons why these objects were selected and shows what their effects have been on the def-inition of these relations); and the treatment of space, because of its fundamental role in the definition of gender. In the films I am considering, representations of time and space constitute an Algerian social imaginary predicated on gender. The cinemato-graphic representation of gender necessarily takes place within the frame of Algerian history, with its constructedness, its privileged referents. To historicize means, in this sense, to identify a specific entity, to base oneself in a past and in a foundational act. But what is the vision of history in the filmic corpus I have chosen? The films refer essentially to the present. The past is simply presup-posed as being known, it is rarely explicitly presented. The past is taken up without interrogation, and is constructed on the *déjà connu,* "preformulated cultural constructs,"[9] on practices and on discursive postulates that do not need to be defined, because they are accepted and deeply rooted in the society. Thus, in these films a pseudo-history surfaces—a history, which is, furthermore, lim-ited to a recent past, to the period of struggle and liberation.

Omar, for example, the main character of *Omar Gatlato,* remembers his father, who died in an explosion in the harbor of Algiers during the war. When he talks directly to the spectator about his father, the camera locks onto the surroundings of the actual docks of the harbor and shows the remains of the past: a wall riddled with bullets, and a timeworn commemorative tablet where the French words are almost erased. Behind this vision of history, another clearly parodic version is drawn. The glorious past is so inflated and deformed it becomes incredible. The story about urban guerrillas (*La bataille d'Alger*), told by Omar's mythomaniac uncle, is met by the members of his family with incredulity and indifference. Even the spectator has been warned by Omar of his uncle's lies, and the story-telling comes to an abrupt end when an American serial is broadcast on television. Fascinated by another myth the uncle abandons his story. The "heroic past," as it is called in official discourses, is henceforth relegated to a phantasmagoric zone, to an ethereal memory.

It is precisely through the metonymical process that the trajectory of history and memory can be best retrieved. The addition and adjustment of metonymical signs give a specific direction to this trajectory, and produce an aggregative totality. For example, when the coalman *(Le Charbonnier),* who is the representative of the people, is immersed in "his" forest, [10] still wearing the clothes of a former *maquisard*, he is unaware of the profound changes going on in Algeria. He does not even realize that Algeria has entered the era of oil and gas. But, when he comes into contact with the city, he leaves his torpor and frees himself from his past. He desperately seeks a job in Algiers. He visits a former war companion (who after independence became the head of a state company) and asks him for help. As the director, ostensibly portrayed as a bourgeois-profiteer, tries to justify the economic crisis by blaming French colonization, the editing renders him voiceless, covering his voice with another sound, which symptomatically belongs to the coalman's universe, that of the forest. The coalman's response appears in a later scene through a voice-over, declaring clearly that "the past is the past, essential is the fight of today in order to construct the future." The reference to the past is thus relative, particularly in light of the requirements of the present and the future. The signs of the character's past, which imply that he belongs with him among those who constantly invoke the past (i.e. bourgeois and rich landowners) in order to legitimate their position, vanish from his universe. Only a certain version of the past is acceptable, the "revolutionary" one. It is because the past contains in itself all the negativities that the present becomes the time of "the true reformulations," of "the new page" (*Premier pas*).

In *Le Charbonnier* as well as in *Omar Gatlato,* history gets lost and is broken down, and it is only presented in ambiguous terms. The remote past is mythologized, a time of tragedy (*Le Vent de sable, Premier pas*), but, because of certain of its values such as the importance of the sexual spatial separation, its evocation serves as a guarantee for the formulation of the new propositions about gen - der. What does it mean for these films to introduce the (remote) past in the formula "Once upon a time" (*Le Vent de sable*) or to dramatize and folklorize it (*Premier pas*), if not to devaluate the past and to assert its inadequacy at the present time? Moreover, it has the effect of erasing former historical gender relations.

The cinematographical treatment of history, which is much more subtle than the political discourse of the same period; invok - ing in the case of women, the recent past involves the mixture of different historical configurations and, without completely erasing them, proposes new gender relations. The treatment of history is essentially functional; selected objects are placed within a positive historical trajectory, while history itself becomes the blind spot of film.

It is clearly the treatment of space and territory that leads us to a better understanding of how gender relations become refor - mulated. The treatment of space, which specifically concerns gen - der, needs to be grounded in another more general space: the Algerian national territory, the place of origin where films specify and modulate their definitions, including those involving the trans- formations of gender. Filmic writing tends to authenticate space, to make it recognizable. Titles such as *Le Vent du Sud* refer explic- itly to regions of Algeria; and *Omar Gatlato* is an idiomatic Algerian expression. The predilection of Algerian films to depict cultural practices in an ethnographic manner (descriptions of engagements, marriages, and matrimonial transactions, maraboutic rites and funeral rituals) leads to the inscription of the films within a concrete geographical entity, that is, Algeria, with all its differ - ences (mainly *vis a vis* France) and its territorial variety. Taken all together as an intertextual framework, these films produce an implicit common discourse on the Algerian national space. The choice of objects, quotations, and "the predilection for the whole ritualized activities of the daily life," [11]: of what is said and the way it is said entails the authentication of space.

The representation of the city and the country also participates in this authentication of space. These localities are not the object of fixed definitions, nor are they directly opposed to each other. The signs that qualify them are both contradictory and complemen - tary. By contrast, in the Maghrebian literature in the mid 1950s, as Charles Bonn has pointed out, the country is rejected as a space of closed identity;[12] instead, as seen in Kateb Yacine's *Nedjma*, the space of the city is adopted as the locus of the heterogeneity of lan-guages, of the plurality of representations; Algerian cinema, which still refers to the country, oscillates between negative and positive representation. What does this mean with respect to gender? The country is not only "shot as the space of origin and moral val-ues,"[13] it is also an obscure place where "feudals" (rich landown-ers) live, and where plots are hatched against such noble and rev-olutionary objectives, as, agrarian reform.

In *Le Vent du Sud* the city is valorized and transformed into a true myth. Nafissa, the principal female character, is completely centered in it; Rabah, her father's shepherd, leaves the country and his dumb mother for the more urbanized North to work in one of the new agrarian cooperatives. *Le Charbonnier* obeys the same logic of devaluating the country, because life in the country fosters dependencies as well as human exploitation. It is during his short passage through the city where he is desperately seeking a job, that Belkacem, the coalman, develops class-consciousness. The country itself is transformed into a living place only after the trans-plantation of the city objects (factory, school, television, radio, etc.) In these films, the world outside brings the dynamic to the country, which is unable to change on its own. Its basic and inad-equate forms of knowledge are threatened by a more scholarly one, one whose language is perfectly in tune with ongoing social change. Its survival depends on admitting and absorbing innova-tions from the city. *Le Vent du Sud* explicitly positions the city as the center of the film's enunciation. Its credit titles—considered by theoreticians of cinema as the locus *par excellence* of the filmic enunciation[14]— show images of Algiers. Despite its ethical and moral struggles, the city is a true and symbolic center through, which one must necessary pass. The references to the city, espe-cially in films, which juxtapose it with the country, work essentially through "citations": books, newspapers, radio and television. The latter even retransmit news footage covering large demonstrations in Algiers in favor of agrarian reform. If the citation is indeed "a trivial operator of intertextuality," and if it "appeals to the com-petence of the reader," it also "always has to do with the discourse of the enunciation. There is no citation that engages only the *énoncé*, and frees itself from the subjects of the enunciation or that does have not the *intention of persuading*."[15]

Furthermore, the country is the privileged frame of the feudal and reactionary forces whose true and symbolic fathers embody its very essence. The big landowner, for example, constantly resitu - ates the coalman within an ancestral tradition, urging him to refuse to let his wife go out and work in the new state textile factory. In contrast, the agrarian revolution means the end of these relations of exploitation. Contesting such relations presupposes challenging the gender relations they sustain: "Stop with this old mentality, it should no longer exist nowadays [...]. The *nif* and the moustache,[16] are for him who works by the sweat of the brow," the teacher reminds the coalman.

The quotations of the city as a center of decisions and the cri - tique of the "fathers" (the landowner in *Le Charbonnier* is but one example) are constitutive of a process of substitution, where the power of the father is replaced by the political power of the city. The systematic use of citation in these films, and the portrayal of educational institutions as a means of effecting women's "eman - cipation," indicates the inability of the country to autonomously give up its onerous fathers. They also testify to its potentially reac - tionary opposition to the advancement of modernity. The accu - mulation and concentration of "the signs of modernity" in the country facilitate and shape the impending change. This substitu - tion of urban for rural values takes place even if the past to be replaced is hardly defined, i.e., if the father is absent or barely present (*Omar Gatlato, Leïla et les autres*). The negating of fathers is accompanied by a massive circulation of the "signs of moder - nity," which invalidates their fathers as well as their references and their laws.

The characteristic qualities of the city speak in favor of a cer - tain modernity. Its proprieties are treated, purged, and reframed according to a targeted alignment of men and women, who must adhere to precise practices and who adapt to precise spaces. Indeed, if the city allows the development of knowledge, particularly the scholarly knowledge from which it takes all its power, it is also an uncontrollable and dubious space since men and women alike share it. It is both an attractive and repulsive place affording its inhabi - tants both creative liberty and the possibility of moral corruption. In contract to the darker side of the urban landscape, rural space is marked by redeeming purity, where the organization of male and female space is fixed. In order to justify the female presence within non-traditional spaces, these films refer to the country and its rigid spatial divisions.

The image of rurality is therefore twofold: it is both negative, justifying the advent of *modernity* (the model of the city) that is inscribed into the ineluctable march of history, and positive since it helps to thwart the negative side effects of modernity. This dialec - tical logic makes clear the limits of the supposedly emancipatory filmic discourses as well as their double argumentation. *Leïla et les autres* shows the danger, which threatens women in the streets of the city; in *Une femme pour mon fils,* the father of the female char- acter recalls the positive values of the country and opposes to them hotels (a metonymy of the city), which hide forbidden encounters and favor debauchery. The city never becomes opaque: every body, particularly the female one, is overexposed, falsely veiled, shame - less.

The street as a sexually charged space constitutes a real threat for women, notably for those workers and students who were among the first to enter it. In comparison to the treatment of male characters, who discover the city and who open it up to the spec - tator's gaze, the treatment of women's presence in the street, and consequently the contiguity of female and male, is rapid and ellip - tic.

Consequently, the films adopt as closely as possible the view - point of the typical (male) spectator unable to conceive of the street as a legitimate space for women. The itineraries of female char - acters are dictated, determined in advance by some important rea - son (work, study, or other customary outings), and their outings do not allow any stops.[17] In so doing, the films are close to the dis - courses of the press in which the street is synonymous with lost morals.[18] The repetition of this term transforms the street into a *cliché* and turns it into *"la parole d'une culture"*;[19] "the *cliché*, as Jenny has pointed out, gets its autonomy and coherence from an 'elsewhere' that it does not name. It is a summary of the ideolog - ical-cultural system from, which it derives."[20] A sign of verisimil- itude, it speaks "the terrorism of the endoxal discourse" and imposes itself through a series of rhetorical, narrative and figura - tive automatisms. as with the scenes of the street, the bus and fac - tory scenes are treated in a way that avoids any action or gesture that might subvert the norm. The women who occupy these spaces are shown as being serious workers or students who do not disturb the established order between men and women.

The argumentative logic, which links the city and the country is both simple and complex. It is simple because it proceeds by a series of soustraction of negative images (the big landowners of the country, the debauchery of the city, etc.), on which it superimposes a series of substitutive elements (the state factory, the agrarian rev - olution, the rights of workers, and the school). It is complex because it maintains some features of the eliminated elements, as the law of spatial separation imposed by the fathers, and integrates them into the new reality. This preservation does not reproduce the canonic separation between men and women; it appropriates the older paradigm in order to mould and regulate it into the new spaces. Seriousness and respect as qualities of the female charac - ters take their meaning from a positive conception of work, grounded in the belief that the reproduction of the labor force comes at the price of sexual gratification. This filmic elaboration shapes the apprehension (in both senses of the term) of the spec - tator, and reinforces the authority of the state, which also provides the authorization for women to occupy the new places. Here, the state is presented in a metonymical form as a sexless entity.

As soon as a space of power opens up to women, it is imme - diately submitted to several limitations. These limitations appear both in the "formal" procedures (of which I will give an example later on) as well as in "ideological" procedures. For example, when female characters keep close to men or are shown alone in the street, it is only because they have been previously identified as workers, unionists or students, all things that carry positive con - notations. As emblem bearers of modern Algeria, filmic narratives portray them as serious and respectable (in opposition to *femmes fatales)*. But as the philosopher Sarah Kofman points out, respect is also a means to keep those who are respectable or inspire respect away from others, and thus to create a certain distance between them.[21]

These films suggest, in a subtle way, the incapacity of female characters to accomplish their objectives or to fulfill their desires. The ending of *Une femme pour mon fils* is a good example of for - mal procedures limiting the woman's will. Instead of living with her husband's parents and waiting for him while he is working in France, the heroine decides to break away from her imposed life and "be free." Shortly after her return to her parents' home, she has a male baby.[22] The film ends with the scenes of her return to her parent's house and the birth of her baby that are linked by a fade-out shot, a form of cinematographic punctuation. This ending shows the hesitation of the filmic argumentation. The power the character begins to acquire is canceled out by the importance of motherhood as a crystallization of society's expectations of women. This power is canceled out by what Julia Kristeva has called "the bio-symbolic latencies of motherhood." [23] The film passes from the demands of woman's emancipation to her reduction into an ideological, sexualized position. The fictional order finds here its projection into the doxa (the specators' beliefs). The encounter of the doxa and the fiction produces the patterns of thought as well as the "truth," which suggests the equation, "woman equals moth - erhood."

Ambiguity and resistance are also found in films, which have been defined as being pro-female. This is the case of *Le Vent de sable* , which tells the story of a young woman, Rogaia, suspected of and then accused of committing adultery with a young poet/singer. The narrator, a young female university professor who witnessed the events as a child, presents the palm grove where she lives to the viewers. The palm grove is a traditional, self-serving and backward-looking space compared to the openness of the city with its university knowledge. The story, which ends with the mur - der of the poet and Rogaia being sent back to her tribe, shows the ineptitude of the harsh code, which defines male-female relation - ships as well as the injustice experienced by women.

I will not go into the extremely illuminating details on the rep- resentation system underlying female speech in comparison to male speech.[24] Instead, I will insist upon the intertwining of image and sound accomplished through editing. Indeed, editing builds arguments and positions them in a double system where the inno- cence of the female character is questioned not only by what is projected on the screen, but also by what is heard. With respect to the characters, there are three basic patterns in *Le Vent de sable* linking shot to reverse shot. The first two express the law and the threat conveyed through by the Rogaia's in-laws, surveillance and persecution; the third expresses seduction, linked essentially to the poet. The sound is the main and the first element of the repre - sentation of the poet. Indeed, the poet seems to excel more with words than with glances and expressions, in contrast to those of the family who rarely speak in the film but control everything with their looks.

In her relations with the characters that dominate her (espe-cially. the mother-in-law), and who occupy positions of authority, Rogaia, the accused, is subjected to close surveillance and is repeat-edly ejected from the action. Sound is used to establish the rela-tionship between the two characters against whom the presump-tions of adultery are leveled. For instance, the first and the last exchange of glances between them occur when the poet is playing a tune on his flute. The tune seems to be directed primarily at the female characters, especially the younger members who show sen-sitivity to it, since they stop working when they hear it. The music evokes a different semantic world and disturbs the normal and acceptable chain of events. The poet's singing and the music throughout the story build a parallel argumentation, carrying mean-ings, which extend beyond the direction taken by the filmscript, thus, denouncing the injustice and showing Rogai's innocence.

This doubling of meaning is based on the modality of expres-sion itself. If it is true, as I have argued, that the poet's gaze is lim-ited, his singing and music invade the camera shot. An example of this can be seen in a way the singing violates inner space (the *harem*), and saps its codes like a parasite by introducing the world of seduction. Seduction, a parasite, for seducing means "taking away, turning off course," writes J. Baudrillard.[25]

How does sound relate to characters? In one of the night scene: Rogaia prepares the bread for dinner, her son seated beside her, when an off-camera voice (from outside) asks the poet to sing. During this time, her husband and her brother-in-law are washing their hands at the doorstep (a series of shots alternate between the inside and the doorstep). When they stand up to enter the house, the off-camera singing of the poet begins. The next shot is a close up of Rogaia, who has a *dreamy look*; she gets a hold of herself with a slight movement of the head, lowers her eyes, and lifts them toward the open door. The brothers enter the house. The brother-in-law glances at Rogaia, whose eyes are lowered. The poet's off-camera voice invades the shot. For each character there is a unique sound/image relationship. The grandmother, who is away from the others, sits at the back of the room behind the loom. The husband's sensitivity is limited to the wind: "The wind is picking up," he says. Still transfixed by the music are the brother-in-law and Rogaia. The singing continues, accompanied by mobile camera (circular panoramic shots and dolly shots), and is replaced near the end of the sequence by the sound of the wind. With the help of sound, this sequence reveals Rogaia to the spectator, through her *dreamy look*. But there is more, for there exists a space reserved exclusively for the spectator that underscores the correspondence of sound with character represented in this sequence —a correspondence that attests to the narrator's work and ultimately the spectators; judgment of the film.

The relationship between the contents of the song and the system of demonstration developed through the plot, is made with the superimposition of the verses of the poet's song and the characters who appear in the sequences.

> The poet (off-camera): "She was good for me and I was for her. I met the woman with the black hair." [the two brothers at the doorsill].

> The poet (off-camera): "Reached the moon when she left the night."[26] [Rogaia].

> The poet (off-camera): "Reached the moon when she left the night," [Young girls].
> The poet (off-camera): "Time is slipping by, I must go." [The brother-in-law].

> The poet (off-camera): "Tomorrow." [Rogaia].

> The poet (off-camera): "Tomorrow I shall return..." [The entire family (circular pan shot)]. His praise continues with a shot of Rogaia. The song becomes provocative and the correspondence more direct.
> The poet (off-camera): " You who pretend to smile, your hearts are burnt..." [The two brothers and Rogaia's son].

> The poet (off-camera): "Stop loving both and choose the best. If I had to choose, I'd choose neither one, but the third." [Rogaia].

Based on the narration and the plot, the spectator's judgment can only be "double." If s/he forms it on the basis of the actions of a family who subjects Rogaia to continuous surveillance, and who show that she possesses no autonomy (each time the brother-in-law or mother-in-law enter the scene, Rogaia automatically leaves), the spectator is to reject the repudiation. But if s/he uses as a basis the juxtaposition of sound and image, then Rogaia's innocence will appear less obvious. The narration functions on two levels and places the spectator in an uncomfortable position. The more s/he identifies with the female character, the more s/he accumulates evidence against her. The building up of the spectator's knowl-edge disturbs the playing out of the story of a woman wrongly accused.

The plot makes Rogaia an object, but a "powerful" object, which makes it possible, by inversion, to pinpoint the normative frameworks of licit activities. As Louis Marin states, "Seduction transgresses the law and, in so doing, we negatively acknowledge the well-founded power."[27] This inversion is all the more signifi-cant because

> the boundary of the sexes [as Abdelwahab Bouhdiba writes] can be transgressed even if the visual function is limited and settled by the hearing of speech, singing or even the sound of a simple footstep. Thus this love from a distance based almost exclusively on hearing or hearsay and, which feeds on imagi-nation and fantasies…[28]

As the film unfolds, its central idea is infiltrated imperceptibly, and a sort of a second text is instituted, parallel to the first one. This second text emphasizes how powerful and strongly anchored the structuring separation of the genders and its impact on the cine-matographic imaginary can be.

Two major contradictory and simultaneous tendencies pervade the films of the corpus under study. On the one hand, gender rela-tions are no longer as they used to be. A "new page" is turned for women. The image of the fathers, that is, the representatives of the old order where honor was the binding element, is weakened and undermined; virility,[29] though "affirmed, is deprived of its car-dinal signs, and the conception of honor is cut off from its former references"; and finally, the community order is replaced by the priorities of the modern couple (*Leïla et lea autres, Premier pas*). On the other hand, the new spaces allowed to women, many of them shared by men and women, are not opened up without a cer-tain suspicion. They are, indeed, redefined on the basis of val-orized social images of women and their opposites, marginalized women who do not correspond to the canon—prostitutes, dancers

(in cabarets or cafés), and French (i.e. Western) women. The latter are the incarnation of the uncontrollable and threatening body;
in a word, they are the "mad body." These redefinitions continue
to reconfigure rules edicted by the very same fathers, who are the
object of the critique in the films. The representation of gender
relations therefore is difficult to reduce to simple terms.

This indecision, which characterizes the filmic discourses on
gender, expresses a transitional moment in which a new (re)dis-
position of the principal figures of authority, the state and the
fathers, is established. The fact that these discourses take into
account (be it only partially), the rationalities guiding the father's
universe, indicates the cultural ascendancy of the latter and of their
legitimate representatives (sons), who defend the traditional law of
the sexual separation of gender.

The power relations of the father/state are sustained by new
terms, which could be apprehended through hesitations and resistances occurring in the films. Although these films can not affirm
radically new propositions on gender relations, they erode the
fathers' position. This moment of transition is potentially deadly
for the power of the fathers, who have already been weakened by
several overturnings (colonization, urbanization, destructuration
of the family, individualization, education, etc.). The symbolic
systems from, which this position draws its strength seem not to
function the way they did before. Following the transformations,
which occurred in Maghrebian societies, Gilbert Grandguillaume[30]
noticed that the Maghrebian languages are *stuck in their words,* that
they are "unable to say what they could not say, [i.e.,] the freedom of the individual desire." He concluded that there exists a
fractured symbolic in these societies. What is at stake is nothing
less than the legitimacy of the fathers.

The filmic *mise en scène* of gender relations thus raises the
fundamental question of the transmission of the symbolic and of
its sustaining parts. The reality staged by cinema is itself represented by cinema as an instrument of modernity. The camera as a
frame, and as a gesture prior to the reception of films, unveils the
feminine universe (be it only in the realm of fiction), which is nevertheless forbidden to the male gaze in the society under scrutiny.
In this timid passage from intimate space to public space, cinema
produces a new reality. It attests to a rupture at the symbolic level
between political and anthropological dimensions, represented
metonymically by the signs of both the Father and the State.

NOTES

1. Gender relations focus on the positioning of men and women, on the definitions and legitimizations of more or less fixed identifiable gender positions as well as on their underlying ambivalent dynamic. To think in terms of gender relations means to detach the notions of "male" and "female" from the metaphysical understanding that confines them to nor-mative and a-prioristic definitions, and to problematize their definitions as the result of an endless negotiation in the social field. According to the philosopher Françoise Collin in her *L'irreprésentable de la différence des sexes. Catégorisation de sexe et construction scientifique*. (Toulouse: Université de Provence, 1989), "men and women occupy different strate-gical positions, places, which are subject to displacements, which should not be confused with essences" (30). Gender relations are the locus where sexed social agents—men or women—confront, contest and test each other in order to trace the symbolic limits, which express that which is think-able and what is acceptable for them. As the historian, J. Scott, in her *Gender and the Politics of History*. (New York: Columbia University Press, 1988) reminds us, gender rela-tions refer to the social organization of sexual difference, which permeates, by means of knowledge, all social dis-courses and practices (2). Furthermore, gender primarily sig-nifies relations of power. Power, here, is not understood as being unified, coherent, and centralized, but rather as form-ing itself; as in Foucault's terms: «on the moving ground of power relations, which constantly induce through their inequality, other states of power, but always local and unsta-ble ones» (122).

2. Before the rise of Islamism in Algeria, this expression was frequently used by so called revolutionary discourses.

3. Pierre Bourdieu: *Esquisse d'une théorie de la pratique*. (Genève: Droz, 1972). Claude-Henri Breteau/Nello Zagnoli: "L'honneur et la vengeance dans deux communautés méditer-ranénnes: La Calabre méridionale et le Nord-Est constanti-nois," *Actes du 2eme Congrès international d'étude des cul-tures de la Méditerranée occidentale*, vol. II. (Alger: SNED, 1978), pp. 460-68. "Le statut de la femme dans deux com-

munautés rurales méditérranéenes La Calabre et le Nord-Est constantinois," *Les temps modernes* 518 (1981), pp. 1954-2007.

4. Fatima mernissi: *Sexe et idéologie en Islam*. [Collection femme et société] (Paris: Tierce, 1983), p. 3.

5. cf. Raymond Jamous: *Honneur et Baraka. Les structures sociales traditionnelles dans le Rif.* (Paris: Maison des Sciences de l'homme, 1981).

6. Rabia Abdelkim-Chikh: "Les enjeux politiques et symboliques de la lutte des femmes pour l'égalitté entre les sexes en Algéria," *Peuples méditerranéens* 48-9 (1989), pp. 257-78; p.262.

7. cf. Mohamed-Salah Yahyaoui: *Discours d'ouverture et de clôture*. 4e Congrès de L'UNfA. (Alger: FLN, 1978), pp. 95-98.

8. For a brief presentation of the contents of these films, see the appendix to this article, pp. 62-64.

9. Jean-Blaize Grize: "Shématisation, représentations et images," *Stratégies discursives*. (Lyon: Presse universitaires de Lyon, 1978), pp. 45-52.

10. The coalman here is not a miner but a producer of charcoal, thus his particular relationship to the forest, which is clearly linked to the guerilla movement *(maquis)* as a site of resistance in the War of Independence.

11. Philippe Hamon "Un discours contraint," *Poétique* 16 (1976), pp. 411-45; 432.

12. Charles Bonn: "L'Ubiquité citadine, espace de l'énonciation du roman maghrébin," *Peuples méditerranéens* 37 (1986): pp. 57-65; 59-60.

13. Nadia Chérabi-Labidi: *Les représentations sociales dans le cinéma algérien de 1964 à 1980*. [Ph Diss. Paris: University of Paris III, 1987], p. 676.

14. Roger Odin: "L'entrée du spectateur dans la fiction, *Theorie du film*, eds. J.J. Aumont/ J.L. Leutrat. (Paris: Albatros, 1980), pp. 198-213; 204.

15. Antoine Compagnon: *La seconde main ou le travail de la citation*. (Paris: Seuil, 1979), pp. 40-211; (italics and translation are mine).

16. *Nif* literally means "nose" and symbolizes the honor of man. Pierre Bourdieu defines it as "point of honor" or "pride" (*self esteem*). The same thing could be said about the moustache.

Bourdieu writes that it "is the symbol of the virility, an essen -
tial component of *nif*" (6, note 4).

17. These remarks are corroborated by several anthropological studies. Cf. Breteau/Zagnoli, *Le statut ...* p. 1958.

18. Ratiba Hadj-Moussa: *Les femmes algériennes entre l'hon - neur et la révolution*. (Laval University, Laboratory of the Department of Sociology, 1984), p. 188.

19. Laurent Jenny: "Structures et fonctions du cliché," *Poétique* 12 (1976), pp. 485-517; 509.

20. *Ibid.*, p. 498.

21. Sarah Kofman, in her *Le respect des femmes (Kant et Rousseau)*, (Paris: Galilé, 1982) says that "To respect women is to see them with a different look than the hooker. It means to put them sufficiently high and afar in order to avoid imme- diate and closed relationships with them, and to be fascinated by them," pp. 41-42. (The translation is mine).

22. I would like to point out that the ending of the film differs from the ending of the novel on, which the film was based, where the heroine has a female baby. This kind of treatment not only constitutes evidence of sexual discrimination and censorship in the film, but also of a series of distinctions: the differences between two cultural modes of expression (film vs. book); between readers and spectators; and between those who master the French language (since the book is in French) and who can easily adopt occidental ideas; in a word the elite and the illiterate.

23. Julia Kristeva: "Hérétique de l'amour," *Tel Quel*, 74 (1977), pp. 30-44; 37.

24. See Ratiba Hadj-Moussa, *Le Corps, l'histoire, le territoire: les rapports de genre dans le cinéma algérien*. Montréal and Paris: Balzac and Publisud, 1994.

25. Jean Baudrillard: *Simulacres et simulations. (Galilée, 1981)*, p.35.

26. To be more precise: "I reached *the moon* when she was in prayer." This passage refers to the dawn prayer, the first prayer of the day for Muslims. Note the erotic allusion, in popular poetry, "the moon" symbolizes a woman and her face.

27. Louis Marin: "Le roi, son confident et la reine ou la séduc - tion du regard." *Traverses*. [*La stratégie des apparences*; 18] (Paris: Centre George Pompidou, 1980), pp. 25-36; 28.

28. Abdelwaheb Bouhdiba: *La sexualité en Islam*.. (Paris: PUF, 1982), p.53.
29. Virility is one of the most important attributes of the logic of honor. Virility means machismo, as it is usually understood in reference to women. It also appeals to noble feelings and actions, where a man has to be considered as one man among others. It refers to a certain equality between men, notably in societies where wealth has no value without a certain "behav-ior of honor."
30. Gilbert Grandguillaume: "Père subverti, langage interdit," *Peuples méditerranéens* 33 (1985), pp. 163-82; 180.

APPENDIX

Le Charbonnier appeared at the beginning of the 70s and is impor-tant because it gave birth to what film historians have termed *"le cinéma djedid,"* or New Cinema. The movie tells the story of a coalman who must find a new trade since he can no longer practice his old one—the new natural gas industry of Algeria had pushed him out of business. He decides to go to the city to look for a job to rescue himself and his family from poverty. While he is gone and despite his strong oppo-sition, his wife starts working at the newly built textile fac-tory in the village that hires only women. Noticing the incred-ible change in their daily life caused by his wife's work, he is finally convinced of the well foundedness of the whole social transformation. He even dreams he defies the old norms of behavior by demanding that his wife take her veil off in the presence of all the inhabitants of the village.

Le Vent du Sud relates the story of a young female student on hol-iday in an isolated village in southern Algeria. Her father, a rich landowner, wants to marry her to the village's mayor in order to avoid the expropriations related to the agrarian reform. She refuses, and flees the village to Algiers with the help of her father's former shepherd who wants to join an agrarian cooperative in the North. When her father discovers their flight, he pursues them on his horseback swearing that he will 'wash his honor," but the two fugitives escape by tak-ing a state transport company bus, which miraculously appears.

Leïla et les autres tells the story of two women: Myriam, who refuses to be married off by her family and pleads the cause of her studies and Leïla, her neighbor, who has two children and works assembling television sets in a private factory. Leïla fights for "the respect and the dignity" of female work - ers. When the foreman humiliates one of her female col - leagues, she provokes a strike. The strike divides the work - ers along gender lines because the male workers are initially reluctant to believe this "women's story," but then they end up understanding that they must have solidarity with their female colleagues if they want their mutual rights protected.

Omar Gatlato is the first film that deals with the problems of the youth. Omar, a civil servant at the gold control office, lives with his large family in a popular neighborhood of Algiers. The title "Omar Gatlato" refers to the virility, *redjla,* and means Omar is killed [by the virility, HMR]. The word viril- ity is presupposed not expressed. The term *redjel,* which means "man," derives from the *redjla. Redjla* refers itself to honor as well as to courage. When it is exaggerated, it sig - nifies machismo.

Omar, the main character, has a passion for popular roman - tic music from the region of Algiers and from India. He always carries with him his tape recorder, be it to a wedding, a concert, or a play. One night, his tape recorder is stolen. His life becomes completely chaotic and loses its meaning. Later, his friend, Moh Smina (Moh the Big), rescues him by find - ing him a tape recorder on the black market, and he offers Omar an empty tape. However, when Omar tries the tape recorder, he is surprised by a female voice. Omar is "shocked" and seduced. He attempts, more or less directly, to get to know the person hidden behind the voice. Moh informs him that it is Selma's voice, a colleague of his, who had pre - viously wanted to buy the tape recorder. Omar arranges an appointment with her. But at the appointment, and despite the encouragements of his friend, Omar hesitates a long time before approaching her. When he finally decides to do so, other close friends appear and tell him to " stay with [them]." He renounces his date and promises to himself to call the woman back.

The story of *Le Vent de sable* is located in an isolated palm grove and relates the life of Rogaia, a young woman who is sus-pected of adultery with a young poet. Her husband's mother and brother continuously watch her. Despite the fact that all the inhabitants of the palm grove talk about it, her husband is not aware of this "affair" until the old poet of the commu-nity sings a song, exhorting him to avenge his honor. Convinced of the "truth" of the allegations, he brutalizes Rogaia and slits the young poet's throat in public. When his mother hears about the murder, she sends Rogaia back to her native tribe.

Une femme pour mon fils tells the story of a young woman in a tra-ditional marriage. While her husband is away working in France, she stays with her husband's parents. Not getting along with her terrible mother-in-law, and unhappy with her life, she claims the right to "be free and to study." Although pregnant with her husband's baby, she decides to leave his family and return to her parents' house. She gives birth to a male baby.

Premier pas is the story of a female teacher who becomes the mayor of her village. Her election to office poses many prob-lems for her—among others the reluctance and the resist-ance of her husband. A teacher as well, he is presented as a man of the left who before she ran for election, had always supported her in making changes in the village. At the end of the film, they are reconciled. The narrative of this film is very complex, because it intertwines with three other stories. One of them is related by a former miner and traces the ori-gins of the village; the two other characters, each relates a story about an unfortunate marriage. These marriages are criticized because they were arranged by families who did not give future spouses the opportunity to choose for themselves. These three stories, which punctuate the main narrative, were collected as material for a drama the teacher couple were about to prepare with their students.

SUB-SAHARAN AFRICAN WOMEN FILMMAKERS: AGENDAS FOR RESEARCH*

Les cinéastes africains ont besoin de leurs soeurs à leur côté et à tous les postes, sans exception, et qu'il y a une grande place à prendre par les femmes dans le cinéma africain.

Werewere Liking (1989, 16)

IF I HAVE LEARNED ANYTHING IN NEARLY 15 years of research on filmmaking by Africans, it is that not enough is known about filmmaking in every Sub-Saharan African country to make generalizations about the subcontinent, and that much that has been written about African filmmaking especially in the West, but also in Africa, is hemmed in by implicit biases about filmmaking being primarily feature films made by a Hollywood-like film indus - try. The result has been many inaccurate generalizations about filmmaking in Africa and endless complaints about what is wrong with African filmmaking when compared to filmmaking in the West, India and other countries where there is a film industry. This kind of writing does not lead to an understanding of filmmaking in Africa.

Women are engaged in filmmaking throughout the subconti - nent, despite published statements to the contrary. This essay focuses on the kinds of research that need to be conducted to iden - tify and learn about *all* women's filmmaking activities. As the quotation above suggests, women are active in many facets of filmmaking, not just as film directors. The filmography at the end

This essay has been corrected and minimally updated since it was first pub - lished in Matatu (Schmidt, 1997). The filmography has been updated from 1995, when it was prepared for Matatu, to include resources I was able to consult through December 1997.

of this essay includes only feature, documentary and television films that I have been able to learn about. It excludes video proj - ects that I am aware of, since I have not had time to do research on the films completed by these projects. However, it is essential that research be conducted on women's self-help video projects spon - sored by governments and non-governmental organizations, since they have potential impact for women as both filmmakers and film viewers.

I read more than 7,000 sources in compiling my *Sub-Saharan African Films and Filmmakers: An Annotated Bibliography* (1988) and *Sub-Saharan Films and Filmmakers 1987-1992: An Annotated Bibliography* (1994). Although I continue to regularly consult newspapers and popular magazines published in Africa, the volume of publication is too vast for any one person to consult. Perhaps as a bibliographer I understand better than most people who write about African cinema that what we know, or think we know, does not represent what really exists.

Basic bibliographic research on African filmmaking remains to be done, for both women and men. What is needed for *every* African country is an audiovisual bibliography/filmography com - parable to Bernth Lindfors's *A Bibliography of Literary Contributions to Nigerian Periodicals 1946-1972*. Only after detailed research[1] has been conducted on all aspects of local film production in all African countries can generalizations be made. The following essay can provide only suggestions about some of the research that is needed.

INTRODUCTION

African and Third World women filmmakers were the focus of Les Journées du Cinéma Africain in Montreal in 1989, the Mannheim Film Festival in 1990, and FESPACO, Festival Panafricain du Cinéma de Ouagadougou, in 1991. This attention represents a significant change from 1976 when Safi Faye, Africa's best-known woman filmmaker internationally, was the only Third World woman who participated in the Festival International de Films de Femmes in Brussels. Yet the participation of African women in international film festivals provides an incomplete and inaccurate perspective of filmmaking activities by African women.

Nearly two decades ago, Paulin Vieyra, the premier historian of African cinema, pointed to the neglect of documentary and tele -

vision films by those who write about African cinema (1990, 63-65, 101-111). More recently Frank Ukadike has argued for the contextual discussion of feature, documentary and short films (1994). At the Carthage Film Festival in 1990 the colloquia empha - sized the worldwide growth of television, the potential of televi - sion film production, and television as a source of film distribution, and called for a more coherent strategy for the future development of film and television in African and Arab countries (Carthage, 1990). Both FESPACO and Les Journées du Cinéma Africain now include television films. Alexis Kalambry has called attention to the important roles of women in television in Mali and the need for new vocabulary to describe the positions they hold: "Comment appelle-t-on une femme à la camera? Et celles qui prennent le son ou font le mixage?" (1994, 4).

Since African women make far more documentary and tele - vision films than feature films, their activities have gained rela - tively little international attention. The potential of television and documentary films has been neglected even in Africa according to Tam Fiofori, who noted the high quality of some 80 Nigerian tel - evision films shown at a national television program festival in 1986 and the high quality of documentary films produced in Ghana (1986, 32). Women are among the makers of television films in Nigeria and documentary films in Ghana, but most are unknown outside of their own countries. [2]

From the available literature it appears that African women started making films in the 1960s. Efua Sutherland, the well-known Ghanaian playwright, made *Araba the Village Story*, a 13 minute film providing a child's view of her village and family, with sup - port from an American television company in 1967, while Thérèse Sita-Bella, a Cameroonian journalist, made *Tam-tam à Paris*, a 30 minute film of a performance of the National Dance Company of Cameroon in Paris, between 1963 and 1966. [3] Since African men supposedly started making films in the 1950s, African women seem to have been active from near the beginning. The real begin - ning of African filmmaking is a subject for further research, as is filmmaking by women in the early years. One need only recall the inaccurate statements made about the "birth" of African literature in the 1950s when literary historians ignored works published on African presses at earlier dates, to encourage caution when read - ing contemporary histories of African film that take as their model histories of feature filmmaking in the West.

When some 50 African women film professionals met at FES-PACO in 1991, more of the participants were actresses than film - makers. Among the participants were five women who at that time were directors of ministries or other national institutions related to film, radio and television: Michèle Badarou of Benin, Danielle Boni Claverie of Côte d'Ivoire, Sokhna Dieng of Senegal, Aminata Ouédraogo of Burkina Faso and Mariama Hima of Niger. Three of these women, Badarou, Ouédraogo and Hima, also are filmmak-ers. The women film professionals recognized that they need to know more about each other and to develop networks among them -selves. One of the four major proposals made at the conclusion of their discussions was to compile an inventory of African women working in film, television and video (Balogun, 1991, 523; Honneur, 1991, 2). The compilation of such an inventory would be a major step in facilitating research on African film, since surveys of African filmmaking usually focus on film or television and exclude video. The directory, *Femmes d'images de l'Afrique fran-cophone* (*Vues d'Afrique*, 1994), is a useful beginning, but is far from complete for francophone Africa.

Although Diaspora filmmakers participate in FESPACO, it is notable that Diaspora women were excluded from making formal presentations at the meeting of women film professionals in 1991, since the African women wanted perspectives from inside Africa (Diallo, 1991, 8-9). The other major proposals that resulted from the discussions were to encourage women to participate in film festivals and to establish and train staff for a mobile film training unit. The latter recommendation is related to the long-standing problem of the paucity of training facilities in Africa.

Les Journées du Cinéma Africain, which has been held annu -ally in Montreal since 1985, has a formal relationship with FES-PACO. The 1989 festival, which focused on African women as film subjects and film professionals, included participation by African women filmmakers, actresses, scriptwriters and journalists. Among the films made by African women which were shown, most were television and documentary films, rather than feature films.[4]

As these film festivals exemplify, the current interest in film -making in Africa occurs in contexts that include television film (whether it is video or film) and documentary as well as feature films. In the following discussion I take the same general approach as I did to the study of Nigerian literature in the early 1960s

(Schmidt, 1965). I survey, to the extent that is possible from written materials, the kind of activities that are taking place, making
no judgment about what is significant or insignificant, "good" or
"bad," and raise some questions that need to be answered if filmmaking by women in Sub-Saharan Africa is to be understood in the
cultural contexts in which films are being made and viewed. In a
short article neither a complete survey can be made nor a comprehensive research agenda outlined.

RANGE OF ACTIVITY[5]

Sarah Maldoror is included in directories of African filmmakers
and widely discussed as an African filmmaker. She is
Guadeloupean by birth, Angolan by marriage and works in Paris.
Only a few of her films have been about Africa, but *Sambizanga*
established her credentials as a maker of revolutionary film about
the Angolan liberation struggle. Is Maldoror an African filmmaker?
As she has observed, her West Indian origin is not relevant;
Africans consider her an African filmmaker (Larouche, 1991, 23).
However, she was excluded from the meeting of women film professionals at FESPACO in 1991 (Diallo, 1991). More relevant is
why some Africans consider her to be an African filmmaker, and
what has been her influence on African filmmakers, including
women. Has her influence been on films with revolutionary
themes? What African filmmakers are included in her personal
networks? Have her Parisian contacts benefited other African filmmakers? How has her presence at African film festivals influenced
African filmmaking?

Ngozi Onwurah, of mixed Nigerian-British parentage, lived for
several years in Nigeria, but has spent most of her life in the UK
where she makes films with her own film company. She is a generation younger than Maldoror, at the beginning of her career. Her
short film *Coffee Coloured Children* about a mixed-race girl in
Britain has been favorably reviewed in the western press ("Coffee
coloured talent," 1990; Cook, 1989), but to what extent has it been
seen in Africa? The same question could be asked about most of
her other films, which also have attracted press attention in Britain
where they are made. Onwurah is one of a growing number of
African filmmakers who work in the UK. One of her mentors is
Spike Lee ("Coffee coloured talent," 1990). Now that Onwurah has
made *Monday's Girls* in Nigeria, shown and led discussions on

281

Behind the Mask in Nigeria, and run workshops on documentary filmmaking in 12 African countries (Anikulapo, 1996, 33), will she be considered an African filmmaker and have influence on African filmmaking? Will the place of her birth have any relevance for her potential influence as an independent filmmaker on Nigerian film? Onwurah's future influence on African film, like Maldoror's past influence, is relevant regardless of her national origin.

Werewere Liking, the well-known Ivorian playwright, has made a television video, *Regards de fous*, of her successful stage play *Dieu-chose*. Because of her experience as a playwright, her participation in filmmaking has included more than making one film. She adapted Bernard Dadié's play *Thogo Gnini* for Sou Jacob's film *Le Grotto*, and designed the puppets for Mambaye Coulibaly's *Le Geste de Ségou* (Werewere Liking, 1989, 16). Coulibaly is Malian and Jacob is Burkinabè, indicating Liking's Panafrican influence. Have other women used their experience as dramatists in making their own films or collaborating with others? How have they developed personal and professional networks among African filmmaking personnel?

Léonie Yangba-Zowe makes documentary films, in super 8, of dances and rituals in the Central African Republic in the tradition of francophone ethnographic film. The French Ministry of Cooperation has provided support for her films, as it has for many African films (Andrade-Watkins, 1990), and her films have been distributed in France. How widely have her films been shown in Africa outside the Central African Republic? What is the reception of her films in the Central African Republic? Has her documentary approach influenced other Centrafrican filmmakers? Yangba-Zowe is among a growing number of African filmmakers who are studying in France and writing theses on African cinema. Her thesis is on the late Nigerien filmmaker, Oumarou Ganda (Yangba-Zowe, 1987). What is the influence of her formal film study and personal contacts she made in Paris on her filmmaking? What will be the influence of greater familiarity with the acting and filmmaking of Oumarou Ganda on her filmmaking?[6] Will the focus of her thesis on women in Ganda's films influence the focus of her future films? Like many African women filmmakers, Yangba-Zowe's films have not had an exclusive female-focus.

Zainab Bitrus, like Yangba-Zowe, incorporates local performance in her films. Hausa oral literature is the basis of her 52 part television series, *Magana Jari Ce*, made in Hausa for the Nigerian Television Corporation and subsequently produced in English for national distribution. The stories are read and acted, and some episodes include stories within stories, as when two chiefs challenge each other regarding whose parrot can tell the best stories. Bitrus's films remain close to familiar Hausa versions of the stories, since the audience would know if she changed the stories. [7] Bitrus is only one of a number of women who make films for Nigerian television. What kind of personal ties exist among women television filmmakers in Nigeria? How are their experiences as filmmakers similar to and different from those of men who make films for Nigerian television? Where do they receive their training and experience before they make their own films?

Gold Oruh, a Nigerian Television Authority news producer, made her film *Away from the Sidewalk* on her own time and partly from private funds, although it had NTA sponsorship (Omotunde, 1985, 36). She made this documentary film to show women's con - tributions to Nigerian politics and to encourage women to realize their political potential by getting off the sidewalk and into the mainstream of political life (Akinosho, 1985, 3). Although the film was shown as part of a Nigerian television series on women, it was made with a foreign audience in mind with United Nations encouragement. What is the influence of Oruh's experience as a tel - evision news producer on her filmmaking? How was official sup - port, like that of the NTA, obtained for independent filmmaking, and how did Oruh obtain private funding for her film?

Women in southern Africa started making films more recently than women in western and central Africa, according to reports in published sources. In Angola and Mozambique women have made films in association with national film centers that since inde - pendence in the mid 1970s have primarily sought to support nation-building and have produced primarily documentary and television films. Fatima Albuquerque's documentaries exemplify the broad range of this documentary activity in Mozambique, from musical performances in *Le Son c'est la vie* to the devastation caused by RENAMO in *No meu pais existe uma guerra*. What is the influ - ence of nationalist ideology on films made by women in Angola and Mozambique? How much choice do women have in the sub - jects of their films? What roles, in addition to those of filmmaker, do women have in these countries and how do these roles influence their filmmaking?

In South Africa women are among the "progressive" film-makers whose work, frequently in video, supports Black liberation. For example, Brenda Goldblatt's, *Grinding Stones*, is about opposition to the "independence" of KwaNdebele and focuses on violence, which occurred between 1986 and 1988 (Leonard, 1990, 11). Elaine Proctor clandestinely shot *Sharpeville Spirit*, which focuses on the continuing impact of the Sharpeville massacre on the township in 1984, and which permits the residents to speak for themselves. Proctor also has made a film in Sotho, with English subtitles, *Re tla Bona*, which depicts rural South Africans who live on the margins of economic existence, and focuses on health and literacy projects for women (*Journées du cinéma africain*, 1988, 34-35). How has apartheid, and recently the official end of apartheid, influenced women's filmmaking in South Africa? How are the activities of "progressive" women filmmakers related to those of other "progressive" filmmakers in South Africa? What are the cinematographic models for South African women's films?

Women in Zimbabwe, like those in South Africa, Angola and Mozambique, are able to complete their films with local production facilities, in contrast to some women in central and western Africa. Zimbabwean women also have obtained local financial sponsorship for their films. *Road to Survival*, a series of films on environmental problems by Pattie Pink, was produced in Shona, Ndebele and English and supported by the Zimbabwe National Conservation Trust and local Rotary Club (Masters, 1987, 9). How does the financial sponsorship of such films influence their content? What are considered appropriate topics for documentary films? Miriam Patsanza made *Woman Cry* on rural disabled women (Mohamed, 1985, 5), but Edwina Spicer was unable to complete *Aids—the Killer Disease*, despite financial support (Ziana ,1988, 3, Spicer 1988, 6). Spicer's *Biko: Breaking the Silence*, was well received in Zimbabwe and also was the first Zimbabwean documentary to be sold internationally, to BBC's Channel 4 (Soper, 1987, 10). What will be the impact of this international recognition on Spicer's career and the future development of documentary film in Zimbabwe? What will be the influence of Miriam Patsanza now that she has become a film producer based in South Africa? What are white women filmmakers doing to share their experience and expertise with other women in South Africa and Zimbabwe?

Student filmmakers are only occasionally the subjects of writ-
ten materials. Afi Yakubu was among the students from Ghana's
National Film and Television Institute who received an award for
Chorkor Smoker, about the building of a fish smoking plant, at
the International Agricultural Film and TV Competition in Berlin
in 1988 (Awards, 1988, 36), the International Medical and
Scientific Film Festival in Parma in 1989, and the Aniwa Africa
Festival in Accra in 1993 (Harvest at NAFTI 1994, 13). The Aniwa
Africa Festival was a student film and television festival accom-
panied by workshops (Peis, 1994:1-2). What additional training
and experience did she receive before making *Bondage* in 1994?
What has been the influence of her participation in the meeting of
Anglophone women film and video producers in Accra in
December 1991 and her role as Secretary-General of the organization on her filmmaking? (Yeboah-Afari, 1992, 129). Short films
made by Ruby Bell Gam, Ijeoma Iloputaife and Anne Ngu when
they were students at the University of California, Los Angeles,
were described in an article on Black women filmmakers (Springer,
1984, 36). All of their films focus on women's issues: stillbirth,
child custody customs and sexual abuse. Yet the article does not
answer such important questions as how their training at UCLA
influenced these women from Nigeria and Cameroon, contacts
with other students and African-American filmmakers.

Much research needs to be conducted on training facilities in
Africa and abroad, on who attends these facilities and which
aspects of filmmaking are studied. Today's film editor or
scriptwriter may be tomorrow's director. For example, before making an animated film, *L'Enfant térrible*, Kadiatou Konaté worked
for Films Cissé for several years in a variety of roles and on
Mambaye Coulibaly's animated film, *La Geste de Segou*
(Coulibaly, 1994). Marguerite Ahyi, a television camerawoman
in Benin, aspires to be a filmmaker (Dagba, 1990). Will she fulfill
her goal and, if so, how? Learning about women from their first
introduction to film, rather than focusing on women only after
their first notable achievement, is essential for understanding filmmaking by Sub-Saharan African women.

THREE PROFILES

Safi Faye is the best known African woman filmmaker internationally, but she is neither the first African woman filmmaker

(Kaboré, 1995, 4) nor the only independent African woman film-maker (Pfaff, 1988, 115, 118). Faye is atypical of most African women filmmakers working in the 1980s and 1990s that I have read about. In some respects she is more similar to African male filmmakers in exile such as Haile Gerima and Med Hondo. Faye has lived and worked in Paris throughout her career, and has far more access to international film networks than do most African filmmakers, women or men. Faye's films are better known to some Europeans than to most Africans, since her films are rarely shown in Africa (Olorunyomi, 1997, 43). More needs to be known about Faye's international film networks, such as those with film editors including Andrée Daventure (Reid, 1991), and on her influence on other African filmmakers. Is Safi Faye a role model for African women filmmakers?

Safi Faye was born in Fad Jal, Senegal, a Serer village south of Dakar, in which she has made several ethnographic films. Educated in Senegal, Faye was a school teacher in Dakar in 1966 when she met Jean Rouch, the foremost French ethnographic film-maker and one of the fathers of cinéma verité, at FESTAC, the World Black and African Festival of Arts and Cultures. Subsequently she played a role in Rouch's *Petit à petit* (1969) and met Damouré Zika, lbrahima Dia and Mustapha Alassane, who also had roles in this film (Pfaff, 1988, 116). With Rouch's encouragement in the 1970s, Faye studied ethnology at the University of Paris where she first earned a diploma and subsequently a doctorate in ethnology based on research on Serer religion, and attended the Louis Lumière Film School. In 1979-1980 she studied video production in Berlin, was a guest lecturer at the Free University of Berlin, and made two videos, *3 ans 5 mois* and *Man Sa Yay*. Faye has received financial assistance for some of her films from the French Ministry of Culture and from television stations and cultural organizations in France and Germany. She has attended many international film festivals, not only in Europe, but also in North and South America and India. However, she has not regularly attended FESPACO, giving as an excuse her filming obligations in Europe (Sawadogo, 1990, 5).

Faye's documentary films on Senegal are related to her thesis research. Although her research focused on Serer religious practice, she found that discussions spontaneously turned to economic problems, which are the subject of *Kaddu Beykat*, *Fad Jal* and *Goob Na Nu*. In an interview, Faye said: "I chose the cinema in order to relate effectively the real problems of people's daily lives. But always looking to the future: won't these documents be nec - essary to my children so that they don't deny their African iden - tity?" (Martin, 1981, 39).

In her documentary films Faye includes some fictional events. For example, she organizes the information about economic life in *Kaddu Beykat* around a love story and includes reenactments of the past in *Fad Jal*. Faye sees no contradiction in including elements of fiction in documentary films: "I base what I do in reality. What I try to film is things, which relate to our civilization. In other words: a typically African culture" (Martin, 1981, 39).

Faye made her Serer documentaries in her own village. In *Kaddu Beykat* she gathered villagers and announced a topic for discussion, and then filmed the ensuing discussion with a station - ary camera and without further "direction." *Kaddu Beykat* reflects both Faye's views in the questions she asks and the villagers' views in the content of the discussions. Faye claims not to have political views, but ideas about reality (Maupin, 1976, 80), which also are evident in other films such as *Man Sa Yay* on an immigrant's life in Germany. *Fad Jal* focuses on life cycle rituals, especially those of birth and death, which are part of the village's history. Because Faye failed to get clearance for making her films in Senegal, the films could not be shown in Senegal at the time they were made (Ruelle, 1978, 49), however, she has subsequently shown them to the people who appear in them (Olorunyomi, 1997, 43).

Faye's first films were made in Paris. *Revanche* made with other students, including the Cameroonian filmmaker Daniel Kamwa, was her first experience in filmmaking (Sawadogo, 1990, 5). Faye acts in her second film, *La Passante*, which reflects in part the solitude she felt in Paris. Some African male filmmakers also have acted in their films (Schmidt, 1991, 37). The solitude of a male student studying at a polytechnic in West Berlin is one of the main themes of *Man Sa Yay*. As in *Kaddu Beykat*, Faye includes documentary and fiction in *Man Sa Yay*, combining views of the man's activities with fictionalized subjective feelings in voice- over narration. This film has both an African significance for Faye in depicting exile and a European significance for its German tel - evision sponsors in depicting problems common to guest workers in Europe.

With sponsorship for her films from such organizations as French television for *Ambassades nourricières*, the United Nations for *Les Ames au soleil*, and UNICEF for *Selbé parmi tant d'autres*, Faye is insured a larger audience for her films than are many film - makers who work in Africa. More needs to be known about how many of her films have been viewed in Africa and how audiences have responded to them. Would African audiences be interested in *Ambassades nourricières*, which is about Chinese, Indian, Hungarian and other ethnic restaurants in Paris, when surveys of African audience preferences show a strong interest in action films?

Although Faye's Serer films were made with very small budg - ets, since the late 1970s her films have been better financed both because of the reputation for excellence established by the receipt of film festival awards for *Kaddu Beykat* and because of her rela - tively easier access to European sources of funding than is avail - able to filmmakers resident in Africa. *Kaddu Beykat* attracted inter- national attention through awards received at FIFEF (Festival International du Film d'Expression Française), FESPACO, and the Berlin Film Festival, as well as the receipt of the Georges Sadoul Prize in France and its selection as an entry at the Cannes Film Festival. However, it was not shown in Senegal when it was first released. Research is needed on the response to *Kaddu Beykat* at European film festivals and FESPACO, and the specific effect of the receipt of European awards on Faye's career.

Safi Faye is an independent filmmaker; for most of her career she has not been restricted by the same infrastructural and finan - cial constraints as most filmmakers who work in Africa. She feels that she has no more difficulties in making films than do African men (Pfaff, 1988, 118). However, Faye recognizes that she has been favored in making films because there were few African women filmmakers when she first started making films (Sawadogo, 1990, 5), and regrets that African films must first win international recognition before being shown in Africa (Schissel, 1978, 73). Even though Faye has made over a dozen films including the fea - ture film *Mossane*, her reputation still rests primarily on *Kaddu Beykat*. *Mossane*, like Faye's documentary films, is based on rural life in Senegal and combines fact and fiction. Faye has said that *Mossane* is in part a vision of herself in her mother's generation (Olorunyomi, 1997, 43). Although she has not been closely affil - iated with filmmaking activities in Africa, she was presented with an award for her filmmaking at the fifth African Regional Conference of Women in Dakar in November 1994 (Kabore, 1995,

4). Research is needed on Faye's contacts with African filmmakers, producers, actors and actresses.

Mariama Hima, recently the Director of Culture in Niger (Mariama Hima, 1991, 6) before her appointment as Minister of Development in 1996 and the Nigerien Ambassador to France in 1997, worked for 12 years as a conservator in the National Museum in Niamey (Diallo, 1989, 28). Like Safi Faye, Hima was trained as an ethnologist in Paris and became a filmmaker through contact with and encouragement from Jean Rouch, as well as Serge Moati. Unlike Faye, Hima makes films in her own country and has influence on others involved in filmmaking in Niger through her administrative positions and such international activities as leading the Niger delegation to Mexico in 1989 and to FESPACO in 1991. Although her official responsibilities and residence in Niger for most of her career may limit the number of films Hima has been able to make, she may have more influence on filmmaking in Africa than does Faye. The impact of all Hima's film-related activities in Niger and elsewhere is a subject which requires research.

Although Faye combines fiction and documentary in her films, Hima is primarily a documentary filmmaker in the more literal sense of the term. Hima originally planned to make a film on women in Niger. However, when she saw a group of tire makers at work in Niamey and was able to obtain use of a camera from Nigerien television (Zouari, 1997:22-23), she began a series of unscripted documentary films on artisans such as tire and barrel-makers in Niamey, which like Faye's Serer films are intended as cultural documents. Hima is interested in the economy of poverty and the fertility of imagination, which enables people to survive (Ouédraogo, 1995). Hima's early filmmaking techniques resembled Faye's in that Hima discussed the purpose of the films with the artisans, encouraged them to behave as if she were not present, and filmed them as they worked without any further "direction." But in-depth research is needed on Hima's and Faye's techniques of filmmaking, and on their decisions to make a feature film. The kind of cultural record that Hima establishes differs from that filmed by Faye, since it focuses on contemporary urban economic activities found throughout the Third World. Hima's approach to filmmaking has won recognition through prizes at international festivals including the Festival du Réel Beaubourg in 1985, Venice Film Festival in 1986 and FESPACO in 1987. Although Hima has not become an international film celebrity like Faye, since both her goals and personal and professional networks are very different, her films have been widely viewed in Niger on television.

Like Faye, Hima has mobilized the financial means to make films, but largely within Africa. Hima has more respect than Faye for the quality of film personnel in Africa and feels that poverty of means should not be used as an excuse for making bad films (Mbarga-Abega, 1987, 63). Hima also feels that Africans are in a position to take control of their cultural development and has per - sonally demonstrated that this is possible in Niger. She has influ - enced women filmmakers outside Niger. For example, Léonic Yangba-Zowe of the Central African Republic acknowledges Hima's assistance in her thesis (Yangba-Zowe, 1987, 8). However, research is needed on the extent to which Mariama Hima has served as a role model for other filmmakers in Niger, for African women filmmakers, and for filmmakers elsewhere in Africa.

Lola Fani-Kayode, who is now using her married name Macaulay, like Safi Faye, is an independent filmmaker, but she makes television dramas in Nigeria. Fani-Kayode has made more films than either Faye or Hima. Her series, *Mirror in the Sun,* alone has 39 episodes. Although Fani-Kayode has experienced her share of financial and legal problems in making films, she has been resourceful in forming a production consortium within Nigeria for making *Iwa,* for example, and is admired both for her perseverance and the quality of her work. Adebisi Aderounmu cited Fani-Kayode as one of the "pillars" of Nigeria's cultural scene who has kept "soldiering on" despite social problems (1991, 37), and Okoh Aihe says she has "spearheaded a revolution" in Nigerian televi - sion (1991, 14).

Mirror in the Sun, a television drama series on contemporary urban and social problems, broke all viewing records for a televi - sion drama in Nigeria (Adinoyi-Ojo, 1984, B7), and had a "mon - umental" impact on the Nigerian public (Tomoloju, 1986, 10). The series deals with such common social issues as widowhood; aban - doned children and materialism in ways that make people think. The script, cinematography, acting, editing and direction were all considered excellent (Adinoyi-Ojo, 1984, B7). Daba Obioha, another Nigerian woman filmmaker, trained at Howard University in the USA and formerly a reporter for the Nigerian magazine *Happy Home*, was inspired by *Mirror in the Sun* to make *Legacy*, another television series on contemporary social problems (Akpederi, 1987, 29). Amaka Igwe, a Nigerian theater actress and video director, producer and scriptwriter also was inspired by *Mirror in the Sun* to make videos (Okungbowa, 1997, B8). *Mirror in the Sun* received recognition outside Nigeria by winning second prize at the URTNA (Union of National Radio and Television Broadcasting Organizations of Africa) competition in Dakar in 1985, one of four Nigerian television series to receive URTNA awards in the 1980s (Ukadike, 1991, 78).

Fani-Kayode's career is only beginning. Her films have been more widely distributed in Nigeria on television, than have Faye's in Senegal. As an independent filmmaker in France, Faye is dependent on commercial film distribution companies, well-known for their discrimination against African directed films, for distri - bution of her films in Senegal and elsewhere in Africa. Although Faye has won international acclaim through her access to interna - tional film festivals and European coproduction of her films, Fani-Kayode has both gained recognition in Nigeria and her films have had an impact on the Nigerian television-viewing public.

Fani-Kayode continues to focus on contemporary mass culture in her work, in contrast to Faye who focuses on rural culture and the problems of individuals in dealing with culture change. Drug abuse is the subject of Fani-Kayode's four film television series, *Mind Bending*, which is based on two years of research at the Yaba Psychiatric Hospital, while *The Dilemma of Father Michael* is based on *Idaamu Paadi Minkaihu*, a Yoruba novel by the well-known writer and television producer Adebayo Faleti. *Drive and Stay Alive* deals with Nigeria's auto accident rate, one of the high - est in the world. The recent series, *Facing Facts*, on family prob-lems stimulated a related radio talk show, *Time Out* (Ayorinde, 1997, 37), and won the award for the best television program at Nigeria's 1996 Thema Awards for media (Okafor, 1996, 33). Much more needs to be known about Fani-Kayode's filmmaking deci-sions, how she works with personnel involved in her films, and the personal networks in Nigeria that have enabled her to finance and direct so many television films, as well as about audience responses to her work.

CONCLUSION

These three profiles of highly accomplished filmmakers suggest how different are the careers of African women filmmakers and the kinds of films they make, and also indicate the lack of detailed information about their careers.[8] Yet they are among the women about whom the most information is available in published sources!

Extensive research is needed to identify and learn about women filmmakers of the subcontinent. Information about successful and unsuccessful filmmakers needs to be collected, both for tracing the development of individual careers and for learning about the specific factors in individual African countries which are relevant for understanding the roles of women filmmakers. Future research needs to be unencumbered by European "industrial" models of filmmaking and as broadbased as possible. If the African contexts of the creation and reception of women's films are the foci of future research, appropriate models for discussing and comparing their work will be developed.

FILMOGRAPHY

This filmography represents only films and filmmakers I have read about or, in a few instances, films I have seen. To make a complete filmography, one would have to scan newspapers, popular magazines, television programs and government publications from broadcasting, communications and information ministries in every African country. There also is difficulty identifying women's names in some cases, so I may have inadvertently omitted some filmmakers whom I could not identify as women.[9]

Adagala, Esther (Kenya). *Women in Health,* 1984.
Adamou, Assiatou (Niger). *La réhabilitation des femmes handicapées,* Niger, 1994.
—. *Les femmes pénitenciers,* 1995.
Adjiké, Sanni Assouma (Togo). *Femme-Moba,* 1995.
—. *L'Eau sacrée,* 1995.
Albuquerque, Fatima (Mozambique). Also listed as Maria de Fatima Silveira Albuquerque. *O ABC da nova vida,* 1985.
—. *As nossas flores,* 1986.
—. *La son c'est la vie,* 1987.
—. *Entre a dor e esperanca,* 1987
—. *No meu pais existe uma guerra,* 1989.
Ambassa, Blandine Ngono (Cameroon). *Miseria,* 1990.
—. *Contes du Cameroun,* 1991.
—. *Passe-Partout Afrique,* with Driss Mrini and Boubacar Ba, 1991.

—. *Silence on joue*, 199?

Arzouni, Linda (Senegal). *Autour du point*, 1996.

Atangana, Rosalie Mbélé (Cameroon). *La production d'Africa Jin*, 1994.

—. *Famille et Sida*, 1994.

Badarou, Michèle (Benin). Also listed as Michèle Badarou Akan and Michelle Huquette Akan Badarou. *Les Tresseuses de natte de Gbangnito*, 1985.

—. *Bénin le temps au féminin*, 1985.

Bekale, Rose (Gabon). Also listed as Rose Elise Mengue- Bekale. *Le Tison enchanteur*, 1988.

—. *Santé en question*, 1992.

Bell Gam, Ruby (Nigeria). *My Child, Their Child*, 1984.

—. *Inyono: The Cult*, with David Uru Iyam, 1985.

Belle, Jacqueline Moustache (Seychelles). *Men and Birds on Cousin Island*, with Ralph la Blanche de Charnoy, 1988.

Biloa, Marie Roger (Cameroon). *Requium pour un président assas-siné*, with Didier Mauro, 1989.

Bitrus, Zainab (Nigeria). *Mangana Jari Ce*, 1989-90.

—. *A dawo Lafiya*, 1997.

Coulibaly, Diatou Cissé (Senegal). *Kew, Stop Danger*, 1992.

—. *Mon combat quotidien à la télé*, with Leo Leysen, 1995.

Coulibaly, Fatoumata (Mali). *N'Golo dit Papa*, 1997.

Coulibaly, Nabintou (Côte d'Ivoire). *La carte d'identité*, 1994.

—. *Coupables traditions*, 1994.

—. *Le cercueil*, with Wintin Wintin, 1994.

—. *L'hôtel*, with Wintin Wintin, 1994.

Cudjoe, Veronica (Ghana). *Suzzy*, 1992.

Dangarembga, Tsitsi (Zimbabwe). *Die Schönheitsverschwörung*. 1994.

—. *Schwarzmarkt*, 1994.

—. *Everyone's Child*, 1996.

Diallo, Assiatou Bily (Guinea). *Le plaisir qui tue*, 1996.

—. *L'amour en larme*, 199?

Diegu, Omah (Nigeria).[10] *Not to My Son*, 1994.

—. *The Snake in My Bed*, 1994.

Diop, Adrienne (Senegal). *Le riz dans la vallée du fleuve*, 1990.

—. *La pêche artisanale au Sénégal*, 1991.

—. *Le sida au Sénégal*, 1992.

Djédjé, Adèle (Côte d'Ivoire). *La Culture de la banane plantain de contre-saison*, 1991.

Djira, Valerie (Côte d'Ivoire) *Afrique étoiles: Kanda Bongoman*, with Youssouf Djira, 1990.
Dlamini, Luvumisa (Swaziland). *Prisoner's Sport and Music*, 1989.
—. *Rose Craft*, 1989.
Dokubo, Hilda (Nigeria). *Another Campus Tale*, with Akaraose Mrakpor, 1997.
Elizabeth, Marie-Claire (Seychelles). *Magazin ekonomik: pti metye*, 1989.
Fani-Kayode, Lola (Nigeria). *Mirror in the Sun*, 1984.
—. *The Dilemma of Father Michael*, 1988.
—. *Iwa*, 1988.
—. *Mind Bending*, series of 4 films: *Last Days, One Edge, Scars Within, Wake to the Night*, 1990.
—. *Drive and Stay Alive*, 1993.
—. *Family Ties*, 1994.
—. *Facing Facts*, 1996.
Faye, Safi (Senegal). *La Passante*, 1972.
—. *Revanche*, with other students, 1973.
—. *Kaddu Beykat (Lettre paysanne)*, 1975.
—. *Fad Jal*, 1979.
—. *Goob Na Nu (La récolte est finie)*, 1979.
—. *3 ans 5 mois*, 1979-83.
—. *Man Sa Yay (Moi, ta mère)*, 1980.
—. *Woman*, 1980.
—. *Les Ames au soleil*, 1981.
—. *Selbé parmi tant d'autres*, 1982.
—. *Ambassades nourricières*, 1984.
—. *La Toile d'araignée*, 1988.
—. *Mossane*, 1996.
Fielou, Michele (Burkina Faso). *Les Mémoires de Binduté Da*, with Jacques Lombard, 1988.
Folly, Anne Laure (Togo) *Le Guardien des forces*, 1991.
—. *Femmes du Niger*, 1992.
—. *Femmes aux yeux ouverts*, 1993.
—. *Entre l'arbre et la pirogue*, 1996.
—. *Les oubliées*, 1996.
Fombé, Margaret (Cameroon). Also listed as Margaret Fombé Fobé. *Portraits de femmes*, 1989—television series that includes:
—. *Les femmes pompistes*, 1989.
—. *Les femmes avocates*, 1989.
—. *Ma'a nwambeng (The Woman Who Collects Palm Nuts)*, 1994.

—. *Sirri Cow (The Woman Butcher)*, 1994.
—. *Femmes et hommes en milieu rural camerounais*, 1995.
Forjaz, Moira (Mozambique). *Uma dia numa aldeia communal,* 1981.
—. *Mineiro Moçambicano*, 1981.
Fresu, Anna (Mozambique). *Jogos e Brinceders*, 1984.
Goldblatt, Brenda (South Africa). *Grinding Stones*, 1990.
Gumedze, Linda (Swaziland). *Point of View: The Drought in Swaziland*, 1992.
Gwatiringa, Agnes (Zimbabwe). *Uchadya Izvzo*, 1991.
Hezumuryang, Melanie (Burundi). *Bichorai (Princes de la rue)*, with Philippe Pierpont, 1994.
Hima, Mariama (Niger). *Baabu Banza (Rien ne se jette)*, 1984.
—. *Falaw*, 1985.
—. *Toukou*, 1986.
—. *Katako (Les planches)*, 1987.
—. *Hadiza et Kalia*, 1994.
Igwe, Amaka (Nigeria). *Rattlesnake*, 1994.
—. *Adamma*, 1995.
—. *Violated*, 1996.
Ilboudo, Martine Condé (Burkina Faso). *S.I.A.O.*, 1992.
—. *Artisanat 1993*, 1993.
—. *Jazz à Ouaga*, 1993.
—. *Féminin pluriel*, 1994.
—. *Un cri dans le sahel*, 1994.
—. *Messages de femmes-messages pour Beijing,* 1995.
Iloputaife, Ijeoma (Nigeria). *African Woman USA*, 1984.
Kaboré, Valérie (Burkina Faso). *Kadoula "la bonne à tout faire,"* 1996.
—. *Les vrais faux jumeaux*, 1996.
Kenmoe Kenyou, Rosine (Cameroon). *Tazibi*, with Augustine Kamani Monkam, 1990.
Kinyanjui, Wanjiru (Kenya). *African Time*, 1991.
—. *The Sick Bird*, 1991.
—. *Black in the Western World*, 1992.
—. *The Battle of the Sacred Tree*, 1994.
Konaté, Kadiatou (Mali). *L'Enfant térrible*, 1994.
—. *Musow Bémi (Rêve de femmes)*, 1995.
—. *La battue des lièvres à Djenné*, 1996.
Kourouma, Suzanne (Burkina Faso). *Branmuso (Belle mère)*, 1994.

◈ Liking, Werewere (Côte d'Ivoire). *Dieu-chose (Regards de fous)*, 1987.

Macaulay, Lola. (See Fani-Kayode, Lola)

Mango, Idi Rakia (Niger). *Femmes et exode,* 1988.

—. *Le Langui,* 1989.

—. *Les Chasses touristes,* 1990.

M'Mbugu-Schelling, Flora (Tanzania). *Kumekucha (From Sun Up),* 1987.

—. *These Hands,* 1992.

—. *Shida and Matatizo,* 1993.

◈ Mekuria, Salem (Ethiopia). *Sidet: Forced Exile,* 1991.

—. *Yewonz Maeibel (Deluge),* 1995.

Melomé, Marie-Constance A. (Benin). *Pudeur de femme,* 1991.

—. *Le Ouassa Ouassa,* 1994.

—. *Youpi,* 1994.

—. *Un groupement pas commes les autres,* 1995.

Mire , Soraya (Somalia). *Fire Eyes,* 1994.

◈ Mouyeké , Camille (Congo). *L'Eprouvé du feu,* 1993. MAN !

Mugugu, Denise (Burundi). *Des anges en fer,* 1991.

◈ Mungai, Anne C. (Kenya). *Nkomani Clinic,* 1980.

—. *The Beggar's Husband,* 1980.

—. *Tomorrow's Adult Citizens,* 1981.

—. *Root 1,* 1981.

—. *Together We Build,* 1983.

—. *Wekessa at Cross Roads,* 1986.

—. *Productive Farmlands,* 1990.

—. *Faith,* 1991.

—. *Saikati,* 1992.

—. *Pongezi,* 1993.

—. *Usilie Mtoto wa Africa (Don't Cry Child of Africa)*

◈ Nacro, Fanta (Burkina Faso). Also listed as Regina Fanta Nacro, *Un Certain matin,* 1992.

—. *Pouc Niini,* 1994.

—. *Le truc de Konaté,* 1997.

Ngu, Anne (Cameroon). *Little Ones,* 1984.

Nkono, Barbara (Cameroon). *Etre veuve et réussir,* 1995.

Obioha, Daba (Nigeria). *Legacy,* 1987.

Okodo, Elizabeth (Kenya). *Immunization Spots,* 1994.

Omaboe, Grace (Ghana). *It's Too Late,* 1995.

Onobrauche, Evelyn (Nigeria). *Oghenetega,* 1996.

◈ Onwurah, Ngozi (Nigeria /UK). *Coffee Coloured Children,* 1998.

—. *The Body Beautiful*, 1990
—. *Yetunde's Gymhaka*, 1991.
—. *Who Stole the Soul?*, 1991.
—. *And Still I Rise*, 1993.
—. *Monday's Girls*, 1994.
—. *Welcome to the Terrordome*, 1994.
—. *Behind the Mask*, 1996.
Oruh, Gold (Nigeria). *Away from the Sidewalk*, 1983.
Osoba, Funmi (Nigeria). *The Dormant Genius*, 1991.
Otuka, Mary Wagturi (Kenya). *Through Women's Eyes*, 1996.
Oubda, Franceline (Burkina Faso). *Accès des femmes à la terre*, 1992.
—. *Sadjo la Sahélienne*, 1994.
—. *Femmes de Boussé survivre à tout prix*, with Benjamin Nama, 1994.
—. *Hommage aux femmes de la Sissili*, 1995.
—. *Elles, pour refaire le monde*, 1995.
Ouédraogo, *Aminata* (Burkina Faso). *L'Impasse*, 1988.
—. *A qui le tour*, 1991.
—. *Alcoolisme*, 1992.
Owen, Charlotte (South Africa). *Mayibuye Africa*, 1993.
Owolabi, Adewunmi (Nigeria). *Gogongo (Wind Pipe)*, 1995.
Patsanza, Miriam (Zimbabwe). *Woman Cry*, 1985.
—. *Beyond Today*, 1988.
—. *The Return*, 1992.
Phoba, Monique (Zaire). *Revue en vrac*, 1991.
—. *Rentrer*, 1993.
—. *In situ*, 1993.
—. *Rêves en Afrique*, 1993.
—. *Une voix dans le silence*, 1995.
—. *Deux petits tours puis s'en vont...*, with Emmanuel Kolawole, 1997.
Pink, Pattie (Zimbabwe). *Road to Survival*, 1987.
Proctor, Elaine (South Africa). *Re tla Bona*, 1984.
—. *Sharpeville Spirit*, 1986.
—. *On the Wire*, 1991.
—. *Friends*, 1993.
Quashi, Veronica (Ghana). *Twin Lovers*, 1995.
—. *Tears of Joy*, 1996.
Rabenirainy, Olga (Madagascar). *Zana-Bazaha (Enfants des étrangers)*, 1994.
Salazar, Denise (Angola). *Marabu*, 1984.

Sanogo, Kadida (Burkina Faso). *Le Joueur de kora*, 1989.
—. *Un Siao des femmes*, 1992.
—. *Une semaine au féminin*, 1994.
Sawadogo, Cilia (Burkina Faso). *La Femme mariée à trois hommes*, with Danielle Roy, 1993.
—. *Naissance*, 1993.
—. *L'Arrêt d'autobus*, 1994.
—. *Le joueur de cora*, 1996.
Selly, Mariam Kane (Senegal). *Cars rapides*, 1990.
—. *Xessal*, 1991.
—. *Femmes rurales*, 1993.
Sinclair, Ingrid (Zimbabwe). *Mothers Don't Forget*, 1986.
—. *Wake Up*, 1989.
—. *Bird from Another World*, 1992.
—. *Flame*, 1996.
Sita-Bella, Thérèse (Cameroon). *Tam-tam à Paris*, 1963.
Sona, Venessa Eboté (Cameroon). *Play Skul*, 1994.
—. *Vivre au Sahe*, 1994.
Spicer, Edwina (Zimbabwe). *AIDS—The Killer Disease (never released)*, 1984.
—. *Biko: Breaking the Silence*, 1987.
—. *A Knock on the Door—The Story of Silveira House*, 1988.
—. *The First Twenty Years*, 1993.
—. *Keeping a Live Voice*, 1995.
Sutherland, Efua (Ghana). *Araba the Village Story*, with Leon Glickman, 1967.
Tan, Florence (Cameroon). *Comment? Comment!*, 1994.
—. *Retirement—Life's End?*, 1996.
Tchakoua, Josephine (Cameroon). *Un mariage riche en couleur*, 1996.
Tchongolo, Blanche (Togo). *Aneho raconte*, 1994.
Thompson, Bridget (South Africa). *An Unwritten Story*, 1989.
Touré, Assiatou Laba (Senegal). *Profession talibé*, 1987.
Wanono, Nadine (Niger). *Demain, au bout du fleuve*, 1987.
Wareta, Josephine (Kenya). *Dreams of a Sweet Tomorrow*, with Mudegu K. Ongusso, 1992.
Wera, Françoise (Burkina Faso). *Fati et les autres*, 1995.
Yacoub, Zara Mahamat (Chad). *Dilemme au féminin*, 1994.
—. *Enfants de la rue*, 1995.
—. *Les enfants de la guerre*, 1996.

Yakubu, Afi (Ghana). *Chorkor Smoker*, with other students at the National Film and Television Institute, 1988.
—. *Bondage,* 1994.
Yambo-Odotte, Dommie (Kenya). *If Women Counted,* 1993.
—. *Towards Autonomy*, 1993.
—. *Women Agenda Kenya/Uganda*, 1996.
Yaméogo, Florentine (Burkina Faso). *Le Jeudi de Gaoussou*, 1994.
—. *Sacrées chenilles (Sacred caterpillars)*, 1994.
—. *Mélodies de femmes*, 1995.
—. *Seni le petit joueur de cora*, 1997.
Yangba Zowe, Léonie (Central African Republic). Also listed as Léonie Yangba Zowe, *Yangba bolo*, 1985.
—. *Lengue*, 1985.
—. *N'Zale*, 1986.
—. *Paroles de sages*, 1987.
Zoulaha, Mme Abdou (Niger). *Santé pour tous en l'an 2000*, 1993.

NOTES:

1. A major problem with the majority of publications on African cinema is that they are journalistic, not scholarly. I have dis-cussed problems with the literature on African cinema, which are too numerous to be discussed here in "The bibliography of films by Sub-Saharan African filmmakers" (Schmidt, 1989), and "The challenges of African film bibliography: content and audience" (Schmidt, 1996).
2. In the written literature about all kinds of African films a clear distinction is not always made between directors and produc-ers. Some producers may have inadvertently been included in this discussion because of inaccurate or incomplete informa-tion in the written sources that were consulted.
3. Three different dates are listed for this film: 1963 by L'Association des Trois Mondes (1991, 92); 1965 by Guy Jérémie Ngansop (1987, 73); and 1966 by Claire Andrade-Watkins (1990, 91). While date discrepancies of a year are not uncommon in published sources, this much discrepancy is not typical. Since I have not seen the film, I cannot resolve the discrepancy.
4. *Les Journées du cinéma africain 1989* (1989). This festival includes Canadian and Diaspora participation. Each year's fes-

tival has a different thematic focus. Women regularly partici -
pate even when the thematic focus is not on women.
5. The discussion that follows is biased by the written sources that
I have been able to consult. It has not been possible to provide
examples from all Sub-Saharan countries.
6. Her thesis and most recent film were completed in the same
year.
7. Comments made by the producer, Debra Ogazuma, at the
showing of several episodes from the series at the African
Studies Association annual meeting, Baltimore, November 2,
1990.
8. There is more published information on Faye and Hima in
European and African newspapers and on Fani-Kayode in
sources on television and in Nigerian magazines than I was
able to consult in preparing this essay.
9. The first version of the filmography was published in Schmidt
(1992), the second version was published in Schmidt (1997).
I have deleted filmmakers from the previous lists who I have
now identified as men or producers. Jane Lusabe is mentioned
as a Kenyan filmmaker (Cham, 1994, 93, 98), but I have not
located the titles of any films she made. Also, there is the prob -
lem of identifying women filmmakers from names when very
little has been written about them. For example, is Mina Bataba
of Togo a woman? I do not know from the minimal published
information I have found.
10. In an interview with Michael Tonfeld in *Uhuru* (1994) she
says that she made *African Woman USA*. This film was attrib-
uted to Ijeoma Iloputaife by Claudia Springer in *Jump Cut*
(1984).

WORKS CITED

Aderounmu, Adebisi. "Pillars in the storm," *Newswatch* March 4,
1991: 36-37.
Adinoyi-Ojo, Shaibu. "A one-way mirror in the sun," *Guardian*
(Lagos) October 28, 1984: B7.
Aihe, Okoh. "Lola, Euzahn, Kathryn, Julia: Amazons on cellu -
loid," *Guardian* Lagos) March 1, 1991: 14.
Akinosho, Toyin. "Television producer screens political contribu -
tions of Nigerian women," *Guardian* (Lagos) June 23, 1985:
3.

Akpederi, Joni. "Pet project on tape," *African Guardian* July, 23, 1987: 29.

Andrade-Watkins, Claire. "France's Bureau of Cinema: financial and technical assistance between 1961 and 1977—operations and implications for African cinema," *Visual Anthropology Review* 6, 2, 1990: 80-93.

Anikulapo, Jahman. "On screen, pains of a distorted past," *Guardian* (Lagos) October 1, 1996:33.

L'Association des Trois Mondes. *Dictionnaire du cinéma africain*. Paris: Karthala, 1991. Vol. 1.

"Awards for African films," *Afrika* 5-6, 1988: 36.

Ayorinde, Steve. "Lola returns with Time Out," *Guardian* (Lagos) May 29, 1997:37.

Balogun, Françoise. "Scope for the future," *West Africa* April 8-14, 1991: 523.

"Carthage 90 le marché à l'honneur," *Unir cinéma* 149, 1990: 33-36.

Cham, Mbye. "African women and cinema: a conversation with Anne Mungai," *Research in African Literatures* 25, 3, 1994: 93-104.

"Coffee coloured talent," *West Africa* September 3-9, 1990: 2393.

Cook, Pam. *Coffee Coloured Children*, *Monthly Film Bulletin* October 1989: 316.

Coulibaly, Inza. "Melle Kadiatou Konaté réalisatrice: L'homme ne vit pas seulement de riz et d'eau, mais aussi de cinéma," *Femme 2000* (Bamako) 00, 1994: 14-16.

Dagba, Edson. "Mlle Marguerite Ahyi la première "camera-woman" de la télévision béninoise," *Amina* 248, 1990: 52-54.

Diallo, Assiatou Bah. "Les femmes à la recherche d'un nouveau souffle," *Amina* 253, 1991: 8-9.

—. "Mariama Hima la championne du cinéma pieds nus," *Amina* 225, 1989: 28-30.

Faleti, Adebayo. *Idaamu Paadi Minkailu*. Ibadan: Onibonoje Press, 1972.

Fiofori, Tam. "The neglect of local films," *Times International* December 22, 1986: 32.

"Harvest at NAFTI," *Concept* (Accra) 2, 1, 1994: 13.

"Honneur aux femmes africaines de l'audiovisuel," *FEPACI Info* 5, 1991: 2.

Les Journées du cinéma africain 1988. Montreal: Vues d'Afrique, 1988.

Les Journées du cinéma africain 1989. Montreal: Vues d'Afrique, 1989.

Kaboré, Françoisc. "Safy (sic) Faye awarded a gold 'Oscar,'" *FES-PACO News* February 20, 1995: 4,8.

Kalambry, Alexis. "Les amazones du son et de l'image," *Les Echos* October 21, 1994: 4.

Larouche, Michel. "Le temps que l'on met à marcher. Sambizanga (1972) de Sarah Maldoror," in *Films d'Afrique*. ed. Michel Larouche. Montreal: Guernica, 1991: 21-39.

Leonard, Charles. "KwaNdebele's anti-homeland battle examined in festival film," *Weekend Mail* (Johannesburg) September 14-20, 1990: 11.

Lindfors, Bernth. *A Bibliography of Literary Contributions to Nigerian Periodicals 1946-1972*. lbadan: lbadan University Press, 1975.

Maiga, Cheick Kolla. "Colloque sur le parternariat audiovisuel. Deuxième journées internationales du partenariat (25-27 février 1991): l'espoir l'hirozon" (sic), *Sidwaya* February 22, 1991:10.

"Mariama Hima," *Africa international* 237, 1991:6.

Martin, Angela. "African Cinema," *South* January 1981: 38-39.

Masters, Reyhana. "Video film series looks at environmental prob-lems," *Herald* (Harare) June 2, 1987:9.

Maupin, Françoise. "Entretien avec Safi Faye," *Revue du cinéma* 303, 1976: 75-80.

Mbarga-Abega, Mathieu. "Mariama Hima," *Bingo* 415, 1987: 62-63.

Mohamed, Shehnilla. "Focus on rural disabled women," *Herald* (Harare) October 11, 1985: 5.

Ngansop, Guy Jérémie. *Le Cinéma camerounais en crise*. Paris: L'Harmattan, 1987.

Okafor, Chido. "Lola returns with facing facts," *Guardian* (Lagos) June 22, 1996:33.

Okungbowa, Andrew Iro. "The future of Nigerian film is bright," *Guardian* (Lagos) March 30, 1997:B8.

Olorunyomi, Sola. "Talking film with cineaste, Safi Faye," *Guardian* (Lagos) August 21, 1997:43.

Omotunde, Soji. "Women on the sidewalks," *Newswatch* 1, 11, 1985: 36.

Ouédraogo, Oumdouba. "Mariama Hima, 'L'Afrique, victime d'un complot économique,'" *Amina* 298, 1995: 18.

Peis, Joe Louis. "Aniwa Africa '93," *Concept* (Accra) 2,1,1994:1-2.

Pfaff, Françoise. *Twenty-five Black African Filmmakers*. Westport: Greenwood, 1988.

Reid, Mark A. "Interview with Andrée Daventure. Producing African cinema in Paris," *Jump Cut* 36, 1991: 47-51.

Ruelle, Catherine. "Lettre paysanne de Safi Faye," *Afrique-Asie* 71, 1978: 48-49.

Sawadogo, Filippe. "Safi Faye l'une des premières cinéastes africaines," *Sidwaya* December 7, 1990: 5.

Schissel, Howard. "Among the peasants," *New African* August 1978: 73.

Schmidt, Nancy J. "An Anthropological Analysis of Nigerian Fiction." Dissertation. Northwestern University, 1965.

—. "The bibliography of films by Sub-Saharan African filmmakers," in *Africana Resources and Collections: Three Decades of Development and Achievement*, ed. Julian Witherell. Metuchen, NJ: Scarecrow Press, 1989: 151-177.

—. "Films by Sub-Saharan African women filmmakers: a preliminary filmography," *African Literature Association Bulletin* 18,4, 1992: 12-14.

—. "The influence of acting on African cinema: agendas for research," *ZAST Zeitschrift für Afrika Studien* 9/10, 1991: 33-47.

—. *Sub-Saharan African Films and Filmmakers: An Annotated Bibliography*. London: Zell, 1988.

—. *Sub-Saharan African Films and Filmmakers 1987-1992: An Annotated Bibliography*. London: Zell, 1994.

—. "The challenges of African film bibliography: content and audience," *African Research and Documentation* 72, 1996:1-8.

—. Sub-Saharan African women filmmakers: agendas for research, *Matatu* 19, 1997:163-190.

Soper, Jane. "Zimbabwe's film industry 'moving into new era,'" *Sunday Mail* (Harare) October 4, 1987: 10.

Spicer, Edwina. "Filmmaker hits back," *Herald* (Harare) May 24, 1988:6.

Springer, Claudia. "Black women filmmakers," *Jump Cut* 29, 1984: 34-37.

Tomoloju, Ben. "*Mirror in the Sun* bows out for new documentary," *Guardian* (Lagos) January 11, 1986: 10.

Tonfeld, Michael. "*Not to My Son*. First German film of Nigerian director Omah Diegu," *Uhuru* 0(Accra) 6, 11, 1994: 69-70.

Ukadike, N. Frank. "Angolphone African media," *Jump Cut* 36, 1991: 74-80.

—. *Black African Cinema*. Berkeley: University of California Press, 1994.

Vieyra, Paulin Soumanou. *Réflexions d'un cinéaste africain*. Bruxelles: Editions OCIC, 1990.

Vues d'Afrique. *Femmes d'images de l'Afrique francophone*. Montreal: Trait d'Union Culturel, 1994.

"Werewere Liking écrivain, metteur en scène." *Les Journées du cinéma africain 1989*. Montreal: Vues d'Afrique, 1989: 15-16.

Yangba-Zowe, Rosette Léonie. "Divers aspects du mariage et le rôle des femmes dans l'oeuvre cinématographique d'Oumarou Ganda (Niger)." Mémoire diplôme de l'EHESS, 1987.

Yeboah-Afari, Ajoa. "African women form guild," *West Africa* January 20-26, 1992: 129.

"Minister explains AIDS film ban," *Herald* (Harare) July 2, 1988: 3. 2.

Zouari, Fawzia. "Le charme discret du Sahel," *Jeune Afrique* 1909, 1997:22-23.

WOMEN IN AFRICAN CINEMA:
AN ANNOTATED BIBLIOGRAPHY

THIS BIBLIOGRAPHY IS DESIGNED TO SERVE as a guide for research on topics related to women in African cinema. On beginning this project, I did extensive bibliographic research and found no single bibliography devoted to women in African cine - ma. Moreover, although in most fields today CD-ROM technol - ogy has made it easy to access literature for research, the index - es available on CD-ROM do not provide many references on this topic. Instead, the researcher has to consult a wide range of sources, including monographic bibliographies, journals, maga - zines, books, and newspapers. The general omission of African women in works devoted to African cinema, women in general, Third World women, and women's studies led me to conclude that either experts in these areas are not aware of the available lit - erature, or they do not consider issues concerning African women important enough to include in their scholarship. Since we are dealing with a visual medium, one cannot ignore the fact that women play focal roles in most African films. By African films, one should understand films directed and produced by an African about Africa in or outside Africa.

Although this bibliography is by no means comprehensive, it attempts to pull together a representative selection of recent research focusing on the themes of portrayal of African women in African films, and the role of women in African filmmaking. Of particular interest in it are works on the question of represen - tation of women in African films.

It includes books, periodical articles, periodicals, and World Wide Web documents published from 1970 to 1997. It is divided into such topics as actresses, approaches, awards, catalogues and listings, costume designers, directories, distribution, education, festivals, filmmakers, filmographies, guides, make-up artists, reception, reviews, treatment of women, and World Wide Web sites. Items, which were available for my perusal, are annotated. Some items are listed under more than one section depending on their relevance to the respective sections.

It is hoped that this bibliography will stimulate widespread use of the films and the scholarship that are available on, by, and about women in African cinema. It is also hoped that it will contribute to research promoting women from their marginal position to a central one in a way that is commensurate with their presence on screen.

ACTRESSES

"Clarisse Keita, héroïne de la *Nuit Africaine.*" *Amina* 250 (February 1991): 8-9, 14. Discussion of how she started acting in film, her acting career, and preference for roles.

"Edith Nikiéma une jeune comédienne." *Amina* 232 (August 1989): 55. Discusses her film roles and training.

"Obituary: 'Mme Art Has Passed Away.'" *FESPACO Newsletter* 13 (September 16, 1997). <http://www. fespaco. bf/newsl13a.htm>. Announcement of the death of cinema and theatre actress Nafissatou Latoundji, also known as "Fifi," from Bénin. She died in a car accident on her way to the 15th FESPACO.

Domingo, Macy, and Klevor Abo. "Une Africaine à Hollywood/An African in Hollywood." *Ecrans d'Afrique/ African Screen* 2.4 (1993): 6-11. An interview with Akosua Busia. Provides biographical information and traces her painting, acting and writing career. Also gives her views on African cinema.

Maïga, Cheick Kolla. "Maysa Marta (actress, Guinée-Bissau)." *Ecrans d'Afrique/African Screen* 1.2 (1992): 36-38. Discusses her acting role in *Les Yeux Bleus de Yonta* of Flora Gomes. Reviews the film.

Mobioh, Dominique. "Stars dites-vous?" *Ivoire Dimanche* (July 14, 1991): 10. Criticism of kinds of women's roles in African films.

N'daw, Aly N'Keury. "Zalika: Star of Niger Films/Zalika: Star des films nigériens." *Ecrans d'Afrique/African Screen* 2.5-6 (1993): 28-31. Traces the acting career of Zalika Souley, including biographical information.

Olufunwa, Bola. "African Women and Cinema." *African Woman* 7 (June 1993): 45-47. Discusses the role of women in African cinema through the work of actress Juanita Ageh (Nigerian-Caribbean), director Anne Mungai (Kenyan whose film—*Saikati*—won two awards at the 1993 FESPACO) and Ngozi Onwurah (Nigerian). Looks at the way these three profes-sionals approach the issues of "women." Comments on the stereotypical portrayal of African women in film. Mentions Twende: African Professional Women in Cinema, a confer-ence organized by the Africa Centre and the British Film Institute.

Oyekunle, Segun. "'The Prodigy' of Wenchi." *West Africa* 3994 (April 18, 1994): 678-. Akosua Busia wins Women in International Film Award. Includes biographical information. Announces her upcoming screenplay *Seasons by Beento Blackbird*.

Speciale, Alessandra. "La triple galère des femmes, Africaines, actrices/A Threefold Trial: African, Female and Actress." *Ecrans d'Afrique/African Screen* 3.7 (1994): 24-29. Félicité Wouassi and Naky Sy Savané talk about the meaning of "African actor" and the difficulty for African women actors to get leading roles for women, as heroines, as women who fight, work, raise children and make their daily contribution; roles that valorize the African woman as such, whether she is traditional or modern.

Tapsoba, Clement. "Oum'Dierryla (actress, Senegal)" *Ecrans d'Afrique/African Screen* 4.12 (1995): 19-20. Traces Oumou Khaltoum Ba's (her real name) training and career.

Wonogo, Zoumana. "N'deye Fatou N'daw: From the Grammar School to Cinema." *FESPACO Newsletter* 14 (December 1997) <http://www.fespaco.bf/newsl14a.htm>. An interview with N'deye Fatou N'daw, the actress who played the role of the suffering barren woman in *Tableau Ferraille* by Moussa Sene Absa. Covers her background, her views on polygamy, and her prospect in cinema.

Yéyé, Zakaria. "Ai Keita le parcours d'une combattante." *Bingo* (March 2, 1989): 6. Actress discusses how she started acting, her film roles, and goals for the future.

—. "Hommage à Edith Nikiéma une comédienne du cinéma Burkinabe." *Sidwaya* (August 17, 1989): 6. Obituary includes biographical background and list of all films in, which she acted.

—. "Hommage aux femmes africaines professionnelles du ciné-ma: Un mérite et un défi." *Sidwaya* (February 26, 1991): 6,8. FESPACO 1991, general statement about the importance of women filmmakers, producers and actresses, photographs of actresses from Mali, Niger, Chad, Benin and Côte d'Ivoire.

Zongo, Célestin. "Afia Mala: Un Rôle dans *Yelbeedo* me fera beaucoup de bien." *Sidwaya* (September 15, 1989): 4. Actress and composer of some music for *Yelbeedo* discusses its theme and her training.

APPROACHES

"La nudité dans le cinéma africain quand le nu chasse le beau." *Amina* 253 (May 1991): 30-31. Comments by women at FESPACO 1991 on nudity in African film in the context of controversy over scenes in *Visages de Femmes.*

"Les années folles de Habiba Msika/The Life and Times of Habiba Msika." *Ecrans d'Afrique/African Screen* 3.8 (1994): 12-13. Interview with Tunisian filmmaker Selma Baccar on her film, *Habiba M'sika.* Includes biographical background and filmography.

"Stories of Women/Une affaire des femmes." *Ecrans d'Afrique/African Screen* 3.8 (1994): 8-11. Interview with Tunisian Moufida Tlatli on her "Les Silences du palais," 1994. Focuses on the feminist nature of the film. Includes biographical background.

"Women in the Place of Honour/Les femmes à l'honneur." *Ecrans d'Afrique/African Screen* 4.11 (1995): 39-40. Discussion of issues raised at FESPACO 95 during the Pan-African Union of Women in the Image Industry (Upafi) sem-inar, Words and Views of Women in Africa Today.

Bakari, Imruh and Mbye B. Cham, eds. *African Experiences of Cinema.* London: British Film Institute, 1996. Contains a chapter by Farida Ayari on cinematic images of women, and a chapter by Sheila Petty on the emergence of feminist themes in African cinemas. It also contains essays by Pfaff on Kaboré's and Ouédraogo's films as anthropological sources, and eroticism in sub-Saharan films.

Balogun, Françoise. "*Visages de Femmes* dans le cinéma d'Afrique noire." *Présence Africaine* 153 (1996): 141-150.

Cham, Mbye B. "Issues and Trends in African Cinema-1989." *African Cinema Now*. Atlanta: np, 1989. 3-6. Brief comments on reconstructing history, economic and cultural history, lan - guage, visual style, women filmmakers, films of literature, inadequate outlets for criticism, distribution problems.

Ecaré, Désiré. "*Visages de Femmes* n'est pas un film à scandale." *Fraternité Matin* (June 7, 1989): 11. A response to a May 29, 1989 "Fraternité Matin" article by K.K. Man Jusu maintain - ing that showing nudity in a film is not scandalous, that "Visage de Femmes" is a militant, feminist film. Mentions the prizes the film has won. See a further response in the June 7, 1989 article, "Fraternité Matin," by K.K. Man Jusu.

Ellson, Betty. "The female Body, Culture and Space/Le corps féminin, la culture et l'espace." *Ecrans d'Afrique/African Screen* 4.11 (1995): 28-35. Discusses the cinematic use of the African female body and how cultural specificities of the body in African space are particularly manifested in visual representation and should be accorded more importance in African film analysis. Uses *Wend Kuuni, Touki Bouki,* and *Saaraba* as examples.

Giddings, Paula. "Third World Activists: Two Women Committed to Change the World." *Encore American and Worldwide News* (June 4, 1979): 20-22.

Hadj-Moussa, Ratiba. *Le corps, l'histoire, le territoire-les rap-ports de genre dans le cinéma algérien*. Montréal: Les Editions Balzac, 1994. Discusses the issue of male-female relations in Algerian cinema, particularly through five films produced between 1972 and 1982: *Le Charbonnier* by M. Bouamari (1972), *Le Vent du Sud* by S.M. Riad (1975), *Omar Gatlato* by M. Allouache (1976), *Leila et les autres* by S.A. Mazif (1978) and *Vent de Sable* by M. Lakhdar-Hamina (1982).

Haffner, Pierre. "No Model, No School, No Tradition, an Introduction to the Identity of African Cinema." *Pensée* 306 (1996): 99-111.

Jusu, K. K. Man. "Des précisions nécessaires." *Fraternité Matin* (June 7, 1989): 11. A reply to Désiré Ecaré's article in the same issue of *Fraternité Matin*. Claims that *Visages de Femmes* is deliberately scandalous.

—. "Festival de Cannes, Idrissa Ouédraogo couronné." *Fraternité Matin* (May 29, 1989): 10. Little attention to African film, comments on *Yam Daabo* and *Visages de Femmes* See reply in June 7, 1989 *Fraternité Matin* article by Désiré Ecaré.

Kindem, Gorham H., and Martha Steele. "Women in Sembene's films." *Jump Cut* May 1991. 52-60. 36. Examines aspects of female characterization in Ousmane Sembene's *Emitai* (1971) and *Ceddo* (1976). Maintains that women are agents of both group solidarity and social change in Africa's devel-opment. Discusses the way the strong cohesive force of women in traditional African society has changed with colo-nialism.

Maldoror, Sarah. "On Sambizanga." *Women and the Cinema*: a *Critical Anthology*. Editors. Karyn and Gerald Peary Kay. New York: E.P. Dutton, 1987. 308-310.

Petty, Sheila. "African Cinema and (Re)Education: Using Recent African Feature Films." *Issue* 20.2 (June 1992): 26-37. Discusses the use of African films in the classroom to devel-op a critical awareness of established, discipline-based meth-ods of observing and interpreting texts. Suggests ways for achieving this goal. Also discusses the "Woman's Point of View" with the example of *Finzan* around the question of whether male filmmakers truly articulate African women's subjectivity or only observe it.

—. "Black African Filmmaking?" *SVA Review* 6.1 (1990): 60-64. Analyzes *Sarraouina* in relation to view that African feminist film should synthesize feminist and Panafrican ideas in order to understand the interconnection of race, gender and class oppression.

—. "Images of Women and Oppression in 'Francophone' West African Film." *Canadian Journal of Communication* 14.3 (September 1, 1989): 17-28. Examines the influence of colo-nization on the image and condition of women in contempo-rary francophone Africa through a study of the content and structure of such films as *Letter from my Village* (Faye: Senegal: 1979), *Wend Kuuni* (Kabore: Burkina Faso: 1982),

The Price of Liberty (Dikongue-Pipa: Cameroon: 1978), *Destiny* (Coulibaly: Mali: 1976), *Muna Moto* (Dikongue-Pipa: Cameroon: 1975), *Yaaba* (Ouédraogo: Burkina Faso: 1988), *Pousse-Pousse* (Kamwa: Cameroon: 1975), *The Polygamous Wazzou* (Ganda: Niger: 1971), *The Money Order* (Sembene: Senegal: 1968). Concludes that subordination and oppression of women stems from the colonial and neocolonial social models that strip women of the autonomy, power, and decision-making they have enjoyed traditionally. Maintains that western cultural and economical and political systems are the major culprits in this shift in agency.

—. *La Femme dans le cinéma d'Afrique noire*. Diss. Paris: Université Paris IV, 1988.

—. "La représentation des femmes dans le cinéma africain." *Films d'Afrique*. ed. Michel Larouche. Montréal: Guernica, 1991. pp. 127-141.

Discusses heroines in *La Noire de, Codou, Sarraouina, Le Prix de la Liberté, Le Destin*, and *Emitai*.

—. "Women's Societal Roles and Their Depiction in Black African Film." *Resources for Feminist Research (Canada)* 17.2 (June 1988): 27-29.

Pfaff, Françoise. "Eroticism and Sub-Saharan African Films." *AST Zeitschrift für Afrikastudien* 9-10 (1991): 5-16. Discusses how intimate scenes and female bodies are treated, verbal expression of sexual desire, examples of eroticism noticed by African, but not Western audiences.

—. "Five West African Filmmakers on their Films." *Issue: A Journal of Opinion* 20.2 (June 1992): 31-37. About the contribution of Souleyman Cissé, Safi Faye, Gaston Kaboré, Idrissa Ouédraogo and Ousmane Sembene to the enrichment of the international film world. Focuses on the sociopolitical and cultural content of West African films, which make them an invaluable tool for the exploration of the continent's history, cultures, and society.

Reid, Mark A. "Dialogic Modes of Representing Africa(s): Womanist Film." *Black American Literature Forum* 25.2 (Summer 1991): 375-389. Presents a "womanist" interpretation of three aspects of Black independent film. Provides a working definition of Black womanist film; theorizing Black experience of womanism and post-negritude.

Robin, Diana, and Ira Jaffe. "Women filmmakers and the Politics of Gender in Third Cinema." *Frontiers: a Journal of Women Studies* 15.1 (1994): 1-19. Introduction to a special issue of *Frontiers* devoted to women filmmakers and third cinema.

Savory, Elaine. "African Women's voices on Film." *NWSA Journal* 9.1 (Spring 1997): 99-105. A critical review of three films by African women filmmakers: Ngozi Onwurah's *Monday's Girl,* Ann-Laure Folly's *Femmes aux yeux ouverts* (*Women with open eyes*), and Flora M'mbugu-Schelling's *These Hands.* Discusses the women's control of their bodies, women's labor within capitalist economies, the significance of modernity within the framework of African identities and community.

Spass, Lieve. "Female Domestic Labor and Third World Politics in La Noire de." *Jump Cut* 27 (1982): 26-27.

Tapsoba, Clément. "Margaret Fombe Fobe (TV filmmaker, Cameroon)." *Ecrans d'Afrique/African Screen* 3.8 (1994): 26-27. Margaret Fombe Fobe's view on the importance of African filmmakers. The role she has played in breaking some of the stereotypical images of women in Cameroon society. Mentions her films, *Sirri Cow* (*The Woman Butcher*), and *Ma'a Nwambang* (*The Woman who Collects Palm Nuts*), which won the first Images de femmes prize awarded by Vues d'Afrique in Montréal, in 1994.

Taylor, Marcella. "Finding a Voice: Film and the Female in Gaston Kabore's Wend Kuuni." *Hurricane Alice: A Feminist Quarterly* 10.4/11.1 (April 1995): 19-.

Ukadike, N. Frank. "Reclaiming Images of Women in Films from Africa and the Black Diaspora." *Frontiers: A Journal of women Studies* 15.1 (1994): 102-122. Discusses the alterna-tive film practices of male and female filmmakers who seek to redefine and reclaim Black/African female subjectivity from a history of filmic (mis)representation.

Vieyra, Paulin Soumanou. "Réflexions d'un cinéaste africain." Bruxelles: Editions OCIC, 1990. A collection of his articles, primarily from the 1970s. Themes include relation of film to television, education, and oral tradition, women in African film, Marxism, and African film.

Williams, Amie. "Dancing with Absences: The Impossible Presence of Third World Women in Film." *Ufahumu* 17.3

(1989): 44-56. Analyzes *Emitai* (1971), *Naitou*, and *Visages de Femmes* in relation to theories of third cinema.

Zannad Bouchrara, Traki. "*Asfour Stah or the Image of the Urban Body/Asfour Stah ou l'image du corps* citadin ciné-matographique." *Revue de l'Institut des Belles Lettres Arabes a Tunis* 56.2 (1993): 329-332. Analyzes Férid Boughédir's *Asfour Stah* (*The Roof Sparrow*). Discusses the way public and private spaces are specifically linked with bodily experi- ence in an urban North African Arab Muslim setting. Looks at female nudity within the social atmosphere of the public bath.

AWARDS

"Blandine Ngono Ambassa (Director, Cameroon)." *Ecrans d'Afrique/African Screen* 1.1 (1992): 33. Educational and professional background, including all her television and film projects. Mentions *Miseria* for which she won a special mention at the 7th Journees du Cinema Africain et Créole.

"FESPACO 93: Awards/FESPACO 93 Palmarès." *Ecrans d'Afrique/African Screen* 2.3 (1993): 56-58. Lists awards given at FESPACO 93. Includes such names as *Saikati* by Anne Mungai for UNICEF and APAC Prizes, *These Hands* by Flora M'mbugu-Schelling for City of Perugia Prize, and *Gito l'Ingrat*" by Leonce N'gabo for Oumarou Ganda Prize, Maysa Marta for best actress in the role of Yonta in the film *Les Yeux Bleus de Yonta* by Flora Gomes of Guinea Bissau.

"Les femmes lauréates du FESPACO 1993." *Amina* 276 (April 1993): 18. Discussion of FESPACO 1993 awards for film- making and acting by Anne Mungai, Franceline Oubda, and Naky Sy Savané.

Bangre, Sambolgo. "Monique Phoba (Director, Zaire)." *Ecrans d'Afrique/African Screen* 3.9-10 (1994): 32-33. Traces the professional career of Monique Phoba. Mentions her two films, *Revue en vrac* made in 1991, which won the Jury's Special Prize at the 1991 Vues d'Afrique festival. Also men- tions her second film, *Rentrer?,* made in 1993.

Kaboré, Françoise. "Zarah Yacoub Keeps a Cool Head." *FESPACO Newsletter* 13 (September 16, 1997) <http:// www.fespaco. bf/newsl13a.htm>. About Zarah Yacoub, the Tchadian TV journalist and filmmaker, her 1996 film *Dilemme au Féminin* on female circumcision, and the negative reception that the film got in her country. The film won awards at the African and Créole film festival, and at Vue d'Afrique in Montreal.

Oyekunle, Segun. "'The Prodigy'" of Wenchi." *West Africa* 3994 (April 18, 1994): 678-. Akosua Busia wins Women in International Film Award. Includes biographical information. Announces her upcoming screenplay *Seasons by Beento Blackbird*.

Tapsoba, Clément. "Ilboudo Conde (Director, Guinea/Burkina Faso): "Quand les femmes se lèvent, le cinéma africain bouge/When Women Stand up, African Cinema Moves." *Ecrans d'Afrique/African Screen* 5.17-18 (1996): 22-23. Biographical background on Martine Ilboudo Conde, including her entry into cinema. Mentions some of her films: *Siao 92* (1992), *Jazz a Ouaga* (1993), and *Un Cri dans le sahel* (1994), a docu-fiction film. This film on the image of women received many prizes, including the Regard de femmes Prize (FESPACO 95), the creativity prize at Vues d'Afrique. Also mentions *Message des femmes pour Beijing* (1995), which earned her the ACCT Prize at Vue d'Afrique in 1996. Her views on African women filmmakers, censorship, and the responsibility of male filmmakers.

—. "Margaret Fombe Fobe (TV filmmaker, Cameroon)." *Ecrans d'Afrique/African Screen* 3.8 (1994): 26-27. Margaret Fombe Fobe's view on the importance of African filmmakers. The role she has played in breaking some of the stereotypical images of women in Cameroon society. Mentions her films, *Sirri Cow* (*The Woman Butcher*), and *Ma'a Nwambang* (*The Woman who Collects Palm Nuts*), which won the first Images de femmes prize awarded by Vues d'Afrique in Montreal in 1994.

BIBLIOGRAPHIES

Gray, John, ed. "Blacks in Film and Television: A Pan-African Bibliography of Films, Filmmakers, and Performers." New York: Greenwood Press, 1990. Lists books, dissertations, unpublished papers, and periodical articles on cinema in Africa and the African diaspora.

Pfaff, Françoise. *Twenty-Five Black African Filmmakers*. Westport, CT: Greenwood Press, 1988. Safi Faye and Sarah

Maldoror are the two women filmmakers included. For each filmmaker, biographical background, major themes, a survey of criticism, a filmography and bibliography are included.

Schmidt, Nancy J. *Sub-Saharan African Films and Filmmakers, 1987- 1992: An Annotated Bibliography*. London: Zell, 1994. Updates a bibliography with the same title published in 1988. Lists books, dissertations, periodicals, and periodical articles on Sub-Saharan films and filmmakers.

CATALOGUES AND LISTINGS

California Newsreel. Library of African Cinema. [*1991 Catalogue*]. San Francisco: California Newsreel, nd [1991]. This film catalogue includes a brief introduction to African film, 6 suggestions for viewing African films in the USA, background on the following films including a map and relat - ed print materials: Cheikh Oumar Sissoko, *Finzan*, Souleymane Cissé, *Yeelen*, Cesar Paes, *Angano...Angano*, Ngangura Mweze and Bernard Lamy, *La vie est belle*, Amadou Saalum Seck, *Saaraba* Thomas Mogotlane and Oliver Schmitz, *Mapantsula* and Gaston Kaboré, *Wend Kuuni*. It also includes a list of other selected African films, and questions to ask about tradition and modernity.

—. *Focus on African Women*. San Francisco: California Newsreel, January 1995. Supplement updating the listings in the Library of African Cinema 1993-94 catalog. Looks at the condition of women in African society through background and reviews of the following films: Djibril Diop Mambéty's *Hyenas*: 1992, Flora M'mbugu-Schelling's *These Hands*: 1992, Jeremy Nathan/Afravisions' *In a Time of Violence*: 1994, Anne-Laure Folly's *Femmes aux yeux ouverts*: 1994, and Ngozi Onwurah's *Monday's Girls*: 1993.

—. *Reimagining Africa*. San Francisco: California Newsreel, August 1995. Supplement updating the listings in the Library of African Cinema 1993-94 catalog. Gives a back - ground and review of recent films including Flora M'mbugu-Schelling's *These Hands*: 1992, Anne-Laure Folly's *Femmes aux yeux ouverts*: 1994, and Ngozi Onwurah's *Monday's Girls*: 1993. Also includes Flora Gomes' *Udju Azul di Yonta* (*The Blue Eyes of Yonta*):1991, which focuses on a young woman.

COSTUME DESIGNERS

Speciale, Alessandra. "Oumou Sy, profession costumière/Oumou Sy, Profession Costume Designer." *Ecrans d'Afrique/African Screen* 1.2 (1992): 102-105. Oumou Sy's biographical and designing career. Interview focusing on her experience work - ing with *Hyenas* (D.D. Mambéty) and *Samba Traore* (I. Ouedraogo) costumes.

DIRECTORIES

Gaye, Amadou. "Women Filmmakers in Morocco = Femmes cinéastes du Maroc." *Ecrans d'Afrique/African Screen* 2.5-6 (1993): 10-12. A historical directory/filmography of such Moroccan women filmmakers as Farida Banlyazid, Farida Bourquia, Izza Genini, Imane Meshahi, and Touda Bouanani.
Shiri, Keith. *Directory of African Filmmakers and Films.* Westport, CT: Greenwood Press, 1992. Lists 259 filmmakers of whom only 8 are women, with biographical background and filmography.
Tlili, Najwa. *Femmes d'images de l'Afrique francophone.* Montréal: Trait d'Union Culturel, 1994. A directory of pro - fessional African women who use French in the cinema and audio-visual sector. In addition to the presentation of women filmmakers and their filmographies, this directory contains the addresses of companies in Canada interested in North-South production and post-production. It also includes infor - mation on funding, distribution, circulation, and training institutions, for the most part Canadian.

DISTRIBUTION

Cham, Mbye B. "Issues and Trends in African Cinema-1989." *African Cinema Now.* Atlanta: np, 1989. 3-6. Brief comment on reconstructing economic and cultural history, language, visual style, women filmmakers, films of literature, inade - quate outlets for criticism, distribution problems.
Moore, Cornelius. "African Cinema in the American Video Market." *Issue: A Journal of Opinion* 20.2 (June 1992): 38-41. Proposes a three-pronged strategy (in universities, public libraries, and African American communities) for wide dis -

tribution of African films in the United States. Mentions efforts of California Newsreel's Library of African Cinema.

EDUCATION

"La 'Cousine Angèle va à l'essentiel...'" *Amina* 253 (May 1991): 27. Opportunities for African women to obtain fund- ing for filmmaking and use film as instrument of develop- ment. Views of Marie-Thérèse Gonçalves, Bénin.

"Régina Fanta Nacro." *Ecrans d'Afrique/African Screen* 1.1 (1992): 35. Her educational and professional background. Her views on the training of women in film schools.

Bakari, Imruh. "D. Elmina Davis." *Ecrans d'Afrique/African Screen* 4.11 (1994): 23. Describes D. Elmina Davis' work in Ceddo Film & video, a Black Independent cinema group of the 1980s, the Black workshop movement, and WAVES (Women's Audio-Visual Education Scheme). Mentions her first film, *Omega Rising: Women of Rastafari*, 1988.

Kaboré, Françoise. "*Le Truc de Konaté*: Fanta Nacro on a Crusade Against AIDS." *FESPACO Newsletter* 13 (September 16, 1997) http://www.fespaco.bf/newsl13a.htm>. Describes Nacro's shooting of her third film, *Le Truc de Konaté*. Discusses her strategy in educating rural masses in Africa about the use of condoms to prevent AIDS.

Landau, Julia. "From Zimbabwe to South Africa: Starting All Over Again/Du Zimbabwe à l'Afrique du Sud: On recom- mence tout." *Ecrans d'Afrique/African Screen* 3.8 (1994): 30-32. Miriam Patsanza talks about her video production company, Talent Consortium, which she set up in Zimbabwe in 1984. This company, which is also a school, has now moved to Johannesburg to take a more active part in "re- difining the media in South Africa."

Moore, Cornelius. "African Cinema in the American Video Market." *Issue: A Journal of Opinion* 20.2 (June 1992): 38- 41. Proposes a three-pronged strategy (in universities, public libraries, and African American communities) for wide dis- tribution of African films in the United States. Mentions efforts of California Newsreel's Library of African Cinema.

Petty, Sheila. "African Cinema and (Re)Education: Using Recent African Feature Films." *Issue* 20.2 (June 1992): 26-. Discusses the use of African films in the classroom to devel-

op a critical awareness of established, discipline-based methods of observing and interpreting texts. Suggests ways for
achieving this goal. Also discusses the *Woman's Point of
View* with the example of *Finzan* around the question of
whether male filmmakers truly articulate African women's
subjectivity or only observe it.

Pfaff, Françoise. "Five West African Filmmakers on their Films."
Issue: A Journal of Opinion 20.2 (June 1992): 31-37. On the
contribution of Souleyman Cisse, Safi Faye, Gaston Kaboré,
Idrissa Ouédraogo and Ousmane Sembene to the enrichment
of the international film world. Focuses on the sociopolitical
and cultural content of West African films, which make them
an invaluable tool for the exploration of the continent's history, cultures, and society.

FESTIVALS

Atelier Femmes, Cinéma Télévision. Vidéo en Afrique.
*Déclarations des femmes africaines professionnelles du ciné-
ma, de la télévision et de la vidéo*. February 27, 1991. Text of
report from FESPACO symposium to FEPACI.

Balogun, Françoise. "Cinema: Scope for the Future." *West Africa*
3840 (April 8, 1991): 523. African women in cinematography, television, and video meet in Ouagadougou to discuss
issues they face in their profession. Development of a proposal for surveying and training of African women in these
fields and for encouraging their participation in film festivals. Summary of their recommendations.

Beaulieu, J., E. Castiel, and Larue J. "Festival International du
Jeune Cinéma, Vues d'Afrique, Silence elles tournent."
Séquences (September 1991): 16-19. Report on the 1991
Montréal festival, with emphasis on African films and those
directed by women.

Biloa, Marie Roger. "Femmes africaines et médias." *Les
Journées du Cinéma Africain 1989*. Montréal: Vues
D'Afrique, 1989. p. 21. Comments on the role of women in
radio, television, and journalism.

—. "*La Citadelle* encore." *Jeune Afrique* 1481 (1989): 56-57.
Discusses the women theme of *Journées du cinéma Africain
1989*, commenting on some of the films shown and improving the quality of African films.

318

Brownstein, Bill. "Vues d'Afrique Shows More than the Horror Stories We're Used to." *The Gazette* (*Montréal*) (April 29, 1995): F5-. On 1995 Vues d'Afrique festival, the historical and cultural background, and film shown.

Diallo, Aissatou Bah. "Les femmes à la recherche d'un nouveau souffle." *Amina* 253 (May 1991): 8-9. Report on symposium of women film professionals at FESPACO 1991, excluding all non-African women.

Diawara, Manthia. "Out of Ouaga." *The Village Voice* (April 19, 1995): 54-.

—. "Report from FESPACO: Recovery vs. Nostalgia" *Black Film.*
Review 7.1 (1993): 22-25. Provides updates from the 1991 Festival of Pan-African Cinema at Ouagadougou in Burkina Faso. Themes in the participating films include the emancipation of women in modern Africa, humanism, and denunciations of colonialism. Titles include *Touki Bouki* by Djibril Diop Mambéty, *Allah Tantou* by Maroff Aschkar.

Hustak, Alan. "She Aims to educate Through Film; Human-Rights Activist Is Promoter of Vues d'Afrique." *The Gazette* (*Montréal*) (July 9, 1995): F4. On Rose Ndayahoze's involvement in promoting Vues d'Afrique and her human rights activism. Some biographical background.

Kaboré, Françoise. "FESPACO 91. Les femmes du cinéma s'organisent." *Sidwaya* (March 5, 1991): 6. Report on meeting of women film professionals.

—. "Scoop féminin à Harare/Female Scoop in Harare." *Ecrans d'Afrique/African Screen* 5.17-18 (1996): 84-85. Report on the third Southern African Film Festival (SAFF) held in Harare Sept 20-26. Nine out of twelve awards went to women.

Maïga, Cheick Kolla. "Entretien avec Aminata Ouédraogo sur les femmes de l'audiovisuel." *Bingo* 455 (February 1991): 12. Discusses FESPACO symposium of women film professionals.

Sackey, Catherine. "African Films and Women." *West Africa* (17 May 1993): 843. Conference in London of 10 women prominent in film and television discussed technical issues, roles for women, concern with Western films saturating African market.

Sama, Emmanuel. "African Cinema in the Feminine: A Difficult Birthing/Cinéma Africain au féminin: Un difficile enfante - ment." *Ecrans d'Afrique/African Screen* 1.1 (1992): 69-71. On the first workshop by African women professional of the audio-visual, which was held during the 12th FESPACO in 1991. Four main priorities were defined: compiling a direc - tory, setting up an itinerant training workshop, training instructors, and seeking support for regular participation of women in film festivals.

Yeboah-Afari, Ajoa. "African Women form Guild." *West Africa* (January 20, 1992): 129. Meeting of film and video produc - ers in Accra, December 1991, from Kenya, Cameroun, Ethiopia, Zimbabwe, Tanzania, Nigeria, South Africa, and Ghana.

Zongo, Jean Bernard. "FESPACO 91: Atelier sur le partenariat et sur les femmes africaines professionnelles du cinéma: La transformation du paysage audio-visuel: une nécessité vitale." *Sidwaya* (February 26, 1991): 6. About two FESPA-CO conferences opened by Gaston Kaboré.

FILMMAKERS

"Anne Mungai le fleuron du cinéma kenyan." *Amina* 253 (May 1989): 16. Personal background on Mungai's training as actress and filmmaker, and professional activities.

"Blandine Ngono Ambassa (Director, Cameroon)." *Ecrans d'Afrique/African Screen* 1.1 (1992): 33.
Educational and professional background, including all her television and film projects. Mentions *Miseria* for which she won a special mention at the 7th Journées du Cinéma Africain et Créole.

"FESPACO 91 hommage aux femmes africaines professionnelles du cinéma." *Souka* 29 (April 1991): 16. Summarizes meeting of women film professionals, asks when a woman will win the grand prize.

"FESPACO 91. Women Workshop. Cinema, Television, Video in Africa." *FEPACI News* 6 (1991): 8-10. Report on meeting of women film professionals, description of forthcoming proj - ects, statement on African women in film.

"Flora M'Mbugu-Schelling: vive la solidarité féminine." *Amina* 253 (May 1991): 22. Her training and activities as a film-maker, producer, and distributor in Tanzania.

"Honneur aux femmes africaines de l'audiovisuel." *FEPACI Info* 5 (1991): 2. Report on meeting of women film professionals at FESPACO 1991. Women who are directors of national radio or television: Michèle Badarou (Bénin), Danielle Boni Claverie (Côte d'Ivoire), Sokhona Dieng (Senegal), Aminata Ouédraogo (Burkina), and Mariama Hima (Niger).

"Karité revu et corrigé par Odile Nacoulma." *Amina* 253 (May 1991): 38. Interview at FESPACO about her academic training, tenure as director of Institut cinématographique, Burkina Faso, and activities after Sankara came to office.

"Kenyan Filmmaker Makes her Way, Camera in Hand, Baby on her Back." *Afrika* 3-4 (1992): 31-32. Anne Mungai discusses filmmaking at AWIFAV meeting, goals of AWIFAV.

"La 'Cousine Angèle va à l'essentiel...'" *Amina* 253 (May 1991): 27. Opportunities for African women to obtain funding for filmmaking and use film as instrument of development. Views of Marie-Thérèse Goncalves, Benin.

"Le parcours de Seipati Bulang Hopa." *Amina* 253 (May 1991): 20. Personal background on South African videomaker and distributor.

"Le pari audacieux de Chantal Bagilishya." *Amina* 253 (May 1991): 11-12. Burundi journalist's training and views on African film.

"Les années folles de Habiba Msika/The Life and Times of Habiba Msika." *Ecrans d'Afrique/African Screen* 3.8 (1994): 12-13. Interview with Tunisian filmmaker Selma Baccar on her film *Habiba M'sika*. Includes biographical background and filmography.

"Régina Fanta Nacro." *Ecrans d'Afrique/African Screen* 1.1 (1992): 35. Her educational and professional background. Her views on the training of women in film schools.

"Stories of Women/Une affaire des femmes." *Ecrans d'Afrique/African Screen* 3.8 (1994): 8-11. Interview with Tunisian Moufida Tlatli on her *Les Silences du palais*, 1994. Focuses on the feminist nature of the film. Includes biographical background.

"The Women of FESPACO 97: Valérie Kaboré or the Filmmaker 'of all Trades.'" (Extract from an item of Clément Tapsoba)

(July 23, 1997) <http://www.fespaco.bf/women.htm>. Mentions films by African women filmmakers at FESPACO 97. Discusses Valérie Kaboré's career. Her film *Kado ou la bonne a tout faire* won the second prize for the best fiction film in the TV and video section.

Amarger, Michel. "Directors Give their Opinions on the State of African Cinema." *Ecrans d'Afrique/African screen* 3.9-10 (1994): 14-24. Includes Farida Benlyazid (*Identité de femme*, 1979; *Une porte sur le ciel*, 1987/88) and Tunisian Moufida Tlatli (*Les silences du palais*, 1994).

Atelier Femmes, Cinéma Télévision. Vidéo en Afrique. *Déclarations des femmes africaines professionnelles du cinéma, de la télévision et de la vidéo.* February 27, 1991. Text of report from FESPACO symposium to FEPACI.

Bakari, Imruh. "D. Elmina Davis." *Ecrans d'Afrique/African Screen* 4.11 (1994): 23. Describes D. Elmina Davis' work in Ceddo Film & video, a Black Independent cinema group of the 1980s, the Black workshop movement, and WAVES (Women's Audio-Visual Education Scheme). Mentions her first film, *Omega Rising: Women of Rastafari*, 1988.

Balogun, Françoise. "Cinema: Scope for the Future." *West Africa* 3840 (April 8, 1991): 523. African women in cinematography, television, and video meet in Ouagadougou to discuss issues they face in their profession. Development of a proposal for surveying and training of African women in these fields and for encouraging their participation in film festivals. Summary of their recommendations.

Bangre, Sambolgo. "Monique Phoba (Director, Zaire)." *Ecrans d'Afrique/African Screen* 3.9-10 (1994): 32-33. Traces the professional career of Monique Phoba. Mentions her two films, *Revue en vrac* made in 1991, which won the Jury's Special Prize at the 1991 Vues d'Afrique festival. Also mentions her second film, *Rentrer?* made in 1993.

Beaulieu, J., E. Castiel, and Larue J. "Festival International du Jeune Cinéma, Vues d'Afrique, Silence elles tournent." *Séquences* (September 1991): 16-19. Report on the 1991 Montréal festival, with emphasis on African films and those directed by women.

Cham, Mbye B. "African Women and Cinema: A Conversation with Anne Mungai." *Research in African Literatures* 25.3 (September 1994): 93-. An Interview with Anne Mungai, a

Kenyan filmmaker, at the 1992 Milan Festival of African Cinema. Mungai talks about African women and society, *Saikati* (1992), her first feature film, which raises issues if female sexuality in urban and rural Kenya, and forced mar- riages.

—. "Issues and Trends in African Cinema-1989." *African Cinema Now*. Atlanta: np, 1989. 3-6. Brief comments on reconstructing history, economic and cultural history, lan- guage, visual style, women filmmakers, films of literature, inadequate outlets for criticism, distribution problems.

Chikhaoui, Tahar. "Kalthoum Bornaz (Director, Tunisia)." *Ecrans d'Afrique/African Screen* 2.5-6 (1993): 38-39. Traces Kalthoum Bornaz' career with biographical background.

—. "Selma, Nejia, Moufida and the Others." *Ecrans d'Afrique/African Screen* 3.8 (1994): 8-9. Features Tunisian women filmmakers Selma Baccar, Nejia Ben Mabrouk, and Moufida Tlatli, with their film career in the broad Tunisian film industry.

Deffontaines, Thérèse Marie. "Music above All/De la musique avant tout." *Ecrans d'Afrique/African Screen* 2.5-6 (1993): 8-15. An interview with Moroccan filmmaker Izza Genini. Discusses how her career evolved from music to filmmaking, the creative possibilities offered by documentaries and the role of music in her films.

Diallo, Aissatou Bah. "Aminata Ouédraogo, coordinatrice de l'atelier des femmes." *Amina* 253 (May 1991): 12. Films she has made. Comments on meeting of women film professionals of FESPACO 1991.

—. "Cheik Doukouré." *Amina* 233 (September 1989): 36-38. Problems of being African filmmakers in France, African filmmakers he admires, opportunities for women in film.

—. "Les femmes à la recherche d'un nouveau souffle." *Amina* 253 (May 1991): 8-9. Report on symposium of women film professionals at FESPACO 1991, excluding all non-African women.

—. "Mariama Hima la championne du cinéma pieds nus." *Amina* 225 (January 1989): 28-30. Nigerian delegate to film festival in Mexico, her training and employment, comments on *Baabu Banza*.

Djebar, Assia. "Behind the Veil." *Africa News* 32.11-12 (December 1989): 6-7. Algerian writer and filmmaker Assia

Djebar explores the importance of having women on both sides of the camera. Mentions her first film, *La Nouba des femmes du Mont Chenoua*, which won the International Critics' Prize at the Venice Biennale in 1979.

Domingo, Macy, and Klevor Abo. "Une Africaine à Hollywood/An African in Hollywood."*Ecrans d'Afrique/ African Screen* 2.4 (1993): 6-11. An interview with Akosua Busia. Provides biographical information and traces her painting, acting and writing career. Also gives her views on African cinema.

Ferrari, A. "Le second souffle du cinéma Africain." *Téléciné* 176 (January 1973): 2-9.

Gaye, Amadou. "Women Filmmakers in Morocco/Femmes cinéastes du Maroc." *Ecrans d'Afrique/African Screen* 2.5-6 (1993): 10-12. A historical directory/filmography of such Moroccan women filmmakers as Farida Banlyazid, Farida Bourquia, Izza Genini, Imane Meshahi, and Touda Bouanani.

Gibson-Hudson, Gloria J. "Through Women's Eyes: The Films of Women in Africa and the African Diaspora." *The Western Journal of Black Studies* 15.2 (June 1991): 79-.

Harvey, Sylvie. "Third World Perspectives: Focus on Sarah Maldoror." *Women and Film* 1.5-6 (1974): 71-75, 110.

Jusu, K. K. Man. "FESPACO 91 Hommage à la femme et à l'environnement." *Fraternité Matin* (February 23, 1991): 12. Meeting of women film professionals planned since 1989, theme of partnership, sale of films, no Ivorian film in competition.

Kaboré, Etienne Mouni. "Safi Faye: Filmmaker, Ethnographer and Mother." *FESPACO Newsletter* 13 (September 16, 1997) <http://www.fespaco.bf/newsl13a.htm>. A short biography on the film director.

Kaboré, Françoise. "Annick Balley Adds Strings to her Bow." *FESPACO Newsletter* 13 (September 16, 1997) <http://www.fespaco.bf/newsl13a.htm>. An interview with Annick Balley, a TV journalist from Benin who is switching to filmmaking. Discusses her project about women, especially the challenges of traditions in the struggle to liberate African women.

—. "Kahena, Profession: Film Editor." *Ecrans d'Afrique/African Screen* 3.8 (1994): 67-68. On the editing career of Tunisian Kahena Attia, who is chief editor and also producer.

—. "La nouvelle génération des cinéastes: Funmi Osoba." *Ecrans d'Afrique/African Screen* 1.2 (1992): 70. Director Osoba's film career debuts with her documentary *The Dormant Genius* presented at FESPACO 91.

—. "Zarah Yacoub Keeps a Cool Head." *FESPACO Newsletter* 13 (September 16, 1997) <http://www.fespaco.bf/newsl13a.htm>. About Zarah Yacoub, the Tchadian TV journalist and film-maker, her 1996 film *Dilemme au Féminin* on female circumcision, and the negative reception that the film got in her country. The film won awards at the African and Creole film festival, and at Vue d'Afrique in Montreal.

Landau, Julia. "From Zimbabwe to South Africa: Starting All Over Again/Du Zimbabwe à l'Afrique du Sud: On recommence tout." *Ecrans d'Afrique/African Screen* 3.8 (1994): 30-32. Miriam Patsanza talks about her video production company, Talent Consortium, which she set up in Zimbabwe in 1984. This company, which is also a school, has now moved to Johannesburg to take a more active part in "redifining the media in South Africa."

Maïga, Cheick Kolla. "Koudil (Director, Algeria): Témoigner malgré la terreur/Tell the World Despite the Terror." *Ecrans d'Afrique/African Screen* 4.12 (1995): 12-16. An interview with Algerian filmmaker Hafsa Zinai Koudil after her first film *Le Démon au féminin*.

Martin, Angela. "Hondo, Med (1936-)." *Women's Companion to International Film* (1990): Gives a brief biography of Med Hondo, followed by overview of his films. Also gives a brief review of *Sarraounia* (1986).

Maupin, Françoise. "Entretien avec Safi Faye." *Image et Son* 303 (February 1976): 75-80.

Novicki, M.A., and D. Topouzis. "Ousmane Sembene: Africa's Premier Cineaste." *Africa Report* 35.5 (November/December 1990): 66-68. An interview with Senegalese novelist-film-maker Ousmane Sembene about the outlook for African cinema as well as about his latest artistic projects. He believes film is the most important medium to reach a large African audience. Talks about new novel about the liberation of African women.

Olufunwa, Bola. "African Women and Cinema." *African Woman* 7 (June 1993): 45-47. Discusses the role of women in African cinema through the work of actress Juanita Ageh (Nigerian-

Caribbean), director Anne Mungai (Kenyan whose film—*Saikati*—won two awards at the 1993 FESPACO) and Ngozi Onwurah (Nigerian). Looks at the way these three professionals approach the issues of "women." Comments on the stereotypical portrayal of African women in film. Mentions *Twende: African Professional Women in Cinema*, a conference organized by the Africa Centre and the British Film Institute.

Ouédraogo, Noufou. "Dommie Yambo Odotte (Director, Kenya)." *Ecrans d'Afrique/African Screen* 4.12 (1995): 20-21. Traces the career of the Kenyan filmmaker who is the first independent woman filmmaker in Kenya.

Relich, Mario. "Chronicle of a Students." *West Africa* 3393 (1982): 2112.

Sama, Emmanuel. "African Cinema in the Feminine: A Difficult Birthing/Cinéma Africain au féminin: Un difficile enfantement." *Ecrans d'Afrique/African Screen* 1.1 (1992): 69-71. On the first workshop by African women professional of the audio-visual, which was held during the 12th FESPACO in 1991. Four main priorities were defined: compiling a directory, setting up an itinerant training workshop, training instructors, and seeking support for regular participation of women in film festivals.

Sezirahiga, Jadot. "Kadiatou Konaté (Director, Mali)." *Ecrans d'Afrique/African Screen* 3.8 (1994): 28-29. Traces the professional career of Malian Kadiatou Konaté who specializes in animated folk tales. Mentions her first work, *L'enfant térrible*.

—. "Maldoror (Guadeloupe-Angola): 'Il faut prendre d'assaut la télévision/We Have to Take Television by Storm.'" *Ecrans d'Afrique/African Screen* 4.12 (1995): 6-11. An interview with Sarah Maldoror after her 1995 documentary, *Léon G. Damas*. Discusses her life career, and gives a filmography.

Speciale, Alessandra. "Viola Shafik (Director, Egypt)." *Ecrans d'Afrique/African Screen* 3.9-10 (1994): 32-33. Biographical background of Viola Shafik tracing her film career, particularly *Le Citronnier*.

Tapsoba, Clément. "Anne Laure Folly (Director, Togo)." *Ecrans d'Afrique/African Screen* 1.2 (1992): 36. Professional background and review of her first film, *Le Gardien des Forces*, which won the Best Feature Film at the 8th Journées du Cinema Sfricain et Créole in Montreal in April 1993.

—. "Franceline Oubda (TV Director, Burkina Faso)." *Ecrans d'Afrique/African Screen* 2.5-6 (1993):41. Traces Franceline Oubda's Career with biographical information.

—. "Ilboudo Conde (Director, Guinea/Burkina Faso): "Quand les femmes se lèvent, le cinéma africain bouge/When Women Stand up, African Cinema Moves." *Ecrans d'Afrique/African Screen* 5.17-18 (1996): 22-23. Biographical background on Martine Ilboudo Conde, including her entry into cinema. Mentions some of her films: *Siao 92* (1992), *Jazz a Ouaga* (1993), and *Un Cri dans le sahel* (1994), a docu-fiction film. This film on the image of women received many prizes, including the Regard de femmes Prize (FESPACO 95), the creativity prize at Vues d'Afrique. Also mentions *Message des femmes pour Beijing* (1995), which earned her the ACCT Prize at Vue d'Afrique in 1996. Her views on African women filmmakers, censorship, and the responsibility of male film-makers.

—. "Joyce Makwenda (Director, Zimbabwe)." *Ecrans d'Afrique/African Screen* 2.5-6 (1993): 39-40. Traces Joyce Makwenda's career with biographical information.

—. "Margaret Fombe Fobe (TV filmmaker, Cameroon)." *Ecrans d'Afrique/African Screen* 3.8 (1994): 26-27. Margaret Fombe Fobe's view on the importance of African filmmakers. The role she has played in breaking some of the stereo-typical images of women in Cameroon society. Mentions her films, *Sirri Cow* (*The Woman Butcher*), and *Ma'a Nwambang* (*The Woman who Collects Palm Nuts*), which won the first Images de Femmes prize awarded by Vues d'Afrique in Montreal in 1994.

—. "Sarah Bouyain (Assitant Director, Burkina-France)." *Ecrans d'Afrique/African Screen* 4.11 (1995): 17-19. Discusses her experience as assistant director, a profession with little visi-bility. Mentions her educational and professional back-ground, including her work with Idrissa Ouédraogo on *Le Cri du Coeur* and *Afrique, mon Afrique*.

—. "SIDA dans la cité/AIDS in the City (produced by Hanny Brigitte Tchelley, Côte d'Ivoire)." *Ecrans d'Afrique/African Screen* 5.17-18 (1996): 88-90. An interview with Hanny Brigitte Tchelley, producer of this series based on the social reality in Africa. The second part puts an emphasis on the role of women in the fight for awareness.

Yeboah-Afari, Ajoa. "African Women from Guild." *West Africa* (January 20, 1992): 129. Meeting of film and video producers in Accra, December 1991, from Kenya, Cameroun, Ethiopia, Zimbabwe, Tanzania, Nigeria, South Africa, and Ghana.

Yéyé, Zakaria. "Hommage aux femmes africaines professionnelles du cinéma: Un mérite et un défi." *Sidwaya* (February 26, 1991): 6,8. FESPACO 1991, general statement about importance of women filmmakers, producers and actresses, photographs of actresses from Mali, Niger, Chad, Benin, and Côte d'Ivoire.

FILMOGRAPHIES

Gaye, Amadou. "Women Filmmakers in Morocco/Femmes cinéastes du Maroc." *Ecrans d'Afrique/African Screen* 2.5-6 (1993): 10-12. A historical directory/filmography of such Moroccan women filmmakers as Farida Banlyazid, Farida Bourquia, Izza Genini, Imane Meshahi, and Touda Bouanani.

Kabous & R.Y. "Mossane: Safi Faye, Senegal, 1996, 35mm 105.'" August 4, 1997. <http://www.fespaco.bf/mossane.htm> (February 26, 1998). A brief review of *Mossane,* with a filmography on Safi Faye.

Pfaff, Françoise. *Twenty-Five Black African Filmmakers.* Westport, CT: Greenwood Press, 1988. Safi Faye and Sarah Maldoror are the two women filmmakers included. For each filmmaker, biographical background, major themes, a survey of criticism, a filmography and bibliography are included.

Schmidt, Nancy J. "Films by Sub-Saharan African Women Filmmakers." *African Literature Association Bulletin* 18.4 (September 1992): 12-14. Lists 89 films by 45 filmmakers from 1972 to 1992.

Shiri, Keith. *Directory of African Filmmakers and Films.* Westport, CT: Greenwood Press, 1992. Lists 259 filmmakers of whom only 8 are women, with biographical background and filmography.

Tlili, Najwa. *Femmes d'images de l'Afrique francophone.* Montréal: Trait d'Union Culturel, 1994. A directory of professional African women who use French in the cinema and audio-visual sector. In addition to the presentation of women filmmakers and their filmographies, this directory contains the addresses of companies in Canada interested in North-South production and post-production. It also includes information on funding, distribution, circulation, and training institutions, for the most part Canadian.

GUIDES

Annecke, Wendy Jill, and Ruth Elizabeth Tomaselli. "South Africa." *Women's Companion to International Film* (1990). Gives an overview of South African cinema, citing various films. Also discusses the portrayal of women, especially Black women, in these films. Ends with a brief discussion of women in the industry.

Boughédir, Férid. *Le Cinéma Africain de A à Z.* Bruxelles: OCIC, 1987. Gives an overview of African cinema through a historical, economic and thematic discussion. Analyzes four films (*Borom Sarret, F.V.V.A., Muna Moto,* and *Finye*) with brief discussion of the role of women. Critiques the traditional patriarchal society in Muna Moto where the woman liberates herself not because she is influenced by western ideas, but because of the very social fabric in which she lives. Closes with a country-by-country annotated list of Black African filmmakers.

Kuhn, Annette, and Susannah Radstone, eds. "The Women's Companion to International Film." London: Virago Press, 1990. An encyclopedic work providing, in a feminist perspective, detailed overviews on concepts, genres, actresses, directors (women and men), national and regional cinemas, and studios. Includes an index of films directed, written, or produced by women.

Martin, Angela. "Africa." *Women's Companion to International Film* (1990): Gives an overview of African cinema before reviewing leading themes of films from different countries. The concluding section briefly discusses women in African filmmaking.

Pfaff, Françoise. *Twenty-Five Black African Filmmakers.* Westport, CT: Greenwood Press, 1988. Safi Faye and Sarah Maldoror are the two women filmmakers included. For each filmmaker, biographical background, major themes, a survey of criticism, a filmography and bibliography arc included.

Srour, Heiny. "Algeria." *Women's Companion to International Film* (1990): Gives a socio-historic overview of Algerian cin - ema, underlining the silence of most filmmakers on women's issues until 1970 when Ahmed Lallem made *Elle/The Women*.

——. "Egypt." *Women's Companion to International Film* (1990): Gives and overview of Egyptian cinema, tracing to important role that women have played in the industry since 1927.

——. "Morocco." *Women's Companion to International Film* (1990): Gives an overview of Moroccan cinema focusing on women's predicament. Such films as Hamid Benani's *Wechma/Traces* (1970), Souheil Benbarka's *Mille et Une Mains/One Thousand and One Hands* (1977) Farida Belyazid's *Bab Ala Al Sama/A Door on the Sky* (1988), and many more.

MAKE-UP ARTISTS

Maïga, Cheick Kolla. "Aminata's 'Beauty'/La 'Beauté' de Aminata (Burkina Faso)." *Ecrans d'Afrique/African Screen* 2.3 (1993): 87-88. Aminata Zoure's professional background including films in which she worked as make-up artist (*Sarraounia*, *Zan Boko*, *Yaaba*, *Mamy Wata*, *La Nuit africaine*, *Les Etrangers*, *Rabi*, *Guelwaar*, *Samba Traore* and *Wendemi*). Her views on the importance of technical jobs in African cinema.

RECEPTION

Werman, Marco. "African Cinema: A Market in the U.S.?" *Africa Report* 34.3 (May 1, 1989): 68-.

REVIEWS

"The Battle of Sacred Tree." *Ecrans d'Afrique/African Screen* 4.11 (1995): 25.

Amarger, Michel and Alessandra Speciale. "Taafe Fanga de Adama. Drabo: la révolte des femmes/Taafe Fanga by Adama Drabo: The Women's Revolt. *"Ecrans d'Afrique/*

African Screens 5.17-18 (1996): 12-13. Reviews *Taafe Fanga* with critical remarks by the director, Adama Drabo.

Aragba-Akpore, Sonny. "Palliating the Silent Sufferers." *Guardian* (April 24, 1993). Reviews *Silent Sufferers* by Ladi Ladebo, video documentary made for UNESCO Committee on Women.

Biloa, Marie Roger. "La tendresse d'une femme." *Jeune Afrique* 1517 (1990): 63. Reviews *Histoire d'Orokia*.

California Newsreel. Library of African Cinema. [*1991 Catalogue*]. San Francisco: California Newsreel, nd [1991]. This film catalogue includes a brief introduction to African film, 6 suggestions for viewing African films in the U.S.A., background on the following films including a map and relat - ed print materials: Cheikh Oumar Sissoko, *Finzan*, Souleymane Cisse, *Yeelen*, Cesar Paes, *Angano...Angano*, Ngangura Mweze and Bernard Lamy, *La Vie est belle*, Amadou Saalum Seck, *Saaraba* Thomas Mogotlane and Oliver Schmitz, *Mapantsula* and Gaston Kaboré, *Wend Kuuni* It also includes a list of other selected African films, and questions to ask about tradition and modernity.

—. *Focus on African Women*. San Francisco: California Newsreel, January 1995. Supplement updating the listings in the Library of African Cinema 1993-94 catalog. Looks at the condition of women in African society through background and reviews of the following films: Djibril Diop Mambéty's *Hyenas*: 1992, Flora M'mbugu-Schelling's *These Hands*: 1992, Jeremy Nathan/Afravisions' *In a Time of Violence*: 1994, Anne-Laure Folly's *Femmes aux yeux ouverts*: 1994, and Ngozi Onwurah's *Monday's Girls*: 1993.

—. *Reimagining Africa*. San Francisco: California Newsreel, August 1995. Supplement updating the listings in the Library of African Cinema 1993-94 catalog. Gives a background and review of recent films including Flora M'mbugu-Schelling's, *These Hands*: 1992, Anne-Laure Folly's, *Femmes aux Yeux Ouverts*: 1994, and Ngozi Onwurah's, *Monday's Girls*: 1993. Also includes Flora Gomes' *Udju Azul di Yonta* (*The Blue Eyes of Yonta*): 1991, which focuses on a young woman.

Fiombo, Angelo, Annamaria Gallone, and Alessandra Speciale. *Saikati. Ecrans d'Afrique/African Screen* 1.2 (1992): 29.

Hill, Heather. "The Widow's Revenge." *Africa Report* 38.2

(March/April 1993): 64-66. Discusses the film *Neria* by Godwin Mawuru. Looks at such issues as women's rights, traditional inheritance law, Zimbabwe's convention for women, personal experience of Mawuru, and feminism in Zimbabwe.

Jusu, K. K. Man. "*Finzan* de Cheikh Oumar Sissoko: la révolte des femmes contre la tradition." *Fraternité Matin* (June 18, 1991): 16. Reviews the film.

Kabous & R.Y. "*Mossane*: Safi Faye, Senegal, 1996, 35mm 105." August 4, 1997. <http://www.fespaco.bf/mossane.htm> (February 26, 1998). A brief review of *Mossane* with a filmography on Safi Faye.

Maïga, Cheick Kolla. "Maysa Marta (actress, Guinée-Bissau)." *Ecrans d'Afrique/African Screen* 1.2 (1992): 36-38. Her acting role in *Les Yeux Bleus de Yonta* of Flora Gomes. Review of the film.

—. "Pouc Niini (by Fanta Nacro)." *Ecrans d'Afrique/African Screen* 4.12 (1995): 59. Reviews Nacro's second short film in which the female gaze is turned on the life of a modern couple.

Maio, Kathi. "A Silence Never Broken." *Sojourner: The Women's Forum* 20.10 (June 1995): 19-21. Reviews *The Silences of the Palace* by Tunisian woman filmmaker Moufida Tlati.

Savory, Elaine. "African Women's voices on Film." *NWSA Journal* 9.1 (Spring 1997): 99-105. A critical review of three films by African women filmmakers: Ngozi Onwurah's *Monday's Girl*, Ann-Laure Folly's *Femmes aux yeux ouverts* (*Women with Open Eyes*)," and Flora M'mbugu-Schelling's *These Hands*. Discusses the women's control of their bodies, women's labor within capitalist economies, and the significance of modernity within the framework of African identities and community.

Speciale, Alessandra. "Un Démon au féminin/Ash-shaytan imra' de/by Hafsa Zinaï Koudil-Algérie/Algeria 1993." *Ecrans d'Afrique/African Screen* 4.12 (1995): 34. Reviews Koudil's first feature film in which a man weakened by depression can succumb to cruelty in the name of religion.

—. "Un Eté à la Goulette de/by Férid Boughédir-Tunisie/Tunisia -1996." *Ecrans d'Afrique/African Screen* 5.17-18 (1996): 24.

Reviews film on the story of three friendships—that of three fathers, a Christian, a Jew, and a Muslim—and that of their three daughters.

—. "Film/Bent Familia: Filles de grandes famille de/by Nouri Bouzid." *Ecrans d'Afrique/African Screen* 5.17-18 (1996): 30-31. Reviews film on the crisis of women behind the show - case of modernity in contemporary Tunisia, and the inability of the Arab world to accept the modern Arab woman.

—. "*Miel et cendres de*/by Nadia Fares-Tunisie, Suisse/Tunisia/Switzerland, 1996." *Ecrans d'Afrique/African Screen* 5.17-18 (1996): 27. Reviews film on the condition of women in Arab society.

Tapsoba, Clément. "Anne Laure Folly (Director, Togo)." *Ecrans d'Afrique/African Screen* 1.2 (1992): 36. Professional background and review of her first film, *Le Gardien des Forces*, which won the Best Feature Film at the 8th Journées du Cinéma Africain et Créole in Montréal in April 1993.

Taylor, Marcella. "Finding a Voice: Film and the Female in Gaston Kaboré's *Wend Kuuni*." *Hurricane Alice: A Feminist Quarterly* 10.4/11.1 (April 1995): 19-.

TREATMENT OF WOMEN

"The Maghreb." *Black Film Review* 6.4 (1991): 6-. In the North African countries of Morocco, Algeria, and Tunisia, cinema has been a tool of cultural liberation since independence in the early '60s.

Bakari, Imruh and Mbye B. Cham, eds. *African Experiences of Cinema*. London: British Film Institute, 1996. Contains a chapter by Farida Ayari on cinematic images of women, and a chapter by Sheila Petty on the emergence of feminist themes in African cinemas. It also contains essays by Pfaff on Kaboré's and Ouédraogo's films as anthropological sources, and eroticism in sub-Saharan films.

Bedjaoui, A. "Approche "féministe" d'un cinéma masculin: le cinéma algérien." *CinemAction* 43 (May 1987): 146-151. On the secondary position given to women in Algerian cinema, from 1959 to the 1986.

Diallo, Aissatou Bah. "L'image de la femme dans le cinéma africain." *Les Journées du Cinéma Africain 1989*. Montréal: Vues D'Afrique, 1989. 17. Reviews images of women in

Mandabi, Pousse-Pousse, Sarraounia, Les Guérisseurs, Bac ou Mariage, Visages de Femmes, and *Yeelen.*

Gabriel, Teshome H. "Ceddo: A Revolution Reborn through the Efforts of Womanhood." *Framework* 15-17 (1981): 38-39.

Gallone, Annamaria. "La Mimosa non e solo un Fiore." *Nigrizia* 108.3 (1990): 58-60. Discusses the condition of African women as portrayed in 13 films made by male filmmakers.

Haffner, Pierre. "La femme dans le cinéma négro-africain." *Les Journées du Cinéma Africain 1989.* Montréal: Vues d'Afrique, 1989. 18-19. Discusses women as theme in African films, with a brief mention of roles in 27 films made in 1970s and 1980s. Expresses need for more women film-makers.

—. "No Model, No School, No Tradition, an Introduction to the Identity of African Cinema." *Pensée* 306 (1996): 99-111.

Hall, Susan. "African Women on Film." *Africa Report* 22.1 (January 1977): 15-17.

Hill, Heather. "The Widow's Revenge." *Africa Report* 38.2 (March/April 1993): 64-66. Discusses the film, *Neria,* by Godwin Mawuru. Looks at such issues as women's rights, traditional inheritance law, Zimbabwe's convention for women, personal experience of Mawuru, and feminism in Zimbabwe.

Kaboré, Françoise. "Zarah Yacoub Keeps a Cool Head." *FESPACO Newsletter* 13 (September 16, 1997) <http://www.fespaco.bf/newsl13a.htm>. About Zarah Yacoub, the Tchadian TV journalist and filmmaker, her 1996 film *Dilemme au Féminin* on female circumcision, and the negative reception that the film got in her country. The film won awards at the African and Creole film festival, and at Vue d'Afrique in Montreal.

Kindem, Gorham H., and Martha Steele. "Women in Sembene's films." *Jump Cut.* May 1991. 52-60. 36. Illustrated, Bibliography. Examines aspects of female characterization in Ousmane Sembene's *Emitai,* (1971) and *Ceddo* (1976). Maintains that women are agents of both group solidarity and social change in Africa's development. Discusses the way the strong cohesive force of women in traditional African society has changed with colonialism.

Olufunwa, Bola. "African Women and Cinema." *African Woman* 7 (June 1993): 45-47. Discusses the role of women in African cinema through the work of actress Juanita Ageh (Nigerian-

Caribbean), Director, Anne Mungai (Kenyan whose film—*Saikati*—won two awards at the 1993 FESPACO) and Ngozi Onwurah (Nigerian). Looks at the way these three professionals approach the issues of "women." Comments on the stereotypical portrayal of African women in film. Mentions Twende: African Professional Women in Cinema," a conference organized by the Africa Centre and the British Film Institute.

Pallister, Janis L. "From *La Noire de…* to *Milk and Honey*: Portraits of the Alienated African Woman." *Modern Language Studies* 22.4 (1992): 7687. The two films in this study are respectively by Sembene Ousmane and Rebecca Yates/Geln Salzman.

Petillat, G., and V. Danglades. "Créteil Soleil? L'aventure au féminin prend le pas sur le social-féministe." *Cinéma (Par)* 456 (April 1989): 2-3. (Festival report) Illustrated. Includes a description of films representing Black women at the 1989 Créteil festival.

Petty, Sheila. "African Cinema and (Re)Education: Using Recent African Feature Films." *Issue* 20.2 (June 1992): 26-37. Discusses the use of African films in the classroom to develop a critical awareness of established, discipline-based methods of observing and interpreting texts. Suggests ways for achieving this goal. Also discusses the *Woman's Point of View* with the example of *Finzan* around the question of whether male filmmakers truly articulate African women's subjectivity or only observe it.

—. *La Femme dans le cinéma d'Afrique noire*. Dissertation. Paris: Université Paris IV, 1988.

Pfaff, Françoise. "Eroticism and Sub-Saharan African Films." *ZAST Zeitschrift für Afrikastudien* 9-10 (1991): 5-16. Discusses how intimate scenes and female bodies are treated, verbal expression of sexual desire, examples of eroticism noticed by African, but not western audiences.

—. "Three Faces of Africa: Women in *Xala*." *Jump Cut* 27 (July 1982): 27-31.

Savory, Elaine. "African Women's Voices in Film." *NWSA Journal* 9.1 (Spring 1997): 99-105. A critical review of three films by African women filmmakers:Ngozi Onwurah's *Monday's Girl*, Ann-Laure Folly's *Femmes aux yeux ouverts (Women with Open Eyes)*, and Flora M'mbugu-Schelling's

These Hands. Discusses the women's control of their bodies, women's labor within capitalist economies, the significance of modernity within the framework of African identities and community.

Sissoko, Foussenou. "Les femmes dans le cinéma africain." *Afrique Nouvelle* 1885.17 (August 1985): 21-27.

Speciale, Alessandra. "La triple galère des femmes, Africaines, actrices = A Threefold Trial: African, Female and Actress." *Ecrans d'Afrique/African Screen* 3.7 (1994): 24-29. Félicité Wouassi and Naky Sy Savané talk about the meaning of "African actor" and the difficulty for African women actors to get leading roles for women, as heroines, as women who fight, work, raise children and make their daily contribution; roles that valorize the African woman as such, whether she is traditional or modern.

Stroller, Joyce. "*Fire Eyes*—Fire Between the Legs." *Monthly Review* 46 (February 1995): 58-60. About Somali filmmaker Soraya Mire's, "*Fire Eyes*," a documentary about female circumcision. Discusses the practice of female circumcision as an ideological mechanism aimed at perpetuating women's sexual, cultural and economic inferiority.

Taylor, Marcella. "Finding a Voice: Film and the Female in Gaston Kabore's *Wend Kuuni*." *Hurricane Alice: A Feminist Quarterly* 10.4/11.1 (April 1995): 19-.

Veysset, Marie Claude. "La Noire de: Un film, deux visions." *Jeune Cinéma* 34 (November 1968): 10-11.

Warren, Ina. "Face of Repression." *Edmonton Journal* C11 (April 1970): Films on women shown at JCA, brief comments on *Ma Fille ne sera pas excisée*, *Finzan*, *Nyamanton*, and *M'Biga*.

WORLD WIDE WEB SITES

African Social Message Films and Videos. <http://catalog.com/dsr/film.htm>. One of the distributors of African films and videos. Provides a list of films and videos by topics such as women's issues.

California Newsreel: The Library of African Cinema. <http://www.newsreel.org/topic.htm#LibraryofAfrican Cinema>. The major distributor of African-made films in the

U.S.A. Lists films by filmmaker, country, and topic—
women's issues. Also provides a review of each movie.
Cinergie. <www.synec-doc.be/MediaCine/cinergie/index.html>.
A Belgian film periodical. Contains reviews and critical
essays of Mweze Ngangura's, *Pieces d'identites* and Boughédir
Férid's, *Un Eté à la Goulette*. Includes bio-filmography of the filmmakers. FESPACO. <http://fespaco. bf/>.
FESPACO's official home page. Contains a wealth of information about
festivals, films, filmmakers, and the industry in general.
Vues d'Afrique. <http://www.vuesdafrique.org>. Information on
upcoming festivals and other related events.

CONTRIBUTORS

Claire Andrade-Watkins is an Associate Professor of film at Emerson College in Boston. She has published extensively in lead-ing academic journals and film publications on French and Portuguese-speaking African cinema. Her current work-in-progress is "A Real Story: History of Cinema in the Cape Verde Islands during the Colonial Era." She is in active production on a one-hour documemoire entitled *Some Kind of Funny Porto Rican*, a multifaceted exploration of the largely unknown and undocu-mented place of Cape Verdeans within America's cultural, ethnic, and historical landscape.

Marie-Magdaleine Chirol is Associate Professor of French at Whittier College. She writes on Francophone African cinema and on the motif of ruins in film and 20th-century literature.

Maureen Eke is an Assistant Professor of English at Central Michigan University where she teaches courses in African, African American, and World Literatures, as well as literature and film. Her articles have appeared in *Callaloo, Visual Anthropology,* and the *South African Theatre Journal.*

Ratiba Hadj-Moussa teaches in the Department of Sociology at York University. She is the author of *Le corps l'histoire, le terri-toire: les rapports de genre dans le cinéma algérien,* and the co-editor of *Algérie: aux marges du religieux* and of *Les convergences culturelles dans les sociétés pluri-ethniques.*

Kenneth W. Harrow is a Professor of English at Michigan State University. He edited a special issue of *Research in African*

Literatures Fall 1995, 26.3, on the topic of African cinema, and *Women in African Cinema*, a special issue of *Matatu*, No. 19, 1997, on the topic of women and African cinema.

Jonathan Haynes is Associate Professor of Humanities at Southampton College. He is the author of *The Humanist as Traveler, The Social Relations of Jonson's Theater, Cinema and Social Change in West Africa* (with Onookome Okome), and editor of *Nigerian Video Films*.

Sylvie Kandé teaches French and Francophone Literatures in the French Department at New York University. She is affiliated with the NYU Africana Studies Program. Her book, *Terres, urbanisme et architecture 'créoles' en Sierra Leone, 18eme-19eme siecles* is in press at l'Harmattan. She is the editor of a collection of essays on metissage, entitled, *En quete d'Ariel: discours sur le metissage, identites metisses,* also to be published by l'Harmattan. She is co-editing a book of essays commemorating the Haitian revolution.

Suzanne H. MacRae teaches English and Humanities, including African literature and film, at the University of Arkansas. Her publications have appeared in *Research in African Literatures, Matatu, African Arts, African American Review*, and elsewhere.

Elizabeth Mermin is a doctoral candidate in the Department of Anthropology at New York University. She has written about cinema for several journals, including *Third Text* and *Nka: Journal for Contemporary African Arts*.

Emilie Ngo-Nguidjol is a librarian with a speciality in Africana bibliography at the University of Wisconsin. She published a bibliography on women in African cinema in *With Open Eyes: Women and African Cinema (Matatu)*.

Nancy J. Schmidt recently retired from her position as Librarian for African Studies at Indiana University. She still is an adjunct Professor of Anthropology at Indiana University.

Arnold Shepperson is a researcher in the Centre for Cultural and Media Studies, University of Natal, Durban. He has published on cultural policy issues, African cinema, and African philosophy.

Keyan G. Tomaselli is Professor and Director, Centre for Cultural and Media Studies, University of Natal, Durban. Author of *The Cinema of Apartheid* (1988), he co-wrote the South African gov - ernment *White Paper on Film (1996),* designed to restructure the industry after apartheid.

Stephen Zacks is a graduate student in the Committee on Liberal Studies at the Graduate Faculty for Political and Social Science, the New School for Social Research, New York City.

INDEX